COMPETITIVE AD\
IN SMEs

D1100608

23

ı_

8·11·2010

COMPETITIVE ADVANTAGE IN SMEs

ORGANISING FOR INNOVATION AND CHANGE

Edited by

Oswald Jones

and

Fiona Tilley

Manchester Metropolitan University

WILEY

Copyright © 2003   John Wiley & Sons Ltd, The Atrium, Southern Gate, Chichester,
West Sussex PO19 8SQ, England

Telephone (+44) 1243 779777

Email (for orders and customer service enquiries): cs-books@wiley.co.uk
Visit our Home Page on www.wileyeurope.com or www.wiley.com

This publication is designed to provide accurate and authoritative information in regard to the
subject matter covered. It is sold on the understanding that the Publisher is not engaged in
rendering professional services. If professional advice or other expert assistance is required, the
services of a competent professional should be sought.

Other Wiley Editorial Offices

John Wiley & Sons Inc., 111 River Street, Hoboken, NJ 07030, USA

Jossey-Bass, 989 Market Street, San Francisco, CA 94103-1741, USA

Wiley-VCH Verlag GmbH, Boschstr. 12, D-69469 Weinheim, Germany

John Wiley & Sons Australia Ltd, 33 Park Road, Milton, Queensland 4064, Australia

John Wiley & Sons (Asia) Pte Ltd, 2 Clementi Loop #02-01, Jin Xing Distripark, Singapore 129809

John Wiley & Sons Canada Ltd, 22 Worcester Road, Etobicoke, Ontario, Canada M9W 1L1

Wiley also publishes its books in a variety of electronic formats. Some content that appears
in print may not be available in electronic books.

Library of Congress Cataloging-in-Publication Data

Competitive advantage in SMEs : organising for innovation and change / [edited by]
Oswald Jones, Fiona Tilley.
     p. cm.
   Includes bibliographical references and index.
   ISBN 0-470-84334-9 (pbk. : alk. paper)
     1. Small business – Management. 2. Small business – Technological innovations. 3.
Business planning. 4. Competition. I. Jones, Oswald. II. Tilley, Fiona.

   HD62.7 .C653 2003
   658.02′2 – dc21

                                                            2002191076

British Library Cataloguing in Publication Data

A catalogue record for this book is available from the British Library

ISBN 0-470-84334-9

Typeset in 10/12pt Palatino by Laserwords Private Limited, Chennai, India
Printed and bound in Great Britain by Antony Rowe Ltd, Chippenham, Wiltshire
This book is printed on acid-free paper responsibly manufactured from sustainable forestry
in which at least two trees are planted for each one used for paper production.

CONTENTS

BIOGRAPHIES

Carol Atkinson is Senior Lecturer at Manchester Metropolitan University Business School (MMUBS) teaching on a wide range of human resource management and organisational behaviour programmes. Her main research interests include employment relationship in small and medium-sized enterprises (SMEs) and she has practical experience as a human resource manager in the financial services, retail and voluntary sectors.

Dr Mark Banks is a lecturer in the Department of Sociology at MMU and Research Fellow of the Manchester Institute for Popular Culture at MMU. His research interests are in the creative industries, work and urban culture.

Steve Baron took up the position of Professor of Marketing at the University of Liverpool Management School in July 2002. He was formerly Professor of Services Marketing at MMUBS. His research is in the fields of retail and services marketing. He is a joint author of a book on services marketing and has published widely in a range of marketing, services marketing and retailing journals.

Pascale de Berranger is a Research Fellow in Business Information Technology at MMUBS. Her research interests include the adoption and usage of information and communication technologies (ICTs) in SMEs, and the role of higher-education institutions in supporting the learning needs of SMEs.

Tony Berry is Professor in MMUBS and is editor of *Leadership and Organisational Development Journal*. His research interests include risk, financial management, consultancy, organisational control and leadership.

Meg Elliott is senior lecturer in human resource management and her main research interests are organisation learning and transformation, alliance working in the public sector, and organisation change interventions.

Carole Forbes joined MMUBS as a lecturer after spending 15 years in financial accounting. Carole's research interests include growth and strategy in SMEs, growth in small to medium-sized enterprises, and business advice needs in small enterprises.

Jitsuo Goto is Professor of Economics at Shiga University, Japan, and is currently visiting Professor in the Department of Accounting and Finance at MMUBS. At present he is working with Professors Bob Sweeting and Tony Berry on an international comparison of accounting practices.

Dr Paul Hooper is a senior lecturer in the Department of Environmental and Geographical Sciences at Manchester Metropolitan University.

Oswald Jones is Professor of Innovation and Entrepreneurship in MMUBS and is responsible for the Centre for Enterprise. He has published widely in the area of innovation and technology management, with a particular focus on smaller firms. Current research interests include entrepreneurial networks, innovation management in mature SMEs, social capital and entrepreneurship, and intrapreneurship/corporate entrepreneurship.

Allan Macpherson recently moved from MMUBS to take up a post as senior lecturer in organisation behaviour (OB) at Liverpool Hope University College. While working at MMU he completed two European Social Fund (ESF) projects on the implications of supply chain management for SME competences and competitiveness. In his previous careers, he has held a position as an HR and project manager in the commercial sector, and several operations and training appointments as an officer in the Royal Air Force.

Alan Marsden is senior lecturer in strategic management at MMUBS, with research and teaching interests in the areas of strategic management and small firms.

Julia Owen is a researcher in the Department of Sociology at MMU, specialising in the creative industries, organisational management and diversity in the workplace.

Dr Krsto Pandza is a researcher and lecturer at the University of Maribor, Slovenia. His research interests include operations strategy and its interaction with strategic management, organisational capabilities and knowledge-based theory of the firm. He is a member of the European Operations Management Association (EurOMA) and is a senior research fellow at MMUBS.

Andrew Pendleton is Professor of Human Resource Management at MMUBS. He has published widely in the areas of HR and industrial relations.

Sue Shaw is Executive Head of Postgraduate Programmes at MMUBS. Sue teaches and researches in the areas of international HRM, careers and performance.

Bob Sweeting is Professor of Accounting and Executive Head of the Finance and Accounting Groups in MMUBS. His research and teaching interests include developments in financial management in a range of organisational settings including SMEs and HEIs (Higher Education Institutes).

David Taylor worked in the advertising industry before becoming a lecturer at MMUBS. His main teaching responsibilities include OB, HRM and entrepreneurship, and his current research interests focus on the role of personal networks in the learning and decision-making processes of owner-managers. David is also visiting lecturer at the University of Zagreb and Business College of Athens.

Dr Scott Taylor is a lecturer in Organisational Behaviour at Birmingham Business School, University of Birmingham. He researched HR issues in small firms for his doctoral thesis (undertaken at MMUBS) and is currently involved in research into the Investors in People initiative, corporate universities and workplace spirituality.

Dr Fiona Tilley recently joined the School of the Environment at Leeds University as a lecturer in Environment and Business. Prior to this, she spent two years as a senior lecturer at MMUBS and three years as a senior research associate at the University of Durham Business School. She has published on topics relating to small firms and sustainable business in a variety of journals.

Jane Tonge's background is in the public relations industry, where she worked in-house at an agency level and freelance, especially dealing with the B2B (business-to-business) sector. Jane is currently in the second year of her PhD, which is concerned with the development of agency–client relationships in the public relations industry, focusing on SMEs.

Liz Walley joined MMUBS ten years ago and currently teaches sustainable development and environmental management modules. Prior to MMU, her 15 years' work experience was in consultancy, banking and industry. Liz has published in the areas of environmental management and transition in Eastern Europe. Her current research focus is organisational 'greening'; specifically the roles of environmental champions and green entrepreneurs.

Alison Wilson is European Regional Development Fund project manager at the Centre for Enterprise (MMUBS). Alison has been responsible for managing a number of ESF supply chain projects with MMUBS.

Dr Paul Windrum is senior lecturer in technological innovation and strategic management at MMUBS. He is also an associate of MERIT (Maastricht Economic Research Institute on Innovation and Technology) at the University of Maastricht. His current research portfolio includes innovation in SMEs, services innovation and the strategic management of Internet-based ICTs.

Richard Warren is Subject Leader in the Human Resource Management and Organisational Behaviour subject group at MMUBS. His main research interests are in corporate responsibility, and he has published two books and a number of journal articles on this topic.

PREFACE

As set out in Chapters 1 and 2, this book originated with our interest in the importance of encouraging small and medium-sized enterprises (SMEs) to adopt a more proactive stance towards improving competitive advantage. Interest was stimulated by a number of projects undertaken at MMUBS (Manchester Metropolitan University Business School) which have addressed this issue. Since 1998, the Business School has carried out three ESF (European Social Fund) projects concerned with improvements to supply chain skills within the SME sector (Homan *et al.*, 2000). The first project focused on mapping management skills and techniques as a basis for implementing management development within manufacturing-based SMEs. The second project concentrated on establishing future management development needs as perceived by SMEs themselves and by lead organisations in their supply chains. The research also included current and future skill needs of craft and technical workers. The main objective of the third project was to design an audit tool to assist companies in identifying staff skill development needs arising from fundamental changes taking place within supply chains. Project success has been aided by the participation of key collaborators, including the North-West Development Agency, which helped to identify the skills needs of SME suppliers. Significant private sector partners included the Forum of Private Business, Kelloggs, BNFL (formerly British Nuclear Fuels Ltd), BAE Systems, the chemical company, Ineos Chlor, and Cussons. Over 300 SMEs have participated in the research to date (see Chapter 12).

'Towards a Healthy High Street' was developed by the Department of Retailing and Marketing at MMUBS. Specifically aimed at independent retailers, the initiative builds on expertise established over the last decade. Independent retailing is an important factor in the vitality of local economies but is under threat from structural economic change, major multiple retailers and changing patterns of consumer expenditure. The first project, Retail Skills Forecasting, was part-financed by the European Social Fund (Objective 4) and focused on sectoral changes and their impact on the skill needs of owner/managers. 'Towards a Healthy High Street' Project I, supported by ESF Objective 4 funding, investigated the take-up of training and support systems designed to improve the sector's competitiveness. The initiative is now in its third stage and 'Towards a Healthy High Street II' (ESF Objective 3) has helped to develop a University Certificate in SME retailing as well as a nationwide mentoring programme for small retailers in light of recommendations made in previous projects. The programme's success can be attributed to the wide range of private and public sector partners involved (British Institute of Retailing, Association of Convenience Stores, Institute of Grocery Distribution, J. Sainsbury plc, B&Q, London Institute and Distributive Trade National Training Organisation and the Bakery National Training Organisation). Partnership ensures each project is relevant and has the 'voice' to influence policy and practice. The initiatives are helping to 'protect and encourage diversity within the sector' by looking at specific barriers to enterprise faced by small retailers including location, race, gender and age. Early in 2002, the partnership obtained substantial ESF EQUAL funding for a further project which will run for three and a half years.

MMUBS recently acquired ERDF (European Regional Development Fund) support for a project, which started in January 2002, designed to improve the competitiveness of SMEs in the north-west of England. This project builds on existing strengths in terms of understanding and interacting with SMEs. The overall project aim is to build better links between MMUBS and the small firm community by focusing on improvements to management practices related to innovation, enterprise, sustainability and performance management. Four experienced business analysts have been employed to engage directly with 300 SMEs and to help introduce new skills aimed at improving the competitiveness of individual firms, as well as impacting on the region as a whole. The project has also led to the creation of a Centre for Enterprise which will help the small business community make better use of resources within MMUBS by encouraging links, both formal and informal, with academic staff, postgraduate and undergraduate students.

Research over the last ten years indicates that entrepreneurs from socially deprived areas are excluded from access to support, advice and finance (Portes and Sensenbrenner, 1993; Greve, 1995; Fielden et al., 2000). The New Entrepreneur Scholarship (NES) is a Treasury initiative that seeks to address this issue through the development of appropriate training materials. MMUBS was responsible for one of three nationwide NES pilots which helped entrepreneurs from socially deprived areas develop their business ideas. The DfEE (Department for Education and Employment) (now DfES) (Department for Education and Skills) together with the Prince's Trust and local enterprise agencies sponsored the scheme, which attracted fourteen participants from the Greater Manchester area. The programme, based on 'action learning' ran for six months, during which time the group met regularly to develop their ideas and also attended seminars given by successful role models from the region (Jones and Boles, 2002). The Learning and Skills Council (in partnership with the Association of Business Schools and the Federation of Enterprise Agencies) rolled out NES Nationwide in autumn 2001, and MMUBS was chosen as one of the institutions to participate in the expanded scheme. To date, three cohorts have attended NES programmes, and more than 100 entrepreneurs have been provided with direct support for their nascent businesses.

The Business School has also been involved in projects carried out within other faculties of Manchester Metropolitan University. For example, SMILE (Skills for Missing Industries, Leaders and Enterprises) was part of the ESF Adapt project undertaken by a multidisciplinary team led by the Centre for Employment Research, part of Manchester Institute for Telematics and Employment (MITER). The aim of SMILE was to identify and develop effective managerial strategies and new models for managerial learning, and highlight skill deficiencies within the sector. In doing so, the intention was to inform the strategies of relevant support agencies, training suppliers and SMEs themselves. The project's start pre-dated the launch of the North-West Development Agency's regional strategy document (Towards 2020) which stresses the importance of investment in businesses and ideas. SMILE's objectives are closely related to the NWDA's strategy as well as to the north-west's regional skills and e-learning strategies. SMILE was preceded by CLIME (Creative Leadership in Media Enterprises) which was an ESF Objective 4-funded project to support 'creative' SMEs operating in Greater Manchester.

Such practical engagement with the small firm community provides MMUBS staff with clear insight into problems associated with managing such firms. As discussed in Chapters 1 and 2, our aim has been to draw on this experience to help provide a better understanding of why competitive advantage is important to SMEs as well as improving understanding of mechanisms by which owner-managers can improve the performance of their firms. The principle on which contributors were asked to reflect was the extent to which 'large firm' concepts such as human resource management (HRM), strategic management and supply chain management are directly relevant to owner/managers trying to improve their firms' competitiveness; although, as pointed out by many experts, small firms are not simply 'little big firms' (Dandridge, 1979; Welsh and White, 1981) and therefore we do not suggest that such concepts can be applied indiscriminately.

References

Dandridge, T.C. (1979) 'Children are not little "grown-ups": small business needs its own organisational theory', *Journal of Small Business Management*, **17**:2, 53–57.

Fielden, S., Davidson, M. and Makin, P. (2000) 'Barriers encountered during the micro and small business startup in north-west England', *Journal of Small Business and Enterprise Development*, **7**:4, 295–304.

Greve, A. (1995) 'Networks and entrepreneurship: an analysis of social relations, occupational background and use of contacts during the establishment process', *Scandinavian Journal of Management*, **11**:1, 1–24.

Homan, G., Hicks-Clarke, D. and Wilson, A. (2000) The Management Development Needs of Owner-Managers in SMEs. European Social Fund Project Report, Manchester Metropolitan University.

Jones, O. and Boles, K. (2002) 'New entrepreneurs and social capital: building support networks through action learning', *Institute for Small Business Affairs* (Brighton).

Portes, A. and Sensenbrenner, J. (1993) 'Embeddedness and immigration: notes on the social determinism of economic action', *American Journal of Sociology*, **98**: 1320–1350.

Welsh, J.A. and White, J.F. (1981) 'A small business is not a big business', *Harvard Business Review*, **59**:4, 18–32.

Chapter 1

INTRODUCTION

Fiona Tilley and Jane Tonge

Since the publication of the Bolton Report in 1971 the contribution of small and medium-sized enterprises (SMEs) to economic growth, job creation, innovation and promotion of enterprise has been widely recognised. While SMEs are important in terms of their overall share of GDP, it is also believed that many smaller firms lack both managerial and technical skills, which inhibits their effectiveness. Therefore, improving the competitive advantage of SMEs is important to individual firms and to the UK economy as a whole. In this chapter we present an overview of research on the growth of small firms, with a view to identifying factors which encourage success and act as barriers to growth. There is also an assessment of strengths and weaknesses related to government policy-making in this area. As discussed below, there has been a plethora of policies aimed at the small firm sector over the last thirty years. It is important to reflect on the extent to which policy initiatives have had a positive impact on the competitiveness of smaller firms.

Over the last thirty years there has been considerable discussion related to the appropriateness of categorising SMEs based on the number of employees (see Curran *et al.*, 1991). In 1996, the European Commission (EC) set out a definition of SMEs which was intended to be appropriate in all member countries (see Table 1.1). UK government agencies have since attempted to harmonise their approach to SMEs by adopting the European Commission's definition. While we acknowledge that using the number of employees as a measure of firm size may create a number of anomalies, we believe it is the most convenient and widely understood categorisation. Therefore, this is the approach which has been adopted throughout this book. This chapter begins with a discussion of those factors which encourage or discourage the growth of SMEs. We then briefly review the main policy initiatives in this area and end with a brief evaluation of SME-related policy-making.

TABLE 1.1   EC definition of SMEs (Source: DTI, 2001)

Criterion	Micro firm	Small firm	Medium firm
Maximum number of employees	9	49	249
Maximum annual turnover	–	7m euros	40m euros
Maximum annual balance sheet total	–	5m euros	27m euros
Maximum percentage owned by one, or jointly by several enterprise(s) not satisfying the same criteria	–	25%	25%

Note: To qualify as an SME, both the employee and the independence criteria must be satisfied, plus either the turnover or the balance sheet criteria.

Understanding SME Growth

According to some experts, there is little justification for many of the government policy measures introduced to improve the competitiveness of SMEs. As Curran (1999, p. 42) points out, 'the alleged existence of shortages of start-up finance or the negative impact of employment legislation on small business expansion and job creation, have been overwhelmingly rejected by research'. Seeking to improve the competitiveness of SMEs is not only about understanding problems confronting businesses in this sector; it is also about a better understanding of how to overcome these barriers. Much research has focused on SME competitiveness and has sought to identify factors which make some SMEs successful, while others fail to grow or go out of business. While this research may contribute to our understanding of SME competitiveness, it also serves to demonstrate the complexity of this task (Storey, 1994; Watson *et al.*, 1998; Perren, 1999; Thompson and Gray, 1999). Although a multitude of factors are hypothesised to impact on business outcomes, there is no consistent pattern to the characteristics which contribute to business competitiveness, success and growth (Ray, 1993; Gibb, 1996). Fascination in the growth of small firms is based on the government's desire to promote opportunities for employment. From a public policy perspective, employment generation may be an appropriate growth criterion (Smallbone and Wyer, 2000). However, not all small firms are growth-oriented, and only a small proportion achieve significant levels of growth in employment. For the majority of owner-managers, day-to-day survival is more important than growth. As pointed out by David Storey (1994, p. 112) 'the numerically dominant group of small businesses are those which are small today and, even if they survive, are always likely to remain small-scale operations.'

Publication of the Bolton Report (1971) stimulated research into characteristics that distinguish owner-managers from other members of the economically active population (Watson *et al.*, 1998). One of the more significant contributions identified sixteen growth factors and four growth drivers including owner's motivation, expertise in growth management, resource access and demand (Perren, 1999). Attempts have also been made to identify the behaviours, skills and attributes normally associated with enterprising people (Storey, 1994). These include opportunity-seeking and persuasion (Gibb, 1996) and commitment of leaders to achieving growth (Smallbone *et al.*, 1995). There is evidence that rapidly growing firms are more likely to be founded by groups than individuals, and team members will have higher levels of education and prior managerial experience (Storey, 1994). However, such findings have been contested by those who argue that there is no ideal type of personality nor set of entrepreneurial attributes that guarantee success for new ventures (Ray, 1993). As Ray goes on to argue, the probability of launching a successful business is not based on a fixed set of factors but on an infinite variety of combinations in which an individual's positive attributes might outweigh her negative attitudes. On the other hand, it is possible to reject the idea that success is equated with entrepreneurial competence and view businesses from an entirely different perspective. This involves a shift from a focus on the personality or characteristics of the business founder to the firm's underlying business concept and capacity to accumulate capital (Osborne, 1993).

In attempting to understand SME success, the characteristics of individual entrepreneurs, such as age, gender, work experience, educational qualifications and family background are frequently hypothesised to influence business performance. Yet, other than education, none of these factors appears to be consistently verified in major empirical studies (Storey, 1994). This suggests support for the Jovanovic (1982) notion that neither the individuals themselves nor other bodies have a clear understanding of whether particular individuals will succeed in business. In trying to identify the factors that help small business, it appears there is no simple pattern which maps growth or potential growth. Rather, the evidence points towards a complex set of interrelated factors that increase or decrease the probability that an individual will establish a successful and growing small business (Stanworth and Gray, 1991). Such complexity serves to illustrate the value of this book in contributing to a broader understanding of competitiveness in SMEs.

Overcoming Barriers to SME Growth

A host of explanatory factors for the growth of SMEs has been advanced, and a number of authors have developed integrated models of the process. Seven sets of authors have made real attempts to conceptualise integrative models of firm growth rather than simply itemising factors or concentrating on one specific aspect of growth. These are:

- Durham University Business School's (DUBS) (Gibb and Scott, 1985)
- Keats and Bracker's (1988) theory of small firm performance
- Bygrave's (1989) entrepreneurial process model adapted from Moore (1986)
- Covin and Slevin's (1991) entrepreneurship model
- Davidsson's (1991) entrepreneurial growth model
- Naffziger et al.'s (1994) model of entrepreneurial motivation
- Jennings and Beaver's (1997) management perspective of performance

However, with the exception of Davidsson (1991), these authors do not conceptualise development of micro-businesses which are the typical 'entrepreneurial start-ups'. There is also a lack of empirical evidence and only Gibb and Scott (1985), Bygrave (1989) and Jennnings and Beaver (1997) attempt to address the full range of factors influencing a firm's development. The remaining models, as pointed out by Perren (1999), concentrate on factors which influence the entrepreneurial process and behaviours. Authors also refrain from commenting on how the various factors actually interact to influence development of the firm. Some element of causality is suggested but there is no real consideration of interactions between the various factors (Perren, 1999). These integrative models also tend to impose rather simplistic stages on the process of development. Kimberley and Miles Associates (1980) argue that there is no inevitable sequence of stages in organisational life. This point is also made by Perren (1999, p. 381), who suggests: 'Development is often much more a process of slow incremental iterative adaptation to emerging situations, than it is a sequence of radical clear steps or decision points.' Firms do not move through a series of stages in incremental fashion (Smallbone *et al.*, 1995): rather, as highlighted above, growth occurs as a result of a number of linked factors (Perren, 1999).

The success, and therefore competitiveness, of any business is dependent on a range of situational and contextual factors (Fielden *et al.*, 2000). Improving the competitiveness of SMEs also involves understanding the problems of such businesses and identifying potential solutions. New businesses encounter a number of barriers to success throughout the start-up period and during their first year of operation. These barriers can be both 'internal' to the firm such as lack of motivation and also 'external' including government controls and lack of skilled labour (Storey, 1994). Owner-managers often perceive barriers to growth as being external in origin. Issues related to 'money management' are regularly cited as the main difficulty for business start-ups (Bevan *et al.*, 1987; Fielden *et al.*, 2000). Problems include a poor understanding of tax, VAT, national insurance and book-keeping, as well as difficulties in obtaining capital and the absence of a guaranteed income. Owners of failed businesses often point to the shortage of working capital as the prime cause of business failure (Hall and Young, 1991; Hall, 1992). Lack of adequate start-up funds has a 'knock-on' effect restricting development and growth by reducing funds available for activities such as advertising, publicity and acquiring suitable premises (Fielden *et al.*, 2000).

Issues of finance are followed by concerns related to the level of demand for products and services as well as the nature of marketplace competition (CSBRC, 1992). Nascent entrepreneurs also express concern about difficulties in identifying and contacting potential customers (Fielden *et al.*, 2000). The strong desire of many small business owners to retain personal control and business independence has long been recognised as a key factor limiting the growth of many small enterprises (Gray, 1990). Hence, key constraints on growth are related to a combination of internal factors, an unwillingness to delegate or bring in external skills, and external factors including finance, employment and competition (Storey, 1994), poor products and inefficient marketing (Cromie, 1991; Smallbone, 1991; Hall, 1992; Watson *et al.*, 1998).

SMEs and Government Intervention

SMEs, however defined, constitute the majority of all enterprises in most of the economies in the world (OECD, 1998). Such firms make significant contributions to private sector employment and output, which appears to be increasing over time (Storey, 1994). From 1980 to 2000, the number of businesses operating in the UK rose by 1.3 million to an estimated 3.7 million (DTI, 2001). SMEs, including sole traders, account for 99 per cent of all businesses, 55 per cent of non-governmental employment and 51 per cent of turnover (SBS, 2001). In the UK, SMEs are now more important than larger companies in their contributions to business turnover and jobs (Curran, 1999). Statistical trends go some way to explaining why SMEs have gained attention from politicians, policy-makers and academics. However, between 1945 and the late 1960s there was little interest in small firms from either the government or academics. SMEs were regarded as being poorly managed, badly organised and reliant on outmoded technologies to produce inferior products and services (Mason and Harrison, 1990). During the corporatist era of the 1950s and 1960s, the state took a direct and active involvement in managing the economy. Cooperation between government, trade unions and employers' representatives (such as the Confederation of British Industry) was almost entirely concerned with large organisations (Crouch and Streeck, 1997) and there was no 'voice' for the small firm community. The common perception was that in industrialised nations SMEs were of little relevance to economic progress or competitiveness (Stanworth and Gray, 1991). Economic planning was based on the premise that 'big is beautiful'. Consequently, SMEs did not figure highly in government economic or industrial policies during this period.

In 1969, Labour Prime Minister Harold Wilson commissioned an inquiry into the state of the UK's small firms sector. The Bolton Report, published two years later, revealed that numbers of small firms were declining in the UK at a much faster rate than in other Western countries. The Commission also reported that small firms were constantly battling against unfair bureaucratic, financial and administrative burdens. With hindsight, the findings from the Bolton Report marked the beginnings of a resurgent interest in SMEs which eventually led to a 'sea change' in attitudes within society and particularly government circles. The 1970s were also notable for wider problems in the UK economy with the emergence of 'stagflation' (high inflation and high levels of unemployment) and trade union militancy, culminating in the 1979 'Winter of Discontent'. As a result of these difficulties, faith in the corporatist ideal began to recede and politicians associated with the New Right began to stress the importance of enterprise and entrepreneurship in stimulating economic growth (Hutton, 1995). At the same time, it was recognised that the economic success of Japan and West Germany was partly based on both countries having thriving small firms sectors (United Nations, 1993). The combination of these factors meant that, since the election of the first Thatcher government in 1979, small firms and enterprise have been important to the policies of both Labour and Conservative parties.

Government Policy and SME Growth

In the first four years of the first Thatcher government, more than one hundred SME-related policies were introduced (Beesley and Wilson, 1984). More recently, the Competitiveness White Papers published during the 1990s acknowledged that small firms, particularly those that were growing rapidly, could make important contributions to competitiveness (Johnson et al., 2000). To date, the rationale and objectives of policy measures have been multidimensional. As most SMEs are privately owned, intervention funded from the public purse needs to demonstrate benefits to wider society. Purists of economic liberalisation associated with the

New Right, under the leadership of Margaret Thatcher, argued that state intervention was only justified when markets fail to allocate resources, goods and services efficiently (Bennett, 1996; Bridge *et al.*, 1998, pp. 207–221). Others argue that government intervention can be justified on the grounds of equity with the removal of barriers that favour large firms in an attempt to provide a 'level playing-field' for SMEs (Johnson, 1990). Restrictions on the operation of free markets include barriers to trade arising from monopoly, imperfect information, problems associated with risk and uncertainty, and difficulties in obtaining finance. Government assistance for SMEs provides potential benefits in creating employment opportunities and establishing a seedbed of growing firms as well as improving innovation and competitiveness (Johnson *et al.*, 2000). The view that SMEs create new jobs is based, *inter alia*, on a study undertaken by Birch (1979) which concluded that small firms (those with fewer than 20 employees) in the USA generated 66 per cent of all new jobs between 1969 and 1976. Like many other claims made of SMEs, Birch's findings have been contested (Storey and Johnson, 1987). Nevertheless, Johnson (1990) maintains that there is a substantial and theoretically defensible case for the inclusion of small firms in public policy interventions.

While there may not be a clear rationale for government policy related to SMEs, it is certainly possible to identify different phases of support since the publication of the Bolton Report (Curran, 1999). The 1970s represented an emergent phase and, from 1971 to 1974, eleven indirect policies were introduced. Among these were a series of deregulation measures aimed at reducing bureaucratic and administrative demands that were burdening owner-managers. The remainder of the decade witnessed further measures to reduce financial failures. In this phase, SMEs were perceived as a balance to set against the excessive bureaucracy and monopoly power of large businesses. The rationale for government intervention was described by the Department of Trade and Industry (DTI) in the following terms: 'The small firms sector is recognised by government as having a vital part to play in the development of the economy. It accounts for a significant proportion of employment output, and it is a source of competition, innovation, diversity and employment' (Frank *et al.*, 1984, p. 257).

In the early 1980s, there was a switch from supporting business start-ups as a way of reducing unemployment to policies aimed at improving competitiveness by growing existing SMEs. There was also a programme of deregulation designed to reduce bureaucratic red tape as a means of saving time and resources for SMEs. By the early 1990s, a further policy shift towards 'software' measures was evident. There was less emphasis on providing tangible financial support through the Enterprise Allowance Scheme and the Small Firms Loan Guarantee Scheme, and more concern with supporting SMEs with advice, consultancy, information and training (Stanworth and Gray, 1991). The proliferation of initiatives and constant changes of emphasis served to create the impression among owner-managers that accessing support was both complex and confusing. The government responded in 1992 by introducing a network of 'one-stop shops' called Business Links intended to provide SMEs with a single, local gateway to advice and assistance (Bennett *et al.*, 2001). The election of New Labour in 1997 appears not to have changed the UK's commitment to SMEs and their contribution to an enterprise culture (Gavron *et al.*, 1998): 'Entrepreneurship and innovation are central to the creative process in the economy and to promoting growth, increasing productivity and creating jobs . . . The government's aim is to create a broadly-based entrepreneurial culture, in which more people of all ages and backgrounds start their own businesses' (DTI, 1998, pp. 14–15).

In their first term of office, the new government set out to build on the growth of SMEs by restructuring business support through the creation of eleven Regional Development Agencies (Shutt and Pellow, 1997). Further to this, the Small Business Service (SBS) was established in 2000 to provide a single governmental organisation dedicated to helping small firms and representing their needs within the government. The overall mission of the SBS is to build an enterprise society in which small firms can thrive and achieve their potential. The four areas of activity on which the SBS focuses are acting as a voice for small firms, providing a business service support network, mitigating regulation that unfairly burdens or hinders small firms, and championing entrepreneurship (Irwin, 2001). Other forms of small-firm support, such as the Small Firms Loan Guarantee Scheme, the High Technology Fund and the network of Business Links, are now the responsibility of the SBS. Looking ahead, Johnson *et al.* (2000, p. 52) maintain: '[I]t is reasonable to conclude that the role of the small business sector in promoting economic growth and competitiveness is at the forefront of current government thinking on small-business policy, and will continue to be so for the foreseeable future.'

It is acknowledged that SMEs make important contributions to the UK economy in terms of technological progress, increased competitiveness, the creation of new jobs and the economic revival of certain regions (Cabinet Office, 1996). However, the dynamism demonstrated by SMEs since the 1980s cannot be taken for granted. It is no longer certain that SMEs can continue to make significant contributions to economic growth in a global economy typified by accelerated technological change and ever-increasing market competitiveness (OECD, 1993). UK Government White Papers on Science, Engineering and Technology and on Competitiveness emphasise the significance of small firms as a catalyst for economic success through innovation and technology transfer (Cabinet Office, 1995, 1996). In the drive to sustain competitiveness among SMEs, there is growing interest within the government in fostering stronger links between the SME sector and Higher Education Institutions (HEIs) (Johnson and Tilley, 1999). It is believed that there are benefits to be gained by small firms from such interactions and partnerships, for example:

- Many small firms lack the time, resources, technology or expertise to research and develop new business ideas and innovations. HEIs can potentially provide access to expertise, technology and resources that could be of assistance to SMEs. Working in partnership with research departments can lead to new commercial developments that an SME may have been unable to achieve on its own. Student projects and placements, such as the Teaching Company Scheme, offer SMEs access to a wide range of knowledge, expertise and resources (Brereton, 1996; Jones and Craven, 2001). Furthermore, recruiting more graduates will result in a greater flow of talent, energy and innovation into the SME sector.
- SMEs may not always operate at the optimal technological level. A study undertaken by the Oxford Trust on technology transfer between SMEs in Oxfordshire and the local research base stated that: 'although technology

transfer is increasingly recognised as being of great importance, getting it to work in practice can be difficult' (Bell *et al.*, 1994, p. 5). The authors concluded that technology transfer was making an important contribution to local manufacturing and technology-based firms, but SMEs were still concerned with their own lack of know-how in accessing assistance from universities. Nevertheless, HEIs are repositories of specialist technology and expertise which can be of enormous benefit to SMEs willing to engage with academia.

- Owner-managers often possess the entrepreneurial drive but lack formal management training (Marshall *et al.*, 1995). This weakness can eventually become a critical factor limiting growth and expansion. Developing high-level workforce skills has been identified by Government White Papers as central to improving UK competitiveness. It can also be argued that SMEs would benefit from improvements in their commitment to management training.

- SMEs could make better use of skills available in the graduate labour market. Graduates are under-represented in the SME sector, but this is seen as the most likely growth area for future graduate employment (DfEE, 1996). Owner-managers are often wary of employing highly qualified staff because graduates are perceived as unlikely to remain committed over the longer term due to ambitious career plans.

- Traditionally, SMEs have struggled to obtain adequate and appropriate finance. However, links with HEIs present opportunities for owner-managers to increase their funding capabilities. Involvement in any SME–HEI initiatives, such as the Teaching Company Scheme (TCS), provides resources, labour and access to funding that would otherwise be unavailable to smaller firms.

Evaluating SME Policy

SME policy has developed incrementally in the UK as the government responded to specific problems and difficulties as they arose (Green, 1992). Despite the growing importance of SMEs to the health and competitiveness of the economy, a constant complaint has been of the ad hoc and piecemeal approach taken to policy-making, resulting in a lack of coherence (Stanworth and Gray 1991; Storey, 1994). Over the years, government interventions have also been criticised for being regionally divisive. Indeed, during the 1980s, it was suggested that a 'north–south' divide was being perpetrated, with small firms located in the south being more likely to benefit from policy measures than similar firms located in the north (Whittington, 1984; Lloyd and Mason, 1984).

The present government remains steadfast in supporting SMEs to promote growth and competitiveness (Johnson *et al.*, 2000); although some critics remain unconvinced of this: 'It is difficult to say very much worthwhile about the impact of small business policy in the UK over the last 20 years' (Curran, 1999, p. 43). This claim is based, in part, on the premise that studies intended to evaluate small firms' policies suffer from inherent methodological problems. In particular, identifying and measuring additionality, the net positive outcomes (desired or otherwise) that can be reliably attributed to individual policy measures, is extremely contentious. A 'before and after' comparison would be an appropriate research design, but this approach is difficult to execute because small firms are extremely sensitive to external influences. The obvious solution would be to use a matched control sample but, because of the sector's heterogeneity, this is not straightforward. With the added complexities of accurate sampling, response bias and self-selection it can be difficult, if not impossible, to assess additionality and, therefore, reach reliable conclusions when evaluating the effectiveness of small firms' policies (Curran, 1999).

The most damning assessment of government policy comes from SMEs themselves. Over the last 20 years, it is estimated that there have been approximately 200 initiatives to support the improved competitiveness of small firms, yet the take-up rate has been low. Even support programmes such as training and business health checks have rarely achieved more than a 10 per cent take-up, and often it is much less (Curran, 1999). Possible reasons for low take-up rates include:

1. Support providers do not understand the needs of owner-managers' businesses and therefore offer standardised support measures.
2. Owner-managers are sceptical of solutions based on large-firm practices which are delivered though top-down support programmes.
3. The largely standardised top-down support described in points 1 and 2 may be administratively convenient but fail to recognise the heterogeneity of small firms and the importance of locality.

The limitations of policy provision and delivery are not necessarily an indication of a lack of demand for assistance. The benefits of introducing policies which are directly relevant to the needs of the SME community are still a concern to all those interested in sustaining the competitive advantages of the UK economy.

Conclusion

This brief introduction to small firms highlights a number of factors that can limit the competitiveness and growth of SMEs. The UK government recognises that the UK has some way to go in resolving these issues.

> The lack of an enterprise culture is a particular handicap in the knowledge-driven economy. Attitudes in the UK to entrepreneurship are less favourable than in the U.S. and in some respects fall short of our European partners. Small firms can face difficulties in gaining access to finance, both at the start-up stage and in achieving sustained growth. Further work is needed to promote a culture of entrepreneurship, particularly among young people, and remove the barriers to the development of a dynamic small firms sector. (DTI, 1999, p. 57)

In part, some of the difficulties in understanding SME competitiveness described in this chapter are related to the sheer complexity of the small firm community. The heterogeneity of SMEs can create insurmountable problems to academics and policy-makers seeking universal explanations for SME growth, success and competitiveness. The first step may be to deepen our understanding of what sustains the competitive advantage of smaller businesses in a more individualistic manner.

The main body of the book consists of thirteen chapters divided into three sections. In the first section, there are four chapters dealing with what are described as strategic issues related to SMEs (competitive advantage, strategic management, corporate governance and sustainability). The second section deals with topics categorised as 'people issues' (HRM, share ownership, creativity, innovation and networks). In the final section, four chapters described as 'functional' approaches to the management of SMEs are included (e-commerce, supply chain management, financial management, and marketing). In selecting these topics, the editors have built on the strengths of staff belonging to MMUBS as a result of their engagement with the small firm community. Some topics such as HRM, innovation, networking and strategy are regularly discussed in books related to the management of SMEs. Other topics, such as share-ownership (Pendleton), corporate governance (Warren), creativity (Banks *et al.*) and supply chain management (Macpherson and Wilson) are rarely examined in the context of SMEs. Therefore, it is suggested that this book will provide new insights into ways in which the owner-managers of SMEs can improve the competitive position of their firms.

Inevitably, in a book of this kind there are likely to be some omissions. At the same time, the editors believe that each of the chapters makes a positive contribution to a broader understanding of how competitiveness can be created and sustained in SMEs. As pointed out in Chapter 15, identifying and exploiting new opportunities demands that owner-managers (or the management team) are outward- rather than inward-looking. Long-term success for any SME means that there must be emphasis on the innovation of new products, services and processes. Owner-managers must strive to create a dynamic, entrepreneurial culture in which there is constant emphasis on the importance of regular access to new knowledge, resources and information. In this way, SMEs in all sectors can improve their prospects for longer-term survival, if not growth.

References

Beesley, W. and Wilson, P. (1984) 'Public policy and small firms', in C. Levicki (ed.) *Small Business Theory and Policy*. Croom Helm, London.

Bell, E.R.J., Stott, M.A. and Kingham, D.R. (1994) *Oxfordshire Firms and Technology Transfer: Interactions between small and medium sized enterprises (SMEs) and the local research base*. The Oxford Trust, Oxford.

Bennett, R.J. (1996) 'SMEs and public policy: present day dilemmas, future priorities and the case of business links', ISBA National Small Firms and Research Conference, Birmingham.

Bennett, R.J., Robson, P.J.A. and Bratton, W.J.A. (2001) 'Government advice networks for SMEs: an assessment of the influence of local context on business link usage, impact and satisfaction', *Applied Economics*, **33**, 871–885.

Bevan, J., Clark, G., Banerji, N. and Hakim, C. (1987) 'Barriers to business start-up: a study of the flow in and out of self-employment', *Department of Employment Research Paper No. 71*.

Birch, D. (1979) *The Job Generation Process*. MIT, Cambridge, MA.

Bolton Report (1971) *Report of the Committee of Inquiry on Small Firms*. HMSO, London.

Brereton, M. (1996) The Birmingham Universities TCS for small firms, *Management Services*, **40**, 26–27.

Bridge, S., O'Neill, K. and Cromie, S. (1998) *Understanding Enterprise, Entrepreneurship and Small Business*. Macmillan, Basingstoke.

Bygrave, W.D. (1989) 'The entrepreneurship paradigm: a philosophical look at research methodologies', *Entrepreneurship Theory and Practice*, **14**:1, 7–26.

Cabinet Office (1995) *Competitiveness: Forging Ahead*. HMSO, London.

Cabinet Office (1996) *Competitiveness: Creating the Enterprise Centre of Europe*. HMSO, London.

Covin, J.G. and Slevin, D.P. (1991) 'A conceptual model of entrepreneurship as firm behaviour', *Entrepreneurship Theory and Practice*, **13**:1, 7–25.

Cromie, S. (1991) 'The problems experienced by young firms', *International Small Business Journal*, **19**:3, 43–61.

Crouch, C. and Streeck, M. (1997) *Political Economy of Modern Capitalism: Mapping Convergence and Diversity*. London, Sage.

CSBRC (1992) *The State of British Enterprise*. Cambridge Small Business Research Centre, Department of Applied Economics, University of Cambridge.

Curran, J. (1999) 'What is small business policy in the UK for? Evaluation and assessing small business policy', *International Small Business Journal*, **18**:3, 36–50.

Curran, J., Blackburn, R. and Woods. A. (1991) 'Profiles of the small enterprise in the service sector'. Paper presented at the University of Warwick, 18 April 1991.

Davidsson, P. (1991) 'Continued entrepreneurship ability, need and opportunity as determinants of small firm growth', *Journal of Business Venturing*, **6**, 405–429.

DfEE (1996) Improving job prospects for graduates. Department for Education and Employment, Skills and Enterprise Briefing, no. 2.

DTI (1998) *Our Competitive Future: Building the Knowledge Driven Economy*. Department of Trade and Industry, Cm. 4176, HMSO, London.

DTI (1999) *Our Competitive Future: UK Competitiveness Indicators 1999*. Department of Trade and Industry, HMSO, London.

DTI (2001) www.dti.gov.uk/SME4/define.htm

Fielden, S.L., Davidson, M.J. and Makin, P.J. (2000) 'Barriers encountered during micro and small business start-up in North-West England', *Journal of Small Business and Enterprise Development*, **7**:4, 295–304.

Frank, C.E.J., Miall, R.H.C. and Rees, R.D. (1984) 'Issues in small firms research of relevance to policy making', *Regional Studies*, **18**:3, 257–266.

Gavron, B., Cowling, M., Holtham, G. and Westall, A. (1998) *The Entrepreneurial Society*. Institute of Public Policy Research, London.

Gibb, A.A. (1996) 'Entrepreneurship and small business management: can we afford to neglect them in the 21st-century business school?' *British Academy of Management*, **7**, 309–321.

Gibb, A.A. and Scott, M. (1985) 'Strategic awareness, personal commitment and the process of planning in the small business', *Journal of Management Studies*, **22**:6, 597–632.

Gray, C. (1990) *Business independence – impediment or enhancement to growth in the 1990s?* Paper presented to the 13th National Small Firms Policy and Research Conference, Harrogate, 1990.

Green, H. (1992) *'The changing role of small business'*, Inaugural Professorial Lecture presented at Leeds Metropolitan University, Leeds.

Hall, G. (1992) 'Reasons for insolvency amongst small firms – a review and fresh evidence', *Small Business Economics*, **4**:3, 237–250.

Hall, G. and Young, B. (1991) 'Factors associated with insolvency amongst small firms', *International Business Journal*, **9**:2, 54–63.

Hutton W. (1995) *The State We're In*. Jonathan Cape, London.

Irwin, D. (2001) Keynote presentation at the ISBA Conference, Leicester.

Jennings, P. and Beaver, G. (1997) 'The performance and competitive advantage of small firms: a management perspective', *International Small Business Journal*, **15**:2, 63–75.

Johnson, S. (1990) 'Small firms policies: An agenda for the 1990s'. Paper presented at the 13th National Small Firms Policy and Research Conference, Harrogate, 14–16 November.

Johnson, D. and Tilley, F. (1999) 'HEI and SME linkages: recommendations for the future', *International Small Business Journal*, **17**:4, 66–81.

Johnson, S., Sear, L. and Jenkins, A. (2000) 'Small business policy, support and governance', in S. Carter and D. Jones-Evans (eds) *Enterprise and Small Business: Principles, Practice and Policy*. Pearson Education, Harlow.

Jones, O. and Craven, M. (2001) 'Expanding capabilities in a mature manufacturing firm: absorptive capacity and the TCS', *International Small Business Journal*, **19**:3, 39–55.

Jovanovic, B. (1982) 'Selection and evolution of industry', *Econometrica*, **50**, 649–670.

Keats, B.W. and Bracker, J.S. (1988) 'Towards a theory of small firm performance: a conceptual model', *American Journal of Small Business*, **12**:4, 41–58.

Kimberley, J.R. and Miles Associates (1980) *The Organisational Life Cycle*, Jossey-Bass, San Francisco.

Lloyd, P.E. and Mason, C.M. (1984) 'Spatial variations in new firm formation in the United Kingdom: comparative evidence from Merseyside, Greater Manchester and South Hampshire', *Regional Studies*, **18**:3, 207–220.

Marshall, J.N., Alderman, N., Wong, C. and Thwaites, A. (1995) 'The impact of management training and development on small and medium-sized enterprises', *International Small Business Journal*, **13**:4, 73–90.

Mason, C.M. and Harrison, R.T. (1990) 'Small firms: phoenix from the ashes?', in D. Pinder (ed.) *Western Europe: Challenge and Change*. Belhaven Press, London.

Moore, C.F. (1986) 'Understanding entrepreneurial behaviour', in J.A. Pearce and R.B. Robinson (eds.) *Academy of Management Best Papers Proceedings*. 46th Annual Meeting of the Academy of Management, Chicago.

Naffziger, D.W., Hornsby, J.S. and Kuratko, D.F. (1994) 'A proposed research model of entrepreneurial motivation', *Entrepreneurship Theory and Practice*, **18**:3, 9–42.

OECD (1998) *Fostering Entrepreneurship*. Paris, Organisation for Economic Cooperation and Development.

OECD (1993) *Small and Medium-sized Enterprises: Technology and Competitiveness*. Paris, Organisation for Economic Cooperation and Development.

Osborne, R.L. (1993) 'Why entrepreneurs fail: how to avoid the traps', *Management Decisions*, **31**:1, 18–21.

Perren, L. (1999) 'Factors in the growth of micro-enterprises (Part 1): Developing a framework', *Journal of Small Business and Enterprise Development*, **6**:4, 366–385.

Ray, D.M. (1993) 'Understanding the entrepreneur: entrepreneurial attributes, experiences and skills', *Entrepreneurship and Regional Development*, **5**, 345–357.

SBS (2001) Small and Medium-sized Enterprise (SME) Statistics for the UK (2000). Small Business Service, press release, 21 June 2001.

Shutt, J. and Pellow, N. (1997) 'Industrial districts and business support strategies – contrasting evidence from the North of England'. Paper presented to the Networking and Small and Medium-sized Enterprises Conference, Università di Bologna, Italy, 19–20 June.

Smallbone, D. (1991) 'Success and failure in new business start-ups', *International Small Business Journal*, **8**:2, 34–45.

Smallbone, D. and Wyer, P. (2000) 'Growth and development in the small firm', in S. Carter and D. Jones-Evans (eds) *Enterprise and Small Business*. Pearson Education, Harlow.

Smallbone, D., Leigh, R. and North, D. (1995) 'The characteristics of high-growth SMEs', *International Journal of Entrepreneurial Behaviour and Research*, **1**:3, 44–62.

Stanworth, J. and Gray, C. (1991) *Bolton 20 Years On: The Small Firm in the 1990s*, Paul Chapman Publishing, London.

Storey, D.J. (1994) *Understanding Small Firms*. Routledge, London.

Storey, D.J. and Johnson, S. (1987) *Job Generation and Labour Market Change*. Macmillan, Basingstoke.

Thomson, A. and Gray, C. (1999) 'Determinants of management development in small business', *Journal of Small Business and Enterprise Development*, **6**:2, 113–127.

United Nations (1993) *Small and Medium-sized Transnational Corporations: Role, Impact and Policy Implications*. New York, United Nations.

Watson, K., Hogarth-Scott, S. and Wilson, N. (1998) 'Small business start-ups: success factors and support implications', *Journal of Entrepreneurial Behaviour and Research*, **4**:3, 217–238.

Whittington, R.C. (1984) 'Regional bias in new firm formation in the UK', *Regional Studies*, **18**:3, 253–256.

GENERAL MANAGEMENT ISSUES

Chapter 2

COMPETITIVE ADVANTAGE IN SMEs: TOWARDS A CONCEPTUAL FRAMEWORK

Oswald Jones

Introduction

This book is concerned with ways in which small and medium-sized enterprises (SMEs) create and sustain competitive advantage. All contributors have had considerable experience of working directly with SMEs and therefore have detailed insights into the strengths and weaknesses of such companies. The editors have drawn on that knowledge to help provide a better understanding of why competitive advantage is important to smaller firms as well as improving understanding of mechanisms by which owner-managers can improve the performance of their firms. At the same time, this is not a practitioner-oriented 'how-to-do' book but rather represents an attempt to reconceptualise some of the key factors, such as human resource management (HRM) and innovation management, which contribute to the competitiveness of any organisation. The basic premise that underpins this book is that many 'large firm' concepts such as HRM, strategic management and supply chain management are directly relevant to owner-managers trying to improve their firms' competitiveness although, as discussed below, the nature of strategic management or supply chain management will be very different in SMEs than in large, well-resourced companies. Equally, SMEs are not homogeneous and differences between owner-managed small firms with 10 or 20 employees and medium-sized, limited companies with over 200 employees will be greater than differences between the latter and large, multi-divisional organisations. Those companies at the upper end of the size band (<249) will tend to have adopted U-form (unitary) structures with professional managers in each of the key functional areas, who are accountable to a board of directors and ultimately to shareholders. Therefore, it would be wildly ambitious to claim that this book can answer all the questions about how to improve management practices in SMEs. Rather, concepts outlined in this book are appropriate to a wide range of smaller firms, although the way in which ideas are implemented will be contingent on a range of factors including the skill, knowledge and motivation of owner-managers and their employees as well as the competitive environment in which firms are operating.

There are likely to be substantial differences between small and large firms in terms of what competitive advantage actually means. According to Fletcher (2000), 75 per cent of SMEs are owner-managed and therefore not under pressure from shareholders to increase profit and turnover. At the same time, it is widely acknowledged that one of the key reasons for low levels of UK productivity is the 'long tail' of badly-managed and under-performing small firms. Our starting point is that the competitiveness of these firms can be improved by managerial recognition of the need for higher-quality products and services. In other words, improved competitive advantage for owner-managed firms need not necessarily be linked to an increase in profits or turnover but should focus on supplying better value to customers. The essence of our argument is that owner-managers of SMEs have to create an environment which encourages both individual and organisational learning. As pointed out by Gibb (1997), perhaps the most original definition of the learning organisation is that of Senge (1992): 'A learning organisation is a place where people are continually discovering how they create their reality. And how they can change it.'

Gibb (1997, p. 17) then goes on to say that this definition fits 'with the currently popular concept that the root cause of competitive advantage is a company's relative ability to learn'. This is a view shared by the editors of this book because it seems unlikely that competitive advantage can be created or sustained in the longer term without commitment to learning across the organisation.

Competitive Advantage in SMEs

The work of Michael Porter is the starting point for any discussion of the term 'competitive advantage'. As he himself points out (Porter, 1985, p. xvi) the idea of competitive advantage, directly or indirectly, underpins many business books. Managers in all types of organisations are under increasing pressure to control costs, as well as seeking to differentiate products and services from those of their competitors. Furthermore, Porter (1985, p. 33) argues: 'Competitive advantage ... stems from the many discrete activities a firm performs in designing, producing, marketing, delivering, and supporting its product. Each of these activities can contribute to a firm's relative cost position and create a basis for differentiation.'

The basic tool for understanding links between various activities within the firm and their contribution to competitive advantage is the *value chain*. The value chain provides a systematic way of 'disaggregating' the firm into its relevant units so that managers are better able to understand the nature of costs and potential sources of differentiation. Porter, like most other writers on corporate strategy, concentrates his attention on large, multidivisional firms rather than SMEs. A key distinction between the organisations which are the focus of this book and those which gurus such as Porter write about is that smaller firms are unlikely to have sophisticated divisionalised structures. In many SMEs, either one individual or a very small team is responsible for the whole range of functional activities. Clearly this has both advantages and disadvantages as far as managers are concerned. The advantage is that coordination issues should be less of a problem in SMEs because regular face-to-face interaction provides many opportunities for communication between members of the management team. The disadvantage is that, because such firms lack managerial resources and functional specialists, many activities are poorly managed (Buratti and Penco, 2001).

Penrose (1959), Ansoff (1965) and Andrews (1971) all used the concept of competitive advantage before Porter. In fact, Klein (2001) argues that the term did not appear in Porter's work until 1985. Other authors, Caves (1984), Day (1984), Spence (1984) and Barney (1986), also used the term around the same time as Porter (see Flint, 2000). Klein (2001) suggests that Porter's attempts to define 'competitive advantage' are tautological because the concept is simply equated with a 'firm's performance in competitive markets' (Porter, 1985, p. xv). In fact, none of the definitions discussed by Flint (2000) appear to add much to our understanding of competitive advantage. According to Knights and Morgan (1991), although rational managerialists such as Porter and Ansoff have tried to legitimate corporate strategy, more critical writers have 'challenged the orthodoxy' (Mintzberg, 1978; Mintzberg and Waters, 1985; Pettigrew, 1987, 1988). These authors all regard corporate strategy as a political process which is socially constructed rather than an unproblematic aid to rational decision-making. In essence, Knights and Morgan (1990) see strategy as a 'discourse of power' which does little more than legitimate hierarchical social relationships.

Jones and Tang (1997) analysed two 'mid-corporate' manufacturing companies using Whittington's (1993) four conceptions of strategy: classical (rational), evolutionary (fatalistic), processual (pragmatic) and systemic (relativistic). Whittington's model is based on two dimensions: the outcomes of strategy (profit-maximising versus pluralistic) and the process of strategy formulation (deliberate versus emergent). It was found that strategy-making in the two companies most closely followed the pattern described by Whittington as 'systemic'. Systemic strategy retains the classical school's (Ansoff, 1965; Porter, 1980, 1985) faith in the ability of senior managers to analyse the environment and plan effective responses. But systemic theory is based on a rejection of profit-maximising because social networks weaken the possibility of rational economic behaviour. Economic activity is embedded in a complex network of social relations including family, state, educational and professional background, religion, gender and ethnicity (Granovetter, 1985). Strategy is not restricted by cognitive bounded rationality but by the cultural rules of local society: 'the systemic perspective challenges the universality of any single model of strategy. The objectives of the strategy and the modes of strategy-making depend on the strategists' social characteristics and the social context in which they operate' (Whittington, 1993, p. 38).

Some industrial economists have focused on competitive advantage in smaller firms especially in north America (Audretsch, 2001). Fiegenbaum and Karmani's (1991) analysis of secondary data confirmed output flexibility as a viable source of competitive advantage for smaller firms in industries typified by large fluctuations in demand and low levels of profitability. A questionnaire survey of CEOs in 445 Quebec-based SMEs (200 or fewer employees) was used to investigate links between innovativeness and competitiveness (Lefebvre and Lefebvre, 1993). Using principal components analysis (PCA) the authors identified three competitiveness factors, quality, diversity and cost, which accounted for 72.9 per cent of total explained variance. These results are 'consistent with dimensions that have previously been identified as important to the competitiveness of the smaller manufacturing firms (Lefebvre and Lefebvre, 1993, p. 300). The authors then identified three groups of firms: 'worst', 'niche' and 'best', based on mean values for each of the three competitiveness dimensions. Hence, firms in the 'worst' category appeared to have no identifiable strategy because they 'lagged' on all three dimensions (Lefebvre and Lefebvre, 1993, p. 301). The second group focused on quality and diversity with high prices while the third group combined quality and diversity with relatively low-cost products. Furthermore, this hierarchy was confirmed by the financial performance of each group. The results for innovation were similar in that the 'worst' group made little effort on either R&D or patents while the 'best' firms scored highest 'which may explain why they can maintain low costs and high product diversity (Lefebvre and Lefebvre, 1993, p. 303). In the UK, Reid et al. (1993) use competitive strategy (Porter, 1980) and competitive advantage (Porter, 1985) to investigate the activities of small firms. The detailed fieldwork over a three-year period was based on structured interviews of owner-managers in 73 Scottish SMEs. According to the authors, strategy in small firms should be based on Porter's (1980) five forces which are 'the essential determinants of industry structure' (Reid et al., 1993, p. 121). Despite an extremely detailed analysis of extensive data, there is little real insight into the ways in which the owner-managers of small firms create competitive advantage.

Man and Chan (2002) argue that competitiveness is concerned with factors that contribute to firms being competitive as well as with ways in which it can be achieved. According to Oral (1986) competitiveness is a function of a firm's industry mastery, its cost superiority and the broader political and economic environment. To illustrate the multidimensional nature of competitiveness, Man and Chan (2002) draw on the work of Buckley et al. (1988) and the World Competitiveness Report (IMDWEF, 1993). Buckley et al. (1988) posit three measures of competitiveness: competitive performance, competitive potential and management processes. Within the small firm context, it is more appropriate to discuss entrepreneurial processes rather than management processes. The approach adopted by Man and Chan (2002) is to emphasise the dynamic nature of competitiveness by focusing on the entrepreneur's behaviours and actions. By examining a wide range of literature associated with competitiveness, the authors identify six competency areas which are briefly described in Table 2.1.

In developing a conceptual model of SME competitiveness (Figure 2.1) the authors argue that these six 'entrepreneurial competencies' comprise the process dimension. Task 1 involves the entrepreneur establishing the firm's competitive scope by scanning a range of external factors which include market heterogeneity, technological sophistication, market attractiveness, product/industry life-cycle, market demand and competitive concentration. In carrying out Task 2, the entrepreneur focuses attention on the firm's internal capabilities which include innovation, quality, cost-effectiveness and organicity (creating flexible organisation structures and systems). Finally, Task 3 involves the entrepreneur setting goals

TABLE 2.1 Competence and competitiveness. Reprinted from *Journal of Business Venturing*, **17**, Man and Chan, 'The Competitiveness of Small and Medium Enterprises: A conceptualization with focus at entrepreneurial competencies', 123–142. Copyright 2002, with permission from Elsevier Science

Competency area	Behavioural focus
Opportunity competencies	Recognise and develop market opportunities
Relationship competencies	Person-to-person, group-to-group interactions based on cooperation, communication and trust
Conceptual competencies	Conceptual abilities related to decision-skills, information absorption, risk-taking and innovativeness
Organising competencies	Internal and internal activities associated with human, physical, financial and technological resources
Strategic competencies	Setting, evaluating and implementing strategy
Commitment competencies	Entrepreneurial drive to develop the business

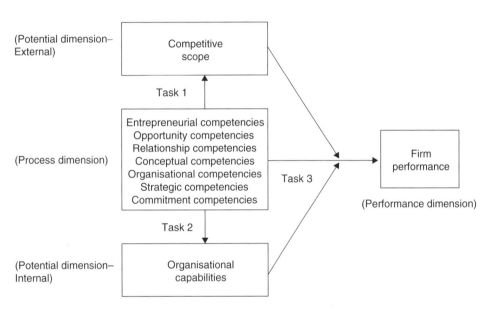

FIGURE 2.1 SME competitiveness. Reprinted from *Journal of Business Venturing*, **17**, Man and Chan, 'The Competitiveness of Small and Medium Enterprises: A conceptualization with focus at entrepreneurial competencies', 123–142. Copyright 2002, with permission from Elsevier Science

for firm performance by ensuring that there are effective linkages between the external environment and the firm's internal competencies. Competitiveness is the means by which entrepreneurs can improve their firms' performance (Hofer and Sandberg, 1987; Horne *et al.*, 1992; Herron and Robinson, 1993) which can be measured according to a number of dimensions including market share, profit, growth and duration. At the same time, Man and Chan (2002, p. 130) stress the importance of links between competitiveness and performance as having a long-term rather than a short-term orientation. The authors conclude by acknowledging that their theoretical framework is complex and therefore difficult to operationalise but is 'higher-level and closer to performance' than lower-level variables such as the entrepreneur's age, education, experience or background. Equally, the framework has broader implications for supporting SMEs: 'A policy implication is that developing competent entrepreneurs in the long term seems to be a more important issue than directly providing them with more resources or a positive environment' (Man and Chan, 2002, p. 138).

Resource-based theories of strategy (Foss, 1997; Grant, 1998) have become increasing influential in recent years and most writers take their inspiration from the work of Penrose (see Rangone, 1999; Lubit, 2001; West and DeCastro, 2001). Generally, as firms grow, new managerial services are created through the acquisition of personnel and by the redistribution of existing employees. Increasing experience gained across the firm shows in resulting changes in knowledge and in the ability to use that knowledge (Bamberger, 1989; O'Farrell and Hitchens, 1992; Penrose, 1995; Chaston and Mangles, 1997; Chawla *et al.*, 1997). A recent study of SMEs in the Netherlands adopted a resource-based approach to identify the source of competitive advantage in a sample of 63 firms representing manufacturing and service sectors (Cobbenhagen, 2000). As this work is discussed in greater detail elsewhere (see Chapter 9) a brief summary of the findings is provided here. According to Cobbenhagen (2000) 'front runners' were distinguished from 'pack members' by the way in which they combined three sets of competencies: market, technological and organisational. Elements of these three competencies included market focus and customer links (market), R&D expenditure and absorptive capacity (technological), multidisciplinary project teams and timing of company policy (organisational) (Cobbenhagen, 2000, p. 244). Resource-based theory, particularly the work of Kay (1993), also influences Wickham's (2001) analysis of competitive advantage in entrepreneurial firms. Four points of 'strategic contact' – costs, knowledge, relationships and structure – are central to the creation of competitive advantage (Table 2.2).

It has increasingly been recognised that the competitiveness of small firms is strongly influenced by the extent of interfirm collaboration (Rosenfeld, 1996). Links with other organisations are important for SMEs because of the increased opportunities they bring for external economies of scale, greater market strength and a wider ability to exploit new opportunities. Networks in which three or more SMEs join together to co-produce, co-market, co-purchase or cooperate in new product development are defined as 'hard' while 'softer' linkages involve the sharing of information or acquisition of new skills. Rosenfeld (1996) goes on to

TABLE 2.2 Establishing competitive advantage (Wickham, 2001)

Factor	Potential competitive advantage
Costs	Importance of price to customers, suppliers, distributors
	Extent of demand elasticity
Knowledge	Stage of industry life-cycle
	Common or localised knowledge
	Tacit or codified knowledge
Relationships	Building links with customers, suppliers, distributors
	Position in network and relative power
Structure	Creating appropriate organisational structures
	Ability to respond to market signals
	Leadership styles (delegation or centralisation)

argue that the economic regeneration of northern Italy was the catalyst for interest in the way in which interfirm collaboration influences the competitiveness of small firms (see Pyke *et al.*, 1990). Others such as Bagchi-Sen (2001) claim that research interest in SMEs increased as a result of the influential work of Birch (1979, 1987) who claimed that such organisations were primarily responsible for the creation of new jobs. Bagchi-Sen (2001) carried out a questionnaire survey of 54 mature SMEs (response rate 24 per cent) in the Niagara region of Canada. The research was designed to investigate two factors: first, the relationship between innovation and business performance and, second, the association between competitive strategy and product innovation. Firms were classified as either 'high' or 'low' innovators according to the number of new or revised products they had introduced in the previous five-year period. It was found that innovators performed 'better in terms of sales and exports' and that there were direct links between increased R&D expenditure and 'innovativeness' in terms of the introduction of new products and in higher levels of export intensity (Bagchi-Sen, 2001, pp. 48–49). In terms of their respective competitive strategies, both low and high innovators regarded process improvements as very important. However, 'non-price' factors such as quality, specialisation, speed of delivery and after-sales' were regarded as much more important in terms of improved competitiveness by innovators in comparison to non-innovators who tended to concentrate on low-price/cost leadership strategies (Bagchi-Sen, 2001, p. 50). High innovators also placed far more emphasis on a wide range of network linkages to access services such as market research, advertising, software, legal, banking, insurance as well as technical support.

According to Gadenne (1998) most studies of 'success' in small firms concentrate on single factors such as 'marketing strategies' (Bharadwaj and Menon, 1993), 'management competence' (Martin and Staines, 1994) or 'good management practice' (Yusuf, 1995). While some authors (Keats and Bracker, 1988; Cragg and King, 1988) have tried to conceptualise the factors which influence small firm performance, Gadenne suggests that it is important to investigate the way in which *different types* of factors interact to help create competitive advantage. In a questionnaire survey of 1500 small firms (response rate 24 per cent) in Queensland, Australia, Gadenne (1998, p. 39) used return on investment (ROI) as the measure of success as 'this more accurately reflects the efficiency with which resources have been allocated'. Principal components analysis was used to select the factors which had most influence (statistically significant at a 5 per cent level) on ROI in three different sectors; retail, service and manufacturing (Table 2.3).

In all three sectors, financial leverage (use of external funds and search for cheaper finance) were negatively related to ROI. This, according to Gadenne (1998,

TABLE 2.3   Management influences on ROI (Gadenne, 1998)

Retail	*Service*	*Manufacturing*
Value for money	Employee relations	Low price strategy
Financial leverage	Financial leverage	Financial leverage
	Working capital	Professional advice

p. 42), indicates that firms which rely on large amounts of external finance (high levels of gearing) perform worse in the shorter term than those which generate funds internally. That other factors, such as innovation, business growth, customer service and marketing, were not common was related to different competitive environments across the three sectors (see Reid *et al.*, 1993). Gadenne also examined links between the personal characteristics and objectives of owner-managers and business success. The 'surprising' result was that 'personal characteristics' had no influence on firm success, which apparently contradicts earlier research (Chell *et al.*, 1991; Chell, 2001). This lack of accord is explained by the fact that previous studies were 'invariably' based on univariate links between individual characteristics and firm success. Furthermore, 'enterprise objectives' were only found to be related to success in those firms operating in service industries. Gadenne (1998, p. 48) summarises his findings in the following manner: 'The fact that there was a common success factor (financial leverage) for all three industry groups, indicates that small enterprises in general tend to be more successful if there are sufficient financial resources either contributed by the owner or generated through profits and cash flows from operations.'

Variation across sectors (Table 2.3) indicates the importance of avoiding simplistic solutions which are intended to improve competitive advantage in any SME regardless of size or industry. In addition, Gadenne's work helps to shift the focus of attention from the owner-manager's characteristics to the importance of wider managerial practices within the organisation.

It is noted by Jennings and Beaver (1997) that independence may be a more important measure of success for owner-managers of small businesses than financial criteria such as growth in sales, profits and cash flow or the number of jobs created. Additionally, management processes in such firms 'bear little or no resemblance to management processes found in larger firms' (Jennings and Beaver, 1997, p. 64). In large firms, strategic decision-making shapes competitive advantage through policies designed to emphasise Porter's distinction between cost, focus and differentiation. But in smaller firms, competitive advantage is more likely to arise as a result of 'accidental circumstances'. In other words, owner-managers are much less able to influence the competitive environment than larger firms. While it would be unrealistic to suggest that strategic management is an entirely rational process in larger firms (Ansoff, 1965) the subjective judgement of owner-managers will have a stronger influence over the smaller firm's strategic direction, not least because owner-managers will be performing a range of functions which in large firms are carried out by professional managers with substantial organisational support: 'Organisation structures, in so far as they exist, are likely to develop around the interests and abilities of the key players. Such organisation structures are likely to be organic and loosely structured rather than mechanistic and highly formalised' (Jennings and Beaver, 1997, p. 65).

The authors summarise what they describe as 'essential management activities' which have been identified by 'a long history of management research' (Figure 2.2). The distinction is that in smaller firms all these roles will either be performed by one person or by a very narrow range of managers who may have been appointed because they are family members or friends, rather than on the basis of ability or education.

ENTREPRENEURIAL SKILLS
(adaptive and organic)

OWNERSHIP SKILLS
(predictive and mechanistic)

STRATEGIC LEVEL

Innovation
Risk taking
Tactical planning

Objective setting
Policy formulation
Strategic planning

COMMON CORE SKILLS

Decision making
Problem solving
Information processing

MANAGERIAL SKILLS
(Managerial level)

Negotiation
Troubleshooting
Interpersonal

Organising
Coordination
Formal communication
Monitoring and stabilising

FIGURE 2.2   Small firm management (Jennings and Beaver, 1997)

Entrepreneurship, Learning and Networks

One common way of examining success in the small firm sector is to study so-called 'supergrowth companies'. An early example (Ray and Hutchinson, 1983) used the growth in stockmarket value to identify firms with unique characteristics. Such companies were defined by a strong emphasis on forecasting financial data such as cash flow, profit and sales. At the same time, the business environment is dynamic and, therefore, successful small firms must possess the managerial capabilities to remain flexible and adaptive (see Greiner, 1972). This, according to Jennings and Beaver, focuses attention on managerial competences which combine entrepreneurship and professional management (Figure 2.2) but at the same time must be transferable to other managers. There have been few other detailed studies of fast-growing small companies. The IRDAC (Industrial Research and Development Advisory Committee) committee of the EU considered a sample of 30 SMEs from seven European countries identified as R&D-intensive and technological leaders (Dodgson and Rothwell, 1987, 1990). More recently, Steward and Gorrino (1997) carried out a study of 22 innovative fast-growing SMEs in six European countries. According to the small firm literature, there are three key resources necessary for growth: financial, technological and human (Steward and Gorrino, p. 18). The availability of financial resources is central to fast growth and a range of different types are used by entrepreneurs: retained profits, grants, loans and equity obtained from a range of sources including self, banks, venture capitalists, government agencies and 'business angels'. Steward and Gorrino found that the most common source of finance was retained profits (50 per cent). Equity investment and government bodies accounted for funding in 30 per cent of firms, with bank loans accounting for 25 per cent (most firms used a combination of sources).

Rothwell (1989) believes that the innovative advantage of small firms are derived from their flexible managerial structures which are more responsive to changes in the marketplace (see Vossen, 1998). However, smaller firms generally have little commitment to R&D and are 'information-constrained' which makes them highly dependent on external knowledge sources. Over 75 per cent of the companies surveyed by Steward and Gorrino drew on external sources for new technology, including suppliers, customers, competitors and research organisations. In some cases acquisition was tightly defined by means of legal contracts whereas in other cases arrangements were more informal. Few of the 22 companies relied on codified legal protection (patents) to retain control of their technological innovations. Instead, the majority placed more emphasis on tacit knowledge and their ability to maintain a 'fast-mover' position through continuous technological development (Steward and Gorrino, 1997, p. 56). The availability of skilled human resources is perhaps the main restriction on the ability of firms to grow rapidly. This may be an especially intractable problem for firms operating in relative geographic isolation or in 'mature' sectors where it may be difficult to attract employees with the appropriate technical skills (particularly IT). Generally, it was possible to identify one individual responsible for initiating change: 'It is evident that a critical role is played in all the cases by entrepreneurial individuals in establishing both the technical and managerial capabilities of the IFSMEs' [Innovative Fast-growing Small and Medium-sized Enterprises] (Steward and Gorrino, 1997, p. 65).

In 75 per cent of cases, 'change agents' were either individual entrepreneurs or 'the team' who had originally founded the firm. In the remainder of the cases, change was initiated by a member of the managerial team or by a newly acquired manager. Effective mobilisation of managerial capabilities was linked to the nature of organisational structure. In the majority of the sample, entrepreneurs retained 'a reasonably flat, communicative and participative organizational style throughout the period of growth' (Steward and Gorrino, p. 76) although, at the same time, there was some evidence of formalisation in terms of the functional division of labour and some element of divisionalisation. A common feature of 'fast growth' was that the firms adopted an 'offensive strategy' involving a proactive search for technical or market leadership. Two distinct approaches were identified by Steward and Gorrino: first, a 'starter strategy' in which growth was important from the firm's foundation, and second, a 'shifter strategy' which involved a conscious move from a 'non-offensive' to an 'offensive' strategy by identifying both market and technological opportunities. IFSMEs were able to exploit opportunities because they were better able to respond more rapidly to market opportunities or customer requirements than their larger rivals.

Many writers on entrepreneurship in smaller firms focus on personality types (extrovert-introvert) and traits (need for control, achievement, etc.) as the explanation for organisational success (Chell et al., 1991; Chell, 1999). Generally such types and traits are regarded as biologically or genetically determined, although occasionally some degree of environmental influence is acknowledged. It is now accepted that there is very little evidence to suggest that any particular trait leads to successful entrepreneurship (Wickham, 2001, p. 16). Rather, as Drucker points out, entrepreneurial capabilities can be acquired in the same way as other managerial skills and competences.

> Innovation is the specific tool of entrepreneurs, the means by which they exploit change as an opportunity for a different business or a different service. It is capable of being presented as a discipline, capable of being learned, capable of being practised. Entrepreneurs need to search purposely for the sources of innovation, the changes and their symptoms that indicate opportunities for successful innovation. And they need to know and to apply the principles of successful innovation. (Drucker, 1985, p. 17)

According to Chandler (1990) 'organisational capabilities' encompassing both physical resources (raw materials, plant and equipment) and human resources (financial, managerial, technical knowledge and skills) are critical to the ability of firms to develop competitive advantage. Chandler's work is important because as well as distinguishing between scale and scope he identifies strategic and functional capabilities. The latter, which include training, motivation, coordination and integration, are central to the exploitation of cost-saving economies which are critical to improved competitiveness (Davies and Brady, 2000). Teece *et al.* (1997) argue that the creation of 'dynamic capabilities' which represent a firm's ability to respond to a changing business environment are dependent on its business processes. Organisations confronted with changing markets or changing technologies have to develop new sets of capabilities to avoid the creation of 'core rigidities' (Leonard-Barton, 1995). The term 'dynamic capabilities' refers to the ability of managers to create innovative responses to a changing business environment. Teece *et al.* (1997) identify three organisational and managerial processes with the creation of dynamic capabilities:

1. The coordination and integration of both internal and external activities.
2. Learning, seen as 'social and collective', is defined as the 'repetition and experimentation which enable tasks to be performed better and quicker.'
3. Reconfiguration and transformation which is based on surveillance of market and technological environments and, according to the authors, 'the more frequently practiced, the more easier accomplished.'

Knowledge and learning networks are central to the transfer of information which occurs through data, documents, softwares and standards (Simmie, 1997). Such transfers are generally associated with the role of 'gatekeepers' who are responsible for the collection, evaluation and dissemination of information (Allen, 1971). Organisational innovation and learning depends on creating mechanisms for the translation of tacit knowledge into codified knowledge (Nonaka and Takeuchi, 1995). Tidd (1997) argues that different network types provide different opportunities for learning and therefore collaboration is an important mechanism for the acquisition of new organisational competences and capabilities. Dussauge *et al.* (2000) adopt a resource-based approach to suggest that 'firms' competitive advantages derive from their preferential access to idiosyncratic resources, especially tacit knowledge.' Results from the study indicate that firms are better able to acquire new capabilities when they have competences in similar areas (Dussauge *et al.*, 2000). This confirms earlier work by Cohen and Levinthal (1990, p. 102) who argue that 'absorptive capacity' depends on having related knowledge and skill that 'confers an ability to recognise the value of new information, assimilate it, and apply it to commercial ends'. Jones and Craven (2001) utilise the concept of absorptive capacity to illustrate ways in which small firms can become more innovative and entrepreneurial by developing links with external sources of knowledge. This case study of a TCS (teaching company scheme) concentrates on how introducing new 'organisational routines' such as regular management meeting and a new product development committee can improve both absorptive capacity and competitive advantage measured by objective factors such as increases in turnover as well as subjective factors that include greater employee involvement and changing customer perceptions of the firm (more innovative and forward-thinking).

As discussed in Chapter 1, recent government small-firm policy, as well as EU initiatives, has been aimed at improving the competitiveness of small firms. Gibb (1997) examines the many training initiatives designed to improve the skills of owner-managers and their employees, concluding there is very little research evidence of any direct impact on organisational performance. This failure of training to improve the competitiveness of smaller firms is attributed to a perception of learning which emphasises the separation of knowledge-creation and context: 'Learning better from experience implies bringing knowledge, skills, values and attitudes together to interact on the learning process; it therefore fundamentally demands an action-learning approach' (Gibb, 1997, p. 16).

Gibb goes on to argue that viewing the firm's business networks (links to customers, suppliers, bankers, accountants, regulatory authorities, family, peers etc.) as a 'learning environment' is central to performance improvements. Network interactions provide opportunities for 'subjective' learning as various actors within small firms make adaptations to operating activities in response to environmental change. The advantage smaller firms have is that there should be fewer communication barriers to sharing knowledge about such activities, which helps to link operational change and the organisation's broader strategic direction.

Conclusion

As pointed out in a recent HM Treasury report (2001), the government's objective of achieving high levels of growth and employment are hampered because the UK is seen to have 'a substantial productivity gap with other major industrialised economies'. The five areas which government believe to be key drivers of productivity are investment, skills, innovation, enterprise and competition. British companies certainly spend far less on capital equipment than their international competitors (Kitson and Michie, 1996) although business investment has risen from 10 per cent of GDP in 1995 to over 14 per cent in 2000 (Treasury, 2001, p. 16). There is still a need for smaller companies to invest, particularly in the area of ICTs (information and communication technologies). Lack of investment in education and training has also limited productivity growth. For example, 55 per cent of the UK workforce is classified as 'low-skilled' compared to only 23 per cent in Germany (Treasury, 2001). The government has initiated a number of changes, including Individual Learning Accounts (ILAs) and learndirect (www.learndirect.co.uk, the UK government's provision of online information and courses), designed to improve workforce skills. It should be noted that ILAs were discontinued in November 2001 due to widespread fraud by training providers (Kingston, 2002). Although levels of literacy in the UK still rank among the lowest in Europe, they are improving, and the proportion of adults with no formal qualifications fell from 18.4 per cent in 1996 to 15.1 per cent in 2000.

The third 'critical input' to productivity is innovation, and again this is an area in which UK companies lag behind. Recent evidence indicates that levels of R&D (research and development) expenditure are beginning to increase, but closing the gap with our main rivals will be difficult (Jones, 2000). According to the Treasury (2001, p. 26): 'the evidence shows ... that spending on R&D is associated with higher levels of innovation and productivity growth.' One of the key government initiatives in this area has been the introduction of R&D tax credits for SMEs. Encouraging smaller firms to be more innovatory through investment in R&D is seen as an important way of improving competitiveness in individual companies and productivity in the economy as a whole. In the other two areas that are linked to productivity, enterprise and competition, there have been a number of government strategies to improve UK performance since New Labour were first elected in 1997. Attempts to create a more entrepreneurial culture include changes to capital gains tax (CGT) to encourage investment in business assets, modifications to bankruptcy law, the £96 million Phoenix Fund (business support for the socially excluded) and the introduction of the Small Business Service (SBS) to ensure that government support for smaller firms is 'simpler and more coherent'. The most important element of the government's approach to competition has been the introduction of the Competition Act which came into force in March 2000 and is intended to 'tackle anti-competitive practices and abuses of a dominant market position' (Treasury, 2001). This attempt to discourage monopolies should provide increased opportunities for smaller firms to compete more effectively with their larger rivals. In his review of UK industrial policy, Wren (2001) discusses a number of government initiatives designed to improve the productivity of SMEs including an additional £10 million for Foresight LINK awards which support partnerships between research and industry, as well as a doubling of DTI funding to encourage technology transfer through TCS (previously known as the Teaching Company Scheme).

Contributors to this book recognise that improving management practices in small firms is an important element in improving national productivity. Furthermore, regardless of the individual owner-manager's motivation, a commitment to innovation through the modification of existing products, the introduction of new products and process improvements designed to reduce costs and improve quality will enhance the firm's longer-term competitive position. However, to be effective any SME change programme must begin with the owner-manager (or management team) establishing a broad **strategic framework** for the company (Figure 2.3). This planning process should help to ensure that change is linked to existing skills and knowledge within the company, while simultaneously identifying those areas of weakness which require training of existing staff or recruitment of new employees. At the same time, strategy-makers should guide the innovation process by identifying markets in which new products or services are expected to compete. Ideally, setting the strategic framework should be based on a wide process of consultation across the organisation. This is important for accessing

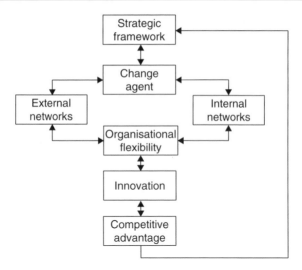

FIGURE 2.3 Conceptualising competitive advantage in small firms

new ideas and for ensuring that all employees are committed to the shift in organisational strategy.

Change agent: the change process should be guided by the owner-manager (or senior management team) but day-to-day responsibility could be delegated to a relatively junior change agent (Jones and Craven, 2001). It is possible that in smaller firms the owner-manager would act as the change agent but, given the operational pressures of managing such organisations, this is not desirable. According to Day (1994), initiators of intrapreneurial actions can adopt one of three roles: top-down champion, bottom-up champion or dual-role champion. Even though change must be a team effort, there will generally be one individual who acts as champion, taking on responsibility for building and motivating 'collective transformational leadership' (Day, 1994). What is more important than status is that the change agent should have access to adequate resources and the wholehearted support of senior managers. Change agents (intrapreneurs) should have the necessary interpersonal skills to build both internal and external networks to help identify, access and disseminate new knowledge and skills. Intrapreneurs need autonomy to operate effectively but at the same time their activities must be guided by requirements set out in the strategic plan.

External networks: key actors within the organisation must recognise the importance of being open to external influences. Smaller firms cannot possibly have internal access to all the knowledge and skills required to remain competitive. Therefore, a willingness to draw on external knowledge sources is a *sine qua non* of the change process as conceptualised here. In other words, the intrapreneur must adopt a 'boundary spanning' role to forge a wide range of external links. These links will include better communications with customers, suppliers and even competitors, but should also include HEIs, TCS, SBS, the local Chamber of Commerce as well as utilising the Internet which is an essential information source for smaller firms.

Internal networks: identifying and acquiring new knowledge must be accompanied by the creation of mechanisms for the dissemination of that information within the organisation. An SME's *absorptive capacity* is a central element in improving organisational competitiveness by ensuring that new information is rapidly disseminated to managers, technical staff, first-line supervisors and shopfloor employees (Jones and Craven, 2001). Intrapreneurship is not based on the activities of a single individual but is essentially a collective effort that demands high levels of collaboration to achieve successful transformation (Denis *et al.*, 1996).

Flexibility: a defining feature of SMEs is that they are unable to influence their operating environment in the same way as larger firms. In addition, one of the major advantages such firms have over their larger rivals is their ability to respond more rapidly to changing signals from the marketplace. Therefore, it is essential that in introducing new routines (working activities) into the firm, emphasis is placed on the importance of flexibility (Figures 2.2 and 2.3). This encompasses managerial activity associated with constantly scanning the environment for threats and opportunities, and employees' willingness to develop new skills. Hence, the company's HRM policies, in terms of both recruitment and reward, should be designed to reinforce appropriate attitudes and behaviours.

Innovation: as Freeman (1982) points out, innovation is the range of organisational activities associated with moving from the conception of an idea to a product or service offered for sale in the marketplace. In other words, innovation is a process rather than a single event and even relatively simple incremental changes to existing products and services require time and resources if they are to be successfully implemented. In a recent paper, Atherton and Hannon (2001, p. 278) use Drucker's (1985) work as the basis of their definition: 'innovation is a business process of managing a bundle of activities which create wealth, in the widest sense of the word, from existing resources.' It is also important to add that innovation does not necessarily involve the adoption of radical new technologies nor the introduction of major new products, services or processes. Instead, particularly for SMEs, concentrating on a range of incremental innovations based on ideas adopted from customers, competitors and suppliers to improve both products and processes is likely to be a more effective way of improving overall competitiveness.

Competitive advantage: the broad strategic direction set by the owner-manager should provide authority for the intrapreneur to begin the change process. This means creating both internal and external knowledge-based networks which lead to greater levels of organisational learning and flexibility. At the same time, the intrapreneur will begin the process or organisational change by encouraging the introduction of new ways of working, and new (or modified) products which strengthen the firm's longer-term competitive position. It is important to stress that the model should not be seen as a linear process but rather that the various factors represent the 'building blocks' of any SME's medium-term competitive strategy and longer-term 'strategic health' (Afuah, 1998). As discussed above, the term 'competitive strategy' is difficult to define, particularly in terms of owner-managed firms which may value independence more than growth in profits or sales (Jennings and Beaver, 1997). However, Tidd (2001) distinguishes between accounting measures of performance (profits, share value, ROI) and market performance (market share and growth). According to Drew (1995), competitive success can be measured by both objective and subjective criteria. Objective criteria include ROI (return on investment), ROA (return on assets), market share and sales revenue. Commonly-used indices of innovatory activity are based on revenues generated from new products:

> Percentage of this year's revenue from products introduced in the last two years;
> Percentage of next year's revenue from products introduced this year and last year;
> Percentage of revenue in five years from products introduced in the next five years.

Subjective measures include improved reputation with customers, suppliers and competitors, improved service quality and better competitive positioning. A combination of objective and subjective factors should help senior managers to judge the effectiveness of their strategic framework. However, of course, it is important to stress that innovation is not the basis of a 'quick fix' for failing companies but something that needs commitment from senior managers over a substantial period of time (Cobbenhagen, 2000). It may be that the best measure of competitive advantage for SMEs is 'value-added' rather than profit, ROI or market share. Improvements in value-added per employee would provide an indication of more effective internal processes (cost reductions) and stronger market performance (the introduction of new or improved products).

To summarise, organisational flexibility is the key source of competitive advantage for most SMEs. While the authors contributing to this book discuss individual factors ranging from innovation management to supply chain management, all activities should contribute to a flexible, learning organisation and eventually to competitive advantage (Figure 2.4). Individual authors attempt to make direct links between their topic and these key issues, and the concluding chapter summarises ways in which managers in SMEs can build more dynamic and successful organisations.

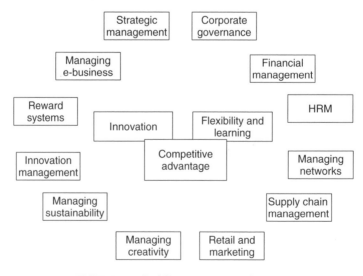

FIGURE 2.4   Building competitive advantage

References

Afuah, A. (1998) *Innovation Management: Strategies, Implementation and Profits*. OUP, Oxford.

Allen, T. (1971) 'Communication networks in R&D laboratories', *R&D Management*, **1**:1, 14–21.

Andrews, K.R. (1971) *The Concept of Strategy*. Richard D. Irwin, Homewood, IL.

Ansoff, H.I. (1965) *Corporate Strategy*. McGraw-Hill, New York.

Atherton, A. and Hannon, P.D. (2000) 'Innovation processes and the small business: a conceptual analysis', *International Journal of Business Performance Management*, **2**:4, 276–292.

Audretsch, D.B. (2001) 'Research issues relating to structure, competition and performance of small technology-based firms', *Small Business Economics*, **16**, 37–51.

Bagchi-Sen, S. (2001) 'Product innovation and competitive advantage in an area of industrial decline; the Niagara region of Canada', *Technovation*, **21**, 45–54.

Bamberger, I. (1989) 'Developing competitive advantage in small and medium-sized firms', *Long Range Planning*, **22**:5, 80–88.

Barney, J. (1986) 'Organizational culture: can it be a source of sustained competitive advantage?' *Academy of Management Review*, **11**, 656–665.

Bharadwaj, S.G. and Menon, A. (1993) 'Determinants of success in service industries: a PIMS-based empirical investigation, *Journal of Service Marketing*, **7**:4, 19–40.

Birch, D.L. (1979) *The Job Generation Process: MIT Project on Neighborhood and Regional Change*. Economic Development Administration, Washington, DC.

Birch, D.L. (1987) *Job Creation in America: How Our Smallest Companies Put the Most People in Work*. Free Press, New York.

Buckley, P.J., Pass, C.L. and Prescott, K. (1988) 'Measures of international competitiveness: a critical survey', *Journal of Marketing Management*, **4**:2, 175–200.

Buratti, N. and Penco, L. (2001) 'Assisted technology transfer to SMEs: lessons from an exemplary case', *Technovation*, **21**, 35–43.

Caves, R.R. (1984) 'Economic analysis and the question for competitive advantage', *American Economic Review*, **74**, 127–132.

Chandler, A.D. (1990) *Scale and Scope: The Dynamics of Industrial Capitalism*. Cambridge, MA, Belknap Press.

Chaston, I. and Mangles, T. (1997) 'Core capabilities as predictors of growth potential in small manufacturing firms', *Journal of Small Business Management*, **35**:1, 47–57.

Chell, E. (1999) 'The entrepreneurial personality; past, present and future', *Occupational Psychologist*, **38**, 5–12.

Chell, E. (2001) *Entrepreneurship: Globalization, Innovation and Development*. Thomson Learning, London.

Chell, E., Haworth, J. and Brealey, S. (1991) *The Entrepreneurial Personality: Concepts, Cases and Categories*. Routledge, London.

Chawla, S.K., Pullig, C. and Alexander, F.D. (1997) 'Critical success factors from an organizational life cycle perspective: perceptions of small business owners from different business environments', *Journal of Business Entrepreneurship*, **9**:1, 47–58.

Cobbenhagen, J. (2000) *Successful Innovation: Towards a New Theory for the Management of SMEs*. Edward Elgar, Cheltenham.

Cohen, W.M. and Levinthal, D.A. (1990) 'Absorptive capacity: a new perspective on learning and innovation', *Administrative Science Quarterly*, **35**, 128–152.

Cragg, P.B. and King, M. (1988) 'Organizational characteristics and small firms' performance revisited', *Enterprise, Theory and Practice*, Winter, 49–64.

Davies, A. and Brady, T. (2000) 'Organisational capabilities and learning in complex product systems: towards repeatable solutions', *Research Policy*, **29**, 931–953.

Day, D.L. (1994) 'Raising radicals: different processes for championing innovative corporate ventures', *Organization Science*, **5**:2, 148–172.

Day, G.S. (1984) *Strategic Market Planning: The Pursuit of Competitive Advantage*. West Publishing Company, St. Paul, MN.

Denis, L., Langley, A. and Cazale, L. (1996) 'Leadership and strategic change under ambiguity', *Organisation Studies*, **17**:4, 673–699.

Dodgson, M. and Rothwell, R. (1987) *Patterns of Growth and R&D Activities in a Sample of Small and Medium-Sized High Technology Firms in the UK, Denmark, Netherlands and Ireland*. Report to IRDAC Working Party III, Brussels.

Dodgson, M. and Rothwell, R. (1990) 'Technology strategies in small and medium-sized firms', in M. Dodgson and R. Rothwell (eds) *Technology Strategy and the Firm*. Routledge, London.

Drew, S.A.W. (1995) 'Strategic benchmarking: innovation practices in financial institutions', *International Journal of Bank Marketing*, **13**:1, 4–16.

Drucker, P. (1985) *Innovation and Entrepreneurship*. Butterworth-Heinemann, Oxford.

Dussauge, P., Garrette, B. and Mitchell, W. (2000) 'Learning from competing partners: outcomes and durations of scale and link alliances in Europe, North America and Asia', *Strategic Management Journal*, **21**:2, 99–126.

Fiegenbaum, A. and Karmani, A. (1991) 'Output flexibility: A competitive advantage for small firms', *Strategic Management Journal*, **12**, 101–114.

Fletcher, D. (2000) 'Family and Enterprise', in D. Jones-Evans and S. Carter (eds) *Enterprise and Small Business: Principles, Policy and Practice*. Addison-Wesley Longman, London.

Flint, G.D. (2000) 'What is the meaning of competitive advantage?', *Advances in Competitiveness Research*, **8**:1, 121–129.

Foss, N.J. (1997) *Resources, Firms and Strategies: A Reader in the Resource-Based Perspective*. OUP, Oxford.

Freeman, C. (1982) *The Economics of Innovation*. Pinter, London.

Gadenne, D. (1998) 'Critical success factors for small businesses: an inter-industry comparison', *International Small Business Journal*, **17**:1, 36–51.

Gibb, A. (1997) 'Small firms' training and competitiveness: building upon the small firm as a learning organization', *International Small Business Journal*, **15**:3, 13–29.

Granovetter, M. (1985) 'Economic action and social structure: the problem of embeddedness', *American Journal of Sociology*, **91**:3, 481–510.

Grant, R.M. (1998) *Contemporary Strategy Analysis: Concepts, Techniques and Applications*, 3rd edition. Blackwell, Oxford.

Greiner, L. (1972) 'Evolution and revolution as organizations grow', *Harvard Business Review*, July/August.

Herron, L. and Robinson, R.B. (1993) 'A structural model of the effects of entrepreneurial characteristics on venture performance', *Journal of Business Venturing*, **8**:3, 281–294.

HM Treasury (2001) *Productivity in the UK: Progress Towards a Productive Economy*. HM Treasury, London.

Hofer, C.W. and Sandberg, W.R. (1987) 'Improving new venture performance: some guidelines for success', *American Journal of Small Business*, **12**:1, 11–25.

Horne, M., Lloyd, P., Pay, J. and Roe, P. (1992) 'Understanding the competitive process: a guide to effective intervention in the small firms sector', *European Journal of Operations Research*, **56**:1, 54–66.

Institute of Management Development and World Economic Forum (1993) *The World Competitiveness Report*. Lausanne, Switzerland.

Jennings, P. and Beaver, G. (1997) 'The performance and competitive advantage of small firms: a management perspective', *International Small Business Journal*, **15**:1, 66–75.

Jones, O. (2000) 'Innovation management as a post-modern phenomenon: the outsourcing of pharmaceutical R&D', *British Journal of Management*, **11**:4, 341–356.

Jones, O. and Craven, M. (2001) 'Expanding capabilities in a mature manufacturing firm: absorptive capacity and the TCS', *International Small Business Journal*, **19**:3, 39–55.

Jones, O. and Tang, N. (1997) 'Networks for technology transfer: linking HEIs and SMFs', *International Journal of Technology Management*, **12**:7/8, 820–829.

Kay, J. (1993) *Foundations of Corporate Success: How Businesses Add Value*. OUP, Oxford.

Keats, B.W. and Bracker, J.S. (1988) 'Towards a theory of small firm performance: a conceptual model', *American Journal of Small Business*, **12**:2, 41–58.

Kingston, P. (2002) 'Spotlight focuses on computer company in ILA debacle', *The Guardian*, 22 January.

Kitson, M. and Michie, J. (1996) 'Manufacturing capacity, investment and employment', in J. Michie and J. Grieve Smith (eds) *Creating Industrial Capacity: Towards Full Employment*. OUP, Oxford.

Klein, J. (2001) 'A critique of competitive advantage', *Critical Management Studies Conference*, Manchester (July).

Knights, D. and Morgan, G. (1990) 'The concept of strategy in sociology: a note of dissent', *Sociology*, **24**:3, 465–483.

Knights, D. and Morgan, G. (1991) 'Corporate strategy, organizations and subjectivity', *Organization Studies*, **12**:2, 251–273.

Lefebvre, L.A. and Lefebvre, E. (1993) 'Competitive positioning and innovative effort in SMEs', *Small Business Economics*, **5**:4, 297–305.

Leonard-Barton, D. (1995) *Wellsprings of Knowledge*. HBS, Boston.

Lubit, R. (2001) 'Tacit knowledge and knowledge management: the keys to sustainable competitive advantage', *Organizational Dynamics*, **29**:3, 164–178.

Man, T. and Chan, T. (2002) 'The competitiveness of small and medium enterprises: a conceptualization with focus on entrepreneurial competencies', *Journal of Business Venturing*, **17**, 123–142.

Martin, G. and Staines, H. (1994) 'Managerial competence in small firms', *Journal of Management Development*, **13**:7, 23–34.

Mintzberg, H. (1978) 'Patterns in strategy formation', *Management Science*, **14**, 934–948.

Mintzberg, H. and Waters, J.A. (1985) 'Of strategies, deliberate and emergent', *Strategic Management Journal*, **26**, 257–272.

Nonaka, I. and Takeuchi, H. (1995) *The Knowledge Creating Company: How Japanese Companies Create the Dynamics of Innovation*. OUP, Oxford.

O'Farrell, P.N. and Hitchens, D.M. (1992) 'The competitiveness business service firms: a matched comparison between Scotland and the South-east of England', *Regional Studies*, **26**:6, 519–533.

Oral, M. (1986) 'An industrial competitiveness model', *IIE Transactions*, **18**:2, 148–157.

Penrose, E. (1959) *The Theory of the Growth of the Firm*, revised edition, 1995. OUP, Oxford.

Pettigrew, A. (1987) 'Context and action in the transformation of the firm', *Journal of Management Studies*, **24**:6, 649–670.

Pettigrew, A. (ed.) (1988) *The Management of Strategic Change*. Blackwell, Oxford.

Porter, M. (1980) *Competitive Strategy: Techniques for Analysing Industries and Competitors*. Free Press, New York.

Porter, M. (1985) *Competitive Advantage: Creating and Sustaining Superior Performance*. Free Press, New York.

Pyke, F., Becattini, G. and Sengenberger, W. (1990) 'Industrial districts and inter-firm cooperation', *Research Series 90* (International Institute for Labour Studies), Geneva, Switzerland.

Rangone, A. (1999) 'A resource-based approach to strategy analysis in small and medium-sized enterprises', *Small Business Economics*, **12**:3, 233–248.

Ray, G.H. and Hutchinson, P.J. (1983) *The Financing and Financial Control of Small Enterprise Development*. Gower, London.

Reid, G.C., Jacobsen, L.R. and Anderson, M.E. (1993) *Profiles in Small Business: A Competitive Strategy Approach*. Routledge, London.

Rosenfeld, S.A. (1996) 'Does cooperation enhance competitiveness? Assessing the impacts of inter-firm collaboration', *Research Policy*, **25**, 247–263.

Rothwell, R. (1989) 'Small firms, innovation and industrial change', *Small Business Economics*, **1**:1, 51–64.

Senge, P. (1992) *The Fifth Discipline: The Art and Practice of the Learning Organization*. London, Century.

Simmie, J. (ed.) (1997) *Innovation Networks and Learning Regions?* Kingsley, London.

Spence, A.M. (1984) 'Industrial organization and competitive advantage in multinational industries', *American Economic Review*, **74**, 356–360.

Steward, F. and Gorrino, I. (1997) *Innovative Fast-Growing SMEs*. Luxembourg, Publication No. 42, European Innovation Monitoring System.

Teece, D., Pisano, G. and Shuen, A. (1997) 'Dynamic capabilities and strategic management', *Strategic Management Journal*, **18**:7, 509–533.

Tidd, J. (1997) 'Complexity, networks and learning: integrative themes for research on the management of innovation', *International Journal of Innovation Management*, **1**:1, 1–19.

Tidd, J. (2001) 'Innovation management in context: environment, organization and performance', *International Journal of Management Reviews*, **3**:3, 169–183.

Vossen, R.W. (1998) 'Relative strengths and weaknesses of small firms in innovation', *International Small Business Journal*, **16**:3, 88–94.

West, G.P. and DeCastro, J. (2001) 'The Achilles heel of firm strategy: resource weakness and distinctive inadequacies', *Journal of Management Studies*, **38**:3, 417–442.

Whittington, R. (1993) *What is Strategy and does it Matter?* Routledge, London.

Wickham, P.A. (2001) *Strategic Entrepreneurship: A Decision-Making Approach to New Venture Creation and Management*, 2nd edition. Pearson Education, Harlow.

Wren, C. (2001) 'The industrial policy of competitiveness: a review of recent developments in the UK', *Regional Studies*, **35**:9, 847–860.

Yusuf, A. (1995) 'Critical success factors for small business: perceptions of South Pacific entrepreneurs', *Journal of Small Business Management*, **33**:2, 68–73.

Chapter 3

STRATEGIC MANAGEMENT FOR SMALL AND MEDIUM-SIZED ENTERPRISES (SMEs)

Alan Marsden and Carole Forbes

Introduction

The field of strategic management consists of the study of strategy and the strategic management process. A strategy can be defined as an action a company takes to achieve one or more of its goals and the strategic management process is the way in which managers develop strategies. In more detail, the strategic management process is often conceived of as consisting of four major steps: analysis, formulation, implementation and evaluation/adjustment. The product of this strategy process is referred to as the strategy content and its study seeks to answer the question of what is, and what should be, the strategy for the company. A third dimension of strategy is the strategy context and the study of this aspect is concerned with the firm and the environment within which the strategy process and strategy content are embedded.

Our knowledge of the strategic management of SMEs derives from two main sources: first from those specialising in the field of small-firm research and second from reflections and research by those involved in the field of strategic management in general. From their early interest in strategic planning, specialists in small-firm research in the UK took a different view from those interested in strategy in general. Instead of a 'top-down' approach in which prescribed planning processes developed in larger organisations were scaled down to suit the smaller firm, they adopted a 'bottom-up' approach (McKiernan and Morris, 1994). In other words, specialists in small-firm research sought to develop strategy-making processes based on a detailed understanding of smaller company operations. The purpose of this chapter is to review the alternative approaches and contributions of these two research groups and to suggest how a combination of their approaches can assist in the development of a more useful analytical framework for the strategic management of SMEs.

Exactly where the cut-off point lies between the small firm and a medium-sized business varies depending on the criteria employed (see Chapter 1) but, however measured, there is general agreement that small firms differ from larger firms in terms of the centrality of the owner-manager, the informality of structure, the limited resource base, the smaller number of products produced and the range of markets served. As we move up the size continuum, the characteristics that distinguish small firms from large firms become less and less pronounced. Professional managers are increasingly employed, the organisational structure becomes more formalised, the resource base is increased and the chance that the firm will be able to offer a wider range of products or services in a range of markets also increases. The 'stage theories' of business growth, though criticised as lacking in explanatory power, do describe the major changes in characteristics as the successful organisation moves from start-up, through survival, success and take-off stages. Churchill and Lewis (1983) for instance, argue that as the firm grows, so the focus of senior management will shift from a concern with operational matters during the survival phase to tactics in the success phase to the strategy in the take-off stage of growth. It is evident therefore that what we are faced with is the task of assessing the applicability of large-organisation strategic management concepts to a range of organisations with differing characteristics. Such a task, however, depends on having knowledge of the strategic management process at different phases of an organisation's growth trajectory. As we do not yet possess such knowledge, we propose the less ambitious task of considering the applicability of large-scale strategy concepts to the small organisation. In doing so, we are making the simplifying assumption that large-scale strategic management concepts will be more relevant as we consider organisations further up the size continuum.

The Strategic Management of SMEs: A 'Bottom-up Approach'

Despite the fact that small-firm research in the UK took off in the 1970s at about the same time as the growth of interest in the general field of strategic management, the model of strategy-making in the small firm has developed somewhat independently of mainstream strategic management. The reason for this has to do with subject specialisation. In the UK, research on small firms tends to have been undertaken by a different set of scholars than those interested in the general field of strategic management. This is of some importance because while models of strategic management owe their development to the work of American scholars, the definition and concept of the small firm is very different in the UK and Europe than in the USA. While in the UK, a small firm is often considered as being one with fewer than 50 employees, in the USA a small business is defined as one with fewer than 500 employees!

Given their different starting points, it is not surprising that the interests and focus of the two groups have diverged. While those interested in the general field of strategic management have sought to develop an analytical framework and set of concepts applicable to all firms, independent of size or industry, those specialising in small-firm research have taken a different view. Indeed, as early as 1959, Penrose observed that because small and large firms are as different from each other as is a caterpillar from a butterfly, it makes little sense to try to apply generalisations developed in the study of large organisations to explain performance and growth in small organisations. Subsequent researchers and writers on small firms have similarly regarded the small firm as unique (see Stanworth and Curran (1976), Milne *et al.* (1982), Gibb and Scott (1985), Storey (1994), Jennings and Beaver (1997) and Smallbone and Wyer (2000).

In their critique of the 'top-down' approach referred to as the 'business management' approach, Smallbone and Wyer (2000) argue that while such an approach may provide guiding insights, it tends 'to be over-rational and systematic and thus incompatible with the idiosyncrasies and informalities of small business management processes.' They justify this view by seeking to show how the internal operating context of small firms differs from that of larger firms and by demonstrating how much more vulnerable small firms are to the external operating context than larger firms. They argue that size-related factors affect the ability of small firms to respond to development opportunities in the external environment. Such factors include the organisation culture which reflects the personality and aspirations of the owner-manager who may be uninterested in growth, the lack of adequate financial resources, the problems of attracting and retaining quality people, and the inability of the owner-manager to understand and cope with the changing environment because of a lack of time and expertise.

The particular vulnerability of the small firm to the external operating context is explained in terms of its inability to cope with change. Given limited resources, it is argued, any particular changes such as that brought about by new government legislation can have a disproportionate effect on the fortunes of small firms. A second problem facing small businesses is the policies and strategies of large firms. The shift in the policy of some large firms 'to make' instead of 'to buy', for instance, can be disastrous for small firms that have built up a trading relationship with them. A third problem is the limited access small firms have to prime locations. In the retail sector, this is of particular importance as small firms find themselves squeezed out of the best locations by larger firms.

Though Smallbone and Wyer (2000) and many others have discussed the unique attributes of the small firm, the discussion by Jennings and Beaver (1997) is particularly relevant because they explicitly reject the application of large-scale strategic management concepts to small firms. On the basis of a review of small-firm research they argue that 'The management process in the small firm is unique. It bears little or no resemblance to management processes found in the larger organisations, which have been the subject of substantial academic research resulting in numerous models, prescriptions and constructs.'

Jennings and Beaver go on to claim that while in larger organisations, competitive advantage is often created deliberately and is primarily a predictive process concerned with the clarification and communication of long-term objectives, in smaller firms, competitive advantage often arises accidentally as a result of the particular operating circumstances surrounding the enterprise. The authors' claims about the nature of the strategic management process in larger organisations is debatable, given recent research, but Jennings and Beaver do provide a useful summary of the general argument for treating small businesses as in some way unique. In their view, strategic management in the small firm has little to do with predicting and controlling the environment and more to do with adapting to the operating environment and devising tactics for mitigating the consequences of any threatening changes that might occur. The reasons why small firms operate in this way, they argue, are to do with the limited resources available to them and to the centrality of the owner-manager as the key decision-maker. In their view, small firms' success is largely dependent on the personal characteristics of the owner-manager and on the closeness of these and other key role-players to the operating personnel and activities being undertaken. This not only provides key role-players with the opportunity to influence activities, but also means that relationships tend to be informal with no precise definition of rights, obligations, duties or responsibilities.

Because of these characteristics, the authors claim, competitive advantage in the small firm often takes an implicit rather than an explicit form, and is enacted instinctively rather than being consciously and deliberately formulated and implemented. This stress on the influence of the owner-manager, the effect of limited resources, the informality of relationships and the vulnerability of the small firm to the environment are typical of the assumptions generally held by writers on small firms.

These constraints on the small firm and its management are undeniable, but they do not make it impossible for small firms to survive and grow. It is also important to note, as several writers have pointed out, that small firms and their owner-managers are not homogeneous. One of the distinctions commonly made in the literature is that between the lifestyle of the owner-manager who has no wish to grow the business and the entrepreneurial owner-manager who is running a small business because she is still in the start-up phase of the firm's life-cycle. It is also the case that some owner-managers of small firms are better educated, more experienced or more gifted in some ways than others, so we cannot assume that either the drive or the ability to seek competitive advantage is the same in all firms. We should be wary, therefore, of assuming that because some small-firm owner-managers are uneducated, limited in experience or lacking skills and resources that this applies to all small firms and their owner-managers and that this will necessarily result in the 'irrational behaviour' of the small-firm owner-manager, as suggested by Jennings and Beaver. We should also be cautious about accepting the claim made by small-firm specialists like Jennings and Beaver. that competitive advantage in the small firm often takes an implicit form and is enacted instinctively, while that in the larger firm it is consciously and deliberately formulated and implemented: in fact, the evidence is unclear, and research on strategy-making in general suggests that there is a variety of modes of strategic decision-making.

Starting with the research on planning in small business, we find that although planning is often regarded as essential by 'how-to-do-it writers' and business advisors the research does not provide clear evidence about its effectiveness. Hannon and Atherton (1998) concluded after an extensive review of the literature that there was, 'no clear consensus that plans and planning, particularly as a formal activity, have a positive impact on small firms' performance.' They also cast doubt on the usefulness of business plans, arguing that these are often produced solely as a means of obtaining external funding from banks and other organisations and are rarely referred to once the necessary funding is obtained.

Commenting on the lack of consistency in the findings on strategic planning, Gibb and Scott (1985) suggested that measurement and conceptual problems might account for the lack of consensus about the value of planning. Writers like Mintzberg (1994) have also argued that definitions of planning are often unclear and imprecise, creating difficulties when trying to compare studies. Hannon and Atherton (in the review already referred to) also claim that 'In general, there is no attempt to conceptualise clearly, and hence define the processes of business planning and strategic planning – nor is there a clearly agreed common definition for a business plan (as opposed to, say an operational plan, a marketing plan, a strategic plan etc.) that is used by different studies.'

Having concluded that it is difficult to say whether or not planning is effective in the small firm, Hannon and Atherton go on to argue that it is the planning *process* rather than the *plan* that is important, and that in the small firm informal planning makes more sense than formal planning. These findings reflect developments in mainstream strategic management in the development of the strategy process. According to Grant (1998), the decline in the popularity of strategic planning began in the late 1970s as a consequence of increasing macroeconomic instability brought about, first of all, by the oil shocks of 1974 and 1979 and then by increased international competition from Japanese, European and South-east Asian firms. This turbulence forced large firms to abandon their long-term corporate plans in favour of more flexible approaches. A relatively recent study of strategic planning in the oil and gas industry by Grant (1999) found that between 1990 and 1996 the number of corporate planning staff had fallen from 48 to 3 in BP, 60 to 17 in Exxon, 38 to 12 in Mobil and 54 to 17 in Shell.

Academic research conducted since the 1970s has also shown that strategy formation is much more complex than the prescriptive, rational planning model would lead us to believe. Research has demonstrated that a range of factors including chance events, management learning and cultural and political processes influence strategy formation. Mintzberg and Waters (1985), in particular, have argued that not all planned strategies are realised because of ineffectiveness in implementation and/or because of unanticipated changes in the external environment. More importantly, they have drawn attention to emergent strategies that develop over time as a consequence of decisions influenced by negotiation and political activity among managers, and/or the impact of culturally established routines, or even from chance events. Such emergent strategies owe little to the deliberate, predictive process and clarification of long-term objectives that Jennings and Beaver and other small-firm specialists have assumed is the norm for strategy-making in larger firms.

Quinn's research (1980) in major multinational businesses suggested that the strategy-making process could best be described as 'logical incrementalism'. According to Quinn, effective managers do have a view of the overall direction in which they wish to go but, realising the difficulties of operating in an uncertain environment, continually scan for signs of potential change and adapt their strategy in response by small-scale steps. This view is very similar to the idea of crafting strategy put forward by Mintzberg (1987). According to this view, strategy develops on the basis of managers' experience, sensitivity to environmental change and what they learn from operating in their market. This discrepancy in the ways in which firms go about the process of strategy formation has been captured to some extent by a typology of modes of strategic decision-making. Mintzberg (1975), for instance, has outlined three modes: entrepreneurial, adaptive and planning mode. A fourth, the logical incremental mode, was added later by Quinn (1980) and was outlined above. The entrepreneurial mode is of particular interest here because it refers to strategy being made by an entrepreneur or chief executive officer (CEO) who has a brilliant insight and is able to quickly convince others to adopt his ideas. Strategy is guided by the founder's vision of direction and is characterised by bold decisions. In this mode, the dominant goal is the growth of the business. The adaptive mode, sometimes known as 'muddling through', is characterised by reactive solutions to existing problems rather than a proactive search for new solutions. In this mode, much bargaining takes place between senior management over the priorities of the business and strategy evolves incrementally rather than in bold steps. The planning mode has already been discussed at some length. If claims by Mintzberg, Quinn and others about the various ways of strategy-making are valid, then the gap between strategy-making in large firms and in small firms is nothing like as great as the small-firm writers would have us believe. Put differently, the similarities between large and small firms are arguably greater than small-firm specialists have been ready to admit. To the extent that this is so, it follows that the concepts developed for competitive analysis and strategy formation in large firms can be applied with appropriate modification to small firms.

The Focus on Growth

In addition to regarding the small firm as unique, small-firm specialists also differ from general strategic management writers in their strategic focus. Unlike the generalist strategy researcher who is interested in developing an analytical framework for the development of any strategy that will yield competitive advantage, small-firm specialists have tended to focus much of their attention on developing a theory for small-firm growth. This effort is evident in the range of models for growth that have been produced.

These include personality-based approaches that look at the entrepreneur as fundamental to the growth process and that connect the success of the firm to their owner-manager's competences and characteristics (Kets de Vries, 1977; Mintzberg and Waters, 1985). This approach also consists of a number of variations such as those that seek to link the personal characteristics of the entrepreneur with the planning and the performance of the company (McClelland and Winter, 1969; Carsrud and Johnson, 1989), while others like Brockhaus and Horwitz (1986) have researched personality types. A second approach led by organisational development theorists and management specialists is based largely on stage models associated with growth and development, and includes models by Greiner (1972), Churchill and Lewis (1983) and Scott and Bruce (1987). A third approach is based on business management, where growth is seen as a function of the marketplace and focuses on financial performance as well as diversification, profitability and product/market development (Penrose, 1959; Ansoff, 1965). A fourth approach is based on the industry or markets, where the factors that impact on growth are external; for example, labour, taxation and regulation. In addition, this approach recognises that the acquisition strategies of large firms will affect the ability of small firms to grow. Industry structure, in relation to the division of power and markets between small and large companies, will also impact on small-firm growth (Oakey and Rothwell, 1988).

A more recent approach is that by Storey (1994) and by Smallbone and Wyer (2000) who suggest that consideration of the growing small firm should be based on a categorisation of three components. Each of these components includes a variety of different elements that should not be considered independently. These include the starting resources of the entrepreneur (e.g. motivation, age, education, management experience, family history, social marginality, training); the firm (e.g. age, sector, location, size, ownership) and the strategy of the firm (e.g. training, market positioning, planning, state support, external equity). Growth according to this theory would occur only where the three components and their relevant elements combined appropriately. Firms that do not experience growth may well have some appropriate characteristics in the entrepreneur, firm or strategy area missing.

It is not our purpose here to evaluate these models, as this has already been carried out by a number of writers, including O'Farrell and Hitchens (1988), Gibb and Davies (1992) and Storey (1994) but simply to demonstrate that the focus of small-firm specialists has been devoted to formulating a theory for the achievement of a particular strategic objective rather than the development of a general strategy framework. It is also of interest to note that small-firm specialists have tended to reject 'top-down' models of small-firm growth. O'Farrell and Hitchens, for instance, argue that a 'micro approach' is required to explain growth in smaller firms, and criticise most previous models because they place too little emphasis upon the difficulties which small owner-managed firms have in meeting the competitive requirements of the marketplace. This concentration of effort is easy to understand for a number of reasons. First, growth is seen as essential for some small firms if they are to reach minimum economies of scale; second, growth is seen as synonymous with success; and third, the growth of small firms is regarded as economically desirable because growing firms are seen as the seedbed of larger firms and as generators of employment.

But growth is not the only strategic objective of a firm, be it small or large. Among other possible strategic objectives are those of stability/minimal change or divestment. This last strategy may take the form of retrenchment, turnaround or downsizing. Gibb and Scott (1985) felt it was important to make the distinction between change and growth, and went on to note that strategic planning may be concerned as much with the maintenance of existing size and capability as with growth. They also make the valuable point that maintaining the existing size of firms may involve much effort as the firm seeks to compete in a dynamic environment. Hence their model is not concerned with explaining how to cope with growth but how to manage change. The model by Gibb and Scott represents one of the more comprehensive attempts by small-firm specialists to develop a framework for the strategic analysis of the small firm (see Figure 3.1) and for this reason will be discussed at some length here. It is also of interest to note that although the authors make little reference to mainstream strategic management writers other than the work of Ansoff and Steiner, their framework is remarkably

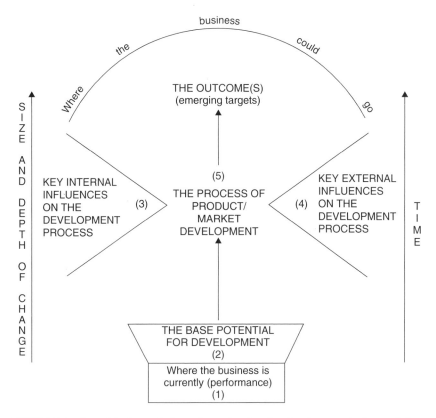

FIGURE 3.1   A model of growth through product/market development in the small firm.
Reproduced from Gibb and Scott (1988)

similar in many respects to the prescriptive planning models that fill many mainstream strategic management textbooks. The diagram makes clear the five key components of the model. The performance base represents a profile of the business in terms of performance to date and is broken down into measures of *market trends* like product mix, marketing mix, competition etc., *production trends*, which include measures of utilisation, efficiency, quality etc. and *financial and management control trends* such as net worth, liquidity and gearing.

In terms of conventional strategic analysis, this part of the model comes nearest to what mainstream strategy writers describe as a 'position audit'. The base potential for development represents the overall in-depth strength of the business incorporating many of the parameters identified as influencing the potential of the firm to change or grow. In the conventional strategic planning model, this comes nearest to what strategy writers call the 'resource audit' and includes

- the resource base consisting of the firm's liquidity, technology, physical assets, human resources and products;
- the accumulated experience base consisting of experience of markets, customers, product development, finance and external agents;
- the control base consisting of the control system, decision-making process, organisation structure and degree of formal planning;

- the leadership base, consisting of the personal objectives of owner-manager, influence of the family on objectives, personal capacity of owner-manager, attitude to change, leadership style etc.;
- the ideas base of the business, consisting of ideas for the development of existing and future products and ideas for new markets, stage of development of ideas and existence of plans for new products/new markets.

The key internal and external influences on development are similar in many respects to those that would be derived from the strengths, weaknesses, opportunities and threats (SWOT) analysis to be found in most mainstream strategic management texts. There are however, a number of differences, including references to external factors such as administrative and institutional blocks that have a particular effect on small firms, such as government-imposed 'red tape' and the influence of assistance given to small firms.

Internal factors over and above those often mentioned in conventional SWOT analysis include constraints on the time of small-firm owner-managers for long-term planning, the influence of the 'perceived' environment as opposed to the 'objective' environment, and the limited strategic awareness of many small-firm owner-managers.

In developing their model, Gibbs and Scott used a small sample of 16 small firms. All of the firms were owner-managed companies, having fewer than 50 employees. This did not mean that there were no other 'layers' of management, although these were obviously limited, but the research underlines the importance of the fact that the owner personally led these companies with his influence very much the dominant managerial factor. This point has important implications for the style of 'planning' encountered. Gibbs and Scott acknowledge that the limitations of their findings derive from the size of the sample and also from the size of company selected, but what they have to say fits in with findings from other research in the field. With these reservations, Gibbs and Scott make the following observations about the planning process in small companies. First, planning in the small business is likely to take place around a specific project or number of specific projects. It is unlikely to be formalised for the organisation as a whole in the large-company planning sense. Second, strategic planning in the formalised sense is unlikely to exist; but the process of development of a specific project will be characterised by varying degrees of strategic awareness, lack of which is likely to lead the company into blind alleys. Third, the absence of formal plans (strategic or otherwise) or, indeed, firm projections over several years, however, may not reflect on the capability of the company. Fourth, the development process is highly dynamic and highly iterative. It is characterised by a great deal of learning by the owner-manager and is influenced considerably by his personal appraisal, knowledge and attitudes. Thus the owner, and the firm, are 'learning' all the time, usually by coming up against problems and solving them rather than by anticipation. This may be the case even when there is a high level of strategic awareness, although such awareness will facilitate 'anticipation'. Fifth, the development process is highly dynamic and is not necessarily reflected in 'growth' as measured by overall output parameters such as employment or turnover. Thus there may be a high rate of change without it ever proceeding through into conventional measures. Sixth, lack of growth (measured in conventional terms) may not mean lack of ideas for development. All the companies studied had a portfolio of ideas. While their detailed development was a function of a variety of push and pull factors, organisational slack in terms of time and resources seems to be an important factor facilitating a proactive approach. Seventh, external information required for successful development is likely to be acquired personally by the owner-manager rather than by formalised 'sweeps' of secondary sources. How adequately this is done will reflect the quality and variety of the contact network of the owner. Finally, the strengths and weaknesses of the existing base (as characterised in the model) will be an important factor in the eventual success of new development, although the development itself may be the means by which the 'base' is explored.

Summing up the 'bottom-up' approach, we find that specialists in the field of small-scale research have focused their attention on two aspects: the particular characteristics of small firms and the single strategic objective of growth. The outcome of this concentration of effort has been the development of a number of competing models of small-firm growth. These models, with the important exception of those by a few writers like Gibb and Scott, make relatively little use of the analytical framework and concepts developed in the field of mainstream strategic management because they are built on the assumption that small firms are unique. That the unique aspects of small firms such as the centrality of the owner-manager, the limitations of time and resources, and a vulnerability to the environment do make a difference to the way small firms develop their strategies is not in doubt, but questions have been raised about how significant these differences are. Research in the field of strategic management in general seems to suggest that the process of strategy formulation varies considerably, ranging from the use of formal deliberate planning based on systematic analysis, through informal rational incremental approaches to adaptive reactive approaches. In other words, organisational size, while it may influence the strategy-making process, is not the only influence on how strategy-making is conducted, and the adoption of a particular mode does not guarantee success. Instead of concentrating on how different small firms are from large firms, it may be more useful to focus instead on how *similar* small firms are to firms of any size. This is the approach of the 'top-down' perspective to which we now turn.

The 'Top-down' Approach

Insofar as those in the mainstream of strategic management are concerned, the major assumption has been that small firms are much like larger firms except that they are small and have proceeded to apply the general model developed for the large business to its smaller cousin. Understandably, this 'top-down' approach has tended to reflect developments in the mainstream of strategic management. With some slight variations in emphasis between different writers, the development of the field of strategic management is broadly as follows. From its origins in military strategy, the application of strategic thinking to business emerged in the USA in the 1960s. Early influences on strategic management can be found in the industrial organisation school of economics (Hitt *et al.*, 1998) and in developments in business policy by writers like Learned *et al.* (1965) and the strategic planning of writers like Ansoff (1965).

According to Mintzberg (1994) the early approaches produced a prescriptive model that generally involved a deliberate step-by-step approach. It commenced with a set of tentative objectives, which the CEO or senior management team considered necessary for the organisation to achieve its goals. The external environment was then analysed to determine potential opportunities and threats; an internal audit was conducted to determine the organisation's strengths and weaknesses. Strategic alternatives were then considered to determine which strategy will best 'position' the organisation so as to capitalise on opportunities and strengths, while minimising threats and weaknesses. Following a process of evaluation a strategy was selected, a plan prepared and the strategy implemented.

In the 1980s the model was added to by the work of Michael Porter with his development of the concept of the five forces model used for industry analysis, the value chain as an instrument for assessing internal organisational strengths and weaknesses, and the generic strategies as a tool to assist in strategy formulation and evaluation. Under Porter's influence, an approach to strategy was evolved which concerned itself with how companies might best *position* themselves in the market, the industry and the wider environment so as to achieve a *strategic fit* with the environment and gain a competitive advantage over rivals. This approach, sometimes referred to as the 'industrial organisation model' (I/O) on account of its being borrowed from the study of industrial economics, is still very influential, although it has been challenged in recent years by a number of alternative perspectives, as we shall see later.

The application of the I/O model to the small firm, as already noted, finds little favour among small-firm research writers, but it has found favour among practitioner-orientated, 'how-to-do-it' writers. In the UK, a good example is the application by Burns and Dewhurst in their books *Small Business and Entrepreneurship* (1989) and *Small Business Management* (1993). In these texts the application comes under the title Business Planning and the owner-manager of a small business is taken through the method of the business plan process as set out in the general prescriptive model. The main elements of the general model remain unchanged (see Figure 3.2).

From the USA, in-depth examples of the application of the general model are provided by Lasher (1999) and a number of mainstream strategy management textbooks (such as that by Wheelen and Hunger, 2002) provide chapters in which the model is applied with very little, if any, adaptation to the small firm. In fact, Wheelen and Hunger argue explicitly that 'the eight steps presented in the strategic decision-making model are just as appropriate for small companies as they are for large corporations.' An examination of their eight-step model reveals that the model varies in only minor detail from the prescriptive model outlined by Mintzberg (1994) and applied by Burns and Dewhurst (1993). It is important to note, however, that there is a big difference between the definition of a small business in the USA and that applied in Europe, as mentioned earlier. Whereas in Europe the small firm is often regarded as small if it has less than 50 employees, the US definition includes organisations with up to 500 employees as small businesses! It is perhaps therefore unsurprising that US strategic management theorists find little difficulty in employing concepts developed for large organisations to their 'small' businesses.

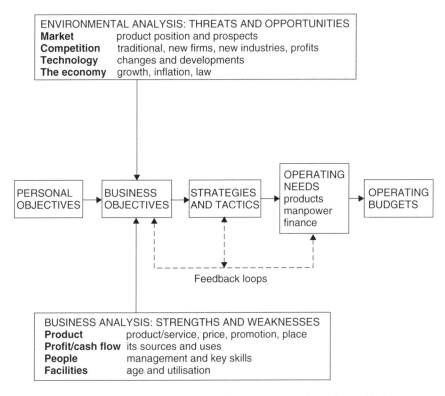

FIGURE 3.2 The planning process. Source: Burns and Dewhurst (1993)

Although the major tendency of the 'top-down' approach has been to apply the large-firm prescriptive model without modification, there have been some attempts by mainstream strategy writers to take account of the particular features of the small firm. Notable contributions have come from the work of Michael Porter with his notions of emerging and fragmented industries and his application of generic strategies. According to Porter (1980), industries can be said to be 'emerging' when a new concept or technology appears to have the potential to create an industry but when the evidence is not yet clear as to whether or not this will be the case. The development of the dot-com firms can perhaps be taken as a recent example of this kind of emerging business form. The computer industry in its early days also illustrates the general idea. The characteristics of an emerging industry are as follows. Initially, these emerging industries provide an opportunity to small firms because entry is relatively easy and there is limited competition. On the other hand, there is little certainty about how or whether the industry's future will develop. Hence being in the field is a gamble in itself. In these situations technical know-how is often critical in determining the winners. Firms also often have problems obtaining resources. Access to adequate financing is also critical. Because barriers to entry are low, new and more powerful players are possible at any time. Customers are difficult to secure because the product is unproven and several years of losses may precede profitable operations. A fragmented industry is said to exist when it is populated by a large number of smaller firms, and no one company has the size or power to dominate the market. Most industries emerge in a fragmented state and slowly consolidate into more concentrated structures. The motor-car industry provides a familiar example. However, conditions sometimes exist that short-circuit the consolidation process and keep the industry fragmented indefinitely. The most common such condition is a local character attached to the product or service being offered. Restaurants, dry cleaners and motor mechanics provide good examples (Lasher, 1999). The market for each is limited to the population within a reasonable travelling distance of the point of sale, so the industries continue to be populated by large numbers of relatively small firms. Other conditions that keep industries fragmented include the absence of scale economies in production (such as in the garment industry and business forms printing); and the high transportation cost and rapidly deterioration of certain products like concrete. According to Lasher (1999), it is important for smaller businesses to understand the fragmentation concept and to know what forces keep the industry they are in fragmented. The value of the idea is especially relevant in defining the industry the firm is in for immediate competitive purposes. A restaurant, for example, competes only with other restaurants within a relatively short driving distance, whereas a garment manufacturer or a parts fabricator faces no such geographic limitation, even though they are in similarly fragmented fields.

Even before Porter developed the classification of generic strategies, writers like Abbanat (1967) concluded in his comparison of the strategies of small companies with the strategies of large companies that, 'if there was a pattern to the results, it was a pattern of difference and in this sense the impression that small manufacturing companies compete directly with large corporations is erroneous. Rather, these companies probed for 'soft spots and gaps in the market.' Similarly, Katz (1970), in attempting to identify strategies associated with different sizes of business, argued that small firms must focus and conserve their resources while larger competitors must play to the advantages of their size. The generic strategies developed by Porter (1980) have been widely adopted by 'top-down' strategists. According to Porter, there are only three fundamental ways of achieving sustainable competitive advantage; *cost leadership*, where the firm sets out to be the low-cost producer in the market, *differentiation*, where the firm sets out 'to be unique in the industry along some dimensions that are widely valued by customers', and *focus*, where the firm focuses on a narrow target market segment combined with either of the other strategies. Cost leadership assumes that costs can be reduced through, for example, economies of scale and technological cost advantages. However, this is risky, because it is difficult to maintain cost leadership as competing firms may easily copy the technology or take advantage of economies of scale. Small firms have difficulty in competing with large organisations in these areas, as often, economies of scale are linked to 'substantial relative market share advantage'. Differentiation is more attractive to small companies, particularly when linked with focus, when it is known as a 'niche' strategy. The company differentiates its product or service with some unique selling proposition in a narrow target market segment. Market power is less of an issue when competing through this type of strategy. However, the risks are that it can be imitated, the segment can become unattractive for some reason, or the basis for segmentation disappears as the differences between segments disappear. Small firms that successfully employ a niche strategy do not compete on price, and consequently are able to sustain a higher margin.

There is some evidence to support Porter's argument that a niche strategy is often the most effective for a smaller business. In a survey of 1500 smaller companies across Europe, the 3i European Enterprise Centre (1994) found that the companies which achieved growth in sales and/or profits had 'better or different products or services' described by Porter (1985) as a differentiation strategy. In 1993, 3i carried out a survey of 3500 UK 'super league companies' and concluded that most of these high-growth companies served niche markets, again following a strategy of differentiation.

Though the positioning approach developed by writers like Porter has been very influential, and still is, it has also been much criticised. The main shortcomings of the approach are first that it relies on a static picture of competition and thus understates the role of innovation (Stalk *et al.*, 1992). Second, it overemphasises the importance of industry structure (Rumelt, 1991) and the wider environment while de-emphasising the significance of individual company differences in the possession of resources, capabilities and competence (Prahalad and Hamel, 1990). The fact that innovation can revolutionise industry structure is now widely recognised. The example of the development of the computer industry is one of the more dramatic recent examples. Other recent examples are in banking, insurance and other financial services.

The undermining of the planning and positioning approaches to strategic management has given rise to the search for alternative perspectives. The variety of perspectives on offer depends on the criteria for classification adopted by a particular author. Henry Mintzberg *et al.* (1998) seems to hold the record, with ten perspectives or 'schools of strategic thought'. These are design, planning, positioning, entrepreneurial, cognitive, learning, political, cultural, environmental and configurational. Richard Whittington (1993), using different criteria, manages to reduce the number of approaches to just four: the *classical*, which stresses rationality and analysis, the *evolutionary*, analogous to the biological 'survival of the fittest' model, the *processual*, which emphasises pragmatism, and the *systemic*, which claims that strategy reflects the social system in which it is formed. Thomas (1993), by adopting a framework consisting of two dimensions, rationality and sectionalism, is able to produce a matrix with conceptual spaces within which schools of strategic management might be placed. In his scheme, strategic approaches are envisaged to range from the rational to the subjectively rational but objectively irrational (practices akin to magic and religion) and from the pursuit of strategic objectives aimed to satisfy the interests of all stakeholders to strategies designed to satisfy the aspirations of just one group. Of this variety of perspectives, however, the resource-based view of strategy-making has been the focus of greatest attention as an alternative to the 'positioning' approach, and will be outlined below.

The Resource-based Alternative

The application of the resource-based view to small firms has to date been relatively limited but a number of papers using the approach are now appearing, and so it is important to understand the nature of the approach. It is also relevant to note that while the application of the resource-based approach has been developed to explain strategy-making in larger firms, there is no reason to think that the concepts cannot be applied with suitable modification to smaller firms. While problems with the positioning approach have been one reason for the search for an alternative, another reason has been the observation that success for many companies appears to have little to do with positioning and much more to do with the exploitation of a company's resources, competencies and capabilities. Thus Prahalad and Hamel (1990) cite the core competence of miniaturisation as the basis for the success of the Sony Company. This competence, it is argued, has allowed Sony to make everything from the Walkman to video cameras to notebook computers. Similarly, Canon's core competences in optics, imaging and microprocessor controls have enabled it to enter markets as diverse as photocopiers, laser printers, cameras and image scanners. These examples have led Hamel and Prahalad and other researchers to focus on the resources, capabilities and competences of the organisation as the source of competitive advantage rather than the environment, as in the traditional approach.

The resource-based approach has its foundation in economics literature. Edith Penrose, in her work *The Theory of the Growth of the Firm* (1959) is often credited with the idea for the resource-based view. Penrose emphasised the managerial constraints on growth. At any given time, she argued, managerial capability limits expansion and this in turn limits the number of new managers that can be employed. This is of course particularly relevant to explanations of small-firm growth. Coming from a separate tradition, the work of Philip Selznick (1957) stressed the role of distinctive competences and Alfred Chandler (1962) demonstrated the importance of organisational structure in the utilisation of a firm's resources. The modern development of the resource-based view has been dated by Foss (1996) to the work of Wernerfelt (1984) and Rumelt (1997).

Because the new approach is still in the process of development, there is as yet limited agreement on the terminology to be employed. Similar terms – core competences, distinctive competences, capabilities, resources, strengths, intangible assets and skills – are used interchangeably by different authors. Currently a number of writers (Sanchez *et al.*, 1996) are trying to derive a vocabulary for discussing what they have called a 'competence-based approach to strategic management'. Whether or not this attempt will provide a vocabulary on which all can agree remains to be seen. Despite the confusing use of terminology, however, it is possible to describe the main characteristics of a resource-based approach. The approach assumes that an organisation is a collection of resources, capabilities and competences that are relatively unique and that these provide a basis for its strategy and its ability to compete. It is also assumed that firms can acquire different resources, skills and capabilities in the process of their development. But because it takes time to acquire and develop such resources and capabilities, it follows that firms which already possess a relevant set of these can gain competitive advantage over rivals. For example, the skills and capabilities required for miniaturisation and considered to be the basis of Sony's core competence take many years to hone to perfection and give Sony an advantage because they are not readily available to competitors.

In contrast to the traditional planning model, which takes the environment as the critical factor determining an organisation's strategy, the resource-based approach assumes that the key factors for success lie within the firm itself in terms of its resources, capabilities and competences. The choice of the firm's strategy is not dictated by the constraints of its environment but is influenced more by calculations of how the organisation can best exploit its core competence relative to its opportunities in the external environment.

The resources of firms in the resource-based approach are typically classified into two types: tangible and intangible resources. Tangible resources are inputs into a firm that can be seen, touched and/or quantified. They include assets like plant and equipment, access to raw materials and finance, a trained and skilled workforce and a firm's organisational structure. Intangible resources range from intellectual property rights such as patents, trademarks and copyrights to the know-how of personnel, informal networks, organisational culture and a firm's reputation for its products. The dividing line between the tangible and intangible is often unclear, and how they are classified varies from one writer to another. Despite the problems with classification, proponents of the resource-based approach are agreed on the relative importance of the two types of resources. Although it is clear that both types of resources are required for any business to operate, resource-based theorists argue that intangible resources are the most likely source of competitive advantage. The reason for this, it is argued, is that being less visible they are more difficult to understand and imitate than tangible resources. As such, they are therefore more likely to be a source of competitive advantage.

Resources alone, however, are not a basis for competitive advantage. It is the way in which resources are integrated with each other to perform a task or an activity that provides the capability for an organisation to compete successfully in the marketplace. This being the case, then the most important resource for any organisation is the skill and knowledge possessed by the organisation's employees. It is this skill and knowledge acquired over time and embedded in the firm's culture that influences how it operates and determines its success. Whether or not resources and capabilities have the potential to become core competences depends on how difficult they are for competitors to acquire and how valuable they are to the firm as a basis for competitive advantage. When they are rare, difficult to imitate or non-substitutable (Barney, 1991) and they allow a firm to exploit opportunities or neutralise threats, then they can be considered core competences and serve as the basis of an organisation's sustained competitive advantage.

As part of this new approach to strategy development, a number of writers have incorporated the notion of strategic intent. This is a term coined by Hamel and Prahalad to mean the leveraging of a firm's internal resources, capabilities and core competences to accomplish what initially appear to be impossible goals in the face of the competitive forces confronting it. Strategic intent is said to exist in an organisation when managers and employees have a fervent belief in their organisation and its products and when they are completely focused on doing what they do better than the competition. Because the idea of strategic intent implies ambitions that at a particular moment in time outstrip the organisation's resources and capabilities for their achievement, theorists have also concerned themselves with how competences might be best acquired. As in the rest of this developing field, a variety of perspectives exist. Thus, some writers such as Senge (1990) and Argyris (1994) stress the acquisition of competences through internal mechanisms of individual and collective learning, while others like Hamel and Prahalad put greater emphasis on strategic tools like alliances, licensing, mergers and acquisitions. Writers who favour internal means of acquiring competences do so because they claim that such means give the advantages of secrecy, exclusivity and surprise. Those who concentrate on external means of acquiring competences defend their approach on the grounds of flexibility and speed.

The idea of strategic intent is particularly relevant to strategy-making in smaller firms because it implies that a lack of resources is not a major obstacle to growth: it is the lack of ambition of the owner-manager that is more important.

As markets change, it is argued, old alliances can be discarded and new ones formed. As new resources, capabilities and competences become necessary for competitive advantage, it is quicker to buy them than to spend years of trial and error in their development. Such is the diversity of approach to the acquisition and building of competences that a contingent approach has been recommended as a way of selecting the most appropriate means of competence acquisition. This approach assumes that the characteristics and direction of the competence-building activity of a company are mainly contingent on its strategic objectives. As with all models, some criticisms have been directed at the resource-based view: first, that it is partial and one-sided and thus in danger of neglecting the environment which is still critical to the survival of organisations; second, that the case for its superiority is based on a few examples of successful companies that have been chosen because they appear to confirm the theory whereas companies that are successful for other reasons have been neglected.

As already noted, the application of the resource-based approach to the strategic management of the small firm has so far been limited. One early attempt, that by Rangone (1999), has attempted to develop a resource-based view of competitive advantage. Rangone argues that the application of the resource-based approach to small firms has to take account of small-firm characteristics. His adaptation of the resource-based theory for application to small firms consists of both adaptations to the strategy process and the strategy content. In process terms, he argues that when applied to small firms it should not be too complex or time-consuming or require specialist skills in strategic analysis. On the basis of a sample study of 14 small firms from different industries, Rangone claims to have developed a model for the competitive advantage of SMEs based on three basic capabilities. These are innovation capability, production capability and market management capability. In a general chapter such as this it is not possible to evaluate his model in any comprehensive manner, but it is difficult to be comfortable with Rangone's claims that such a model does not require specialist skills in strategic analysis. It depends, of course, what is meant by 'specialist skills', but we would argue like (Gibb, Scott, Hannon and Atherton) that strategic awareness is critical if the owner-manager of the small firm is to survive and prosper in today's dynamic business environment. As to the capabilities that Rangone argues are essential for the small firm's competitive advantage, it is difficult to argue with any of these. But then one could argue that innovation, production and management capabilities are required for success by any firm, irrespective of size, and so the claim that these refer specifically to a model for SMEs' competitive advantage becomes difficult to sustain.

To date, therefore, we must conclude that we are some way off a useful specific resource-based model for explaining how small firms can secure competitive advantage. What we have, it seems, is a general framework that provides us with some guiding principles as to what factors can help to give a firm of any size a competitive advantage. The characteristics of the resources and competences that can provide an advantage have been elaborated above, and include those specified by Barney as rare, difficult to imitate and non-substitutable. But just what these resources and competences will consist of will necessarily vary from firm to firm depending on a range of factors such as industry structure and the extent to which critical resources/competences are possessed by competitor firms. Much as it would be useful to be able to specify in advance the factors that would give a competitive advantage, it is difficult to see how this would be possible without a prior analysis of the firm's competitive situation.

Conclusion

The attempt to develop a framework for the strategic management of SMEs has come from two main sources: first from specialists in small-firm research adopting what has been described as a 'bottom-up' approach and second from researchers in the field of strategic management in general who have adopted a 'top-down' approach. In general, those adopting a 'bottom-up' approach have argued that the small firm is unique and as such cannot be understood by concepts developed for the analysis of the larger organisation. More particularly, small-firm specialists committed to the 'bottom-up' approach have argued that the framework for strategic planning developed for the larger firm cannot usefully be applied to the smaller firm. In this chapter, it has been argued to the contrary that the tools of analysis and concepts developed in the general field of strategic management can usefully be applied, provided the constraints operating on the small firm are taken into account. The arguments for adopting many of the tools and concepts applied by 'top-down' theorists are as follows. First, there are more similarities between the small firm and the larger firm than there are differences. Second, research on the process of strategic management has demonstrated that strategic planning is only one of a number of modes of strategic decision-making and that even in larger firms strategy is sometimes an unintended emergent phenomenon that develops from decisions that are far from deliberate and rational but instead are the outcome of political activity and cultural influence. The outcome of this research is the finding that strategy-making in small firms is not so different from that in large firms as small-firm specialists make out, and it is therefore argued here that the concepts adopted by the 'top-down' theorists can be usefully applied to small firms.

It has also been observed that small-firm specialists have been preoccupied with the single strategic objective of small-firm growth rather than with the more general objective of devising an analytical framework for developing small-firm competitive advantage. For most small-firm specialists, the concern with growth has thus had the effect of deflecting attention from a concern with a general framework for small-firm strategy-making. Exceptions to this include Gibb and Scott, who have made use of concepts from the general field of strategic management together with their own ideas to take account of small-firm constraints to produce a useful model for coping with strategic change.

In reviewing the 'top-down' approach to the strategic management of small firms, it was noted that most writers pay little, if any, attention to the constraints faced by small firms and argue that the strategic management framework developed for larger firms is just as applicable to smaller firms. Again, however, there are exceptions to the general picture and here the relevance of concepts such as emerging and fragmented industries and the generic strategies were found to be useful for strategy-making in small firms. Finally, the development of the resource-based approach was discussed at length since it is increasingly regarded as the dominant approach to strategic management. It was noted, however, that to date, no distinctively small-firm resource-based view had been developed but that the model provided useful general insights for strategy-making in any size of organisation including the small organisation, provided that owner-managers were trained in the approach.

References

3i European Enterprise Centre (1994) *Report 12: Winners and Losers in the 1990s*. April.

Abbanat, R. (1967) 'Strategies for size', PhD dissertation, Harvard University.

Ansoff, H.I. (1965) *Corporate Strategy: An Analytic Approach to Business Policy for Growth and Expansion*. McGraw-Hill, New York.

Argyris C. (1994) 'Good communication that blocks learning', *Harvard Business Review*, **72**: 4, 77–85.

Barney, J.B. (1991) 'Firm resources and sustained competitive advantage', *Journal of Management*, March, 99–120.

Brockhaus, R.H. and Horwitz, P.S. (1986) 'The psychology of the entrepreneur', in D.L. Saxton and R.W. Smitor (eds) *The Art and Science of Entrepreneurs*. Ballinger, Cambridge.

Burns, P. and Dewhurst, J. (1989) (eds) *Small Business and Entrepreneurship*. Macmillan, London.

Burns, P. and Dewhurst, J. (1993) *Small Business Management*, 3rd edition. Macmillan, London.

Carsud, A.L. and Johnson, R.W. (1989) 'Entrepreneurship: A social psychological perspective', *Entrepreneurship and Regional Development*, **I**:1, 21–31.

Chandler A. (1962) *Strategy and Structure*. MIT Press, Cambridge, MA.

Churchill, N.C. and Lewis, V.L. (1983) 'The five stages of small business growth', *Harvard Business Review*, **6**:1.

Foss N.J. (1996) 'Research in strategy, economics and Michael Porter', *Journal of Management Studies*, **33**:1.

Gibb A.A. and Davies L.G. (1992) 'Methodological problems in the development and testing of a growth model of business enterprise development', *Recent Research in Entrepreneurship*, Avebury, Aldershot, pp. 286–323.

Gibb A.A. and Scott, M. (1985) 'Strategic awareness, personal commitment and the process of planning in the small business', *Journal of Management Studies* **22**, 597–631.

Grant, R.M. (1998) *Contemporary Strategy Analysis*, 3rd edition. Blackwell, Cambridge.

Grant R.M. (1999) 'Strategic planning among the major oil and gas corporations', Working Paper, McDonough School of Business. Georgetown University, Washington DC.

Greiner, L.E. (1972) 'Evolution and revolution as organisations grow', *Harvard Business Review*, **50**, July–August.

Hannon, P.D. and Atherton, A. (1998) 'Small firm success and the art of orienteering: the value of plans, planning and strategic awareness in the competitive small firm', *Journal of Small Business and Enterprise Development*, **5**:2, 102–119.

Hitt, A.T., Ireland, R.D. and Hoskisson, R.E. (1995) *Strategic Management*. West Publishing Company, St. Paul, MN.

Jennings, P. and Beaver, G. (1997) 'The performance and competitive advantage of small firms: a management perspective', *International Small Business Journal*, **15**:1, 66–75.

Katz, R.L. (1970) *Cases and Concepts in Corporate Strategy*. Prentice Hall, Englewood Cliffs, NJ.

Kets de Vries, M. (1977) 'The entrepreneurial personality: a person at the crossroads', *Journal of Management Studies*, **14**, 34–57.

Lasher, W.R. (1999) *Strategic Thinking for Smaller Businesses and Divisions*. Blackwell, Malden, MA.

Learned E.P., Christensen, C.R., Andrews, K.R. and Guth, W.D. (1965) *Business Policy: Text and Cases*. Irwin, Homewood, IL.

McClelland D.C. and Winter, D.G. (1969) *Motivating Economic Achievement*. Free Press, New York.

McKiernan P. and Morris C. (1994) 'Strategic planning and financial performance in UK SMEs: does formality matter?' *British Journal of Management* **5**, special issue, 31–41.

Milne, T., Lewis, J., Thorpe, R. and Thompson, M. (1982) 'Factors for predicting success in small companies', *Management Studies Working Paper 1*, University of Glasgow.

Mintzberg, H. (1975) 'Strategy-making in three modes', *California Management Review*, Winter, 44–55.

Mintzberg H. (1987) 'Crafting Strategy', *Harvard Business Review*, July–August, 66–75.

Mintzberg, H. (1994) *The Rise and Fall of Strategic Planning*. Prentice Hall International, London.

Mintzberg, H. and Waters, J.A. (1985) 'Of strategies deliberate and emergent' *Strategic Management Journal*, **26**, 257–272.

Oakey R. and Rothwell, R.S. (1988) *Management Innovation in High-Technology Small Firms*. Pinter Publishers, London.

O'Farrell, P.N. and Hitchens, D.M.W.N. (1988) 'Alternative theories of small-firm growth: a critical review', *Environment and Planning A*, **20**, 1365–1383.

Penrose, E.T. (1959) *The Theory of the Growth of the Firm*. Basil Blackwell, London.

Porter, M.E. (1980) *Competitive Strategy: Techniques for Analysing Industries and Competitors*. Free Press, New York.

Porter, M.E. (1985) *Competitive Advantage: Creating and Sustaining Superior Performance*. Free Press, New York.

Pralahad C.K. and Hamel G. (1990) 'The core competence of the corporation', *Harvard Business Review*, May–June, 79–91.

Quinn, J.B. (1980) *Strategies for Change: Logical Incrementalism*. Irwin, Homewood, IL.

Rangone, A. (1999) 'A resource-based approach to strategy analysis in small and medium-sized enterprises' *Small Business Economics*, **12**:3, 233–248.

Rumelt, R.P. (1991) 'How much does industry matter?' *Strategic Management Journal*, **12**, 167–185.

Rumelt R.P. (1997) 'The evaluation of business strategy', in H. Mintzberg and J.B. Quinn (eds) *The Strategy Process: Concepts, Text and Cases*, 3rd edition. Prentice Hall, Englewood Cliffs, NJ.

Sanchez, R. Heene, A. and Thomas H. (1996) 'Towards the theory and practice of competence-based competition', in R. Sanchez, A. Heene and H. Thomas (eds) *Dynamics of Competence-Based Competition: Theory and Practice in the New Strategic Management*. Elsevier, Oxford.

Scott, M. and Bruce, R. (1987) 'Five stages of growth in small business', *Long Range Planning*, **20**:3, 45–52.

Selznick, P. (1957) *Leadership in Administration: A Sociological Interpretation*. Row, Peterson, Evanston, IL.

Senge P. (1990) 'The leader's new work: building learning organisations', *Sloan Management Review*, Fall, 7–23.

Smallbone, D. and Wyer, P. (2000) 'Growth and development in the small firm,' in S. Carter and D. Jones-Evans (eds) *Enterprise and Small Business: Principles, Practices and Policies*. Financial Times/ Prentice Hall, Harlow, Essex.

Stalk, G., Evans, P. and Scholman, L.E. (1992) 'Competing on capabilities: the new rules of corporate strategy', *Harvard Business Review*, March–April, 57–69.

Stanworth, M.J.K. and Curran, J. (1976) 'Growth and the small firm – an alternative view', *Journal of Management Studies*, **13**:2, May, 95–110.

Storey, D.J. (1994) *Understanding the Small Business Sector*. Thomson Business Press, London.

Thomas, A.B. (1993) *Controversies in Management*. Routledge, London.

Wernerfelt, R. (1984) 'A resource-based view of the firm', *Strategic Management Journal* **5**, 171–180.

Wheelen, T.L. and Hunger, J.D. (2002) *Strategic Management and Business Policy*, 8th edition. Prentice Hall, London.

Whittington, R. (1993) *What is Strategy and Does it Matter?* Routledge, London.

Chapter 4

CORPORATE GOVERNANCE FOR COMPETITIVE ADVANTAGE IN SMEs

Richard Warren

Introduction

The concept of corporate governance is a popular one at the moment, although only a few years ago the term had barely been coined. Today, the term is mainly used in relation to large companies or to use the Americanism, 'corporations'. Consequently, the use of this term in the context of discussions about SMEs might be thought to be inappropriate; after all, in many SMEs, the owner-managers are also the shareholders. In this situation the corporate governance process might amount to little more than an almost schizophrenic internal dialogue between the same people. However, this chapter will argue that corporate governance is increasingly relevant to SMEs, and, that even in the case of the smallest firms, some important lessons for better corporate governance can still be learnt. The notion that this aspect of organisation can lead to competitive advantage for SMEs might also seem to be questionable, but it will be argued that this is an often-neglected dimension of SME performance management. First, the question of what enterprise form is most appropriate for SMEs will be briefly discussed. Then the meaning of 'competitive advantage' will be defined and the contribution improved corporate governance could make to this notion will then be identified. The nature and scope of corporate governance will be briefly outlined before its importance in the context of SMEs is explored. The chapter will then identify aspects of best practice that will give SMEs competitive advantage in corporate governance terms. Finally, the policy implications for corporate governance development in SMEs will be considered.

SME Enterprise Form and Corporate Governance

While it is acknowledged by many commentators on SMEs that there is no satisfactory definition of a small business, there are some common characteristics of SMEs that are given to help define the category of business under consideration. The definition used in the Bolton Report in 1971 was that a small firm had a small share of the market, was managed by its owners in a personalised way but independently of outside control, and that, statistically, it employed fewer than 200 employees and had a limited turnover (Bolton, 1971). This common-sense definition has now been superseded by the European Union variable criteria definition. SMEs are generally firms that employ under 500 employees and are subdivided into three categories: micro (0–9 employees), small (10–99 employees), and medium-sized enterprises (100–499 employees). The recent Company Law Review in the UK has defined a small company as one which meets two of the following criteria: turnover of no more than £4.8m; balance sheet total of no more than £2.4m; and number of employees of no more than 50 (DTI, 2001). The review estimated that on 31 March 2000 there were around 1.3m private companies and 12 400 public companies registered in the UK. This does not take into account the number of non-company enterprise forms there are in the UK. The review's definitions are likely to become very significant, however, because the review has proposed substantial changes in company law in favour of the small private company.

Identifying the reasons for choice of enterprise form is a difficult area in which to attempt any generalisations because of the scope and variety of small businesses. Choice of enterprise form is, however, a key issue in the growth and development of SMEs. However, it should be remembered that most SMEs are not destined for growth and evolution into a larger business. Hakim's study of 747 970 firms in 1989 found that the typical no-growth firms were unincorporated businesses which were home-based and which employed only one or two people including the owner-manager (Hakim, 1989). The faster-growth firms were much more likely to be limited companies. Freedman and Godwin also concluded from their surveys that the main benefit of corporate status is limited liability and the resulting perceptions of increased credibility which the business has with customers and banks (Freedman and Godwin, 1994). Storey also notes that empirical studies suggest that limited liability companies are associated with more rapid rates of employment growth than sole traders or partnerships (Storey, 1994). Choice of the corporate form may be a response to growth or a sign that growth is an aspiration of the business from the outset. Consequence or cause is therefore difficult to distinguish in this field of research. Limited companies also have higher failure rates, so they might not be always be conducive to good management.

Corporate governance issues such as directors' responsibilities, shareholders' rights and accountability mechanisms really only become relevant to the corporate form of the business enterprise. There are limited applications of some of these concepts to partnerships and sole traders, particularly as these forms are being refined and developed in the USA to have some of the qualities of the incorporated and unincorporated form. In the USA, the Limited Liability Partnership and Limited Liability Company have been developed to encourage SMEs to take more risks and grow faster. In the UK, the Limited Liability Partnership has also been developed and the Company Law Review steering group has considered giving access to limited liability to more SMEs to make enterprising activity more attractive.

Choice of Corporate Form for the SME

In the UK in 1986, the numbers of SMEs in the following enterprise forms were recorded as:

Sole proprietorships	1 351 000	54.7%
Partnerships	633 000	25.6%
Incorporated	459 000	18.6%
Other	28 000	1.1%

(Source: Bannock and Perkins, 1989, quoted in Storey, 1994)

The enterprise forms noted in VAT figures for 1990 were:

38% Sole traders
26% Partnerships
34% Companies

In 1998, according to the Modern Company Law Review; there were:

1 320 000 companies in the UK on the Companies Register
12 000 Public Limited Companies
2450 shares listed on the London Stock Exchange
740 000 on the register were actively trading
506 000 had fewer than five employees
3380 companies had 500 or more employees and contributed to 54% of employment
The majority of trading companies had only one or two shareholders

The choice of enterprise form is an important issue for the SME. Over the past two decades there has been a tendency for SMEs to adopt the company form in greater numbers than previously. It is often assumed that the more limited liability companies there are, the better for SME growth and development. However, Judith Freedman has for some time been raising important concerns about this trend, and has identified a number of reservations in a range of studies (Freedman, 2000). She has summarised the advantages and disadvantages of encouraging SMEs to adopt the company form as follows. The advantages for the early adoption of the limited liability company form are several. Most importantly, the law affords the firm legal personality to be able to hold property in its own name, to be able to sue, be sued and outlive its founders. Limited liability reduces the risk for shareholders when they invest in a firm. This will make it easier for the SME to attract investment and increase the capital resources available to the business. Limited liability promotes the free transfer of shares and the establishment of market prices for those shares. It also allows owners to realise some of their wealth tied up in their business and the transfer of the business to other owners as a gradual process (very useful for distribution and family succession planning in some firms). There can also be limited taxation advantages. Empirical studies have shown that prestige and credibility are also given as reasons for incorporation into a limited liability company by many owners of SMEs (Freedman and Godwin, 1994).

The disadvantages of incorporating the SME are often neglected and are frequently underemphasised in advice given to SMEs. Freedman has often been a lone voice in bringing these to the policy-maker's attention. Her principal argument is that the unrestricted access of SMEs to limited liability in effect shifts the risk of failure on to creditors from shareholders, thereby creating a moral hazard. And, although there is a climate that seeks to encourage risk-taking in business, she argues it is important to draw a line at irresponsible risk-taking. The social balance to be weighed in these circumstances makes this a political question rather than an economic one. For many firms the form of sole trader, partnership or unlimited liability company may well be the most appropriate and responsible option, particularly bearing in mind that for the majority of SMEs the intention of the owner is to earn a living rather than to grow an expanding empire. As Freedman notes,

> The political rhetoric surrounding small business can lead to an undue emphasis on limited liability because this will be of value to those that do grow. As a result, the importance of catering for the non-growth business can be forgotten and growth may be highlighted at the expense of other values, such as the need to protect third parties (including other small businesses). (Freedman, 2000, p. 321)

There are also other practical drawbacks to incorporation, such as the need for the limited liability owners to offer personal guarantees as security for loans or investments. Having thought that they were limiting their risk of losing their personal wealth by adopting the corporate form, the reality for many entrepreneurs is that they are personally liable for risks and have to pay the extra costs of incorporation into the bargain. To prevent small businesses that are undercapitalised from incorporating themselves, Freedman has suggested that the imposition of minimum capital requirements upon registration should be retained in company law. These requirements are still in place in several European countries so as to protect creditors and prevent the premature incorporation of SMEs. However, the difficulty of drawing a line on minimum capital requirements is said by many commentators to be insurmountable for their adoption in the UK. Nevertheless, the conclusion of Freedman and Godwin's survey of SMEs, conducted in 1994, asking about why SMEs had chosen incorporation, was that, 'for a sizeable minority of small companies, the cost of operating in corporate form is likely to exceed the benefit' (Freedman and Godwin, 1994, p. 266). The competitive advantage of many SMEs might be undermined by the failure of policy-makers and entrepreneurs to heed this warning not to make the company form a universal prescription for all SMEs, particularly for those SMEs not destined for growth and expansion. The contribution that good corporate governance can make to competitive advantage will now be explored for those SMEs where incorporation is appropriate.

Corporate Governance as an Aspect of 'Competitive Advantage'

The term competitive advantage is associated with the work of the business strategist Michael E. Porter (1985). It is not enough for firms to make a profit, they also need to be able to analyse their position within their markets so as to determine their competitive position and to understand the source of their advantage, and whether it can be sustained in the longer term. Porter sets out a framework for conducting this analysis and its key concept is the notion of the 'value chain' for analysing the firm's sources of value enhancement of its products or services. One constituent part of the value chain is the infrastructure of the firm. This includes its organisation structure, systems and processes. While most attention in the work of Porter and others has been given to the organisation's structure, the apex of the organisation's structure, the board of directors and its performance has been a neglected area of investigation. Only in recent years has the contribution of the board of directors to the performance of the organisation been studied in more detail. This process might be widened to include the other corporate governance mechanisms of the firm such as shareholder meetings and communications and the inclusion of other stakeholder groups. Studies are beginning to show that efficient governance arrangements can make a significant contribution to the value chain and so ought not to be a neglected area of analysis in the firm's overall value chain. As Porter noted in his original conceptualisation of the value chain, 'Firm infrastructure is sometimes viewed only as "overhead", but can be a powerful source of competitive advantage' (Porter, 1985, p. 43). The extension of value chain analysis to the corporate governance arrangements in SMEs is therefore a new and important development and a new consideration in many studies.

Evidence about this important area of competitive advantage is hinted at in a recent study of the factors behind high-growth companies in the UK (Storey, 2001). A study of high-growth small businesses from the University of Warwick's Centre for SMEs looked at 6786 companies with turnover between £5m and £100m in most cases for the five years between 1993–94 and 1997–98. To qualify as high-flyers, those companies with sales up to £10m had to achieve a growth of 25 per cent or more a year. For those with sales of more than £10m, the threshold was 15 per cent. Only 317 companies met these criteria and were then subject to an analysis as to why they were high-flyers. Only one in eight of the fast-growth companies were in the high-technology sector; most were in other industries, including wholesale distribution, manufacturing, retailing and construction. When investigating the relationship between growth, ownership, changes in ownership status and acquisitions, the findings were often contrary to expectations. Most of the companies in the survey were privately owned (91 per cent) with only 8 per cent having a full London Stock Exchange listing, and only 1 per cent were listed on the junior AIM (Alternative Investment Market). The growth rates of private and listed companies were virtually indistinguishable. But high-growth companies were much more likely to be listed on the stock exchange (14 per cent for high-flyers compared with 8 per cent for middle market companies) than the AIM (4 per cent for high-flyers compared with 1 per cent for middle market companies). The listed companies had growth rates that were roughly double the average on turnover, value added and profits, and nearly triple the average on employment. And contrary to popular belief, the study found that 81 per cent of the high-flyers had achieved their status through organic growth rather than through mergers and acquisitions. The evidence suggests that the take-up of incorporated status and the influence of corporate governance practices from stock exchange listings is weak, but indicates that better corporate governance factors may play a part in helping companies achieve competitive advantage. Before pursuing this question in more detail and its relationship with SMEs, the meaning and scope of what is meant by corporate governance needs to be outlined a little more fully.

What is Corporate Governance?

The term 'corporate governance' has gained ground in recent years as the debate over the legitimacy of the ownership of business and its social responsibility has grown once more (Warren, 2000). Today, there are many books and journals devoted to the modalities and repercussions of changing debate about corporate governance. The report on *Financial Aspects of Corporate Governance* (Cadbury Committee) defined this term as 'the system by which companies are directed and controlled' (Cadbury, 1992). The term includes two aspects of governance: to rule and to control. They are not synonymous but often are treated as such in many of the discussions on the subject. The basic mechanisms of corporate governance have evolved from our company statutes first created in 1859 and 1862, the latest incarnation of which is the 1985 Companies Act.

Under the Companies Act, assets and liabilities are owned by a company, which in turn is owned by the shareholders. The shareholders appoint directors to run the company as agents on their behalf and the directors are then required to report annually to shareholders on their stewardship. Directors can, in turn, delegate their powers to managers but they are still ultimately responsible to the shareholders. One of the reasons why the company system is so attractive to investors is that they get to reduce their exposure to risk by forming joint stock companies to 'limit' this investment exposure. The shareholders are not liable for the debts of the company beyond the fully paid-up price of the shares, nor are they duty-bound to take any interest in the running of the company. However, they do enjoy a number of rights: to dispose of the stock at will; to receive dividends; to share any surplus capital should the company be wound up; to voting rights in the AGM (annual general meeting); to information on the fortunes of the company; and to the right to subscribe to new shares if more capital is required. Shareholder rights tend to be proportional to the number of shares held in a company, but not always, particularly when different classes of share are issued with different voting rights attached to them. The small shareholder has the opportunity to influence company directors at the AGM albeit all the directors are not obliged to attend, nor does the board chair have to answer shareholders' questions. Institutional investors and large shareholders often enjoy private meetings with managers and directors, but these meetings should not disclose information that would contravene the rules of insider trading.

At the AGM, shareholders vote on the report and accounts presented by the board and accountants and to reappoint members of the board, the auditors and their remuneration, and on other motions that are put to them. Information reported to shareholders is limited under the Companies Acts and the accounting conventions of the accounting professions. Most registered companies are required to have at least two directors. Under the law all directors are treated equally as having a duty to prepare annual reports and accounts and provide sound stewardship of the company, regardless of what particular functional responsibility they may be designated. The board of directors is collectively responsible for all the company. Although the Companies Act has nothing to say about the way a company board is to be run, in reality, the chairman of the board tends to play an important role in reporting to the shareholders and others through the issuing of a chairman's statement and other comments. In private companies, protection is not as extensive as shareholders are insiders and often family members although such companies still enjoy the privilege of limited liability and legal personality.

Problems with the Operation of the Present Structure

Criticisms of the governance structures in many large companies are that they are out of shareholder control; that they allow for too much management self-dealing; and that they are detrimental to the environment and to human rights (Charkham, 1994). Fraud and scandal also brought the topic of corporate governance into the spotlight in the 1990s. The Guinness share manipulation scandal and the theft of pensioners' assets in the Maxwell empire highlighted the potential for corruption in this system. Successive committees were set up to explore these issues and to try to bring in better standards of conduct. The Cadbury, Greenbury, Hampel and Turnbull reports have all formulated rules and processes to help to improve corporate governance in British companies in the future (Greenbury, 1995; Hampel, 1998).

The collective result of these reviews was the Combined Code on Corporate Governance, which was made a listing requirement for companies quoted on the London Stock Exchange. This code sets principles on the separation of chairman from the chief executive, the provision for at least a third of the board to be independent directors, and that committees should oversee the remuneration, appointments and audits of the company. The expectations of institutional investors for improved corporate performance has brought many firms into compliance with this combined code. Other international reports have also developed the theme of more checks and balances in the boardroom to avoid executive domination of decision-making and to protect the rights of shareholders. In 1998, the OECD developed a set of global guidelines on corporate governance (OECD, 1999).

In 1998 the New Labour government announced the launch of a fundamental review of the framework of core company law to be conducted by the Company Law Review steering group and funded by the Department of Trade and Industry (DTI). The terms of reference for the review are to modernise the framework of company law to take into account the globalised economy and the competitiveness of British industry (DTI, 1998). The review published its own summary of what it saw as the drawbacks of the present 1985 Companies Act: it is couched in over-formal language, is complicated by excessive detail, tends towards over-regulation, has a complex structure, making it difficult for businessmen to understand, and is costly to interpret (DTI, 2000). The review was keen to explore the needs of small and closely-held companies, which it did not consider were well served by the present companies act. They have favoured the merits of free-standing legislation for such companies, as opposed to an integrated rewrite of the existing law. The final report recommends a rewriting of the proposed legislation on a 'small-business first' basis, with appropriate flexibility to suit the needs of such small companies, while retaining integrated legislation which provides for all companies. The most significant recommendations regarding SMEs are that private companies should be offered a number of ways to reduce formal decision-making methods – so that AGMs, the laying of accounts and the annual reappointment of auditors should not be required unless companies wish to do so, and that shareholders in unanimous agreement should be able to avoid the need for written resolutions and the formalities of the company's constitution.

Under a new Companies Act it is hoped that information and communications technologies (ICTs) can be incorporated into company decision-making and in the presentation and holding of company information. The form and contents of accounts, directors' duties and responsibilities are to be identified and clarified, and company decision-making is to be made more transparent and accountable. The review recommends that a much clearer distinction be made between the statutory requirements for private and public companies.

Research Perspectives on Corporate Governance

The importance of the theoretical perspective used to analyse and prescribe for changes in corporate governance cannot be overemphasised. The notion about board functioning derives from perspectives about what its function is and should be. The fact that most studies are informed by agency theory tends to overemphasise the importance of contractual and incentive structures in the governance process (Tricker, 2000). This may be to the neglect of service functions and the building of a wider set of relationships within which the company needs to perform for a range of third-party satisfactions. Agency theory is also irrelevant in the owner-director situation, where other perspectives might be more fruitful.

The study of corporate governance is marked by a diversity of theoretical approaches and as yet lacks an orthodox paradigm (Turnbull, 1997). The best candidate for this title is agency theory, which is a development of the kernel of Ronald Coase's ideas into an economics of transaction costs, most notably by the American economist Oliver Williamson. Specifically on the implications for corporate governance of the divorce of ownership from control are contributions by Jensen and Meckling, and Fama and Jensen (Coase, 1937; Jensen and Meckling, 1976; Fama and Jensen, 1983; Williamson, 1991). Agency theory presents governance relationships as a contract between the director and the shareholder. The former are seeking to maximise their own personal utility and are likely to take actions that are to the disadvantage of the latter. To reduce these transaction costs, a set of mechanisms is therefore needed: checks and balances on boardroom power, adequate disclosure to shareholders, and the use of independent directors, to name but a few. Critics of agency theory argue that corporate practice involves a wider set of relationships than those in a mere contractual relationship, and that the theory takes a limited and reductionist view of these relationships (Turnbull, 1997). Stewardship theory has been proposed as an alternative, taking a wider view of the corporate governance process based on the fiduciary duty of directors to act in the best interests of the company as a whole (Donaldson and Davis, 1994) and that the emphasis on compliance detracts from the functions of the board to ensure that there is good performance and forward thinking. The notion that corporations are to be managed on behalf of stakeholders has also been the subject of increasing debate in recent years (Freeman, 1984). The view that shareholders are but one (albeit an important) group of stakeholders in the firm has brought attention on to the other stakeholders who are deeply affected by corporate decision-making and so should be shown moral concern in the governance process. Stakeholder representation and analysis has the benefits of allowing firms to accommodate growing demands for business to be more responsible from consumers, environmental and human rights groups.

How Might Corporate Governance Research Contribute to SMEs?

Corporate governance problems for SMEs are different in many ways from those experienced by a large company (Mileham, 1996). At the start of a firm's existence, its directors' and owners are likely to be the same people. All their attention is likely to be taken up with getting going and surviving in the initial years. Worrying about board structure and procedures will take second place to keeping the business going. The business is likely to have only one or two directors, and board meetings will be informal and unrecorded. However, as a firm begins to expand and grow, and particularly when it needs injections of outside capital, the directors will have to contemplate how the firm is governed, rather than managed. The directors will need to begin to separate their operating tasks from the strategic role of building the firm's long-term future. Many investors will consider the quality of a growing firm's corporate governance mechanisms before they are willing to invest in the company.

The difficulty of making the transition from owner-control to corporate governance, and to allow other stakeholders interest in the governance process is a formidable challenge for the SME. The transition is, in effect, a gradual change from the private to the public in conceptions of ownership and governance. One of the crucial points of transition is the introduction of non-executive directors into the boardroom. They are able to help the firm's executives take a longer and wider view of their activities and help to monitor and improve the performance of the firm's management. In short, outside directors can help to bring focus and expertise to an SME development.

Most corporate governance research today is concerned with those decisions made by the owners and executives of the firm and the impacts of their decisions on various stakeholder groups (Clarke, 1998). The main forum for taking this kind of decision is the company board. Corporate governance is particularly interested in the relationship of the board to the firm and to the owners and shareholders. The structure and process of boards of directors is one of the main areas of study in corporate governance. In most Anglo-American influenced systems of corporate governance, the boards of directors are composed of a mix of inside and outside directors. Inside directors are company employees; outside directors are non-executive or independent individuals who are not employees of the company. Historically, boards have been dominated by outside directors but in the twentieth century professional or executive managers began to replace founder directors in larger firms.

In the case of SMEs, this is a process that has only been apparent in recent years. Owner-directors still tend to predominate in the boardroom. Recent studies of corporate governance focus on a variety of issues such as how transparent should boards be in their decision-making and to whom should they be accountable;

who are boards there to serve – the shareholders or stakeholders; what competencies should directors possess; and how do companies hold their managements accountable? Various problems and issues have been noted in the operation of the present system of corporate governance: many boards are self-perpetuating and control the nomination of new members; many directors are appointed to boards as a reward for long service or loyalty and are less than competent as independent directors; and many board processes are not assessed in the same performance terms as the rest of the firm's activities (Monks and Minow, 1996).

Much of the research and policy analysis in this field has come from a limited range of approaches, mainly agency theory and pragmatic responses. Agency theory is economically orientated and presents a set of theoretical claims about the agent/principal problem in the corporate form. This approach has proved fruitful in opening up the corporate governance problems of large firms where the divorce of ownership and control is most evident. But its assumed applicability to the SME needs to be questioned and a wider range of approaches reconsidered in our understanding of governance problems in this area. The policy of encouraging the incorporation of SMEs has often been based upon the agency analysis of governance and its assumed advantages, which lack rigorous demonstration from the studies on this topic. The next section will consider this evidence and some of the alternative approaches that might be developed in this area.

The Limited Range of Research into Best Practice in this Field

Best practice notions tend to be drawn from a wide range of sources: the anecdotes of SME owners are useful for gauging the variety and distinctive nature of the governance problems in this sector. The SME sector is the home of many family firms and the creation of a private company is often an important device for the perpetuation and development of these businesses. As family firms develop, the difficulty of succession often becomes a problem, along with the founder members needing to take wealth out of the business. The need for the introduction of professional management to supplement or replace family members is also a tricky issue to negotiate. The introduction of corporate status can help to bring experienced and independent outside directors on to the board of the family firm, but as Sir Adrian Cadbury notes in his reflections on the fortunes of his own family firm, all parties have to accept the need for such changes and agree to abide by arbitration if such board appointments are made (Cadbury, 1994). He comments favourably upon making the family firm a public company, as this can help unlock the family's investments in the firm and help to reward long-standing employees with shares and other incentives. Additional capital for the expansion of the company can also be found, and the increased scrutiny of performance can act as a spur to better company management in the longer term. The obvious down-side may be that the control and domination of the company from family interests has to decline, and a more professional relationship between the company and family be allowed to develop. There are some recent examples of private family-dominated companies (Virgin, Amstrad) going public and then being brought back to private status, because leading figures regarded the demands of wider accountability and loss of control as too onerous.

Best practice can also be drawn from the codes of practice on corporate governance (London Stock Exchange, 1999). For example, board sub-committees feature prominently in the combined code but when an SME board consists of only three people (chairman and chief executive, finance director and one non-executive director) the scope for sub-committees might seem to be a little limited. Nevertheless, there comes a point in the growth of an SME when the need to set up sub-committees to help delegate some of the board's work might arise. An audit committee might be needed. This could be facilitated by the one or two non-executive directors meeting with the auditors without the executives present. Here, concerns over company practices can be raised independently of the executives. In time, other committees might be set up for overseeing executive remuneration, nominations to the board, or preparations for listing or changing into a public company.

Some studies of the governance problems in SMEs are driven by theoretical assumptions and research strategies, which can contribute to the development of best practice. A recent study by Mallin and Ow-Yong examined the corporate governance practices of small companies listed on the Alternative Investment Market, which was set up in the UK in 1995 (Mallin and Ow-Yong, 1998). Under the stock exchange rules for this market, the company to be listed must have a nominated advisor and broker who will play an important role in the small firm in terms of monitoring the management of the company as well as offering advice about best practice. The study looked at the disclosures in admission documents lodged by companies with the AIM in matters related to corporate governance. The findings of the study suggested that companies with an advisor paid more attention to the Cadbury code on corporate governance, had more directors appointed to the board, had more non-executive directors, had split the roles of chairman and chief executive, had set up audit and remuneration committees, and had drawn up policies on corporate governance. The benefits to the corporate governance procedures adopted in companies with an advisor led the authors to conclude that the stock exchange should encourage more companies to take on an advisor who can help an SME make the transition to better corporate governance procedures and structures.

A study by Zahra *et al.* into the entrepreneurial qualities of SMEs and the effect of ownership and governance structures on this activity was published recently in the USA (Zahra *et al.*, 2000). The study was informed by agency theory assumptions and sought to explore (in an empirical investigation of 231 SMEs in manufacturing) whether more successful companies had senior executives that had stock in their companies and/or had a substantive shareholder who actively monitored and contributed to the company's deliberations over strategy. Data from the study led the authors to conclude that the more enterprising companies were the ones where executives owned stock in their companies, where the chairman and chief executive were different individuals, where the board was medium in size (6–11 members), and where the outside directors owned stock in the company. Much of this study tends to confirm its own assumptions with regard to agency theory, namely that ownership has a positive value-enhancing effect upon the company, and that this relationship often gets into trouble when the transition is made from owner-managers to professional managers.

Another study based on the framework of agency theory is that of Lee *et al.*, which looks at the value of outside financial directors on corporate boards in the USA (Lee *et al.*, 1999). The dataset used in the study was of 146 firms that had announced during the period 1981–85 that they were appointing an outside director from a commercial bank, insurance company or investment bank. This was then correlated with changes in the firm's share price a month later. From this limited study, the authors concluded that the appointment of an outside financial director to the board was associated with positive abnormal returns for the SMEs in the sample. They also found that investment bankers were appointed to the boards of smaller companies more frequently than commercial bankers or insurance executives. They concluded that smaller firms, which may have limited access to financial markets and less financial expertise, benefit substantially from these appointments. The assumptions of agency theory are thereby affirmed: that board composition is a factor in company valuation by the stock market, and that outside directors in general, and financial directors in particular, are selected in the interests of shareholders.

A recent survey conducted by Berry and Perren in the UK into 1103 SMEs found that when a firm had more than 50 employees it was twice as likely to engage a non-executive director (Berry and Perren, 2001). SMEs with fewer than 50 employees, when they had appointed non-executive directors, particularly valued their financial advice; whereas SMEs with over 50 employees and non-executive directors placed more emphasis on their outside objectivity, contribution to structured board procedures and the director's personal reputation. The authors of this survey suggested that an SME might need to change its non-executive directors as its development progresses, to help the board deal with new challenges and opportunities. While the study did not gather enough evidence to demonstrate a significant difference in performance in SMEs that had non-executive directors, managing directors who had engaged them claimed that their inputs were valued. Most non-executive directors were engaged through personal networks, or through banks and accountancy firms. Berry and Perren concluded by suggesting that a large number of in-depth case studies need to be conducted to shed more light on the role and influence of non-executive directors in SMEs, and to help policy-makers decide on how to make further improvements in SME corporate governance.

Another source of insight into the problems of SMEs and the search for best practice can be found from comparative studies of corporate governance. Such studies in other competitor nations have shown that there are often interesting differences between the institutional arrangements in the conduct of corporate life (Charkham, 1994). Law review bodies are often charged with a duty to examine the governance regimes of what appear to be successful nations in terms of their economic performance to see if alternative structures can bring better results, particularly in the small-business sector. A brief mention of some of the major characteristics of the different systems of corporate governance will now be given.

In the USA, company law is a matter of state jurisdiction and the laws in states can differ considerably, although there is some federal oversight on securities regulation and a general willingness to follow the leading states; New York, California and Delaware. Consequently, the Model Business Corporations Act which came into force in 1984, and the American Law Institute Principles of

Corporate Governance 1994, tend to guide most aspects of US practice. However, states compete for incorporations and Delaware is one of the most competitive centres for this administrative activity. This competitive contest has tended to give favourable terms for directors, enabling them to claim indemnity for breaches of duty, and scope for the preferment of outside interests over those of shareholders in some circumstances. In comparison with the UK, the interests of shareholders are not as closely protected but in terms of the performance of share values this does not seem to have caused any detrimental impact. Company law in Delaware is very flexible in other ways: part of the proceeds of a capital issue can be distributed, and there are extensive provisions for informal operations and decision-making in small firms. There is a willingness to experiment with different versions of the corporate form, such as closed companies and limited liability, so as to be favourable to new business development.

In Europe, there is an attempt to harmonise company law under Article 54 of the Treaty of Rome, but progress to date has been blocked by various member states. In terms of individual European countries, the German system is the most highly developed and has had an impact on other countries companies acts. German company forms are divided between 'share' companies (Aktiengesellschaften) and limited companies (Gesellschaften mit beschrankter Haftung). The former tend to have detailed and prescriptive constitutions and are similar to public companies, with power to raise funds publicly; the latter have limited numbers of members and allow for more flexible internal constitutions and are the nearest equivalent to the private company in the UK.

Until the 1970s most Commonwealth countries tended to follow UK company law with adaptations of the 1948 or 1927 Acts. However, since then a process of reappraisal and simplification has been taking place in many countries, moving them in the direction of the US model. In Australia, the First Corporate Law Simplifications Act was passed which relaxed the rules for small businesses including single member companies, accounting exemptions, liberalised share buy-backs and relaxed requirements for company registers. Another Company Law Review Act in 1998 allowed for the formation of a company without the need for a constitution, simplified the process for conducting shareholder meetings, facilitated the use of electronic technology for meetings, eased changes to share capital values and reduced administrative burdens for company returns.

Competitive Advantage in Governance: Compliance and Performance

As was noted above, most studies of corporate governance are compliance-oriented and tend to lead in the direction of the formalisation and codification of good practice. Compliance becomes a hygiene factor in the corporate governance debate and often revolves around the agency theory of boardroom roles. In this theory, the governing board acts as a ratifier of the decisions to be implemented by the management, and as a controller in monitoring their implementation and performance. These prescribe the following activities as appropriate for the board: the selection of the board; the evaluation of compensation for senior executives; the selection, monitoring and removal of executives; the review of the company's financial objectives, plans and policies; the reviewing and monitoring of the company's auditing and accounting practices; and ensuring the company is in compliance with regulatory demands and requirements. What is often underemphasised is the need for performance and the creation and maintenance of a complex set of relationships around the firm. In the growing firm, it is very important that these are developed and broadened as the business develops. The transition from owner-manager to professional management and the incorporation of outside perspectives on the management and efficiency of the business are crucial steps towards successful growth. The need for business performance and relationship management in corporate governance should not be neglected.

Performance is often felt to be the key to competitive advantage; the actualisation of the SME. It is recommended that the board's role in this respect is to ensure that the management is effectively and continuously striving for above-average performance, taking into account the risk factors (Hilmer, 1993). In this respect the board should pay attention to the following activities: the selection and appointment of the chief executive; the formulation of strategies and policies; budgeting and planning; reporting to shareholders on regulatory compliance; and ensuring the board's own effectiveness.

If we study corporate governance from the agency theory perspective, then control becomes the most important function of the process. But there are other equally important roles for the board to perform, and other theories that would put them in the forefront of their analysis and prescription. Stakeholder theory is a sociological approach that describes the nature of the relationship and interactions between the company and society and the variety of interests which are served. As yet, there is no coherent and consistent framework of theory which covers all the functions of the board and the scope and processes of corporate governance specifically in SMEs (Hung, 1998). Such a theory would need to integrate the functional aspects and provide a valid explanation of the major roles and processes in the corporate governance arena for both large and small companies.

Policy Issues for Corporate Governance in SMEs

As the result of this brief analysis, a number of policy implications for the development of best practice in SME corporate governance are considered. First, best-practice guidelines for SME corporate governance. These guidelines would be similar to the Cadbury code but written specifically with SMEs in mind. They would issue guidance on the following issues: the need to conduct an annual review of the chief executive; an annual review of the firm's strategy to determine if it is working and what changes need to be made; an annual appraisal of the organisation's efficiency, and the performance of the board itself, including the appraisal of individual directors, processes and membership. Another important device for improving SME corporate governance is the drawing up of shareholder agreements or family constitutions, which lay down detailed provisions that will guide dispute resolution in the firm or family, should they develop. Shareholder agreements typically cover issues such as definitions of the business to be pursued by the company; intended capitalisation and the financing structure of the company; composition of the board; the intended policy for the distribution of profits; procedures for the resolution of disputes between shareholders; the transferability of shareholdings, suitable exit routes and the method of valuing the shares being sold or transferred.

Second, there is clearly a need for more research using different perspectives on corporate governance. The new stakeholder agenda in corporate governance should not be ignored by the SME sector. SMEs need to take advantage of the positive and active environmental strategies that can lead to both immediate and longer-term benefits for businesses of all sizes. Customers are increasingly screening potential suppliers for their 'green' credentials. SMEs should not ignore this development and should obtain environmental standards accreditation and certification. Even if the cost of this is prohibitive in some SMEs, then smaller steps in this direction can be taken. Starting with energy efficiency initiatives, companies can then move on to reviews of their packaging and waste disposal policies. This can lead to cost savings and recycling opportunities as well as minimising the SME's risk of exposure under the duty of care provisions of the Environmental Protection Act. Increasingly, access to new sources of capital may be heavily influenced by the social and environmental stance of the firm. All main UK clearing banks are in the process of building social and environmental issues into their credit management policies. SMEs looking to list on the AIM (Alternative Investment Market) also need to start building environmental concerns into their listing strategies because the due-diligence procedures of the reporting accountants and lawyers take into account environmental risk. Helping SMEs embrace this new agenda should be an important aim of the government's business advisory services.

Third, a review of the appropriate corporate forms to be recommended for SMEs. Freedman has brought to wider attention the fact that, although the case for limited liability is widely accepted for larger companies, for the SME the efficiency arguments are less clear-cut. For SMEs, the allocation of risk to those most capable of bearing it tends to be weakened by the adoption of limited liability. Creditors, employees and owners are often more liable than shareholders. This could in fact slow down the growth of the small-business sector since the failure of one SME frequently pulls down other SMEs. SMEs which think that they are limited in their exposure may find themselves taking undue risks and yet still end up as personally liable. This was most recently highlighted in the case of the employees in the private company Easy Group, where the owner, Stelios Haji-Ioannou, reduced the value of employee shares from £1 to 1p at an extraordinary meeting of shareholders by casting his 75 per cent voting rights in the company. Employees who had taken shares in place of higher salaries ended up taking a substantial part of the risk (and losses) in this business (Finch, 2001). Moreover, the role of limited liability in reducing monitoring and transaction costs in SMEs is much less than is often imagined. Without the divorce of ownership from control, the agency problem does not arise, and the business has merely added a layer of disclosure cost that it could have done without. The encouragement of SMEs into incorporation should be carefully considered as this is only appropriate for growth-oriented businesses, rather than a blanket measure for all SMEs. Indeed, the call to deregulate and simplify company law for small businesses has to be tempered, since these regulations and requirements are also there to protect other stakeholders in society and to avoid the creation of moral hazards.

Finally, training for governance and clarification of board roles in SMEs can help the growing firm manage the difficult transition to limited liability and its ultimate public company status. A manager who has succeeded in running a business using command and control skills often finds that when he creates a board of directors that this approach to decision-making is no longer appropriate. What is required is the effective use of personal power, and the ability to influence others by reasoned argument and persuasion. Consequently, directors must learn new types of behaviour: advocacy and consensus building. Board members are all collectively responsible for the fortunes of the business, so all members of the board need to become familiar with all aspects of the business, even those outside their functional expertise. The perspectives of objectivity and collective responsibility also have to be developed. Training and mentoring can help, and gaining experience on the boards of other companies is invaluable. Helping SME directors gain this experience and training would be a real contribution to improving SME governance processes. Help for SMEs with contacts and lists of outside directors in the difficult transition period would also make a useful contribution.

References

Berry, A. and Perren, L. (2001) 'The role of non-executive directors in UK SMEs', *Journal of Small Business and Enterprise Development*, 8:2, 159–173.

Bolton, J.E. (1971) *Report of the Committee of Inquiry on Small Firms*, Cmnd.4811. HMSO, London.

Cadbury, A. (1992) *The Financial Aspects of Corporate Governance – A Report of the Committee on Corporate Governance*. Gee & Co, London.

Cadbury, A. (1994) 'The role of directors in family firms', in R.I. Tricker (ed.) *International Corporate Governance: Text, Readings and Cases*. Prentice Hall, London, pp. 392–402.

Charkham, J. (1994) *Keeping Good Company; A Study of Corporate Governance in Five Countries*. Oxford University Press, Oxford.

Clarke, T. (1998) 'Research on corporate governance', *Corporate Governance: An International Review*, 1:6, 57–66.

Coase, R. (1937) 'The nature of the firm', *Economica*, **4**, 386–405.

Department of Trade and Industry (1998) *Modern Company Law for a Competitive Economy*. URN98/654, London.

Department of Trade and Industry (2000) *Modern Company Law for a Competitive Economy: Developing the Framework*. URN00/656, London.

Department of Trade and Industry (2001) *Modern Company Law for a Competitive Economy: Final Report Vols 1 & 2*. URN01/942, London.

Donaldson, L. and Davis, J. (1994) 'Boards and company performance – research challenges the conventional wisdom', *Corporate Governance: An International Review*, **2**:3, 151–160.

Fama, E. and Jensen, M. (1983) 'Separation of ownership and control', *Journal of Law and Economics*, **26**, 301–326.

Finch, J. (2001) 'Stelios gives staff a lesson in capitalism', *The Guardian*, 27 September.

Freedman, J. (2000) 'Limited liability: large company theory and small firms', *The Modern Law Review*, 3:63, 317–354.

Freedman, J. and Godwin, M. (1994) 'Incorporating the micro business: perceptions and misperceptions', in A. Hughes and D. Storey (eds) *Finance and the Small Firm*. Routledge, London, pp. 233–283.

Freeman, R. (1984) *Strategic Management: A Stakeholder Approach*. Pitman, Boston.

Greenbury, R. (1995) *Directors' Remuneration: the Report of a Study Group*. Gee & Co, London.

Hakim, C. (1989) 'Identifying fast-growth small firms', *Employment Gazette*, January, 29–41.

Hampel, R. (1998) *Committee on Corporate Governance: Final Report*. Gee & Co, London.

Hilmer, F. (1993) *Strictly Boardroom: Improving Governance to Enhance Company Performance*. Information Australia, Melbourne.

Hung, H. (1998) 'A typology of the theories of the roles of governing boards', *Corporate Governance: An International Review*, **2**:6, 101–111.

Jensen, M. and Meckling, W. (1976) 'Theory of the firm: managerial behaviour, agency costs and ownership structure', *Journal of Financial Economics*, **3**, 831–880.

Lee, S., Rosenstein, S. and Wyatt, J. (1999) 'The value of financial outside directors on corporate boards', *International Review of Economics and Finance*, **8**, 421–431.

London Stock Exchange (1999) *Principles of Good Governance and Code of Best Practice*. London.

Mallin, C. and Ow-Yong, K. (1998) 'Corporate governance in small companies – the alternative investment market', *Corporate Governance: An International Review*, **4**:6, 224–232.

Mileham, P. (1996) 'Boardroom leadership: do small and medium companies need non-executive directors?' *Journal of General Management*, **22**:1, 14–27.

Monks, R. and Minow, N. (1996) *Watching the Watchers: Corporate Governance for the 21st Century*. Blackwell, Oxford.

OECD (1999) *OECD Principles of Corporate Governance*. SG/CG(99)5, Paris.

Porter, M.E. (1985) *Competitive Advantage: Creating and Sustaining Superior Performance*. Free Press, New York.

Storey, D. (1994) *Understanding the Small Business Sector*. ITP Business Press, London.

Storey, D. (2001) *A Portrait of Success: the Facts Behind High Growth Companies in the UK*. Deloitte & Touche, London.

Tricker, R.I. (2000) *Corporate Governance*. Ashgate/Dartmouth, Aldershot.

Turnbull, S. (1997) 'Corporate governance: its scope, concerns and theories', *Corporate Governance: An International Review*, **5**:4, 180–205.

Warren, R.C. (2000) *Corporate Governance and Accountability*. Liverpool Academic Press, Liverpool.

Williamson, O.E. (1991) *The Nature of the Firm: Origins, Evolution and Development*. Oxford University Press, Oxford.

Zahra, S., Neubaum, D. and Huse, M. (2000) 'Entrepreneurship in medium-size companies: exploring the effects of ownership and governance systems', *Journal of Management*, **26**:5, 947–976.

Chapter 5

SUSTAINABILITY AND COMPETITIVENESS: ARE THERE MUTUAL ADVANTAGES FOR SMEs?

Fiona Tilley, Paul Hooper and Liz Walley

'The environment is now considered to be a critical competitiveness issue, considered more important than exchange and interest rates, finance or labour costs. Confusion surrounding exactly what represents best practice, however, prevents many companies from realising substantial cost savings ... confusion was most pronounced among small and medium-sized companies (SMEs) – those less likely to have the time and resources available to investigate the relevant issues.' (Envirowise, 2000)

Introduction

This chapter will chart the relationship between SMEs and the natural environment and demonstrate how the sustainability (or what is sometimes referred to as the sustainable development) agenda is relevant to the competitiveness of SMEs. It begins with a general discussion of the win-win link between sustainability and competitiveness and the rise of corporate environmentalism. This is followed by an examination of the factors that have weakened the ability of SMEs to take advantage of potential win-win competitive gains. Government and non-governmental agencies in response have developed measures to raise awareness and assist SMEs in their efforts to improve their environmental performance. This chapter examines why it is that such initiatives, more specifically demonstration projects, have been largely ineffective. The final section assesses what this all means for the management and competitiveness of SMEs.

There are numerous definitions of sustainability and sustainable development, but the best known is that provided by the United Nations World Commission on Environment and Development (1987) which suggests that development is sustainable where it meets the needs of the present without compromising the ability of future generations to meet their own needs. The bridging of economic prosperity and environmental quality gave rise to the belief that sustainable development is a source of new innovations, market opportunities and wealth creation, *ergo*, the sustainability agenda is viewed as a pathway to a new era of competitive advantage. The first stages of the greening of business focused mainly on environmental protection, but over the last ten years or so it has been recognised that sustainability requires a broader focus; namely, the simultaneous pursuit of economic prosperity, environmental quality and social equity. In other words, these three dimensions or pillars are interdependent and it is not possible to attain one without recognising the importance of the others. However, the primary focus of this chapter will be the environmental quality component of sustainability.

The relationship between business and the environment has been classified into different stages of development by Frankel (1999) and placed along an industry sustainability learning curve by Nattrass and Altomare (1999). Figure 5.1 demonstrates the way in which the corporate response to environmental pressures has evolved from being unprepared before the 1970s, reactive through to anticipatory by the 1980s, reaching a proactive state in the 1990s and forecast to be high-integration in the 2000s. Each stage represents the environmental/sustainability activities of the leading companies. Pre-1970s, it was felt that economic growth and environmental protection were incompatible. Environmental advocates were perceived by mainstream businesses to be anti-growth. By the 1980s, this adversarial stance had been replaced by the concept of sustainable development which, by definition, saw sustainability and economic development going hand in hand. The 1990s have been described as a period of strategic action (Welford, 1996), both by governments, emanating from the Rio Earth Summit in 1992, and by some leading companies which began to see environmental management as a strategic tool for gaining competitive advantage. Companies of all sizes can be found at each stage along this sustainability learning curve. The majority of SMEs in the UK can be categorised as being in one of the first three stages (Tilley, 1999a).

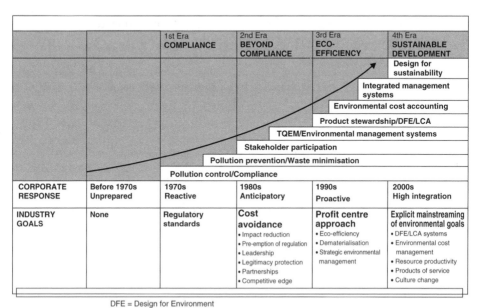

DFE = Design for Environment
LCA = Life Cycle Analysis
TQEM = Total Quality Environmental
Management

FIGURE 5.1   Industry's sustainability learning curve. Source: Nattrass and Altomare (1999)

The 'Win-Win' of Corporate Environmentalism

The advent of sustainable development has presented the business community with the so-called 'win-win' of corporate environmentalism. As popular as this concept has become, it is also contentious; the reasons for this will be discussed below. The win-win approach is based on a belief that businesses which pursue environmental performance improvements can also derive economic benefits from the same activities. This is also referred to by some as environmental efficiency (or eco-efficiency), which relates to an organisation's capacity to find efficiencies in resource use and/or the minimisation of waste outputs.

Porter and van der Linde (1995) have become advocates of the win-win approach to corporate environmentalism. In rejecting the prevailing view that there was an inherent and fixed trade-off between economics and the environment, they advocated that businesses of all sizes must start to recognise environmental improvement as an economic and competitive opportunity, not as an annoying cost or threat, and emphasised the early-movers benefit. Contrary to the level playing-field argument, they supported the need for high environmental regulatory standards in developed countries, but emphasised that this needs to be 'good' regulation, the kind that is innovation-friendly, focusing on outcomes not technologies. In classic Porter terminology, the constituents of competitive advantage that can be attained by becoming more environmentally responsible are improved materials efficiency, improved product quality, increased staff commitment, cheaper finance, lower insurance premiums, reduced risk exposure, assured present and future compliance, improved media coverage and positive pressure group relations (Welford and Gouldson, 1993).

Porter's approach to regulation is predicated on the idea that:

> To believe that environmental regulations improve corporate competitiveness, it is necessary to believe that the average company routinely misses profitable opportunities to develop environmental products or install anti-pollution processes. Moreover, it is necessary to believe that these missed business opportunities are likely to be more profitable than opportunities that companies overlook for other reasons. Otherwise, competitiveness would presumably be best improved in other, perhaps non-environmental areas. (Cairncross, 1995, p. 197)

Clearly these circumstances cannot hold true in all cases, and thus it seems unrealistic to fully regulate the environmental practices of businesses including SMEs. So notwithstanding the merits of regulation to maintain a threshold of acceptable social, environmental and economic activity, the practical difficulties of implementing and enforcing such a regime suggest that alternative methods of sustaining competitiveness should be considered.

A number of commentators (for example, Welford, 1992) and companies such as Procter & Gamble Inc (Shrivastava, 1996) and Westfield (see case study below) have drawn on the analogies and synergies between environmental management and total quality management (TQM). Zero defects in TQM equates to zero negative impacts on the environment; the prevention of defects (environmental accidents) is better and cheaper than after-the-event remedies. Both approaches need to be integrated and holistic and require total managerial commitment. Companies have also recognised the benefits of emphasising the synergy between TQM and environmental objectives. Indeed, the British environmental standard, BS 7750 (introduced in 1992, but now superseded by the international standard, ISO 14001), was modelled on the quality standard BS 5750. From an acceptability and process perspective, companies have found that piggy-backing environmental initiatives on quality programmes has been pragmatically successful. In the context of corporate greening, this has been termed 'greenjacking' (Walley and Stubbs, 1999) to differentiate it from 'hijacking', which has a negative connotation (Welford, 1997). 'Greenjacking' means taking another agenda and giving it a 'green' spin. An SME example of successful 'greenjacking' by an environmental champion is provided in the Westfield case study (Walley, 2000).

Notwithstanding the pragmatic benefits of greenjacking, the down-side is that a systems-based, continuous improvement type approach such as an environmental management system (EMS) is a necessary but not a sufficient mechanism for a significant environmental improvement. A similar critique is made of the strategic, win-win approach to corporate environmentalism. While an EMS does ensure the audit, monitoring and management of organisations' environmental activities, it does not necessarily drive companies towards continuous improvement or sustainability. Walley and Whitehead (1994) make the point that environmental improvements which result in cost savings for a company will eventually decline and decrease. It is erroneous to believe that the costs of investing in environmental improvements will always result in a positive financial payback. The win-win approach to sustainability is therefore not necessarily an endless source of competitive advantage.

Westfield – An SME Greening Success Story

Westfield is a small UK insurance/healthcare business employing around 60 staff in Sheffield. The starting point for their greening initiative was an objective in their 1996 Business Plan to move towards a paperless office by 2000. Whilst this objective came from the CEO, it was the Corporate Planning Manager who was the 'champion' behind the idea to broaden this objective to include a wider environmental agenda. Westfield sought the advice of the National Centre for Business and Sustainability to carry out an environmental review. This review provided baseline data on the company's impact on the environment and made recommendations on environmental priorities in the areas of environmental management systems, purchasing, paper use, transport, IT, waste, energy, water and staff training.

During the first year, their environmental policy was published and paper reduction measures and environmental training took place. In the second phase (through to 1999), an EMS was implemented, they gained the environmental standard ISO 14001 and won the *Sheffield Telegraph* Green Business Award. This case illustrates how much can be achieved in a short period of time by an environmental champion with vision and the interpersonal skills to work within a predetermined context, and network effectively and operate sensitively and pragmatically with different audiences. 'Greenjacking' the IT and quality programmes helped gain acceptance to make a start on environmental initiatives but, once started, it was equally important to sustain the emerging green culture by reinforcing connections to the core values of the company and publicising green gains. Adapted from Walley (2000).

Despite the concern for the scope of the win-win approach to corporate environmentalism, it is fundamental to the eco-efficiency business philosophy advocated by, *inter alia*, the World Business Council for Sustainable Development (Willums and WBCSD, 1998). Eco-efficiency in the simplest terms is doing more with less. This means the delivery of competitively priced goods and services that satisfy human needs and bring quality of life, while progressively reducing environmental impacts and resource intensity throughout the product/service life-cycle, to a level in line with the earth's estimated carrying capacity (Willums and WBCSD, 1998). The concept of 'natural capitalism' as the next industrial revolution (Hawken *et al.*, 1999) expands on eco-efficiency ideas but sets them in a much wider biological and social framework. Given the view, of some, that industrial capitalism as currently practised is not considered to be environmentally or socially sustainable, the natural capitalism model provides a route map of practical and technical solutions to enable a shift from the present 'industrial' form of capitalism to a form of capitalism which operates within the ecological limits of nature. In addition to radical resource productivity, the guiding principles of natural capitalism are biomimicry (redesigning business processes to reflect the circularity of biological systems), service and flow (shifting the focus of the economy from goods and purchases to the provision of quality services) and investing in the restoration of natural capital (by promoting businesses that achieve the first three principles). Because natural capitalism focuses on radical resource productivity rather than human productivity, it provides a basis to increase worldwide employment with meaningful jobs.

A practical way to operationalise the 'natural' or 'sustainable' capitalism model at the level of the company is being developed by Elkington (1997) using the idea of 'triple bottom line' accountability. As mentioned previously, sustainable development involves the simultaneous pursuit of economic prosperity, environmental quality and social equity. Companies aiming for sustainability need to perform not just against a single, financial bottom-line but also against this triple bottom-line. Some leading UK organisations such as Shell and the Co-operative Bank are already experimenting with this notion and reporting against the triple bottom-line in their sustainability reports. The emergence of corporate environmental reporting over the last decade provides further concrete evidence that a small number of leading-edge companies are attempting to maximise the commercial benefits to be derived from more proactive environmental and social policies and practices. Unfortunately, it is primarily larger international companies that make up the vanguard of this environmental and social best practice; SMEs, in contrast, have generally shown a marked reluctance to exploit the 'win-win' scenarios outlined earlier.

SMEs and Sustainability

A plethora of surveys in the 1990s demonstrated that SMEs are not responding to the sustainability agenda to the same extent as larger companies. For example, a survey undertaken by the Institute of Management concluded that while '[a]ccepting that environmental concerns can no longer be treated as a passing phase was perhaps the easy part – however, difficulties have often arisen, especially for smaller concerns, in adopting such principles. Environmental action programmes are closely related to size of organisation and the survey revealed that small concerns of up to 50 employees are far less likely to describe themselves as fully committed' (Charlesworth, 1998, p. 33).

Given the importance of the SME sector from both economic and environmental perspectives, this is of particular concern for those charged with steering economic development on to a more sustainable course. The statistics presented in Chapter 1 outline the economic significance of SMEs as a group. It is hardly surprising, therefore, that the prosperity of the sector is inextricably linked to the economic and social health of the UK and consequently to one of the UK's primary sustainable development objectives, which is the 'maintenance of high and stable levels of economic growth and employment' (DETR, 1999, p. 9). Despite the size of the sector, little attempt has been made to date to assess the scale of environmental impacts associated with SME activity. One such indicator of the sector's cumulative impact was published in Lord Marshall's report on economic instruments and the business use of energy, in which he claimed that SMEs, the commercial sector and non-energy-intensive industries taken together account for around 60 per cent of total carbon dioxide emissions from business, and may offer scope for significant improvements in energy efficiency and reductions in emissions (Marshall, 1998).

Despite the lack of concrete evidence to quantify the full extent of the SME environmental burden, concern has grown as to the apparent reluctance of the sector to respond positively to the emerging sustainability agenda. Possible explanations for this resistance to change have been identified by a number of researchers:

- A lack of environmental awareness. This was evident in early survey work (Hooper and Gibbs, 1995; Hillary, 1995). However, more recently, Petts (2000) has reported that the attitudes of management and non-management of SMEs has correlated closely with general public attitudes to the environment. Annual surveys sponsored by the Department for Environment, Transport and the Regions tracked public concern about environmental issues relative to other policy issues of the day over a ten-year period from 1986 to 1996/7. Significantly, the proportion of respondents viewing the environment as an important issue fell from a 30 per cent high in 1989 to around 15 per cent in the later years (DETR, 1998).

- A gap between environmental attitudes and subsequent behaviour (Tilley, 1999b); this is often explained by the perceived irrelevance of environmental issues to small organisations (Hooper and Gibbs, 1995) and a lack of organisational capacity for change (Petts, 2000). In particular, Petts identified a series of barriers to improved environmental performance associated with inflexible working habits; the inability to relate complex environmental regulations into individual responsibilities and thus actions; and a potential conflict between environmental messages and production and survival pressures.

- Limited access to resources, including finance, expertise and information (O'Laoire and Welford, 1996). Earlier surveys of SMEs confirmed that commercial realities act as a restraint; lack of available finance and other business demands provide a barrier to behavioural change and are causal factors in the resistance to change (Nash, 1990; Hendry, 1992; Holder, 1993).

- Inappropriate environmental management techniques. Environmental management practices are increasingly being adopted by larger businesses (Smith,

1993, Dodds, 2000). However, the general reluctance of SMEs to adopt the management solutions offered (Hutchinson and Chaston, 1994) has in part been explained by the mismatch between the requirements of environmental management systems and the limited strategic management capabilities of the SME sector.

Policy Responses

As a result of these barriers to change, a compliance culture has governed the SME response to environmental challenges in which short-term responses to immediate regulatory stimuli dominate. Acknowledgement of this failure to exploit environmental opportunities rather than simply guard against business threats has resulted in a plethora of supply-side policy initiatives. Emanating from local and central government and supported by the work of a host of non-government organisations and larger companies (for example Rover, B&Q and the National Westminster Bank), these initiatives have sought to demonstrate the commercial benefits derived from improvements to environmental performance.

Arguably the most high-profile and extensive examples of this policy drive are waste-minimisation demonstration projects. Two of the earliest examples of this approach in the UK, the Aire and Calder Project and Project Catalyst (see box below), were able to demonstrate substantial financial benefits resulting from waste avoidance and/or recycling. The success of these widely publicised demonstration projects spawned a whole series of similar schemes up and down the country (Cardiff Bay, Humber, Leicester, Merseyside, Thames Valley and the West Midlands), all of which were able to quantify waste reductions and consequent financial savings (ENDS Report, 1995).

However, despite the impression of success given by the catalogue of waste-minimisation opportunities identified by these schemes, these demonstration projects and other attempts to encourage environmental improvement in the SME community have been criticised for:

- Very low take-up rates for the support being offered. While this is true for all general business support provisions (for example, Curran and Storey (2000) report that Business Links only achieved a 7 per cent penetration rate of the SME sector), recruitment of firms into environmental initiatives is notoriously difficult.

The Benefits of Waste Minimisation

Two landmark projects in the UK funded with public and private money and involving a range of service providers demonstrated the commercial advantages to be derived from waste minimisation.

The Aire and Calder Project

This initiative ran between May 1992 and March 1993 and was intended to demonstrate the benefits of reduced use of process water, energy and raw materials among a group of

11 companies drawn from the Aire and Calder catchment area. Applying a systematic methodology for the quantification of waste streams and the identification of waste reduction possibilities, the key achievements of the project were:

- The identification of some 542 waste minimisation opportunities, this figure rose to 671 some two and a half years after the launch of the project;
- That some 10% of the initiatives were categorised as cost-neutral with a further 60% offering a payback in less than one year;
- Total savings of £3.3m per annum, three years after the launch of the project.

Project Catalyst

Based in the North-west of England, this waste-minimisation project ran from June 1993 to May 1994 and involved 14 companies. Applying a very similar methodology to the Aire and Calder Project, this initiative was also able to demonstrate considerable financial benefits arising from waste reduction. In particular, the project:

- identified some 399 options for improving process efficiency;
- achieved savings of £2.3m by the end of year one, with the potential for £8.9m per annum worth of savings if all options were implemented;
- demonstrated that the exploitation of 30% of the waste minimisation opportunities was cost-free, with a further 30% paying back investment within one year.

Source: Johnson and Stokes (1995).

- A lack of dissemination of learning experiences outside the project participants. Spatially discrete demonstration projects have largely failed to affect the behaviour of companies in the surrounding areas (Johnson and Stokes, 1995).
- A failure by project participants to maintain the momentum of environmental improvements at the end of the start-up schemes. Evidence suggests that any impetus created by initiatives quickly dissipates once the formal period of support and encouragement has ended (Shearlock et al., 2000).

This last point is probably the most damning as it conflicts with the logic of the 'stages of greening' (Welford, 1996; Frankel 1999). These stages imply that when a company experiences the commercial benefits of proactive environmental management it will invest additional resources into more radical environmental improvement and thus become more willing and able to exploit environmental opportunities. Unfortunately, the experience of environmental support initiatives targeted at SMEs suggests that while organisations may be willing to pick the 'low-hanging fruit' (the easy win-win savings gained from inexpensive environmental improvements) this does not inevitably lead to reinvestment in environmental improvement and a change in organisation priorities. More importantly, it does not necessarily lead companies to make larger, more long-term, changes and investments to achieve the gains offered by 'higher-hanging fruit'. Such gains typically require a more radical effort to re-engineer business processes to achieve the advances in eco-efficiencies regarded as essential to sustainability (as reflected, for example, by the principles of natural capitalism discussed earlier in this chapter).

Research by Hooper *et al.* (2000) used organisational learning literature as a framework to investigate why there appears to be so much resistance to the wider (or double-loop) learning necessary to engender a shift in corporate culture, which many see as essential if a real shift towards a more sustainable pattern of development is to be achieved (Ballard, 2000). Drawing upon surveys of SMEs and business support providers, the research demonstrates the potential benefit to recruitment derived from presenting the business support in terms of solving problems that arise from the dominant win-win business agenda. Unfortunately, while this approach has the merit of increasing the perception that the support available is relevant, it necessarily confines the experience into a 'problem-setting, problem-solving' framework. Once the environmental problem has been solved, it is hardly surprising that further environmental improvements are rare after specific initiatives have finished. So, incremental environmental improvements are seen to occur, but they do not create any sustained momentum for change. Furthermore, the very fact that the sustainability agenda has been made relevant by an explicit attempt to relate environmental issues to dominant business norms means that it is also likely to reinforce rather than challenge prevailing corporate values. Even in cases where the experience of environmental improvement was found to have begun to challenge the existing business agenda, the potential for change was profoundly curbed by organisational defence routines triggered when that original agenda was threatened.

So we are left with a conundrum: the very changes to the provision of environmental support which make it more relevant to the needs of SMEs, and thus would encourage greater uptake, appear to inhibit more radical organisational change. So what is to be done? If one option is to accept that SME business support networks have a limited power to influence a more radical response to the sustainability agenda, then business support organisations could simply focus on those changes that will encourage a wider range of SMEs to utilise this service provision and, consequently, start on a path of incremental environmental improvement. In essence, this means doing more of the same by focusing activities on the wider diffusion rather than the deeper penetration of the sustainability agenda. From a pragmatic viewpoint, this scenario is preferable to the existing situation, in which the majority of environmental services on offer fail to find their market and/or engender continual improvements. However, this does not even hint at the 'revolutionary change' (Ballard, 2000) required to shift development patterns on to a more sustainable footing. If the business support network is to make any contribution to this more fundamental change, perhaps the findings by Hooper *et al.* (2000) that suggest utilising the SME capabilities for learning could point to a possible way ahead. In particular, the latter research demonstrates that organisations with higher capabilities for learning have a greater capacity to assimilate training inputs, which suggests that in appropriate circumstances it may be possible to extend training/business support beyond the immediate needs of problem-solving to a wider environmental agenda that challenges the deeper cultural roots of the organisation.

The Importance of Education and Training

An important implication of the discussion is that business education and training with an environmental or sustainable development component has a key role to play in generating a stronger internal demand within SMEs to seek environmental performance improvement. Training has been a subject of much interest and discussion in the SME research and policy community (Storey, 1994); the lack of general formal training provision has been identified as a problem capable of damaging the growth potential and competitiveness of the SME sector (Curran *et al.*, 1996). A number of environmental training programmes targeted specifically at SMEs have been piloted in the UK (Kemp *et al.*, 1996). Green business clubs and other environmental and business support agencies deliver seminars and training programmes, and the government has organised environmental roadshows, all aimed at disseminating environmental training, information and business support (Smith, 1996). These initiatives to date have gained only limited success in targeting and attracting participation from SMEs.

SMEs in the UK have a reputation for undervaluing and under-investing in training (Hankinson, 1994). This is a serious obstacle to improving SME demand for change because without the requisite knowledge and skills relating to the sustainability agenda, SMEs are always going to be placed at a disadvantage. To take advantage of the improvements to competitiveness that the sustainability agenda offers SMEs, owner-managers and employees need to possess greater levels of awareness and understanding of the issues and the possible solutions. To quote the UK government's 1999 strategy for sustainable development; '[to] meet the challenges for sustainable development, we need a skilled and adaptable labour force ... better education and training are essential' (DETR, 1999, p. 36). As the objectives of the sustainability agenda become more pressing, SMEs will increasingly be required to engage with the sustainability challenge. At present many SMEs do not have the necessary in-house knowledge and expertise to understand the issues at stake. An inability to understand and identify environmental problems, to be unable to communicate in the language of the environment and ecology, presents a serious barrier to the implementation of appropriate sustainable business solutions (Tilley, 1999b). As Hutchinson and Hutchinson (1997, p. 134) have noted, 'staff training and education is essential if the SME sector is to become more involved in the move towards sustainability.' The environmental literacy skills of the workforce of SMEs are, therefore, an important determinant of the total environmental performance of the firm.

The importance of environmental education and training is exemplified by the following comment from the first report by the government's Sustainable Development Education Panel (1999, p. 13), which stated that: 'Employers are enormously influential, not just in providing learning opportunities for their employees, but also in educating their customers, their suppliers and the world at large. We believe that all businesses should be actively addressing the challenges of sustainable development.'

Research on sustainable development education initiatives in the workplace has revealed that such initiatives are not widespread, currently affecting only a small proportion of the country's workplaces. Many existing projects also lack clear stated objectives or objectives against which progress and success can be measured (Impactt, 1999). The Impactt study went on to observe that small firms rarely seek training of this nature because of time and cost constraints, nor do they respond well to advice that is paper-based. Education and training on sustainable development and environmental management has flourished in small firms where practical benefits and an added value to the core business are identifiable. Although it is recognised that SMEs need environmental education and training to raise levels of awareness and environmental performance, in general there is little external pressure being placed upon them to warrant them taking up training in this area (Haile *et al.*, 1999). Research, therefore, shows that SME demand for environmental education and training is low; other barriers to take-up are a reflection of inappropriate provision in terms of content and delivery. This further demonstrates that there is scope for improvement in all aspects of SME education and training.

Sustainability and the Competitive Advantage of SMEs

So far it has been suggested that the win-win goals of the sustainability agenda can contribute to the competitiveness of SMEs. However, it is also recognised that firms in the SME sector need external assistance and encouragement to take up the challenge. It would be unfair to paint too bleak a picture of the failures of business support. There have been some gains and some successes: for example, Envirowise (formerly the Environmental Technology Best Practice Programmes), Groundwork initiatives and local Green Business Clubs have been able to target specific help and guidance at SMEs. Nevertheless, the question remains: why is it that so few small firms have grasped the competitive advantages of sustainable development, and how can this situation be remedied in future?

To begin to understand the way forward, it is essential to appreciate that there are few, if any, generic solutions. Environmental solutions designed for larger firms cannot necessarily be applied to SMEs. Therefore, to begin with, measures to support the sustainability of SMEs must be built on a platform of a sound understanding of the SME: its problems, its conditions and its needs. In order to achieve this, greater emphasis ought to be focused on truly understanding the complexities and problems from a SME perspective. That means not forcing top-down solutions, but instead designing and delivering solutions that appreciate local needs and involve small and medium-sized enterprises from inception. The second consideration is how can SME business support build capacity for change at an organisational level and more broadly across industry sectors? Initiatives such as the Aire and Calder waste minimisation project were successful for those businesses directly involved. Unfortunately, in too many cases projects like this fail to build on their initial success and cannot sustain involvement beyond the life of the demonstration projects once funding has been withdrawn. The Advisory Committee on Business and the Environment (1998) point out that overcoming the barriers to change is not just about raising awareness; it is also about understanding the difference between overcoming the barriers within the SME to action and implementation.

The government's use of regulatory control and economic instruments acts as a powerful external driver for change. The necessary transformation will not be fuelled by regulation alone. All firms, including SMEs, need to accept that their environmental management practices need to go beyond compliance standards. In addition, stakeholder pressure (particularly via the supply chain) can and has motivated action to change. However, external pressures and business support initiatives have had limited success in promoting the environmental performance improvements of SMEs. It would appear that if SMEs are to fully assimilate the sustainability agenda into their day-to-day operational and managerial practices, it is just as important to generate a much stronger internal drive for change. Unless SMEs want to respond responsibly to environmental and social, as well as conventional, economic priorities, business support initiatives will continue to find it difficult to build the necessary capacity needed to generate substantial change in the sector. More importantly, the longer these conditions continue, the longer it will take for the SME sector to realise the competitive advantages the sustainability agenda offers.

Research has yet to find an effective solution to the problem of generating sufficient organisational capacity for change. Figure 5.1 may provide a route map of where SMEs need to go, but it does not tell them or others how a critical mass of firms are going to become sustainable organisations. Small and medium-sized firms which have taken responsibility for their environmental impacts have recognised that ignoring the sustainability agenda could put them at risk of becoming uncompetitive. Doing nothing may not be a viable business option for some SMEs.

Conclusion

Theoretical and practical evidence indicates that the sustainability agenda need not be a business threat or cost burden to SMEs. This agenda has steadily gained momentum since the 1960s, and can no longer be perceived as another business fad. The win-win approach to sustainability provides significant scope for competitive advantage. It is also evident that SMEs en masse are not responding to the sustainability agenda and therefore not benefiting from potential competitive advantages. This is in part due to environmental business support initiatives targeted at the SME sector not realising their potential. To address this deficiency, policy-makers, SMEs and other parties interested in the environmental performance of businesses need to build capacity for change, both within individual firms and across the sector. A key element in this is recognising the role that training and education can play in creating the capacity and desire for change. Training and education will fuel the momentum and capacity for change needed to make the necessary shifts in behaviour, culture and values advocated by Ballard (2000).

It is one thing to recognise the nature of the solution, but another to deliver it. This chapter has highlighted the difficulty of engaging SMEs in the sustainability challenge and, clearly, capacity-building cannot be imposed; SMEs need to be involved and take ownership of the agenda. Given the heterogeneity of this sector, there is a need for much more consultation. Significantly, capacity-building will not only have implications for ways in which SMEs respond to business support measures such as demonstration projects and regulation, but also for the scale of that response. Increasing capacity for change will also have implications for the SME demand for support and assistance. Although organisations seeking to assist SMEs can help create the conditions for change, ultimately it is the SMEs themselves who have to embrace the sustainability agenda. The ultimate responsibility for seizing the opportunity to change lies with the SMEs themselves. It is for them to seek out the know-how to improve their resource efficiency, minimise waste, design products and services that are less harmful to the environment, and create management systems to achieve these ends. In smaller organisations, it can be easier for would-be environmental champions to drive the necessary changes and make a significant impact.

References

ACBE (1998) *The Eight Progress Report*. Advisory Committee on Business and the Environment, DTI 3680. HMSO, London.

Ballard, D. (2000) 'The cultural aspects of change for sustainable development', *Eco-Management and Auditing*, 7:2, 53–59.

Cairncross, F. (1995) *Green Inc.: A Guide to Business and the Environment*. Earthscan, London.

Charlesworth, K. (1998) *A Green and Pleasant Land: A Survey of Managers' Attitudes to, and Experience of, Environmental Management*. The Institute of Management, London.

Curran, J. and Storey, D. (2000) 'Small business policy: past experiences and future directions'. Paper presented at the Kingston Small Business Service Seminar Series, 12 December, DTI.

Curran, J., Blackburn, R., Kitching, J. and North, J. (1996) 'Small Firms and Workforce Training'. Paper presented at the 19th ISBA Conference, Birmingham.

DETR (1998) *Digest of Environmental Protection and Water Statistics*, No. 20. HMSO, London.

DETR (1999) *A Better Quality of Life: A Strategy for Sustainable Development for the UK*. CM4345. HMSO, London.

Dodds. O.A. (2000) 'Foreword', in R. Hillary (ed.) *ISO 14001 Case-studies and Practical Experiences*. Greenleaf Publishing, Sheffield.

Elkington, J. (1997) *Cannibals with Forks: The Triple Bottom Line of 21st Century Business*. Capstone, Oxford.

ENDS Report (1995) '*Waste minimisation culture begins to take root*', *ENDS Report*, **243**, April.

Envirowise (2000). *Attitudes 2000*, EN305, Department for Trade and Industry, London.

Frankel, C. (1999) *In Earth's Company*. New Society Publishers, Gabriola Island.

Haile, S., Manns, H. and Marshall, J. (1999) *Report of the Provision of Environmental Training to SMEs in the North-East Region*. University of Newcastle upon Tyne.

Hankinson, A. (1994) 'Small firms Training: The Reluctance Prevails', *Industrial and Commercial Training*, **26**:9, 28–30.

Hawken, P., Lovins, A. and Lovins, H. (1999) *Natural Capitalism*. Earthscan, London.

Hendry, E. (1992) *A Survey of Environmental Pressure on Small and Medium Sized Businesses in the Eastern Region*. Compiled by the University of Cambridge, the University of East Anglia, the University of Hertfordshire and Anglia Polytechnic University.

Hillary, R. (1995) *Small Firms and the Environment: A Groundwork Status Report*. Groundwork, Birmingham.

Holder, A.T. (1993) 'Environment and the SME', *Integrated Environmental Management*, **18**, 22–24.

Hooper, P.D. and Gibbs, D.C. (1995) *Profiting from Environmental Protection: A Manchester Business Survey*. Report for the Co-operative Bank, Manchester.

Hooper, P.D., Jukes, S. and Stubbs, M. (2000) 'SME environmental performance and business support networks: problem solving not panacea', *Proceedings of the Business Strategy and the Environment Conference*, September, 173–178.

Hutchinson, A. and Chaston, I. (1994) 'Environmental management in Devon and Cornwall's SME sector', *Business Strategy and the Environment*, 3:1, 15–22.

Hutchinson, A. and Hutchinson, F. (1997) *Environmental Business Management: Sustainable Development in the New Millennium*. McGraw-Hill, London.

Impactt (1999) *Review of Sustainable Development Education Initiatives in the Workplace*. Prepared for the Government's Sustainable Development Education Panel, Impactt Limited, London.

Johnson, N. and Stokes, A. (1995) *Waste Minimisation and Cleaner Technology: An Assessment of Motivation*. Centre for the Exploitation of Science and Technology, London.

Kemp, R.G., Bardon, K.S. and Smith, M.A. (1996) 'Environmental training for the SME sectors'. Paper presented at the Eco-Management and Auditing Conference, July, University of Leeds.

Marshall Report (1998) *Economic Instruments and the Business Use of Energy*. HMSO, London.

Nash, T. (1990) 'Green about the environment?', *Director*, February, 40–44.

Nattrass, B. and Altomare, M. (1999) *The Natural Step for Business*. New Society Publishers, Gabriola Island.

O'Laoire, D. and Welford, R. (1996) 'The EMS and the SME', in R. Welford (ed.) *Corporate Environmental Management: Systems and Strategies*. Earthscan, London.

Petts, J. (2000) 'Smaller enterprises and the environment: organisational learning potential?', in S. Fineman (ed.) *The Business of Greening*. Routledge, London.

Porter, M. and van der Linde, C. (1995) 'Green and competitive: ending the stalemate', *Harvard Business Review*, Sept/Oct, 120–137.

SDEP (1999) *First Annual Report 1998*. Sustainable Development Education Panel, Department of Environment, Transport and the Regions, London.

Shearlock, C., Hooper, P.D. and Millington, M. (2000) 'Environmental improvement in small and medium-sized enterprises: a role for the business support network', *Greener Management International*, **30**, Summer, 50–60.

Shrivastava, P. (1996) *Greening Business: Profiting the Organisation and the Environment*. Thomson Executive Press, Cincinnati, OH.

Smith, D. (1993) 'Towards a paradigm shift?', in D. Smith (ed.) *Business and the Environment*. Paul Chapman, London.

Smith, M.E. (1996) 'Stimulating environmental action with small-medium sized enterprises'. Paper presented at the Eco-management and Auditing Conference, July, University of Leeds.

Storey, D. (1994) *Understanding the Small Business Sector*. Routledge, London.

Tilley, F. (1999a) 'Small-firm environmental strategy: the UK experience', *Greener Management International*, **25**, 67–80.

Tilley, F. (1999b) 'The gap between environmental attitudes and the environmental behaviour of small firms', *Business Strategy and the Environment*, **8**, 238–248.

Walley, E.E. (2000) 'The environmental champion: making a start' in R. Hillary (ed.) *Small and Medium-sized Enterprises and the Environment*. Greenleaf Publishing, Sheffield.

Walley, E.E. and Stubbs, M. (1999) 'Greenjacking' – A tactic for the toolbag of environmental champions? Reflections on an SME success story', *Eco-Management and Auditing*, **6**:1, 26–33.

Walley, N. and Whitehead, B. (1994) 'It's not easy being green', *Harvard Business Review*, **72**:3, May–June.

Welford, R. (1992) 'Linking quality and the environment', *Business Strategy and the Environment*, **1**:1, 25–35.

Welford, R. (1996) *Corporate Environmental Management: Systems and Strategies*. Earthscan, London.

Welford, R. (1997) *Hijacking Environmentalism: Corporate Responses to Sustainable Development*. Earthscan, London.

Welford, R. and Gouldson, A. (1993) *Environmental Management and Business Strategy*. Pitman Publishing, London.

Willums, J. and WBCSD (1998) *The Sustainable Business Challenge*. Greenleaf Publishing, Sheffield.

World Commission on Environment and Development (1987) *Our Common Future*. Oxford University Press, Oxford.

Section 2

MANAGING PEOPLE

Chapter 6

HUMAN RESOURCE MANAGEMENT: MANAGING PEOPLE IN SMALLER ORGANISATIONS

Scott Taylor, Sue Shaw and Carol Atkinson

Introduction

Personnel management and human resource management (HRM) are just two of the many labels used to bring together the theories and practices of managing people. In this chapter, we explore HRM techniques and philosophies and how to seek competitive advantage through them in smaller organisations, suggesting that previous studies have sought to apply conclusions as to the nature of effective people management techniques reached through studying large companies, into smaller organisations. The 'culture' of HRM established in the UK, through research in large companies, management development and education, and initiatives such as Investors in People, may not be relevant to managing people in smaller companies. We argue that the owner-manager or manager trying to accomplish the practical 'essences' (Eccles and Nohria, 1992) of people management (recruitment and selection, training and development, payment systems and performance appraisal) may be excluded from this culture.

However, we also outline the 'structure' of managing people manifest in recent employment legislation. Awareness and use of this employment regulation, if mediated through the use of the expertise of business support services (Klaas *et al.*, 2000) or informal support networks, may enable managers in smaller companies to manage people more effectively. The discussion and analysis presented in this chapter is informed by a study of managerial and employee experiences of people management in four case study companies employing fewer than 50 people, in both manufacturing and services, and by survey data collected on the implementation of recent employment legislation in smaller organisations. Qualitative data is presented through four 'exhibits' through the chapter, each dealing with a different aspect of personnel management, while quantitative data is presented in the sections dealing with employee relations legislation.

The Culture of People Management: HRM as a Collective Noun

[HRM is] no more than a collective noun for the multitude of concepts-and-methods devised . . . to manage and control the employment relationship. (Keenoy, 1999, p. 17)

When industrial production began to require the concentration of people in purpose-built factory environments, the owners began to develop techniques to manage the newly constituted employees to maximise their time and effort (Jacques, 1996). This led to the introduction of performance measurement and management, target-setting for employees, and motivational techniques. More recently, managerial initiatives claiming to enhance performance and produce competitive advantage have come in three parts, giving rise to 'three letter acronyms' (Watson, 1995) such as Total Quality Management (TQM), Investors in People (IiP), Business Process Reengineering (BPR) and, perhaps the most widespread and well recognised, Human Resource Management (HRM). The latter is the only one to have become an accepted part of business school curricula in its own right, with courses, course modules, professorial chairs and departments all using the acronym (Noon, 1992). Despite the phrase having been in use for more than fifty years before it attained its current high profile (Storey, 1989), it is generally accepted that HRM came to have a clearly differentiated meaning in the 1980s and 1990s.

However, questions were asked as to how the 'new-fangled, faddish HRM' (Legge, 1995, p. xiv) differed from more established methods of people management. If there was no clear distinction between HRM and other managerial techniques, then it could have no serious academic or practitioner interest (Guest, 1987). A series of papers and books in the early 1980s sought to demonstrate that new management course modules in US business schools under the title of HRM were significantly different from previous philosophies (Tichy et al., 1982; Fombrun et al., 1984; Beer et al., 1984, 1985). This version of HRM began as a means for general managers to engage with the strategic issues involved in the management of people, with the aim of introducing 'people issues' at board-level in large companies.

HRM was also put forward by American academics as the sensible managerial response to a range of societal changes. Tichy et al. (1982) state that technological, economic and demographic changes which demand the input of the human resource into organisational strategy formation and performance enhancement must be recognised and exploited, drawing comparisons between successful Japanese and unsuccessful American corporations. Fombrun et al. (1984) claim that automation, increasing global competition and scarcity of resources, a sociocultural shift from production-driven to knowledge-based economies, and increasing political regulation and intervention, all mean that the managed human resource will make a crucial difference to organisational performance. Beer et al. (1984, 1985) provide an even more comprehensive list of reasons for the introduction of HRM into organisations and business schools, including increasing international competition, the increasing complexity and size of organisations, slower economic growth, higher levels of education and the changing values of workforces.

In addition to these rather broad societal rationales for introducing HRM into management courses and organisations, there are a number of practical commonalities identified as underpinning the early manifestoes for change. The first is the notion of HRM as oriented towards *'exploiting* the labour resource more fully' (Storey, 1989, p. 9, emphasis in original). In order to achieve this, organisational change introduced under the banner of HRM encourages employees to adopt a more individualistic stance towards the employment relationship, and to maximise production in the hope of personal gain and advancement (Guest, 1987). This is reinforced through the promotion of a unitarist view of organisational and employee goals, achieved through the active management of 'the culture' in the workplace, 'winning the hearts and minds' (Willmott, 1993) of employees to encourage greater commitment to organisational goals. This message was disseminated at a populist level through the ideas presented in the best-selling 'airport lounge' books of Peters and Waterman (1982) and Deal and Kennedy (1982), which explained how to achieve increased levels of inclusion and production through cultural integration (Legge, 1989). Thus, in this, its broadest sense, HRM is an amalgam of all management decisions that 'affect the nature of the relationship between the organisation and its employees' (Beer *et al.*, 1985, p. 1), founded on a clearly and consistently articulated 'philosophy about people' (Fombrun *et al.*, 1984, p. 41) which 'requires considerably more sophisticated approaches to the human resource input' (Tichy *et al.*, 1982, p. 47), focusing on the management of people to provide a competitive advantage in difficult marketplaces.

The emphasis on the individual in HRM encourages managers to treat employees less as a collective mass and more as a grouping of self-directing entities. This was supported by a new entrepreneurial discourse that managers were expected to commit to, and the dismantling of bureaucracy as the central feature of work organisations (Du Gay *et al.*, 1996). This was in turn supported by changes to British labour law, as formal income policies were abandoned, trade union rights were curbed, and employment contract law encouraged employee flexibility. The redefinition of employees as market-driven individuals is seen in HRM practices such as individually based performance-related pay, the encouragement of entre- and intrapreneurship, and an emphasis on task-based working. In addition, employees are told that the notion of lifetime employment has broken down, and are encouraged to take responsibility for developing their own careers through lifelong learning.

Case Study 1: Gearbox – Recruitment of real and fictive kin

Recruitment processes control the structure and culture of an organisation in a very direct way. The methods of recruitment and selection can define the 'kind of person' that a company employs in many different ways, and it is the area of managing people that has historically been most closely controlled by legislation. Smaller organisations are often singled out for recruiting through family relations, even if growth is achieved into something as large as, for example, Cadbury's. Managers also recruit 'fictive' kin, however, bringing friends and social acquaintances into the company.[1] There are many positives to this method: the maintenance of cultural continuity, social support if there is external pressure on the organisation, and generation of a sense of shared destiny and obligation.

Gearbox, a manufacturing subsidiary of a Danish parent, recruited on just such a basis. Family recruitment was common on the production shopfloor, with several brothers working alongside each other, and many employees related how they had applied for jobs after 'getting the nod' from a friend working in the company. Managers at Gearbox sanctioned this practice, letting existing employees know about upcoming posts and encouraging them to ask family and friends to apply. The world, as one manager put it, is not your oyster twenty miles to the north of Manchester, and this method also saved significantly on advertising and selection costs. Managers also claimed that locals could be relied upon not to 'rip the company off' as most employees lived locally too.

Some employees, however, reflected on the potentially negative aspects of this. One in particular resented the leakage of work relations into her leisure time, suggesting that managers found out more about employees in the pubs in the village than in the factory. She also felt pressure to conform to her work role outside work time.

Finally, it should be noted that during this research, none of the managers or employees in the organisations mentioned the legal aspects of recruitment and selection conducted in these ways. Yet this is the area of people management that has been most closely monitored and heavily regulated, and all companies employed enough people to make them subject to legal obligations in this area. The attractions of recruiting through real and fictive kin may be strong, but the dangers are significant, legally outside the company and culturally inside it.

It may be that these societal shifts in attitudes to work and employment have little relevance to managers and employees in smaller companies; after all, it has long been noted that collective structures, such as trade unions, are less often found in small companies, and that employees in smaller companies choose to avoid larger organisations in order to remain relatively free as individuals. Further, smaller companies were often held up as models of individual creativity and employee innovation by unwieldy, stifling multinationals, and the 'happy ship' image of working life in a family company is brought out as evidence of individual contentment in a coherent collective. As we outline in more detail below, this vision of the smaller company as a happy family of fulfilled individuals is not one which many employees or managers recognise in their daily working lives (Rainnie, 1989; Ram, 1994; Holliday, 1995). The idealistic vision is not supported either by detailed analyses of 'working lives in small firms' (Ram, 1994), or by the frequency of appearance of small-company owners in industrial tribunals (Earnshaw et al., 2000).

The second practical commonality in theories of HRM relates to the location of personnel administration. Within multinational organisations, HRM was put forward as a means of treating people management strategically; senior managers would be responsible for the philosophies of recruitment and selection, appraisal, reward and employee development, and line managers would accomplish the tasks on the ground. This was argued to provide a more generalist viewpoint on the issues involved at a business level, functioning as an aid to developing long-term trust and higher production levels, pro- rather than reactive (Beer *et al.*, 1984; Fombrun *et al.*, 1984). In the words of the originators, '*HRM is the development of all aspects of an organisational context* so that they will encourage and even direct managerial behaviour with regard to people' (Beer *et al.*, 1984, p. 4, emphasis in original), so that the organisational managers are 'concerned with the identification of what it is the people ... must do (behaviour) to be proficient in their respective functions' (Fombrun *et al.*, 1984, pp. 88–89). The separation of analysis of 'how best to manage the people' in the organisation, from the action of 'accomplishing the tasks' and delegating them to line managers at a behavioural level, was aimed at enabling senior non-specialists to circumvent the detail involved in the practicalities of personnel management and to identify the fundamental implications or problems of policies and practices.

Case Study 2: Diamondcom – Managing the managers

Taking on managers as a smaller organisation grows was central to the management of Diamondcom. The company provides high-tech services to individual customers and businesses, and grew from an idea to a company employing more than 40 people in less than five years. This rapid expansion also brought headaches for the four owner-managers, however, as they had to go into the employment market for supervisors and line managers to take control of the small teams set up as business expanded. The owners of Diamondcom were constrained in this, as many smaller organisations are, by perceptions of company status (with larger organisations seen as providing more perks and potential for individual development), inability or reluctance to pay what seemed to be high salaries, and finally by the location of the company.

A traditional solution to these issues in smaller organisations might be to develop managers within the company, through the kind of informal training that is so widespread. Staff resisted this for two reasons; the primary reason, as one salesman put it, was that he would 'always plump for making money as opposed to being a senior manager that's walking around all day looking in cupboards and stuff like that ... I can't sit in all day and go through papers.' Another staff member from purchasing also doubted that any more managerial position would provide him with a more interesting or rewarding job than his present post.

The owner-managers decided then to take on people from outside the company and the area, in an attempt to get over these barriers and to grow the company beyond the 30 employees point. This strategy, however, did not go well: a series of managers came and went, as the owner-managers found them wanting in various respects. In particular, the 'imported' managers had their commitment to the company questioned, and their understanding of the work of employees also provided a point of resistance for employees. In short, their professional identities were in doubt from both above and below.

At the time of this research, Diamondcom's owner-managers had not definitively solved this problem. Some success was had through recruitment of people with previous connections to the company, who either had experience of working in supervisory positions or (frustrated) aspirations towards managerial jobs; some success was had

> by putting people through short courses with management development organisations like Dale Carnegie or the local Chamber of Commerce. As the company grew, and as teams began to need more autonomy from the owner-managers, only one thing was certain – that 'somebody has to be the boss', as one supervisor put it, and that they will have to learn somehow.

Once again, in the context of companies employing fewer than one or two hundred people, the relevance of this is questionable. HRM gained rapid popularity in the USA in part as a result of allowing higher-level managers to devolve responsibility for the practical accomplishment of personnel tasks to line managers and administrative specialists. The senior HR manager then became the representative on the board, bringing the 'people issues' to the notice of finance, operations and marketing managers. However, the initial division of administrative and strategic personnel management that HRM is designed to achieve is problematic if an owner-manager interviews all potential new recruits, has control over training opportunities and feels able to appraise employee performance by walking around the building. In a context where employing one new line manager is a key decision that will significantly impact on the conduct of the business, separating the strategy and administration of people management tasks will be difficult.

However, it is important to note that these high-level strategic aims that HRM sought to achieve were not sustained in practice. In the first major empirical study of HRM in the UK, Storey (1992) focused on the linkages to broader notions of enterprise and managerial initiative, arguing that a codified set of interrelated practices could be set down as indicating whether HRM philosophies were being practised. This study marks a shift in the analysis of HRM; over less than a decade, it changed from a set of propositions concerning the structure of an organisation and the organisation of people management, to a set of operational techniques to be implemented. HRM thus reabsorbed the operational, and researchers began to investigate in detail the performance improvement hypotheses on which the approach was initially based. Initial claims of HRM practitioners and academics that individual and organisational performance would improve if HRM philosophies were implemented now began to be tested through large-scale questionnaire surveys based on managerial practice (e.g. Huselid, 1995).

However, as Pfeffer (1997) argues, in seeking precision of measurement, substantive meaning may well be lost in the numbers. It has been argued that HR professionals in large organisations sought to gain a 'place on the board' (Purcell, 1993) through proving that their area of management can contribute to the bottom line as much as operational decisions or marketing strategies. However, the measurement of people management may only 'provide the illusion of precision' (Pfeffer, 1997, p. 363) to be used in micro-political battles, with the ultimate result being that HR managers lose sight of the original basis for their employment: to provide an alternative view of the organisation that is not reliant on assets, costs or trading results. Accounting for the management of people financially may undermine a key rationale for personnel, as well as being something of a dead end given the difficulty of proving causal (or even correlative) linkages in the assessment of what is primarily a social activity.

More recently, Keenoy (1999) identified four sources of ambiguity in the discourse of HRM. First, he argues that there is a conceptual–theoretical elision, in which the term HRM is characterised by indeterminacy and ambiguity, to the extent that it may not denote anything. Second, there is a continuing empirical elusiveness, with many researchers not finding what they have gone out to look for. Third, representations of HRM rely on language, which is bounded by understandings of situated meanings developed in a previous employee relations context. Finally, HRM has been investigated in institutionally narrow locations, neglecting non-standard organisational contexts beyond the larger, corporate organisation. HRM is thus characterised by 'conceptual fragmentation, empirical incoherence, and theoretical vacuity' (Keenoy, 1999, p. 1), and searches for it have been guided by the sought, rather than the seen or experienced.

We would suggest that this has clear implications for the study of people management in concrete organisational contexts, and particularly smaller companies. First, it suggests that we acknowledge and accept that empirical refutations of the existence of normative HRM do not lessen the cultural impact of the discourse (Keenoy and Anthony, 1992). Thus, even if we fail to 'find' HRM being practised, there is still a need to be aware that managers and employees work within a context that is in part defined by the language of HRM (Katz et al., 2000) – in other words, there is a culture of HRM. Second, it implies that studies which utilise the language of HRM, in organisations where employees and managers are not already familiar with the academic or practitioner norms that the terms refer to, may fail to establish shared meaning. As Alvesson and Sköldberg (2000, p. 272) note, in organisational research:

> Interviewees are … inclined to use the models and language they had once learnt in order to explain 'how things are'; not necessarily because they 'fit' particularly well, but because they seem appropriate for use in an interview situation, in which an established and adapted vocabulary is used in order to create order and facilitate mutual understanding of a messy world difficult to account for.

This means that research which imposes a set of people management issues and problems on managers in smaller organisations may miss the issues that managers deal with in everyday practice (Heneman et al., 2000). This in turn raises the danger that managers and academics will fit into each other's accepted understanding of how the world is and fail to bring new insights to research and practice. Finally, it raises questions as to the relevance of research within the HRM discourse to organisations which are not part of the establishment (Heneman et al., 2000). Keenoy (1999), for example, cites the emergence of a significant but volatile 'small business sector' as one of the locations in which the meaning and language of HRM may not be agreed. Notwithstanding these objections, HRM as a performance-enhancing practice and philosophy has been sought in smaller companies; the next section explores the results of this quest.

Searching for HRM in Small Companies

Following frequent calls for HRM researchers to consider organisations outside those large and prestigious companies that appear in accounts of best practice, some have targeted smaller companies. In North America, a series of studies proposed that managers in smaller companies do not implement good HRM practice and assert that organisational performance suffers through this neglect (McEvoy, 1984; Amba-Roe and Pendse, 1985; Gatewood and Field, 1987; Ng and Maki, 1993; Deshpande and Golhar, 1994; Golhar and Deshpande, 1997; Chandler and McEvoy, 2000; Hornsby and Kuratko, 1990). However, all of these studies share fundamental flaws. First, researchers concentrate on the views of managers through either self-administered questionnaires or structured telephone interviews. Thus, the existence of HRM techniques is assumed simply when managers report that initiatives such as team-working are in place. Second, smaller companies are regarded as primitive and backward compared to the sophistication of larger firms. Third, and perhaps most importantly, there is no agreed definition of what a small firm is, leading to a vague notion of employee numbers as a variable that defines managerial practice (Heneman *et al.*, 2000).

In the UK, there has also been a concerted effort made to gauge whether HRM is being practised in smaller companies. The Chartered Institute for Personnel and Development (CIPD), the professional body for qualified HR practitioners, surveyed 300 managers in small companies and concluded that a majority were aware of current good practice in people management and perceived the issues as important, but that few had implemented initiatives to achieve the competitive advantage available through HRM (IPD, 1994). The authors argued for better presentation of HRM initiatives to emphasise the positive contribution to business performance, and the need for more management development to convince small-firm managers of the benefits of HRM. Also in the UK, Bacon *et al.* (1996) surveyed more than 200 companies employing fewer than 200 people, asking about managers' experience of innovative techniques such as culture change programmes, devolved managerial responsibility, team briefing and psychometric testing in the selection process. Take-up was found to be high for most techniques, with 75 per cent of owners and managers using team-working, and 61 per cent using team briefings. The study concluded that 'the new management agenda has penetrated deep into the economy and . . . innovative and progressive employee relations are no longer restricted to large mainstream companies' (Bacon *et al.*, 1996, p. 87).

Case Study 3: Zincpipe – Paying for skills

Training and development of employees has been found to be the area of people management that small business owners find most difficult, particularly during periods of expansion. It may be that the processes of bringing employees to the point where they can work effectively is seen as a hurdle to get over; it may be that training and development are seen as 'happening' naturally within the working context, and therefore not something to be isolated and dealt with separately. At Zincpipe, getting 'trained up', as one employee put it, was central to managing people; in part, this was a result of linking judgements of competence with pay levels.

Several employees related how they had arrived on their first day with the company to find that the person responsible for their induction or training was absent. Sometimes travelling, sometimes absent through illness, sometimes present but buried under a pile of work, many new employees and managers found it very difficult to start work and pick up their new duties without structured training. Senior managers and Zincpipe owners explained this practice in two ways: first, they suggested, lower-level production work was often not complex or difficult to pick up. Second, they argued that managerial work was not context-specific – a new shopfloor supervisor, in particular, was held up as someone who had come in from another industry (recruited through a friend already working at Zincpipe) and been able to pick up operational details as he went along.

However, shopfloor employees at Zincpipe made a clear distinction between high-level managers and company owners, and those responsible for directing the work processes. Those at the top of the company were expected to do their jobs, managing the organisation and making decisions about the direction of work; lower-level managers and supervisors were expected to be both managerially competent and to understand the production processes in some detail.

This was especially clear when the payment system in Zincpipe was changed, to better reflect skills differences and reward those with the ability to perform multiple tasks. Shopfloor employees often rejected the judgements of the managerial staff as to their abilities, and as training often took place on an ad hoc, 'sitting with Nellie' basis, managers had little external authority on which to draw to support their judgements. Some employees even hinted that their colleagues were skilled at manipulating the new payment-skills system to individual benefit.

Employees recognised that training and development could be efficient and effective when conducted on an informal basis, and that much knowledge could be lost through people leaving or retiring. However, they also expressed strongly the idea that Zincpipe as an organisation was not stable or permanent, and that formal training and development for employees was part of a managerial responsibility that could form part of satisfying the customer's demands.

Once again, the vision presented here in both studies is of the smaller organisation running to catch up with innovation and progression in larger organisations, improving practice and performance through following the leaders. This approach, defining HRM as a set of practices, testing for its existence, and taking reported practice in larger companies as an ideal, positions the management of people as a mechanical operation. Again, it does not explore the implementation of techniques and the introduction of new philosophies beyond the managerial assertion that they are doing 'it'. Finally, this approach does not allow for the possibility that HRM techniques and language may not be appropriate for the smaller company.

As Heneman et al. (2000) note, despite some research evidence on people management practices in small companies, there remains a dearth of information and analysis around the world. They suggest that most academic analyses focus on issues that are not primary concerns of owner and managers of smaller companies. This means two things: first, that the research community is failing a key user community, and second, HRM researchers are ignoring a fundamental methodological limitation in their studies. However, Heneman et al. (2000) go on to recommend the application of HRM theory developed in studies of larger organisations, rather than working from the basis that smaller organisations can develop people management practices and philosophies that perhaps do not draw on experience in larger companies.

In sum, then, we suggest that researchers seeking HRM in smaller organisations should move away from comparison with practice in larger companies. Such a project inevitably highlights dimensions of people management dynamics in larger organisations, framing the concept of best-practice HRM as transferable and static. This detracts from the possibility of developing our understanding of the management of people in smaller organisations as experienced by practitioners. It may be that researchers should spend less time verifying the existence of a linguistic construct through 'the empirical forms adopted in the name of HRM by managerial elites in particular organisational locales' (Keenoy, 1999, p. 8). More positively, we suggest that HRM can inform our understanding of the management of people in two ways. First, HRM could be seen as a means of managing people which can be historically, conceptually and practically located in multiple organisational settings, rather than a language which defines practice. Thus, the culture of HRM within which employee relations currently exist could be seen as a conditioning influence, rather than as an ideal to be achieved. Second, we can see the way that HRM conditions understanding of the nature of the employment contract through the dissemination of notions such as a discourse of people as resources. Thus, through initiatives like Investors in People, which emphasise that training interventions must be related to profit or strategic goals, HRM may be seen as contributing to the instrumentalisation and individualisation of the employment relationship – to the redefinition of people as resources to be exploited. However, we would also emphasise that the management of people in smaller organisations owes as much to structural as to cultural considerations. As noted above, there have been significant changes to the legal conditions of employment during the establishment of the culture of HRM. Consequently, we see employment legislation playing an important role in the embedding of HRM philosophy and practice across organisational contexts, and it is to an analysis of such regulation that we now turn.

Structures of People Management: Employment Regulation and Managerial Action

As suggested in Chapter 1, in the early 1970s smaller companies were perceived as drowning in a sea of bureaucracy imposed by the state. The election of the Conservative government in 1979 saw the introduction of much new employment legislation (e.g. Employment Acts 1980, 1982, 1988, 1989, 1990, Trade Union Act 1984, Trade Union Reform and Employment Rights Act 1993, Trade Union and Labour Relations (Consolidation) Act 1992, Employment Rights Act 1996), some of which contained derogations exempting businesses with fewer than a certain number of employees from the legislation. Not surprisingly, there is evidence that employment regulation is seen as onerous by small employers (Westrip, 1986) and studies have often confirmed that owner-managers in small companies view the law as one of the most important and difficult aspects of people management. In this section, we aim to examine how regulation can be applied to managing the employment relationship within small companies to improve performance and competitiveness, in particular the importance of addressing the provisions of the legislation to avoid the costs of non-compliance.

Between 1945 and 1980, employee relations in the UK were dominated by a collective approach involving employers and trade unions. Initially, this was a period of voluntarism, although the mid-1960s and 1970s saw an increase in the level of state intervention. However, broad trends in employee relations from 1980 to 1997 have been towards less direct state and collective intervention in the conduct of management and the organisation of work (Hollinshead *et al.*, 1999). This was in line with general Conservative philosophy regarding the responsibility of the individual to self-regulate, and the importance of letting market forces regulate all areas of the economy so as to increase flexibility and competitiveness in the global marketplace. The shift away from collective intervention has led to a decline in multi-employer bargaining across work contexts (Purcell, 1993), and brought about an era in employee relations known as 'liberal individualism' (Rose, 2001) where the focus is on the relationship between manager and individual employer. Indeed, this shift has been so marked as to lead some to observe that the 'problem' of employee relations is no longer the role of the trade union in the market economy, but rather the role of the individual in the employment relationship (Beardwell, 1996). Legislative reforms in the 1980s aimed at increasing flexibility and competitiveness coincided with the emergence of HRM and provided the employee relations context in which certain people management practices could be enacted. The underpinning notion of individualism is entirely consistent with the philosophical considerations of HRM.

The arrival of a new Labour government in 1997 heralded a new approach to workplace legislation and employment relations. The most recent piece of legislation to affect people management practices and philosophies is the Employment Relations Act, or ERelA (1999), intended to create partnerships between employers and employees while retaining labour market flexibility. Further, this Act has as a stated aim the introduction of minimum standards and security for all employees in all work organisations regardless of size, to provide greater fairness in the employment relationship. In its philosophies and aims, it could be argued that the Act seeks to combine 'hard' and 'soft' HRM, bringing together the employer's dream of labour flexibility and the employee's vision of security and fairness at work. As such, it may provide a valid framework for managing and enhancing the employment relationship.

Employment Legislation and Smaller Companies

Research into the impact of employment legislation on small businesses and their attitude to regulation reveals a complex but predominantly negative picture (Westrip, 1986; Scott *et al.*, 1989; Walsh 1999; Harris, 2000; Earnshaw *et al.*, 2000). Recent research in small companies regarding employment legislation identifies the volume and complexity of the law, and being aware of changes to the law, as most significant concerns (Harris, 2000). This contrasts with earlier work indicating that many small businesses made little or no effort to keep up to date with legislative changes (Westrip, 1986). We would suggest that this indicates a shift in the mindset of owner-managers in small businesses towards legislation, and recognition of the need to be aware of it. Nevertheless, there continues to be evidence that many managers in small companies do not understand or cannot cope with the detail of the legislation (Walsh, 1999), and that this results in breaches of legal requirements due to ignorance of those requirements (Scott *et al.*, 1989). In short, managers in many small businesses ignore or avoid legislation until pushed to take action.

Case Study 4: Bodywork – Organising workspace

The organisation of workspace may be the first HRM-related aspect of managing that is faced within a smaller organisation. Bodywork provides business services to larger companies; the managing director of Bodywork, Stephen, started the business in an office above a shop, but as the number of employees increased from two to forty space became central to the management of business expansion and employees. Expansion in employee numbers placed strain on the space available for each individual, and Stephen was forced to choose between moving the business or making the best of the available space in the building. He chose to remain in the bulging building, excavating a large basement area and squeezing more people into the space. As his wife remarked, it would be difficult to take on more people in her department unless they were hanging from the ceiling.

In terms of managing people within Bodywork, this dynamic had a significant impact on the employee experience of appraisal. Managers worked alongside their teams in small rooms, and each could see how and how much each of the others worked. Members of one department, renowned throughout the company for their relaxed attitude to performance targets, complained that they had acquired a reputation because their office was in fact a corridor that others had to pass through on their way to the toilets. This kind of peer appraisal caused resentment among employees, however.

Stephen spoke of the need to introduce formalised systems of appraisal and tracking of work when the company spread beyond a couple of rooms – when the employees became too spread out and he could no longer 'just shout to attract someone's attention', as he put it. These annual appraisal systems in fact ran in parallel to managerial presence; employees dealt with both the formal, and managers 'knocking around' the office. Employees 'had to work' in this context, and as a consequence felt more pressure to perform to the standards of the managers and owners. Some resented this, preferring the freedom to demonstrate a higher level of trust rather than 'babysitting' them in every action. Managers emphasised the coaching potential of being in this kind of workspace in which 'channels are open all the time, treating people as grown-ups'. As one of the owner-managers at Bodywork emphasised, however, control can only really be achieved over the activity, not the outcome – that is often beyond the limits of an appraisal system.

This may underlie the finding that employment regulation has a disproportionate impact in managing smaller organisations (Harris, 2000), and that a disproportionate number of employment tribunals involve small businesses (Earnshaw *et al.*, 2000). Smaller organisations may thus be more vulnerable to litigation and more likely to lose employment tribunals (Harris, 2000). Ignoring or avoiding legislation may significantly detract from performance where financial costs are incurred at employment tribunals and managerial time is taken up with dealing with complex cases before and during proceedings.

Employee Relations in the Smaller Company

Employment relations in smaller companies are characterised by informality (Wilkinson, 1999), reflected in the approach to employment regulation described above. The employment relationship is often perceived to be good by employers, with a generally paternalistic approach evident (Duberley and Walley, 1995). However, while the employment relationship is largely driven by employers (Matlay, 1999), employees often do not share their positive view of the relationship (Dundon *et al.*, 1999). Across the small business sector, it is most often general managers who make decisions on people-management issues. Almost 50 per cent of companies have no personnel specialist (Duberley and Walley, 1995), and there is often little consultation with employees (Atkinson and Curtis, 2001). Many have argued that the paternal nature of the small, often family-owned, firm benefits from this less procedural approach to people management, and hence a more flexible, profitable and pleasant work organisation results. Indeed, this was the basis of much research into the dynamics of managing and working in small firms through the 1970s, with smaller companies held up as an alternative to larger organisations. The 'happy ship' scenario developed by Ingham (1970) and others, and supported by arguments relating to the unsustainability of 'big business' (Schumacher, 1974), has however been extensively questioned, especially by those whose research includes the experiences of the managed as well as the managers (Rainnie and Scott, 1986; Rainnie, 1989; Ram, 1994). This in turn led to the development of the 'bleak house' scenario where it is noted that poor employee relations in small companies is the norm, and that workers are often deemed to be exploited by their employers. However, a more nuanced view of the relationship acknowledges that employers and employees both bear responsibility for the conduct and maintenance of employment relations in small companies (Ram, 1994).

Despite the preference for informality in small companies, previous employment legislation has led to increased formality in employment relations. The Industrial Relations Act (1971), for example, led to more formalised disciplinary procedures in order to avoid unfair dismissal claims (Earnshaw *et al.*, 2000). Marlow and Strange (2000) argue that recent legislation, such as the ERelA, may have a similar impact. Certainly, an informal and reactive approach to managing people appears to be less of an option as the law expands and the penalties of non-compliance increase (Harris, 2000). Work by Brown *et al.* (2000), however, has indicated that while the increase in the role of statutory employment law has led to the growing legalisation of employee terms and conditions, this has been only partially applied in smaller firms. Further, recent research carried out into employer awareness and implementation of the ERelA by one of the authors of this chapter (reported in more depth in Atkinson and Curtis, 2001) indicates that informal approaches to personnel issues continue to dominate in smaller companies.

Crucially, high levels of awareness of the individual requirements of the ERelA were not supported by high levels of managerial action in implementing the requirements. This is perhaps unsurprising, taking into account the low levels of personnel professionals employed in companies with fewer than 50 employees, and the increasingly high expectations placed on personnel professionals. In addition, many of the respondents in this research expressed negative views of both the ERelA and its central tenets, in particular the increase in emphasis on employee rights in the workplace that it represents. It is often suggested that the owners of smaller companies resist legislation, management development and education because they perceive their independence and autonomy to be threatened, but in adopting this approach to both the culture and structure of contemporary people management, managers may well be overlooking opportunities to improve performance through enhanced workplace relations.

Contribution to Performance and Competitiveness versus the Costs of Non-compliance

It might be expected that the new trend in employment relations and regulation towards individualisation of the employment relationship could potentially benefit the small business in two ways. First, individualisation and the decreasing participation of trade unions should allow the small-business owner to continue to adopt an informal approach. Second, a more laissez-faire approach to employment relations should mean more flexibility of contractual relations, allowing smaller companies to take on and let go employees as levels of work fluctuate, in line with the overall philosophy of increasing flexibility and competitiveness. Such an approach would be consistent with a 'hard' approach to HRM, defining employees solely as a resource to be managed. However, in failing to deliver the provisions of the legislation or acknowledge that there is a 'soft' side to people management, small-business managers may risk missing the opportunity to develop partnerships with their employees and so continue in a more paternalistic mould unmediated by employee participation. As has been discussed, significant questions have been raised as to the effectiveness of this approach. Further, the disproportionate impact on small companies of employment legislation must be taken into account. The potential cost of employment tribunal claims has increased significantly since the ERelA was established, with the maximum award now in excess of £50 000 – and even the average award of £2000 is likely to be significant in a small company. Thus, we conclude this section by suggesting that managers in smaller organisations need to consider whether the benefits of informality are really so great – and perhaps to consider the challenge of retaining the benefits of relative informality while avoiding the costs of legislative non-compliance.

Conclusion

We have suggested in this chapter that there is a culture of HRM in the UK that is problematic for managers in small organisations. The ambiguities within the concept and the practices associated with it and a preoccupation with testing for 'its' existence in smaller organisations, using a set of prescribed practices, fails to acknowledge the complexities of people management within smaller organisations. We would argue that managers in smaller organisations are most concerned with the practical aspects of recruiting, training, appraising and rewarding individuals within an often resource-poor and rapidly changing working environment. However, we have also indicated that it is possible to develop a notion of HRM within small organisations. If we see HRM as individualised managerial practice and not simply as a 'linguistic artifact', then it can be practically located in a small organisational setting. Such an approach locates the management of people within a dynamic operating context, conditioned by context inside and outside the organisation.

However, we have also argued that employment relationships are conditioned through structural means as well as cultural considerations. Changes in employment regulation, a feature of the last two decades, and the impact of people management philosophies and practices have clearly shifted the managerial focus to a more individualist approach. Indeed, the most recent piece of legislation, the ERelA, reflects the dualism of hard and soft HRM in the way it seeks to bring together flexibility with fairness and security. Awareness and use of employment regulation may help smaller organisations in their task of managing staff, from recruitment and selection through training and development to the management of performance. At the same time, the extent to which employment regulation can provide a framework for managing and even improving the employment relationship is dependent on how it is perceived and utilised within companies. Arguably, there is a considerable way to go before small employers perceive its value – indeed, the threat of financial penalties for non-compliance may not outweigh the burdens of navigating the complexities of employment law, something recognised by and acted upon by the small-business support services and employer federations.

From the review above, and the empirical research that informs the arguments and analysis, we would suggest that there are useful comparisons to be made across the cultural and structural aspects of people management. That is, the understanding of HRM in business schools, and the ways in which employment relations are legally defined, may be seen as two aspects of the same perspective on managing people in smaller organisations. This is best seen in Table 6.1.

TABLE 6.1 Overlap between HRM and ERelA

Aspect of cultural and structural conditions of managing people	Reflected through
Response to trading or social environment	HRM as managerial change vehicle; ERelA as latest in series of legislative changes
Response to changes in organisational structures	HRM emphasis on, e.g., delayering; ERelA emphasis on individual responsibility in the workplace
Response to competition from abroad	HRM defined in answer to Japanese management techniques; ERelA as response to European legislative changes
Personalised responsibility for managing skills development and training	HRM operationalised in the UK through IiP as a vehicle to encourage 'employability'; ERelA emphasis on labour flexibility

As can be seen from Table 6.1, and as we have suggested throughout this chapter, the ERelA can be seen in part as a structural support for the culture of HRM. The philosophies underpinning HRM techniques, such as individualism, an instrumental approach to work combined with unitarist expectations of commitment to organisational ideals, increased personal responsibility for career development and skills maintenance, and response to environmental change, are all present to some degree in both aspects of employee relations conditions that managers work within. Although the managers of smaller organisations may resist HRM and employment legislation, actively through employers' federations, or passively through ignoring legislation and management education, it is our contention that such a reaction is not in the interests of employees, managers, owners or business. However, urging managers in small companies to adopt a range of management practices labelled as HRM may not be the best way to promote effective people management in small organisations. Nor, we would suggest, is the 'special pleading' for smaller companies from employers' federations which often results in exemption from legislation. We would suggest that the most fruitful approach is one which seeks to understand and reflect on practice and how and why that is changing, rather than focusing narrowly on how HRM can be applied or ensuring compliance with employment legislation.

References

Alvesson, M. and Sköldberg, K. (2000) *Reflexive Methodology: New vistas for qualitative research*. Sage, London.

Amba-Roe, S. and Pendse, D. (1985) 'Human resources compensation and maintenance practices', *American Journal of Small Business*, Fall, 19–29.

Atkinson, C. and Curtis, S. (2001) 'The impact of the ERelA (1999) on the formality of employment relations in SMEs'. Paper presented at the Work, Employment and Society Conference, University of Nottingham.

Bacon, N., Ackers, P., Storey, J. and Coates, D. (1996) 'It's a small world: Managing human resources in small businesses', *International Journal of Human Resource Management*, 7:1, 82–100.

Beardwell, I.J. (1996) *Contemporary Industrial Relations*. Oxford University Press, Oxford.

Beer, M., Spector, B., Lawrence, P., Quinn Mills, D. and Walton, R. (1984) *Managing Human Assets*. The Free Press, New York.

Beer, M., Spector, B., Lawrence, P., Quinn Mills, D. and Walton, R. (1985) *Human Resource Management: A general manager's perspective*. The Free Press, New York.

Brown, W., Deakin, S., Nash, D. and Oxenbridge, S. (2000) 'The employment contract: from collective procedures to individual rights', *British Journal of Industrial Relations* 38, 611–629.

Chandler, G. and McEvoy, G. (2000) 'Human resource management, TQM and firm performance in small and medium-sized enterprises', *Entrepreneurship Theory and Practice*, Fall, 43–57.

Deal, T. and Kennedy, A. (1982) *Corporate Cultures: The rites and rituals of corporate life*. Addison-Wesley, London.

Deshpande, S. and Golhar, D. (1994) 'HRM practices in large and small manufacturing firms: A comparative study', *Journal of Small Business Management*, 32:2, 49–56.

Duberley, J. and Walley, P. (1995) 'Assessing the adoption of HRM by small and medium-sized manufacturing organizations', *International Journal of Human Resource Management*, 6:4, 891–909.

Du Gay, P., Salaman, G. and Rees, B. (1996) 'The conduct of management and the management of conduct: Contemporary managerial discourse and the constitution of the "competent" manager', *Journal of Management Studies*, 33:3, 263–282.

Dundon, T., Grugulis, I. and Wilkinson, A. (1999) 'Looking out of the black hole. Non-union relations in SMEs', *Employee Relations* 21, 251–266.

Earnshaw, J., Marchington, M. and Goodman, J. (2000) 'Unfair to whom? Discipline and dismissal in small establishments', *Industrial Relations Journal*, 31, 62–73.

Eccles, R. and Nohria, N. (1992) *Beyond the Hype: Rediscovering the essence of management*. Harvard Business School Press, Boston, MA.

Fombrun, C., Tichy, N. and Devanna, M. (1984) *Strategic Human Resource Management*. Wiley, New York.

Gatewood, R. and Field, H. (1987) 'A personnel selection program for small business', *Journal of Small Business Management*, October, 16–24.

Golhar, D. and Deshpande, S. (1997) 'HRM practices of large and small Canadian manufacturing firms', *Journal of Small Business Management*, **35**:3, 30–38.

Guest, D. (1987) 'Human resource management and industrial relations', *Journal of Management Studies*, **24**:5, 503–521.

Harris, L. (2000) 'Employment regulation and owner managers in small firms, seeking support and guidance', *Journal of Small Business and Enterprise Development*, **7**, 352–362.

Heneman, R., Tansky, J. and Camp, S. (2000) 'Human resource management in small and medium-sized enterprises: Unanswered questions and future research perspectives', *Entrepreneurship Theory and Practice*, Fall, 11–26.

Holliday, R. (1995) *Investigating Small Firms: Nice work?* Routledge, London.

Hollinshead, G., Nicholls, P. and Tailby, S. (1999) *Employee Relations*. Financial Times/Pitman Publishing, London.

Hornsby, J. and Kuratko, D. (1990) 'Human resource management in small business: Critical issues for the 1990s', *Journal of Small Business Management*, July, 9–18.

Huselid, M. (1995) 'The impact of human resource management practices on turnover, productivity, and corporate financial performance', *Academy of Management Journal*, **38**:3, 635–672.

Ingham, G. (1970) *Size of Industrial Organization and Worker Behaviour*. Cambridge University Press, Cambridge.

IPD (1994) *People Management in Small and Medium Enterprises*. Institute of Personnel and Development, London.

Jacques, R. (1996) *Manufacturing the Employee*. Sage, London.

Katz, J., Aldrich, H., Welbourne, T. and Williams, P. (2000) 'Human resource management and the SME: Toward a new synthesis', *Entrepreneurship Theory and Practice*, Fall, 7–10.

Keenoy, T. (1999) 'HRM as hologram: A polemic', *Journal of Management Studies*, **36**:1, 1–23.

Keenoy, T. and Anthony, P. (1992) 'HRM: Metaphor, meaning and morality', in P. Blyton and P. Turnbull (eds) *Reassessing Human Resource Management*. Sage, London.

Klaas, B., McClendon, J. and Gainey, T. (2000) 'Managing HR in the small and medium enterprise: The impact of professional employer organizations', *Entrepreneurship Theory and Practice*, Fall, 107–124.

Legge, K. (1989) 'Human resource management: A critical analysis', in J. Storey (ed.). *New Perspectives on Human Resource Management*. Routledge, London.

Legge, K. (1995) *Human Resource Management: Rhetorics and Realities*. Macmillan, London.

Marlow, S. and Strange, A. (2000) 'Regulating labour management: the effect of the Employment Relations Act upon small firms'. Paper presented at the 23rd International Small Business Association Conference, University of Aberdeen, 15–17 November.

Matlay, H. (1999) 'Employee relations in small firms. A micro-business perspective', *Employee Relations*, **21**, 285–295.

McEvoy, G. (1984) 'Small business personnel practices', *Journal of Small Business Management*, October, 1–8.

Ng, I. and Maki, D. (1993) 'Human resource management in the Canadian manufacturing sector', *International Journal of Human Resource Management*, **4**:4, 897–916.

Noon, M. (1992) 'HRM: A map, model or theory', in P. Blyton and P. Turnbull (eds) *Reassessing Human Research Management*. Sage, London.

Peters, T. and Waterman, R. (1982) *In Search of Excellence: Lessons from America's best-run companies*. Harper & Row, New York.

Pfeffer, J. (1997) 'Pitfalls on the road to measurement: The dangerous liaison of human resources with the ideas of accounting and finance', *Human Resource Management*, **36**:3, 357–365.

Purcell, J. (1993) 'The end of institutional industrial relations', *Political Quarterly*, **6**, 6–23.

Rainnie, A. (1989) *Industrial Relations in Small Firms*. Routledge, London.

Rainnie, A. and Scott, M. (1986) 'Industrial relations in the small firm', in J. Curran, J. Stanworth and D. Watkins (eds) *The Survival of the Small Firm*, Vol. 2. Gower, Aldershot.

Ram, M. (1994) *Managing to Survive: Working lives in small firms*. Blackwell, Oxford.

Rose, E. (2001) *Employment Relations*. Financial Times/Prentice Hall, Harlow.

Rose Ebaugh, H. and Curry, M. (2000) 'Fictive kin as social capital in new immigrant communities', *Sociological Perspectives*, **43**:2, 189–210.

Schumacher, E. (1974) *Small is Beautiful*. Abacus, London.

Scott, M., Roberts, I., Holroyd, G. and Sawbridge, G. (1989) *Management and Industrial Relations in Small Firms*. London, Department of Employment Research Paper 70.

Storey, J. (1989) 'Introduction: From personnel management to human resource management', in J. Storey (ed.) *New Perspectives on Human Resource Management*. Routledge, London.

Storey, J. (1992) *Developments in the Management of Human Resources*. Blackwell, Oxford.

Tichy, N., Fombrun, C. and Devanna, M. (1982) 'Strategic human resource management', *Sloan Management Review*, **23**:2, 47–61.

Walsh, J. (1999) 'Firms give working time regulations the thumbs up', *People Management*, **5**, 10.

Watson, T. (1995) 'In search of HRM: Beyond the rhetoric and reality distinction, or the case of the dog that didn't bark', *Personnel Review*, **24**:4, 6–16.

Westrip, A. (1986) 'Small firms policy: the case of employment legislation', in J. Curran, J. Stanworth and D. Watkins (eds) *The Survival of the Small Firm*, Vol. 2. Gower, Aldershot.

Wilkinson, A. (1999) 'Employment relations in SMEs', *Employee Relations*, **21**, 206–217.

Willmott, H. (1993) 'Strength is ignorance: Slavery is freedom: Managing culture in modern organizations', *Journal of Management Studies*, **30**:4, 515–552.

Note

1. The notion of fictive kin originates in anthropology, and has been applied in analysis of other social groupings (see especially Rose Ebaugh and Curry, 2000).

Chapter 7

EMPLOYEE SHARE OWNERSHIP IN SMEs

Andrew Pendleton

Share ownership offers employees a real stake in their company with shareholders, managers and employees working towards common goals.
Gordon Brown, Foreword to
Consultation on Employee Share
Ownership. (HM Treasury, 1998)

Introduction

In the last five years, there has been considerable interest among policy-makers in the use of share-based rewards in small and medium-sized enterprises (SMEs). Several initiatives have been taken to stimulate the use of this instrument among small firms, and these have formed an integral part of the government's drive to assist small firms, to promote entrepreneurship, and to improve the UK's level of productivity (Treasury, 2001a,b). However, in the UK, as in the rest of Europe, equity-based employee rewards are still rare in small firms (see Pendleton *et al.*, 2001).

In this chapter we suggest that the limited use of share ownership schemes in small businesses can be attributed to two main reasons. The first is that the typical rationale for the use of share-based rewards (incentives, alignment of interests and commitment) is less relevant in small-firm settings, and this may help to explain their apparent lack of appeal to small-business owners and managers. The second is that there are significant obstacles to the use of these schemes in small firms, some of which emanate from the regulatory framework governing share schemes and some of which derive from the culture of small-business management. Recent policy initiatives have attempted to address these issues by providing generous tax incentives to stimulate the appeal of share ownership schemes and by amending regulations governing share schemes to facilitate their adoption in small, private business contexts. However, it is difficult in the short term for government policy to tackle wider problems in small-business management, such as the culture of informality.

The use of share schemes in small firms appears to be growing, though it is difficult to assess precisely the impact of these recent policy initiatives. We find that employee share schemes are concentrated in certain types of small firms and in certain types of contexts. We identify four main contexts and rationales for the use of share schemes: as a risk-sharing instrument in management buy-outs and related restructuring transactions; as an instrument of pay substitution in 'new economy' start-ups; as a means of protecting firms and workforces when owners exit; and as a device for ameliorating managerial recruitment and retention difficulties in SMEs. We account for the use of share schemes in each setting and highlight both the benefits and problems arising from the use of this instrument.

Incidence of Share Ownership in SMEs

Employee share ownership schemes can take a number of forms in the UK, and all are in principle open to SMEs. Given the relatively extensive statutory framework for employee share schemes and the substantial tax concessions available to share scheme participants in the UK, the majority of share schemes are Inland Revenue-approved operated in accordance with the relevant legislation. Share options (whereby employees are granted rights to acquire shares in the future on favourable terms) are the most widespread form of share scheme. The main schemes are as follows:

Approved Profit Sharing (APS): Established in 1978, this scheme enabled profit-sharing payments to be made in shares via the use of a trust. A variant allowed employees to receive free shares via this route for each one bought – 'buy one, get one free' or BOGOF. This scheme was superseded by the Share Incentives Plan in 2002.

Save As You Earn share options (SAYE or Sharesave): This scheme enables employees to take out options to purchase shares in three, five or seven years time, at up to a discount of 20 per cent on the market price at the time of grant. Meanwhile, the employee makes regular savings using a SAYE savings contract, with the terminal sum being used to acquire the shares if the employee so wishes.

Company Share Options Plan (CSOP): This is a discretionary option-based plan (i.e. it is not necessarily open to all employees). Participating individuals take out options to acquire shares in 3–10 years' time.

Share Incentives Plan (formerly All-Employee Share Ownership Plan (AESOP)): Introduced in the 2000 Finance Act, this plan has a number of strands. Employees may buy shares using a regular payment plan ('partnership shares'), or may receive 'free shares' (in a similar way to the APS scheme). Those buying partnership shares may receive 'matching shares'. Dividend payments for shares held in trust may be made in 'dividend shares'. There are also a number of innovations in this plan aimed specifically at SMEs, such as a relaxation of the typical share scheme requirement that shares be voting shares.

Enterprise Management Incentives: Also introduced in the 2000 Finance Act, this scheme is aimed specifically at SMEs (those with gross assets under £15 million). This provided for options to be granted to up to 15 employees (subsequently extended to all employees) subject to a total ceiling (after the 2001 Finance Act) of £3 million. It has been announced recently that the gross assets limit will be doubled to £30 million so as to expand the number of companies eligible to participate in the plan (see Treasury, 2001b).

The main principles of the taxation regime governing these schemes is that employees are exempt from income tax on share acquisition as a benefit from employment, and are instead subject to a capital gains tax (CGT) regime on the eventual sale of their shares. Recent policy initiatives have enhanced CGT concessions by making share scheme gains subject to the CGT business assets 'taper' so that the effective rate of taxation diminishes over time. The longer that shares are held (once they are acquired by the employee), the lower the rate of capital gains tax liability when the shares are sold. Currently the rate tapers from 40 per cent for sales in year one to 10 per cent for those after year 2. The capital gains tax arrangements are even more favourable in the case of Enterprise Management Incentives, where the starting point for the taper is the grant (rather than the exercise) of the option.

The take-up of share schemes among small firms is difficult to measure precisely, as Inland Revenue statistics are not organised on a size basis, except where the scheme is explicitly based on company size (as in the case of EMI). Our main source for information is the Workplace Employee Relations Survey 1998, which provides a representative survey of workplaces with 10 or more employees. WERS data indicates that one per cent of firms[1] with fewer than 100 employees in total have an all-employee share ownership scheme, and none have a share-based profit sharing scheme (APS) (Cully *et al.*, 1999, pp. 260–261). Since WERS was conducted, Enterprise Management Incentives has boosted the use of share options among smaller firms. As of March 2002, 2179 companies had issued stock options under the EMI scheme, and 21 377 employees had received options (an average of 10 per company). Around half of the options awarded had a market value of £25 000 at the time of grant, and 5 per cent were at the maximum individual limit.[2]

Given that share schemes are widely used by larger firms (24 per cent of all workplaces were covered by a share scheme in 1998 according to WERS data), it is interesting to consider why this form of employee reward is not widely used by SMEs. We do this by considering the theoretical rationale for share schemes and relating this to a small-firm context. This provides a 'demand-side' explanation for the limited use of employee share ownership schemes. We then go on to examine obstacles to the use of this form of employee reward.

The Rationale for Employee Share Ownership

The attraction of employee share ownership to the Blair government resides in its apparent performance-enhancing capabilities. This process operates by giving employees a stake in the success of the firm. As the Financial Secretary to the Treasury put it in 1999:

> There is a clear link between employees owning shares in the company they work for and an increase in productivity ... employee share ownership can bridge the gap between employees, managers and shareholders by aligning more closely the interests of the

> workforce with the owners of the company ... Employee owners have an incentive to contribute more actively to the development of the business by raising productivity from which they can benefit directly. (Adjournment Debate on Employee Share Ownership, 14 July 1999)

The incentive-based rationale for share ownership schemes outlined above should be more compelling (at least in theory) in small rather than large businesses. The problem facing all collective forms of remuneration is the '1/n' or 'free rider' problem. The essence of this problem is that with n members of the group, extra profit-sharing reward associated with marginal effort on any single worker's part is diluted by a factor of 1/n (Weitzman and Kruse, 1990, p. 98). Thus, the temptation to 'free-ride' on the efforts of others increases as the size of the workforce increase. If it is assumed that those running the firm are aware of the potential for free-riding then, all things being equal, employee share ownership schemes should be more common in small firms.

A counter-argument is that employee share ownership and other collective forms of remuneration are less 'necessary' in small firms because of certain characteristics associated with their 'smallness'. As we saw above, the economic rationale suggests that, in a principal-agent setting, collective remuneration potentially aligns the interests of principals (the firm, its owners, its managers) and agents (the workforce), leading workers to work harder, to share information and to cooperate with managers. However, work discipline, information-hoarding and non-cooperation may all be less pertinent problems in small firms. The 'personal' or 'direct' control of work tasks that characterises many small firms may obviate the need for instruments such as employee share ownership. In owner-managed firms (43 per cent of firms with fewer than 100 employees, according to WERS), the owner's direct involvement in work discipline helps to ensure that the interests of principals are 'reflected' in agents' behaviour. The personal and informal character of hierarchy relationships may also encourage information-sharing between workers and bosses. In any case, in owner-managed settings, those in authority are also likely to be highly knowledgeable about work processes (especially in firms characterised by 'fraternal' employment relations i.e. where owner-managers work alongside employees on the 'shop floor').

So, there are conflicting expectations on the attractions of instruments such as employee share ownership (ESO) in SMEs. On the one hand, conventional economic discussions suggest that employee share ownership ought to be more widespread in smaller rather than larger firms. On the other, the typical work and employment relationships found in small firms suggests that the problems which ESO might be used to ameliorate are dealt with in different ways. The very limited use of share schemes in SMEs suggests that the latter may be more important.

Barriers to Share Ownership in SMEs

Policy-makers have been acutely conscious of the barriers to the use of share ownership schemes in SMEs, and have attempted to refine the regulatory framework to lower some of them. They are found in three main areas: the finance and ownership structures of SMEs; the approach to people management that typifies many SMEs; and the implications of share ownership for management and control.

The finance and ownership structures of most SMEs is not conducive to the use of employee share ownership. Around two-thirds of small companies over the VAT threshold are either partnerships or sole proprietorships, and hence have neither a share capital nor a workforce. About half a million SMEs are companies, with employees (Cosh and Hughes, 1994), and most of these are very small. Only about 2500 of these companies are listed (though this is high by European standards). Thus, not many firms have the equity 'infrastructure' to readily operate an employee share scheme, and a decision to operate such a scheme may well require major changes to the equity base and the legal form of the company. Thus, there are likely to be high set-up costs to the introduction of a share scheme, over and above the direct costs of establishing the scheme.

This reflects broader issues and constraints concerning the financing of small firms. The main source of external finance for SMEs in the UK is short-term loans and overdrafts from banks (Storey, 1994). Equity is rarely used, especially among start-ups, because equity providers are generally unwilling to shoulder the level of risk involved. A related problem is that venture capital providers are unwilling to participate in equity offerings because the transaction costs are high relative to the level of finance involved. The costs of undertaking risk assessments are relatively high for equity acquisitions of under £500 000 million or thereabouts (Gavron *et al.*, 1998), and hence venture capitalists tend to shun equity issues (except in the case of MBOs). Institutional investors (pension funds, insurance companies, etc.) are also reluctant to invest in the small firm and private equity sector, as the Myners Report showed recently (Treasury, 2001c). On the whole, then, the financial context in which small firms operate does not encourage the development of company structures that are facilitative of share ownership schemes.

A major issue for any non-listed company with an employee share scheme is how to provide a market for shares. Employees need to have a way of divesting their shares, especially since in small companies with high growth potential the potential capital gains from selling shares may far outweigh the value of dividends. In these cases, flotation may provide the vehicle for liquidity. However, only a tiny minority of SMEs aspire to take this route. Most SMEs intend to remain privately owned, and here the problem is how to create a market which does not create the opportunity for outsiders to gain control of the company (by acquiring shares from divesting employees). One solution is to establish an employee benefits trust with the power to purchase and sell equity to employees. In effect, the trust acts as a 'market-maker' and also possibly as a 'warehouse' for shares. But the establishment and operation of employee benefits trusts is perceived to be costly, and the set-up costs are a barrier to many companies. Furthermore, the trust clearly has to have a source of finance to acquire shares in the first place (where shares are initially located in trust) and to re-acquire them from divesting employees. In most cases, either the company will gift or loan the money required, or else underwrite a loan to the trust. In some circumstances, this can be a major drain on company cash-flow. To limit this, it is common for small private firms with share schemes to place tight limits on trading activity. Typically, trading days might be held on one or two days per year. Furthermore, divestments might be limited to departing employees, with the trust buying back shares when employees leave the firm (this will typically require modifications to the Articles of Association and will therefore impose a further cost on the firm).

In private firms, where there is no external market for equity a major issue concerns the valuation of shares. Clearly, shares will have to be valued periodically to operate trading days. It is not usually feasible to allow a free internal market in shares because most participants lack the information to make sound trading decisions and, knowing this, would simply choose not to participate. Share valuations are also necessary where schemes are operated in accordance with Inland Revenue schemes because of limits to the total value of shares that can be awarded/placed under option, and because of the need to calculate individual tax liabilities. Valuation by the Inland Revenue is seen by some firms as an additional hurdle to contend with, though the Inland Revenue has recently emphasised the speed with which valuations can be conducted.

An interesting issue concerns the level at which shares are valued, and movements in this value. Employee preferences may well be for a steeply rising share value since this provides the opportunity to make a significant capital gain. However, an employee's gain can be the company's 'loss' in so far as the company has to underwrite or even cover the trust's expenditure in re-acquiring shares where necessary from employees. If shares become highly valued, it may then prove difficult for the trust to sell on these shares to other employees (due to liquidity constraints, perceptions of risk, etc.). In circumstances where share price has risen sharply, there may well be a drift of shares from individual employees to trusts. From a company point of view, then, a more or less stable share price may be preferable since it provides a stable environment for share schemes to operate, and hence enables the company to make sound estimates of corporate liabilities.

A second major set of barriers may be located in the approach to human resource management in SMEs. On the whole, SMEs are not noted for well-developed human resource management strategies, institutions and policies. For instance, the Workplace Employee Relations Survey 1998 found that just nine per cent of small businesses (of under 100 employees) have a specialist personnel manager. The reasons for this state of affairs include employer aversion to formal employee involvement, lack of belief or knowledge that HRM practices are relevant to the small business situation, and an emphasis on the merits of informality (see Bacon et al., 1996). Two particular aspects of this may be viewed as antithetical to the use of employee share schemes. The first is that pay practices in SMEs tend to be ad hoc and responsive to the imperatives of short-term labour and product market pressures at the micro level (Gilman et al., 2002). Where contingent forms of payment system are used, they tend to take the form of individual Payment By Results, and tend to be used in an ad hoc and mechanistic fashion (Cox, 1999). Overall, that strategic dimension to reward systems which is necessary to justify the investment in the establishment and operation of a share scheme tends to be absent. The second is that there is an aversion to formal structures of employee involvement in most SMEs. The industrial relations literature on small firms has emphasised the autocratic or 'unitary' nature of employment relations in small firms (Rainnie, 1989; Goss, 1991; Ram, 1991). Employment relationships of this sort, whether they take a paternalistic, fraternalistic or clearly autocratic form (see Scase, 1995) are not conducive to formal kinds of employee involvement. This emphasis on informality is a major barrier to employee share schemes because typically the operation of these schemes is inevitably highly bureaucratised, especially where Inland Revenue-approved schemes are used. It is necessary to operate these schemes within statutory parameters, to maintain formal records and to formally communicate with employees to meet statutory financial services requirements.

However, small firms are extremely heterogeneous in their character (Dundon *et al.*, 2001), and not all SMEs can be criticised in this way. Bacon *et al.* (1996), in a survey of SMEs, found that the take-up of 'sophisticated' HRM instruments was higher than would be expected given the prevailing consensus in the literature. Similarly, the WERS survey found a relatively high incidence of formal employee involvement mechanisms (between 20 and 33 per cent) in SMEs (Cully *et al.*, 1999). The WERS researchers suggest that many small firms do not rely wholly on informal means of communication, and instead use a blend of formal and informal practices. On the whole, those SMEs that adopt more extensive and more formal approaches to human resource management and employee involvement seem more likely to be favourably disposed to the use of employee share schemes.

A third obstacle concerns the attitude of owners to sharing control of the company with others. Typically, owner-managers are highly reluctant to share control with others, and ownership tends to be highly concentrated. The Cambridge Small Business Survey conducted in the early 1990s found that in firms with 500 or fewer employees, 75 per cent of company boards held on average over 75 per cent of the stock, with a median level of 100 per cent ownership (Cosh and Hughes, 1994). The danger of extending ownership further is that new owners will seek to exercise influence on how the company is run and to challenge the prevailing management policies and practices of executive directors. For employees, there may be a particular anxiety in that ownership rights may run directly contrary to autocratic or paternalist employment relationships, leading to direct challenges to management prerogatives. Once again recent policy initiatives have attempted to engage with this issue. The Share Incentives Plan, for instance, allows companies to use non-voting shares for employee share schemes.

ESO Scenarios

For the reasons outlined above, employee share ownership is a rare phenomenon among SMEs. However, as Dundon *et al.* (2001) emphasise, the SME sector is heterogeneous in its composition and there are some circumstances where share ownership is more widely used. Four types of context where share ownership is more common or is seen to be more readily applicable are discerned: management buy-outs (and its variants), dot-coms and new economy firms, exits (retirements, etc.), and firms experiencing difficulties in recruitment and retention. We deal with each of these in turn.

Management Buy-outs: Employee Share Ownership in Restructuring Transactions

A management buy-out is where the management of a subsidiary or business unit of a firm buy out the parent company. In many cases the new company that is created can be classed as an SME. Research by the Centre for Management Buy-Out Research shows that over three-quarters of management buy-out transactions in 1997 were less than £10 million in value (CMBOR, 1998). The role of share ownership in these new enterprises is linked to the financing of buy-outs and the approaches taken to devise appropriate incentive structures. Typically, MBOs are mainly financed by venture capitalists. Given their short time-frame for returns, coupled with the level of risk attached to the finance contract, venture capitalists tend to seek more explicit contracts with managers of the firm than is usual in other circumstances. In this sense, MBOs are a solution to the agency costs of investor–manager relationships in larger firms (Wright and Robbie, 1996).

A key element of the performance contract adopted in most MBOs is that the managers mounting the buy-out acquire some of the equity in the new firm. Often the loan finance is made available on a 'ratchet' basis: as the firm repays the loan to the venture capitalists, the equity stake of these financiers is transferred to those within the firm. The evidence suggests that MBO contexts are often favourable to the introduction of all-employee share ownership. Employee share ownership is seen as a way for binding employees to the success of the firm. Recent work by the Centre for Management Buy-Out Research (CMBOR) finds that equity participation by employees in MBOs is relatively high. In a survey of buy-outs that took place between 1991 and 1997, Bacon and Wright found that 33 per cent of MBOs had introduced an all-employee share scheme compared with a national average of 15 per cent. A further noteworthy finding from this survey was that two areas where financiers tended to be more involved was in the selection of the management team and the design of reward strategies for employees (Bacon and Wright, 1999).

An extreme, and rarer, case is where employees take on such a stake that the buy-out can be seen as a management-employee buy-out or employee buy-out. The primary economic argument for significant employee participation in ownership resides in the potential for alignment of interests. Against this, there are a set of counter-arguments. It can be argued that employee ownership can lead to under-performance because participation by ill-qualified employees in key decisions leads to sub-optimal decision-making. In addition, participation in decisions by diverse workforces leads to high coordination costs as institutions and processes need to be created to reconcile conflicting interests and objectives (Hansmann, 1996). A further argument, derived from the literature on workers' cooperatives, is that employee-owners' preferences may be for current consumption rather than long-term investment, i.e. in other words they prefer to divert profits into 'excess' wages.[3]

Management-employee buy-outs are not common, and there appear to be no more than a handful created each year. There was a flurry of activity in the early 1990s connected to privatisation initiatives (i.e. where firms were sold or where activities were divested from state corporations or public service organisations). Two types of scenario can be observed in these cases (see Pendleton, 2001). Where firms were already trading entities, and had good cash flow, high-leveraged buy-outs were feasible. Typically, management and workers would create a new firm to mount the buy-out and would borrow the money necessary to purchase their employing firm. In these cases, employee subscriptions to equity were not necessary as such to finance the buy-out and shares were passed to employees free of charge. Use of trusts was common to handle the transaction, with the employees' shares initially being held in trust. Examples of MEBOs of this sort were most notably found in the bus industry during the privatisation of that industry in the late 1980s/early 1990s. Local authority owners and unions favoured employee ownership as an alternative to trade sales, on the grounds that it was more likely to protect jobs and services. The other instance of MEBOs in privatisation contexts can be found where firms were newly created at the buy-out. In these cases – where there was no trading record and hence a high level of risk – those organising the buy-out typically found it difficult to raise external finance. In these circumstances, employee subscriptions to equity may form an important part of the raising of the cash needed to secure the buy-out.

'Dot-coms' and New Economy Firms: Employee Share Ownership as Pay Substitution

The second main set of cases where employee share ownership can be observed is in the Internet-based companies that sprang up towards the end of the 1990s (the so-called 'dot-com' companies). The function of employee share ownership is typically rather different from that found in the management buy-outs considered above, and there is a different set of theoretical arguments to explain the popularity of share ownership schemes in these companies. In fact, employee share ownership has been seen as central to the nature and functioning of 'new economy' firms. Charles Leadbetter, an influential figure in government policy-making, has argued that employee ownership is the 'glue' that binds knowledge economy companies together (Leadbetter, 1998).

There is now considerable evidence that share ownership schemes (especially share options) are widespread in 'new economy' firms. A recent study by the Involvement and Participation Association (2001) found that 63 per cent of 'dot-coms' operated a share ownership scheme for non-managerial employees. Similarly, a survey of Internet companies by IRS (2001) found that 66 per cent had a share ownership scheme open to non-management staff. Although share option schemes in dot-coms have attracted a lot of attention, they are not a new phenomenon in 'new economy' firms. Over a decade ago, Smith found that 82 per cent of firms in the United States INC 100 Fastest Growing Publicly Held Firms (mainly high-technology SMEs) had a share options scheme (Smith, 1988).

Share options are attractive in firms with high growth potential because of the benefits that will flow from increases in company value. This was exemplified by dot-com companies, which experienced huge rises in market valuation in 2000. At one stage, the market valuations of dot-com companies was such that several were admitted to the FTSE 100.[4] The remarkable feature of these companies was that in terms of turnover, number of employees and gross assets they clearly met all of the criteria to be considered SMEs. Some had very little in the way of physical assets, and many were loss-making. Between them, the new economy entrants to the FTSE 100 in March 2000 earned just £516 million, compared with £3.5 billion of the 'blue chip' companies they replaced (*Financial Times*, 8 March 2000). Nearly all of their market capitalisation was dependent on market assessments of their potential, based on the 'knowledge economy' attributes of their products and human resources.

The primary purpose of employee share schemes in these firms was provision of deferred compensation or pay substitution. Employees were paid partly in share options rather than 'cash' salaries, on the basis that the options would provide considerable returns in the future, given the prevailing patterns of capital growth. This use of share options contrasts sharply with the case of larger firms, where share schemes are nearly always supplements to, rather than substitutes for, salary. This use of share options met the needs of both employer and employee. The problem of meeting the wage bill out of the profit and loss account, when revenue was tiny, was met by transferring it, in effect, to the balance sheet. From an employee point of view options were highly attractive. Many dot-com workers were young, often recent graduates, with relatively few fixed outgoings. Thus, they could take on a higher level of salary risk than many employees. The potential rewards, given that what appeared to be a potentially huge market was only just emerging, outweighed the level of risk and the short-term limits on salaries and consumption.

Some more theoretical arguments can be advanced to demonstrate the value of employee share option schemes in dot-com firms. Drawing on arguments put forward by Margaret Blair in *Ownership and Control* (1995), share options helped to deal with the problem of firm-specific human capital investments. The danger of asset specificity, as has been shown by Williamson (1985), is opportunism and 'hold up'. From an employer point of view, in knowledge-based firms in rapidly developing markets there is a high dependence on the knowledge of key employees. It is vital that employees commit to building up their human capital, in circumstances where the firm's capacity to develop training programmes is decidedly limited. In other words, they need employees to make the investments. The danger with this is that, in the particular market context of the dot-coms, employees could take their knowledge of the firm's products and plans elsewhere (perhaps even establishing their own firms, given low barriers to entry) or could use their pivotal position to 'hold up' the firm (Smith, 1988). In these circumstances, employee share schemes provide an important means to align employee interests with those of the firm and to encourage cooperation. More specifically, option schemes also 'lock in' the worker because options are typically not vested until a year or more after the options are awarded. From an employee point of view, share options are a control on managerial opportunism. Given the huge potential market growth of dot-com firms, there is the possibility that the managers and primary owners of dot-coms could make a fortune on the back of worker investments in human capital. Employee share schemes provide a signal that the benefits of growth will be shared with employees. They also counter the opportunity costs of concentrating personal investments in one firm where alternative opportunities are available. It is for these kinds of reasons that observers such as Leadbetter emphasise the role of share schemes as 'corporate glue'.

The potential rewards from option schemes featured heavily in the news in the year 2000, but since then the gloss has worn off this form of reward. With the collapse in market value of many dot-com PLCs, the value of share options has plummeted. For those dot-coms planning to realise value by floating, the fall in capitalisation has inevitably led to the postponement of Initial Public Offerings, thereby preventing option holders from realising value. Worse still, many dot-coms have gone bankrupt so that employees have both lost their jobs and the value of their options (the 'double risk' that opponents of employee share ownership schemes have traditionally emphasised).

Even without these difficulties, problems had arisen with the operation of share schemes in these firms. Many dot-coms firms did not use the tax-approved options schemes, probably because they would have found it difficult to get employees to subscribe to a savings plan when the options formed an implicit part of their salaries. Also, the short-term time horizons of dot-coms do not sit easily with the stipulated option and deferral periods of Inland Revenue-approved schemes. The problem with this, however, is that such employers could not receive the National Insurance exemptions associated with the approved schemes, and were instead liable to employers' NIC charges when their employees exercised their options.[5] Given the huge potential increases in share value, many dot-coms faced an unquantifiable but potentially enormous NIC liability. Some 'new economy' firms threatened to scale back their UK operations as a result. To deal with this problem, the government introduced regulations in the Social Security Act 2000, which allows firms and their employees to reach an agreement that employees will meet the employer's NIC charges when gains are made from share option schemes.

However, there are events looming which will present major difficulties for the use of employee share options in 'new economy' companies (and indeed in other companies). Currently, the Accounting Standards Board is considering (along with accounting standards setters in other developed nations) whether to require firms to enter the 'real' costs of options on to their profit and loss accounts. Clearly, if there is an increase in share value between award and exercise, the firm can be said to have suffered an opportunity cost equivalent to the difference between the two prices. It is argued that current accounting standards, which do not register this loss on the profit and loss account, give a misleading picture of the economic health of the company. It is said that Microsoft would never have made a profit if it had been required to enter the full value of its employee option schemes on to its profit and loss account. If the new accounting standard is enacted, the attraction of options as a way of providing off-profit and loss account rewards in a context of limited revenue will be eliminated.

Employee Share Ownership at Exit

A third set of circumstances where employee share ownership is relevant, though rare in practice, is where a major owner wants to exit, either fully or in part. A common problem facing those owning small or unlisted firms is how to exit. Private buyers may not be readily found, and there is the danger that a sale to a competitor will result in restructuring or even a wholesale disbandment of the business. Competitors may be more interested in the customer base than the human or physical assets of the company.

From the point of view of the owner of a small business, the possibility that sale of the business will lead to downsizing poses two major problems. One, it is a destruction of all that has been worked for over the years, and hence is emotionally unappealing to the owner. Two, closure of the business would violate any paternalistic or fraternalistic sense of obligation on the owner's part towards the workforce. In these circumstances, the appeal of employee share ownership is not hard to see. Employee share ownership passes ownership of the business to those that have the biggest stake (other than the departing owner) in the success and continued existence of the firm. This solution therefore resolves the two problems outlined above: it protects the workforce and it also protects the firm in its present form, at least for the time being. A further benefit of employee share ownership is that it permits gradual or phased exit by the major owner. The owner can divest some of the firm but still retain effective control.

An illustrative case of employee share ownership in these circumstances is provided by a small perfume company in Manchester. In this case the owner was nearing retirement and wanted to partially exit (to realise value for the benefit of his younger wife) but to retain control. He also wanted to gradually transfer ownership in a way that the company could readily 'digest'. If the company had been sold on the open market, it would probably have been acquired by a competitor so as to gain access to its recipes, and then shut down. The answer was to set up a QUEST and a Profit Sharing Trust to distribute shares to employees (using a BOGOF scheme), and an EBT to hold shares for a discretionary options scheme. The QUEST acquired 10 per cent of the equity and the EBT 15 per cent, with the owner retaining 75 per cent. Eligibility for the BOGOF scheme is one year's employment. In the distributions that have occurred to date, over 60 per cent of eligible employees have participated.

However, this is not a widespread solution to exit and succession problems. The most obvious barriers are those of liquidity, risk and coordination. Employees may not have the money to acquire the firm, and may be unwilling or unable to take the risk of borrowing to fund the acquisition. A further problem is the transaction costs, especially for the vendor in selling potentially small parcels of the firm to each employee. In the circumstances, by far the most sensible option is to use an employee benefits trust to effect the transaction. Even then, there is the problem of acquiring the financial resources to purchase shares from the owner. One solution is to use a loan-note mechanism, whereby the owner's equity is passed to the trust, which then pays the owner in instalments over time as company profits are passed to the trust. However, this is not suitable when the owner wants to realise value quickly. These difficulties of raising finance to effect ownership transfers appear to outweigh the tax advantages that are available to owners who sell their businesses to employee trusts.[6]

Share Schemes as an Instrument for Recruitment and Retention

The final use of share ownership schemes is as a tool for recruiting high-calibre employees. Aside from dot-com companies, where shares were widely targeted at all levels of employees, this mainly affects managerial employees. Here, the argument derives from the influential findings of the Bolton Committee on SMEs in the 1960s. Bolton found that SMEs lacked managerial skills, and that the major challenge was to import and develop management skills in these firms. The evidence shows that fast-growth SMES are much more likely than other SMEs to have managers with a large-firm background (Stanworth and Gray, 1991, p. 226). Even where they attract high-quality managers from outside, they find it difficult to keep them. Management turnover in SMEs is relatively rapid (Stanworth and Gray, 1991, p. 213). This is not at all surprising. By virtue of their size, SMEs typically lack the well-developed and extensive internal labour markets found in many large firms, with the result that promotional opportunities are typically limited. The challenge for SMEs is to attract experienced managers, and retain them once they have them.

One way of attracting experienced managers to small and medium-sized firms is the provision of share ownership or share option schemes. By providing these rewards, SMEs can imitate the typical reward packages of large PLCs, and also provide the potential for major capital gains should the SME do well. They may also help to close the gap in average pay levels between small and larger firms: research has shown that there is a wage premium of around 30 per cent in larger firms (Storey, 1994). Once these managers have been attracted to the SME, the deferral provisions of share ownership schemes or the gap between grant and exercise in stock options schemes provide a degree of 'lock-in'. The manager needs to maintain employment with the SME for a period of time to access share-based rewards. In this way, share schemes can help with managerial retention as well as recruitment. However, another way of looking at these schemes is that they have an element of risk. These rewards may not be realised if the SME does not perform well, and this may amplify the risk of exchanging well-remunerated employment in a larger firm for that in a smaller, perhaps less stable, company.

The desirability of attracting experienced managers to SMEs was an explicit and important policy objective for the Enterprise Management Incentives scheme introduced by the 2000 Finance Act. Each firm operating this scheme could allow up to 15 individuals to participate (since widened to all employees). The taxation arrangements are extremely favourable since the capital gains tax taper relief clock starts ticking when the options are granted. Thus, much of the CGT liability may well have been dissipated by the time the option is exercised. In a sense, the EMI scheme is an employment version of the Enterprise Investment Scheme (EIS). Whereas the latter is about investments of finance capital, EMI can be seen as being aimed at encouraging human capital investments.

A further element of the scheme aimed particularly at small businesses is a 'light touch' approvals regime. In fact, unlike other share schemes, firms operating EMI do not have to seek scheme approval from the Inland Revenue. Instead, firms simply make awards to individuals in keeping with the rules of the schemes, while information on individual tax returns ensures that the limits for each individual are adhered to. This was designed to keep the bureaucratic burden on small firms to a minimum.[7] It is too early to tell whether EMI will have a major impact on recruitment and retention in SMEs, but the take-up rate so far (over 1000 companies in the year since it was introduced) certainly suggests that it is a popular scheme.

Conclusion

Overall, the evidence suggests that the use of share-based rewards is growing in the SME sector, albeit from a very low base. The current government's policy of promoting such schemes is clearly enjoying some success, though it is far too early to assess whether the objectives behind the policy (e.g. recruitment and retention of experienced managers) are being met. However, it is clear that share schemes are attractive to only a very small segment of the total SME population, for the reasons outlined earlier. Most SMEs do not perceive a need for them, and there are also a host of reasons why share schemes are difficult to operate in typical SMEs. The government has attempted to make share ownership plans more attractive, but it is difficult for the government to alter the prevailing culture of management in SMEs in the short term (though there has been a package of measures aimed at improving management capabilities, such as Business Links). The formalised nature of employee share schemes, especially those aimed at all employees, does not sit easily with the informality and flexibility that are central to the management of SMEs and which are often seen as integral to the appeal of SMEs. So, while we can anticipate further growth in the use of share-based rewards in SMEs, share ownership will remain a minority pursuit in the SME sector.

References

Bacon, N. and Wright, M. (1999) 'Buy-outs and human resource management', *Management Buy-Outs: Quarterly Review from the Centre for Management Buy-Out Research*, Summer.

Bacon, N., Ackers, P., Storey, J. and Coates, D. (1996) 'It's a small world: managing human resources in small firms', *International Journal of Human Resource Management* 7:1, 82–101.

Blair, M. (1995) *Ownership and Control: Rethinking corporate governance for the twenty-first century*. Brookings Institution, Washington, DC.

Centre for Management Buy-Out Research (1998) 'Market overview', *Management Buy-Outs: Quarterly Review from the Centre for Management Buy-Out Research*, Autumn.

Cosh, A. and Hughes, A. (1994) 'Size, financial structure and profitability: UK companies in the 1980s', in A. Hughes and D. Storey (eds) *Finance and the Small Firm*. Routledge, London.

Cox, A. (1999) 'Supporting performance? The role of variable pay systems in medium-sized enterprises in the engineering sector', Manchester: UMIST (unpublished mimeo).

Cully, M., Woodland, S., O'Reilly, A. and Dix, G. (1999) *Britain at Work: as Depicted by the 1998 Workplace Employee Relations Survey*. London, Routledge.

Dundon, T., Grugulis, I. and Wilkinson, A. (2001) 'New management techniques in small and medium-sized enterprises', in T. Redman and A. Wilkinson (eds) *Contemporary Human Resource Management: Text and Cases*. Financial Times/Prentice Hall, Harlow.

Gavron, R., Cowling, M., Holtham, G. and Westhall, A. (1998) *The Entrepreneurial Society*. Institute for Public Policy Research, London.

Gilman, M., Edwards, P., Ram, M. and Arrowsmith, J. (2002) 'Pay determination in small firms in the UK: the case of the response to the National Minimum Wage'. *Industrial Relations Journal*, **33**, 52–67.

Goss, D. (1991) *Small Business and Society*. Routledge, London.

Hansmann, H. (1996) *The Ownership of Enterprise*. Belknap, Cambridge, MA.

HM Treasury (1998) *Consultation in Employee Share Ownership*. HM Treasury, London.

HM Treasury (2001a) *Productivity in the UK: Progress towards a Productive Economy*. HM Treasury, London.

HM Treasury (2001b) *Productivity in the UK: Enterprise and the Productivity Challenge*. HM Treasury, London.

HM Treasury (2001c) *Institutional Investment in the UK: A Review*. HM Treasury, London.

Industrial Relations Services (2001) 'E-reward: a share of the losses', *Pay and Benefits Bulletin*, **526** (August).

Involvement and Participation Association (2001) *HR Strategy in the New Economy*. Involvement and Participation Association and Equity Incentives Ltd, London.

Leadbetter, C. (1998) 'Who will own the knowledge economy?' *Political Quarterly* 69:4, 375–385.

Pendleton, A. (2001) *Employee Ownership, Participation and Governance: A Study of ESOPs in the UK*. Routledge, London.

Rainnie, A. (1989) *Industrial Relations in Small Firms: Small isn't Beautiful*. Routledge, London.

Ram, M. (1991) 'The dynamics of workplace relations in the small firm', *International Small Business Journal*, 4:4, 42–60.

Scase, R. (1995) 'Employment relations in small firms', in P. Edwards (ed.) *Industrial Relations: Theory and Practice in Britain*. Blackwell, Oxford.

Smith, S. (1988) 'On the incidence of profit and equity sharing: theory and an application to the high tech. sector', *Journal of Economic Behaviour and Organization*, **9**, 45–58.

Stanworth, J. and Gray, C. (1991) *Bolton Twenty Years On*. Small Business Research Trust, London.

Storey, J. (1994) *Understanding the Small Business Sector*. Routledge, London.

Weitzman, M. and Kruse, D. (1990) 'Profit sharing and productivity', in A. Blinder (ed.) *Paying for Productivity: A Look at the Evidence*. Brookings Institution, Washington, DC.

Williamson, O. (1985) *The Economic Institutions of Capitalism: Firms, Markets, Relational Contracting*. Free Press, New York.

Wright, M. and Robbie, K. (1996) 'The investor-led buy-out', *Long Range Planning* **29**:5, 691–703.

Notes

1. This part of the WERS analysis focuses on firms as well as workplaces.
2. This information kindly supplied by the Inland Revenue.
3. The empirical literature on UK cooperatives suggests this is not a major problem in practice. Cooperative members tend to under-pay themselves.
4. Freeserve, Thus, Baltimore Technologies, Psion, Nycomed Amersham, Celltech Group, EMAP and Capital Group were admitted to the FTSE 100 in March 2000.
5. The position until April 1999 had been that employers' NICs were payable on the discounts on market rates given to unapproved share options at the time of grant. The government then shifted the point of taxation to the gains at the time of exercise.
6. The Share Incentives Plan and the 1989 QUEST legislation provide capital gains tax rollover relief to owners who sell substantial portions of equity to qualifying employee benefits trusts and reinvest the proceeds in other business assets.
7. However, there is some anxiety among SMEs that, in the absence of prior approval by the Inland Revenue, they cannot be sure that they have not violated the rules of the scheme.

Chapter 8

MANAGING CREATIVITY AND COMPETITIVE ADVANTAGE IN SMEs: EXAMINING CREATIVE, NEW MEDIA FIRMS

Mark Banks, Meg Elliott and Julia Owen

Introduction

The chapter analyses the definition and management of creativity and how the creative resources of small and medium-sized enterprises (SMEs) can define their competitive advantage. The notion of creativity is increasingly being perceived as a major influence and determinant of economic success and, as such, is a major issue of concern for managers (Rickards, 1999; Davis and Scase, 2000). The shift towards a more service, design and information-led economy (Castells, 1996) requires SMEs to become more flexible, adaptable and innovation intensive – the nurturing of 'soft' skills, such as creativity, is seen as being a vital part of this process. Using the 'creative industries' as an example, we will attempt to show how managing creativity is, however, far from straightforward and that defining, mobilising and managing creativity to enhance competitive advantage is possible, but may be problematic and uncertain. We present data to support and develop our argument from two projects we have recently completed which focused upon gaining a greater understanding of management development within SMEs in the creative industries.

We argue that a managerial perspective such as that described by the resource-based theorists (Grant, 1991; Christensen, 1996) offers a more potent model and approach for the effective management of creativity necessary in securing competitive advantage in SMEs. Much of the literature around the capabilities approach is, however, set within the context of large firms. More recent research (Yu, 2001) uses this approach to explore the 'exceptional attributes' or 'resources' of small firms which allow them to sustain a competitive advantage. Yet, as we will show, managers of SMEs in the creative industry sector do not uniformly build on these 'distinctive intangible assets' (Yu, p. 187) or subscribe to this view as crucial to securing competitive advantage. Many of the managers interviewed saw competitive advantage arising out of, or directly attributable to, formal managerial activities, which involved strategic, top-down decision-making about the goals and objectives of an organisation. For those managers who advocate this more classical perspective on securing competitive advantage, the crucial issue is the matching and fit of internal resources with their own, and the firm's, strategic goals. We offer examples to demonstrate the differing extent to which managers perceive the organisation's internal resources as inherent to securing the firm's 'creative' competitive advantage. We also explore different emphases in managerial approach and the use of formal and informal organisational mechanisms and routines which may enable or constrain the development of these resources over time. In our conclusions we show that attempts at harnessing and directing what is generally perceived to be such an elusive and, at times, ephemeral concept as 'creativity' can often result in tensions and conflict, in that there is an inherent mismatch between the organisation's 'creative' skills and resources and managerial intention and goals. If creativity is to be effectively realised for competitive advantage, much closer attention needs to be paid to understanding how creativity exists as an array of contextual and unique company resources and relationships, not simply as a commodity which can be acquired in the marketplace and factored in at will to defined stages in the production process.

Creativity and its Uses

Whilst there is increasing concern to account for the role of creativity in the management process (Stacey 1996; Rickards 1999), there remains little consensus on how to define and mobilise this enigmatic resource. Creativity is often seen as a psychological phenomenon, an aspect of behaviour; for others it is an outcome of social processes, embedded and realised in communication and collective activity (Davis and Scase, 2000). Concepts such as innovation and problem-solving are often conflated with creativity – yet creativity is perhaps more directly concerned with generating ideas, while innovation is more concerned with the actions and outputs of those ideas (Higgins and Morgan, 2000). Neither is creativity wholly the same as problem-solving: while creativity may contain problem-solving elements, the former is about taking action to bring something into being, the latter about taking action to make something go away (Fritz, 1989, cited in Higgins and Morgan, 2000). But it is inevitable that definitions of creativity vary – indeed, our data and research experiences bear this out. What is perhaps more important is how firms develop and make use of this resource for company development and growth.

How is creativity defined and utilised for competitive advantage? Whilst it is commonly thought to reside in such hazy activities such as 'thinking outside the box' or 'thinking the unthinkable', others have tried to more systematically pin down the means to mobilise creativity. For example, Tan (1998) identifies 'dispositional' theories whereby creativity is seen to be the possession of key individuals with unique capacities for creative action. To tap into this resource, managers can devise criteria that identify the 'creatives', or devise selection procedures to identify creative candidates for the company (Singh, 1996). There is a widespread belief that by 'freeing up' the creative individual – even the outsider, the non-conformist or the eccentric (Shirley, 1997; Rickards, 1999) – firms can realise a unique competitive advantage. Others have concentrated on devising team-based theories of creativity, whereby (through structured intervention) firms can collectively identify and harness creative potential. It has become increasingly common for firms to ensure that some or all of their employees are given instruction in formal training programmes or structured techniques to enhance creativity in their organisations – for example, Edward de Bono's (1982) lateral thinking, Tony Buzan's (1995) mind-mapping techniques and Isaksen's (1989) creative problem-solving process spring to mind here (see McFadzean, 1998).

Why has creativity become so important? We argue that the fundamental shift from a mode of production dominated by industrial activity to one dominated by post-industrial, service-led activity can explain the new emphasis on creativity in the business context. Long-term structural changes associated with the shift from 'Fordist' to 'post-Fordist' economies (Amin, 1994) have led to the growth of service and design-led, information-rich companies which work within a new 'flexible' mode of production (Harvey, 1989; Lash and Urry, 1994). Here the margins of a firm's competitiveness increasingly depend on the generation and exploitation of new products, new knowledge and a commitment to total flexibility. This transformation has impacted on all sectors, and successful firms are those that are research-, development- and innovation-intensive, highly tuned to market shifts, and capable of swift manoeuvre – in short, they are seen to be proactive and *creative* firms. In this 'creative age' (Bentley, 2000), firms across all sectors and sizes now place more emphasis on developing their creative and innovative capabilities, in order to stay cutting-edge and ahead of the pack (Lash and Urry, 1994; Scott 2000). Creativity is part of that bank of 'soft' assets that firms must employ to realise their potential – alongside other subjective attributes such as imagination, intuition and play (Higgins and Morgan, 2000).

In order to examine the role of creativity in enhancing competitive advantage, we need to identify firms or sectors where creativity is both visible and accessible. While our aim is to offer some general observations on the role of creativity as a competitive asset, we need to pinpoint cases where creativity and creative management is both pronounced and amenable to analysis. To this end, we have chosen to examine creativity in the context of SMEs in the so-called 'creative indus-tries' – a sector in which creativity clearly exhibits a strong influence at the levels of management and organisational practices (Banks *et al.*, 2000, 2003). The sector is chosen specifically to reveal the complexities of dealing with the creativity prob-lem, not because the sector is necessarily representative of SMEs more generally. We feel it is particularly pertinent to examine the creative industries, first, because we assume that creativity is most likely to be found within this sector, and, sec-ond, because we hypothesise that the intellectual and practical resources required to manage and mobilise creativity may be more advanced here than in other sectors. Whilst we acknowledge the dangers of generalising from single cases, we hope to generate findings and observations that could be tested or examined by researchers interested in the role of creativity in other industry sectors.

The Creative Industries

The creative industries have emerged as part of the shift towards more 'symbolic', 'informational' and 'knowledge-based' modes of production (Castells, 1996; Scott, 2000). In the UK, the Department of Culture, Media and Sport's Creative Industries Task Force (CITF) and its 1998 *Creative Industries Mapping Document,* identified 13 sub-sectors as comprising the creative industries.[1] In 2001 an update of this report claimed that over £112 billion of revenue are generated by a sector that now employs over 1.3 million people, the majority in SMEs. The CITF defines creative industries thus: '. . . those industries which have their origin in individual creativity, skill and talent and which have a potential for wealth and job creation through the generation and exploitation of intellectual property' (DCMS, 2001, p. 5).

We might expect that the creative industries would emphasise the importance of enabling and managing creativity in the generation of new products, increased productivity and competitive advantage. Yet, surprisingly, little work has been done to identify just *how* and *why* creative industries are creative. The DCMS definition locates creativity within the creative individual – not the creative firm or the creative process – yet, as our review will indicate, it is far from clear-cut just who possesses creativity, where it is found and how it is mobilised and managed. We may assume that 'creativity' is out there – but what it looks like is less clear. The creative activities of this sector ought to be more thoroughly investigated at the level of everyday practice – only then might we learn more about how creativity is defined and mobilised for competitive advantage.

To do this, we feel that creativity is best conceptualised, not as a commodity or resource freely available in the marketplace to be strategically 'bought in' as and when required, but as a key and integral – but often latent or underdeveloped – internal human resource. This reflects some of the concerns identified by resource-based theorists (Christensen, 1996). Essentially, the approach highlights the unique components and skills embedded within firms and individuals as crucial to securing the firm's competitive advantage. It emphasises the importance of managers understanding and developing processes by which these resources might be supported and enhanced over time. We argue that this approach offers a model that can be applied within the context of small firms to increase our understanding of how creativity can be more effectively fostered and managed to secure their competitive advantage.

The Resource-based View: Key Issues and Themes

The resource-based view challenges the more traditional, classical perspective on securing competitive advantage and market share through the processes of rational decision making and planning. Whittington (1993) describes how the processes and strategies within the classical perspective are: '. . . presented as emerging from a conscious, rationalistic, decision-making process fully formulated, explicit and articulated, a set of orders for others, lower down the organisation to carry out.'

However, in an environment where product cycles are shortening, technologies are converging and industry structures are becoming more diffuse, a growing belief has been that the focus for building competitive advantage lies in the development and fostering of distinctive internal capabilities that are relatively enduring. The resource-based view of the firm argues that an organisation's competitive advantage comes from the unique capabilities of its resources, which not only define but also generate an organisation's strategic capacity. Its origins lie with Edith Penrose's (1959) economic theory of the competitive advantages to be gained from exploiting the heterogeneity of firms. This heterogeneity can best be sustained (and is at its most inimitable) when based upon the core competencies and skills of its resources (both human and otherwise), since other factors of production are replicable and substitutable. Resource-based theorists such as Grant (1991, 1998) and Boxall (1996) argue that management strategies purporting to maximise opportunities are constrained by imperfections of the market and the fact that not all resources necessary for securing competitive advantage can be found and bought in markets. Furthermore, in an environment where customer preferences are ephemeral and the pace of technological change is accelerating, simply having an external focus does not provide a secure foundation for formulating long-term strategy. It is therefore argued that an organisation's competitive advantage lies in what is unique and embedded in its resources; that is, its core distinctive capabilities. These distinct capabilities inform, shape and mould but also generate an organisation's strategic capacity. Grant (1998) offers a cogent definition of the relationship between resources and capabilities as the constituents of competitive advantage:

> There is a key distinction between resources and capabilities. Resources are inputs into the production process – they are the basic units of analysis ... but on their own, few resources are productive. Productive activity requires the cooperation and coordination of team resources. A capability is the capacity for a team of resources to perform some task or activity. While resources are the sources of a firm's capabilities, capabilities are the main source of its competitive advantage. (Grant, 1998, p. 177)

For small firms to successfully compete with larger organisations they must possess distinctive capabilities and assets. Yu (2001) suggests that the most distinctive intangible assets possessed by small firms are 'entrepreneurship' and a 'simple capital structure'. 'Entrepreneurial alertness and judgement' are, Yu argues, particularly crucial assets of a small firm, because entrepreneurship is inherently non-contractible and immutable. Given that the (human) resources of small firms often consist of entrepreneur/owners and a small number of employees, the entrepreneur's vision and influence on the direction of the firm is often greater than in larger firms that make collective decisions and communicate via a hierarchy. Furthermore, Yu argues, in general, small firms have better personal links, a more unified culture and a stronger collective identity. Owners of small firms tend to employ staff whom they perceive hold similar cultural or knowledge bases, thus allowing more straightforward synergies in internal communication and the shared understanding of firm-specific routines. The specific form of idiosyncratic human relationships in small firms can therefore facilitate organisational efficiency, contributing to flexibility and competitive advantage (Monteverde 1997; Yu 2001).

Creating capabilities involves, however, complex patterns of coordination and collaborations between people and other resources over time. As with individuals, the skills and capabilities of an organisation are learned and enhanced through experience and repetition and developing what Grant (1998) and Nelson and Winter (1982) refer to as 'organisational routines'. These are described by Nelson and Winter as 'regular and predictable patterns of behaviour' (p. 97). They are defined by the work context, and influence both current conceptions of appropriate action and future choices about change. As Jones and Craven (2001) point out, our understanding of routines is hampered by the fact that they are emergent, tend to be associated with many actors, and are often reflected in tacit knowledge. In their in-depth study exploring the social processes involved in the emergence of new organisational routines in a manufacturing SME, Jones and Craven highlight how these routines influence the ability of organisational actors to respond to unfamiliar situations by modifying existing routines or developing new ways of working, and point out that innovation occurs through the creation of appropriate organisational routines. Our data indicate that organisational routines are important in influencing creative activity in the SMEs in our study and that there was considerable variation in the extent that they constrained or enabled creativity. Furthermore, we suggest that where managerial approaches and firm-specific routines reflected increased control they dissipated those capabilities that might be considered particularly important in enabling the small firm to be competitive.

Managing Creativity

If the argument is that creativity is a key and unique internal resource for small firms in the creative industries and one which must be effectively mobilised in order to ensure competitive advantage, we identified the following as being the fundamental questions to pose in analysing the data from our work with SMEs in the creative industries sector:

- How is creativity defined in the context of a creative industry SME?
- What value is placed on creativity as an internal resource and to what extent do managers encourage the essential collaborations and cooperation necessary for generating creative capabilities?
- Are managers guilty of chasing what *they* believe to be the key opportunities, out in the marketplace, and often demoting the skills and resources within the organisation – which, if encouraged and enhanced, would in themselves generate the capabilities necessary for securing competitive advantage?

It should be noted that questions such as these have begun to be addressed elsewhere. In *Managing Creativity* (2000), Davis and Scase explore approaches to managing creativity in creative industry organisations. They discuss how creativity is managed within different kinds of organisation – from the 'formal/hierarchical' approach of 'cultural bureaucracies' (such as the BBC) through to the 'informal and collegial' management mechanisms found in 'network organisations' such as broadcast and new media micro and small enterprises. Throughout they argue that management in creative industries – at all scales – is 'less clearly defined', managerial identities are 'underplayed' and management proceeds not through formal control or principles of scientific management but through what Davis and Scase term 'mutual adjustment' (see Mintzberg, 1983); a kind of informal negotiated consent. This approach is necessary because of the need for flexibility in an uncertain and fast-moving marketplace: 'Mutual adjustment is a means of coordinating inputs into the work process from those with a wide variety of talents and skills. Organised around projects, these elements are constantly reconstituted so that the organisation can be adaptive and therefore, innovative' (Davis and Scase, 2000, p. 15).

In this way, creativity is seen as an internal resource that can be effectively managed through appropriate 'adjustments' – by necessity, managers must relinquish their status as 'controllers' and become the 'facilitators' of a diverse and often disparate array of skills, aptitudes and abilities. Managers must work to facilitate creativity, defined by Davis and Scase as the ability to tolerate and, indeed, cultivate three key elements:

- autonomy: individuals are encouraged to experiment within their broad roles;
- non-conformity: encouraging non-standard methods and solutions;
- indeterminacy: enable organisational goals to be led by creative practices.

Concerning this third element, Davis and Scase (2000, p. 20) offer this most optimistic analysis: 'Indeed, in many work settings, the goals of the organisation will be shaped by the creative work process, with senior managers having an almost entirely supportive or facilitative function...[t]he creative work process which depends on the interactions of relatively autonomous employees determines the management process rather than vice versa'.

While there is some truth in this, our own research leads us to suggest that it somewhat overplays the extent to which managers are surrendering control – even in creative and cutting-edge 'network organisations'. We further argue that Davis and Scase (2000, p. 147) underestimate the role of workplace conflict in creative organisations: 'The emphasis is on trust, informality, flexibility and cultures of participation...trust and internalised commitment are fundamental ... relations between colleagues are necessarily cooperative and harmonious.'

Our data can confirm this – but only to a limited degree. While we have evidence to support the existence of firms where creativity is allowed to flourish, we also show how processes of 'mutual adjustment' and managing creativity are often marked by managerial control, conflict and uncertainty, and how creativity – even in the creative industries – can often be blocked, inhibited or in some instances eradicated. Our aim is not to disregard or undermine any notion that creative industries can provide a template for other sectors to follow: quite the contrary. Instead, we wish to show that the creativity issue is far from straightforward and unproblematic. Even in a sector where creativity is so central to securing competitive advantage, how creativity is effectively defined, managed and mobilised remains contested and difficult. If we are to take seriously the creativity issue, we must be clear that managing creativity for competitive advantage is not a conflict-free process.

The data are derived from two projects undertaken at MMU[2], both focusing on SMEs operating within the creative sector. The first project, Creative Leadership in Media Enterprises (CLIME), involved initial research to identify the issues for managers in small businesses operating in the creative sector in the north-west of England. This included the sub-sectors of broadcast and 'new' digital media, graphic and fashion design and the music industry. Twenty-three semi-structured interviews were conducted with owner-managers to identify their concerns in relation to change, business growth, collaborative networks and the management of multi-skilled teams. From these interviews four were selected for a company-based action learning and research programme. The second project, Skills for the Missing Industry's Leaders and Enterprises (SMILE), built on and extended information obtained from CLIME, but concentrated solely on creativity/management issues in new media and multimedia enterprises – a growing sub-sector. In-depth interviews were conducted with over 20 SMEs in the region and further data were collected through:

- observation of day-to-day exchanges;
- shadowing employees in everyday interactions and practices;
- attending in-house meetings;
- informal interviews with key employees and members of production teams;
- charting product life-cycles.

In both projects, firms were drawn from a range of sub-sectors including advertising, fashion, popular music, e-learning software, interactive leisure software and publishing. Firms varied from micros operating within a loose collaborative network (nine firms) to a few firms employing over 20 individuals (six firms). Most firms had been in existence between two and ten years (28). Eight had been operating for over ten years. Our specific focus here is one sub-sector, 'new media',[3] the dominant group in our sample over the two projects. The following findings focus on the definition and management of creativity and prevailing perceptions as to the part creativity plays both in terms of production process and securing SME competitive advantage.

How Managers Defined Creativity

The value placed on creativity varied in relation to how it was perceived and defined. The majority of managers interviewed perceived creativity to be a mixture of individual skill and organisational capacity necessary to facilitate innovation in product development and enable effective problem-solving. Managers rarely differentiated between the concepts of innovation and problem-solving; instead definitions of creativity detailed how they were inextricably linked and how they as a firm were devising something 'different' and unique as a solution to a problem. Managers' definitions consistently described how they saw the firm's core business to be the provision of technical solutions to client problems, not simply the production of quality products and services. All quotations in the remainder of this chapter are from managers we interviewed in our study.

On the whole, the managers of new media firms within both advertising and marketing tended to favour definitions of creativity that promoted the performance of key business functions such as marketing and customer relations. One manager said, 'Creativity is in the way "you market", the way you create your markets and secure a share of what is increasingly becoming a highly competitive marketplace.'

Although the concept of creativity was often referred to as a process that arises out of a collaboration between organisational members and the dynamics of team-working, several owner-managers and managers from sales, advertising and marketing backgrounds emphasised their own creative qualities in the areas of client management and played down the role of creativity at other stages of the production process. This often brought them into conflict with other staff who practised a different definition of creativity: 'The client relationship is what's really important – designers come with differing creative skills and ideas but most of it is subsumed by the customer requirements – it's not about fantastic whizzy stuff, it's actually about functionality.'

For firms specialising in the creation and imparting of 'knowledge', such as e-learning, training, business consultancy or management development, creativity also encompassed innovation in relation to the content development and the mechanisms for promoting new knowledge and understanding. In contrast, managers from an art or design background were more inclined to insist on the autonomy and eminence of 'pure' aesthetic creativity and defined it in terms of its distinctiveness from more functional or business elements of the business.

How Managers Managed Creativity

Just as participating managers in our study all defined creativity differently, so there were clear differences in the way creative employees were managed. Variations in the management and facilitation of creativity reflected whether managers identified creativity as being associated with particular individuals and groups or as part of wider social processes. This latter perspective tended to involve greater emphasis on fostering a work environment where mechanisms and routines were introduced to enable individual and group creative activity.

Project teams and team-working are inherent to the sector (Banks *et al.*, 2000; Davis and Scase, 2000). The nature of the work necessitates a diverse range of skills and expertise which a sole individual is unlikely to possess. Collaboration, exchange of ideas and collective problem-solving are generally seen as essential to both the creative and the production process. Only one manager in our study suggested that creativity could not be managed and that creatives needed to be 'left to get on with it'. A significant number of managers, however, particularly those from a human resource management (HRM) background, said how, as managers, they focused on providing 'creative direction' – directing a collaborative process to facilitate creativity – arguing that the 'process itself must be creatively managed'. The research indicated several different approaches to managing creatives.

Managing 'organised looseness'

Of those managers who stressed the importance of fostering and managing the creative process, several were explicit in identifying this as crucially concerned with developing and managing a wide range of disparate skills and collaborations, exchanges and interactions among and between these organisational resources. One manager, describing in detail the process and practices he used to encourage and capture creativity, emphasised the need to be facilitative rather than overly directive or controlling: 'One guy is, in his own estimation, not very creative, but if the problem is defined to him he is actually very creative in coming up with a solution but you've got to define the problem very tightly otherwise he is totally confused.'

Another owner-manager commented: 'You end up with a much more fluid organisation, less hard definitions in terms of people's roles, in terms of work process and work content. What I have to do as a leader is provide support structures and overall direction, not prescriptive procedures.'

Within this approach there appeared to be less concern about enabling the generation of new and alternative ideas and more concern with facilitating the direction of the creative effort so that it didn't dissipate, and met organisational goals. Several owner-managers and managers emphasised that, although direction was important, employee involvement and trust was crucial. This was underpinned by respect rather than control: 'Organisations that aren't prepared to respect their employees, aren't prepared to give them the opportunity to make mistakes, aren't going to grow the right skills or right people.'

Several managers described how, in facilitating and supporting creativity, it was often necessary to introduce challenge, uncertainty and risk through, for example, considering alternative ways of approaching a problem, organising individuals into different groups or using different 'technical' tools to persuade individuals 'to step outside their safety zone' and to encourage them 'to think outside of the box'. To do this, it was important to have 'flexibility in the system' or what was referred to as 'organised looseness'. However, managers had to be mindful that this 'looseness' be compatible with, and capable of integration into, the other organisational and business processes, most crucially the business objectives of customers and clients.

Generally, the research indicated little recognition of the importance of developing individuals as an aspect of building organisational capability. Although we argue that the enhancement of individual capabilities and their contribution to a firm's growth and capacity is crucial to securing business competitiveness, for small businesses which may prefer to subcontract work as and when needed, it is not such a crucial concern. There was, however, a clear distinction between managers operating within this perspective who adopted a more developmental approach to fostering creativity and those who emphasised reviewing performance and achieving targets.

Managerial perspectives and practices appear loose in terms of control, with managers adopting a more facilitative than managerial role. There is a conscious concern to maintain an enabling work environment in which organisational routines support creative activity. Creativity is not limited to a certain group, and the creative process arises out of dynamics within the wider organisation that engage all members (Davis and Scase, 2000; Banks *et al.*, 2003).

Organising and Controlling

Other managers argued that certain types of individuals and groups were, by definition, creative. These managers acknowledged the need to ensure that creativity was harnessed within the production process, but insisted that this had to be 'controlled' and often constrained to ensure realisation of the firm's business objectives and meeting of customer expectations. The challenge is defined as 'directing' and 'focusing' creative activity, with an emphasis on control rather than facilitation. In several of these firms, the owner-manager or a creative director tended to keep tight control over work. Others described how they perceived their role as 'setting the scene' for designers and graphic artists and acting as a 'gate-keeper' between the customer and the creative through 'interpreting' customer requirements.

In this model it was apparent that both formal and informal organisational structures, roles and routines were used to manage and constrain creativity. There was a sense within these firms that, although flexibility within teams was considered crucial, to enable the generation of ideas and their realisation in the production process, overall direction and control of projects and production lay with managers. The definition and allocation of individuals to specialist discipline areas, perceived to reflect areas of expertise and skill, tended to be used to bound creativity, as one manager put it: 'Creatives have to be given certain freedom but within an organised structure.'

While managers (often in graphic design and advertising firms) seemed particularly concerned about the importance of developing an image and identity for the firm and ensuring the firm promoted its creative/design staff, several expressed a tension around delegating responsibility to 'creatives' within the organisation. While it was considered important to maintain an atmosphere of 'openness' and 'transparency' to enable individuals to feel they could make a contribution, several managers highlighted the importance of maintaining an 'appropriate' internal environment. In several of these organisations, established routines reinforced what were considered to be appropriate behaviours. For example, it was accepted that employees should attempt to complete projects on time. This often involved working (at short notice) overtime, weekends and unsocial hours as the job demanded. Also, experimentation and autonomy for the 'creatives' had to be curtailed as often designers would be seen to be 'designing for themselves' and not for the client. Beyond this, the emphasis is on maintaining an almost de-politicised environment where individuals aren't 'hassled' and could focus on their task and the production process. Fitting in to the existing way of doing things is perceived as crucial: '. . . it's about the individual's ability to connect to the organisation, to assimilate with the culture of the organisation.'

Through ensuring that new staff were 'like the others', problems could be filtered out at the start. Disruption is minimised – certain kinds of personal expression and autonomy are tolerated but work is treated as a serious business and the individual 'must conform to the demands of the company or risk being seen as a bad apple'. Within this perspective the processes of managing creativity tend to take place within the implicit (if not explicit) boundaries of constraint and managerial control.

'Laying it on the Line': Rejecting Creativity

A third perspective identified among firms could be described as a 'formal rejection' of any managerial obligation to facilitate or manage creativity. This is not to say that creativity went unrecognised – but that the emphasis in these firms was on attracting and retaining highly qualified 'creative individuals' who had innate and fully realised creative skills that did not need special attention or nurture. Here creativity was accounted for within individual performance evaluation, and achievement of targets using formalised review processes was in evidence. Organisational processes and routines generally emphasised completing tasks within set budgets and time constraints, with creativity being a kind of fixed variable to be factored into the production equation. Managers regarded these controls as internalised and to be accepted without question by employees if they wanted to remain with the firm: 'Everybody has a chance to expand into as much risk as they want to take because you get fired if you screw up or you lose money.'

Within this perspective, organisational success involved delivering the client's requirements within the required constraints. Individual autonomy was tolerated to a degree, but targets and budgets were used to maintain control. The emphasis was on conforming and delivering managerially prescribed targets, or failing and losing one's job. Finally, at the extreme end of this perspective, no recognition was given that the firm was in fact 'creative' or worked in the 'creative sector' – creativity was not part of the discourse or practice of the new media firm.

Discussion

Our research indicates that SMEs in the new media sub-sector vary considerably in their definitions of creativity and the extent to which they recognise creativity as an important contributor to competitive advantage. The majority of owner-managers did consider creativity, regardless of the specificity of its definition or role, as an important but not the primary determinant of organisational success and competitive advantage. Where creativity was valued, most managers in our study emphasised the importance of an organic structure, flexibility, an open culture where employees identified with the objectives of the business, a work environment of high mutual trust and the importance of collaboration and cross-functional communication – all of which would appear to contribute to innovation and competitive advantage. The data, however, indicate considerable variation in approaches to managing creativity.

Those managers operating in what we have described as a model of 'organised looseness' usually had a clear view of the direction the business should take but seemed prepared to manage a disparate array of skills (Davis and Scase, 2000). The emphasis is on facilitating rather than controlling. Within this model, owner-managers foster a climate and firm-specific routines that reflect some of the following characteristics associated with enabling creativity: a respect for diversity, open-mindedness in the encouragement of flexibility and involvement, the ability to stimulate the expression of ideas, and a willingness to give clear objectives and relevant, developmental feedback (Majaro, 1988). Attention is given to stimulating creativity, encouraging individuals and teams to own problems, tolerating mistakes and risk-taking. Considerable effort is made to create informal and formal mechanisms to enable individuals to get involved and contribute in suggesting new ideas and alternative ways of working, thus challenging existing routines and establishing new ones (Jones and Craven, 2001). Employees appeared more actively involved in contributing to the organisation's strategy in an incremental way through a more enabling alignment of their actions with organisational goals. We would argue that this model emphasises the 'distinctive capabilities' that enable small firms to be successful (Jones and Craven, 2001; Yu, 2001).

For many small companies in our research, however, creativity was confined to specific individuals and groups, and needed to be 'organised and controlled'. Although managers acknowledged its importance in the production process, the language and actions associated with creativity are more indicative of control. In this model the owner-manager or creative director often kept a tight control over all project work. Employee involvement, particularly around the generation of ideas, was limited to specific, task-related contributions. Organisational routines reinforced what were considered to be appropriate individual behaviours, group activities and established legitimate ways of doing things within the firm. For example, temporal limits were often placed on the generation of ideas, to discourage designers from spending too much time perfecting an idea at the onset of a project. The creatives were often split up or monitored more closely than their technical or managerial counterparts. There was little in these firms to suggest an awareness of the benefits of challenging or exploring alternative routines or involving employees in the process. Rather, managers in these firms described the explicit expectation that staff should adapt to the expected way of working and commented that they often resorted to removing 'bad apples' either temporarily or permanently. In this model, the congruence between strategy, structure, people and culture (Tushman and O'Reilly, 1997) is through reliance on controls, incentives or attempts to place creative processes into systemic sequences that emphasise targets.

Finally, the data indicate that despite the emphasis placed on information and knowledge exchange in the creative work environment, for many, the focus tends to be task-related, solution-driven and short-term. In our third type of managerial approach, firm-specific routines controlled and limited communication synergies and the way individuals were actively able to contribute to the creativity of the business. If recognised at all, creativity was seen as a calculable, knowable and rationally manageable given. We would suggest that this model at best neglects, and at worst constrains, the ability of these small firms to make the most effective use of their capabilities. Generally we found the size and maturity of company to be important indicators of creative 'freedom'. The smaller the company, the more scope and freedom owner-managers perceived they had to take creative risks. Firms working in new media art, graphic design or education-based enterprises tended to consciously prioritise 'staying small' to help maintain creativity, ensure employee involvement and maximise flexibility. As firms expanded, creativity generally becomes less central and firm-specific routines tend to emphasise managerial control and constraint.

Our research has several implications for SMEs generally. Even within SMEs in a creative sector, where it might be anticipated that attention is given to ensuring that managerial style, routines and mechanisms are enabling rather than constraining, there would seem to be considerable variation in how this is operationalised in practice. Similarly, there is variation in the emphasis on control apparent in managerial style, the way the work is organised and coordinated, the degree and nature of employee involvement and the influence of organisational routines. We would argue that the managerial approach reflected in the model characterised as 'organised looseness', builds on those 'distinctive capabilities' that enable SMEs to be competitive with other larger firms. As small firms mature and grow, however, there is likely to be greater pressure to increase control. At this point, owner-managers need to pay particular attention to encouraging formal and informal mechanisms and routines that allow adaptation and continuous learning (Senge, 1990; Jones and Craven, 2001).

Conclusion

Our research identified differing approaches to managing creativity within SMEs in the sector. The culture of these firms is often described as cooperative and collaborative, empowered and facilitative, team-based, conducive to creativity, solving problems, reaching 'solutions' and so on. The reality in many of these firms, however, may involve routine and control. In this sense, many managers do not appear to be willing to relinquish their status as controllers and become facilitators of a diverse array of skills. Furthermore, the encouragement of autonomy, non-conformity and indeterminacy in a harmonious and cooperative work environment as suggested by Davis and Scase (2000) would not seem to be the norm. In reality, creativity is more typically constrained by inflexibility of budgets, deadline cultures and operational time regimes, and little attention is paid to building individual capability for improved organisational performance.

If creativity is to be harnessed for competitive advantage it is essential that firms move beyond the notion that creativity is easy to define, is unproblematic and can be factored in as and when required. Interventions designed to nurture creativity need to engage more fully with how creativity is defined, mobilised and managed in specific firm contexts. The politics of creativity – in terms of who holds it and how it is contested – need further investigation. Creativity should be seen as an internal resource – a capacity held and negotiated by the individuals and culture of the firm itself – and one that can only be mobilised for competitive advantage through detailed analysis and self-reflexive critique; it can be a difficult and painful process. Our findings from one sub-sector of the creative industries show that, even in a sector where creativity is widely assumed to be crucial for competitive advantage, considerable variation exists in managerial attitudes and understanding of creativity and its perceived centrality to the production process. We would therefore suggest that broader cross-sector or sector-specific interventions which assume that encouraging more creativity a good thing need to recognise that creativity is a much more complex and multifaceted phenomenon than hitherto assumed. The relationship between creativity and competitive advantage requires closer scrutiny in order to ensure that firms are able to usefully identify and mobilise creative resources to expedite growth and competitive advantage.

References

Amin, A. (1994) *Post-Fordism: A Reader*. Blackwell, Oxford.

Banks, M., Lovatt, A., O'Connor, J. and Raffo, C. (2000) 'Risk and trust in the cultural industries', *Geoforum*, **31**:4, 453–464.

Banks, M., Calvey, D., Owen, J. and Russell, D. (2003) 'Where the art is: defining and managing creativity in new media SMEs', *Creativity and Innovation Management* (forthcoming).

Bentley, T. (2000) *The Creative Age*. Demos, London.

de Bono, E. (1982) *Lateral Thinking for Management*. Pelican, Harmondsworth.

Boxall, P. (1996) 'The strategic HRM debate and the resource-based view of the firm', *Human Resource Management Journal*, **6**:3.

Buzan, T. (1995) *The Mindmap Book*. BBC Books, London.

Castells, M. (1996) *The Rise of the Network Society*. Blackwell, Oxford.

Christensen, J. (1996) 'Analysing the technology base of the firm: a multidimensional resource and competence perspective', in N.J. Foss and C. Knudsen (eds) *Toward a Competence Theory of the Firm*. Routledge, London.

Davis, H. and Scase, R. (2000) *Managing Creativity: The Dynamics of Work and Organisation*. Open University Press, Buckingham.

Department of Culture, Media and Sport (2001) *Creative Industries Mapping Document*. DCMS, London.

Fritz, R. (1989) *The Path of Least Resistance: Learning to Become the Creative Force in your own Life*. Fawcett Columbine, New York.

Grant, R. (1991) 'The resource-based theory of competitive advantage: implications for strategy formulation', *California Management Review* **33**:2, 114–135.

Grant, R. (1998) 'The resource-based theory of competitive advantage: implications for strategy formulation', in S. Segal-Horn (ed.) *The Strategy Reader*. Open University and Blackwell, Milton Keynes.

Harvey, D. (1989) *The Condition of Postmodernity*. Blackwell, Oxford.

Higgins, M. and Morgan, J. (2000) 'The role of creativity in planning: "the creative practitioner"', *Planning Practice and Research*, **15**: 117–127.

Isaksen, S.G. (1989) *Creative Problem Solving: a Process for Creativity*. Centre for Studies in Creativity, Buffalo, New York.

Jones, O. and Craven, M. (2001) 'Beyond the routine: innovation management and the teaching company scheme', *Technovation*, **21**, 261–279.

Lash, S. and Urry, J. (1994) *Economies of Signs and Space*. Sage, London.

Majaro, S. (1988) *The Creative Gap: Managing Ideas for Profit*. Longman, London.

McFadzean, E. (1998) 'The creativity continuum: towards a classification of problem solving techniques', *Creativity and Innovation Management*, **7**:3 131–139.

Mintzberg, H. (1983) *Structures in Five: Designing Effective Organizations*. Prentice Hall, Englewood Cliffs, NJ.

Monteverde, K. (1997) 'Mapping the competence boundaries of the firm: applying resource-based strategic analysis', In H. Thomas *et al.* (eds) *Strategy, Structure and Style*. John Wiley, Chichester.

Nelson, R.R. and Winter, S.G. (1982) *An Evolutionary Theory of Economic Change*. Harvard University Press, Cambridge, MA.

Penrose, E. (1959) *The Theory of the Growth of the Firm*. Blackwell, Oxford.

Rickards, T. (1999) *Creativity and the Management of Change*. Blackwell, Oxford.

Scott, A.J. (2000) *The Cultural Economy of Cities*. Sage, London.

Senge, P.M. (1990) 'The leader's new work: building learning organizations', *Sloan Management Review*, Autumn, 7–23.

Shirley, D. (1997) *Managing Creativity: A Practical Guide to Inventing, Developing and Producing Innovative Products*. See www.managingcreativity.com.

Singh, B. (1996) 'The role of personality versus biographical factors in creativity', *Psychological Studies*, **31**, 90–92.

Stacey, R. (1996) *Complexity and creativity in organizations*. Berrett-Koehler, San Francisco.

Tan, G. (1998) 'Managing creativity in organizations: a total systems approach', *Creativity and Innovation Management*, **7**:1, 23–31.

Tushman, M.L. and O'Reilly, C. (1997) *Winning through Innovation: A Practical Guide to Leading Organizational Change and Renewal*. Harvard Business School Press, Boston, MA.

Whittington, R. (1993) *What is Strategy and Does it Matter?* Routledge, London.

Yu, T. Fu-Lai (2001) 'Towards a capabilities perspective of the small firm', *International Journal of Management Reviews*, **3**:3, 185–197.

Notes

1. Advertising, architecture, arts and antique markets, crafts, design, designer fashion, film, interactive leisure software, music, performing arts, publishing, software, and television and radio.

2. Both CLIME and SMILE were partly sponsored under the ESF Adapt programme and undertaken by multidisciplinary teams led by the Centre for Employment Research, part of Manchester Institute for Telematics and Employment Research (MITER) at Manchester Metropolitan University.

3. A contested term but one we use to refer to firms involved in the production of Internet-based designs, services and applications. This may include educational and training materials, business and systems software, computer and video games, advertising and marketing materials, and digital art.

Chapter 9

INNOVATION IN SMEs: INTRAPRENEURS AND NEW ROUTINES

Oswald Jones

Introduction

Kurt Lewin (1947) is attributed with initiating the terms 'change agent' and 'action research' in his quest to unite scientific inquiry with democratic methods. The first definition is credited to Lippitt *et al.* (1958, p. 10): 'The planned change that originates in a decision to make a deliberate effort to improve the system and to obtain the help of an outside agent in making this improvement. We call this outside agent a change agent.' Bennis (1964, p. 306) advanced the concept of change agents by defining them as professionals that, on the whole, 'have been trained and hold doctorates in the behavioural sciences' (see Bennis *et al.*, 1969). According to Beckhard (1969, p. 101) change agent refers to 'people, either inside or outside the organisation, who are providing technical, specialist or consulting assistance in the management of a change effort.' Writers on organisational change generally present different interpretations of the term: some describe change agents as those who aid others 'with their *processes* of problem-solving and change, without themselves becoming involved in its content' (Dale, 1974, p. 102). According to Rogers and Shoemaker (1971, p. 35) 'a change agent is a professional who influences innovation decisions in a direction deemed desirable by a change agency.' One of the most influential views is that a change agent's 'primary role is to deliberately intervene in social systems' to facilitate social change (Tichy, 1975, p. 772). Havelock and Havelock (1973, p. 60) argue that there are four distinct roles which change agents adopt: catalyst, solution giver, process helper or resource linker. Initiators and facilitators of change, whether they act alone or a part of a team, can be grouped into four categories: external pressure groups, internal pressure groups, organisational development consultants and internal change agents or consultants (Duncan, 1978). Others such as Beer (1980) use the terms 'manager', 'change agent' and 'consultant' interchangeably in referring to individuals responsible for generating and leading organisational change. One of the most widely quoted authors uses the terms 'change master' and 'corporate entrepreneur' in her work on organisational change (Kanter, 1983, 2000), while Cummings and Worley (1997) equate change agent with 'OD (organisational development) practitioners' in their work on the change process.

Whether they are internal or external, change agents need to identify key stakeholders and accept 'ownership of change' (Leigh and Walters, 1998). Internal change agents have the advantages of being familiar with systems, knowing where power lies and understanding norms within the system (Greiner and Schein, 1988). Some argue that CEOs play a leading role in encouraging innovation and change (Stein and Pinchot, 1998). Others (Bird, 1992; Hussey, 1998) provide practical guides to effective change leadership and change. Hartley *et al.* (1997, p. 62) state that literature on change agents 'has tended to produce idealised lists of skills rather than detailed studies of the actual roles, activities and performance of change agents in practice.' It is also evident that the majority of the change agent literature focuses on external consultants, particularly when action research is employed (Eden and Huxham, 1996).

My objective in this chapter is to examine the role of change agents in developing organisational practices conducive to innovation. Empirical data are drawn from two longitudinal studies of innovation in mature firms. MFD is a medium-sized manufacturing company based in a small town in north Wales. A range of new technologies were introduced into the company over a three-year period and these have been utilised to develop new products, improve manufacturing processes and improve organisational communication. Change in MFD was initiated by the owner, who was concerned about a decline in MoD (Ministry of Defence) contracts. The second firm, RSL, which was founded in 1954 to produce a unique office-filing product known as the Rotary Vertical, has two sites employing about 70 people and manufactures office supply equipment. The main site, in Birmingham, manufactures a variety of sheet manila files, folders and wallets and also houses an increasing important print department which now accounts for 20 per cent of turnover. Sheet metal products such as cabinets and trolleys are manufactured at the Bristol site. The chapter begins with a discussion of the 'innovation process'. This is followed by an examination of literature associated with entrepreneurial networks and intrapreneurship. The research methods are briefly outlined, and then activities in the two companies are analysed and discussed.

The Innovation Process

Although the general SME literature is 'large and diverse', treatment of innovation is 'underwhelming, both theoretically and methodologically' (Hoffman *et al.*, 1997, p. 42). However, a number of recent literature reviews have been carried out including the work of Hoffman *et al.* (1997) who identify links between SME innovation and profitability. Vossen (1998) provides a brief summary of small firms' innovation strengths and weaknesses. The relationship between competitive advantage and SME 'capabilities' is the subject of Yu's (2001) literature review.

This resource-based approach stresses the importance of entrepreneurial vision and the need to build organisational flexibility. Although Tidd (2001) does not focus on SMEs, he discusses a range of mechanisms for measuring both innovation output and organisational performance which are relevant to smaller firms (see Tidd *et al.*, 2001). A recent study of innovation (Barnett and Storey, 2000, p. 319) reported on detailed interviews with SME managers in which three narratives were identified: reconfiguring customer relations, organisational evolution and 'the central part played by human resource development'. A more consultant-oriented approach to SME innovation is outlined in a book from the European Commission (1999) which sets out ten innovation management techniques (IMTs).

It is now generally accepted that innovation is a process rather than a single event. The most complex mapping of the innovation process is based on seventeen years of research carried out by the Minnesota Innovation Research Programme (MIRP). Unfortunately, the studies were almost entirely based on large, high-technology firms and the process model developed by Van de Ven and his colleagues (1999) is inappropriate for the majority of SMEs in which new product development is likely to be less complex. Nevertheless, given the depth of information acquired by MIRP researchers it would be arrogant to suggest that there are no lessons for smaller firms. Three factors stand out as being worthy of consideration for those managing innovation in SMEs. First, once the 'gestation' period is over it is essential that the innovation process is guided by careful plans and the allocation of appropriate resources. Second, no matter how careful the planning process, there will be setbacks and it is likely that criteria will change as projects progress. Third, even in large, well-resourced firms project participation is generally fluid rather than fixed (Van de Ven *et al.*, 1999, p. 44): 'In almost all cases studied by the MIRP team, personnel on the innovation teams only worked part-time, experienced high turnover rates and although technically competent, lacked experience in innovation.'

This should reassure those responsible for managing innovation in SMEs that many of the problems they face also apply to larger firms. Another approach to the innovation process is described in a study of the development of CAPM (computer-aided production management) technology (Robertson *et al.*, 2000). Some recent attempts have been made to reconcile the role of individual agents with organisational structures during the innovation process (Jones *et al.*, 2000; Edwards, 2000).

Despite the acknowledged importance of innovation to national competitiveness and the significant role played by SMEs in most developed economies there has, according to Atherton and Hannon (2001), been a 'paucity of research' related to how innovation can be managed in smaller firms. Where studies of the SME sector have been carried out, there has been a tendency to concentrate on 'product development' rather than trying to understand 'less tangible aspects of the small business, such as building capacity or developing awareness' (Atherton and Hannon, 2001, p. 277). The authors attempt to remedy this omission by reporting on five detailed case studies, utilising in-depth, semi-structured interviews with owner-managers, which produced a 'general process framework for innovation in smaller businesses' (p. 280). An action-research approach was then utilised to verify the framework by piloting innovation programmes in a further 16 small firms. As a result of this work, Atherton and Hannon modified their original

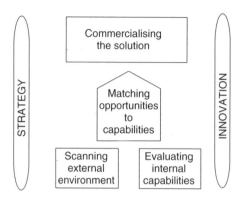

FIGURE 9.1   The innovation process

framework to produce a model which has three distinct phases: building blocks, developing innovative responses and commercialisation (Figure 9.1).

Figure 9.1 is a simplified version of Atherton and Hannon's original model in which, for example, 'internal capabilities' contains five factors ranging from 'technical know-how' to 'personal success formula'. Although Atherton and Hannon ignore key UK contributors to the innovation literature such as Dodgson and Rothwell (1993) their model is useful in conceptualising the important activities associated with such organisations becoming more effective in managing innovation.

Freel (1999, 2000) used data from a postal questionnaire to investigate the barriers to innovation in 238 manufacturing SMEs based in the West Midlands. Drawing on the work of Rothwell (1984, 1989) Freel suggests that there are four constraints on the ability of SMEs to innovate: finance, management and marketing, labour, and information. Evidence from the study indicated that innovative firms found it difficult to access external finance and often had to rely on overdrafts to fund product development. In addition, owner-managers in many firms were unaware of long-term equity finance, which was compounded by the West Midlands being a net exporter of venture capital (Murray, 1997). More positively, innovative firms in the sample were much more likely to have established contacts with Business Links/TECs (Training and Enterprise Councils) and universities than less innovative firms. Also, in many firms managers had tried to develop internal competences by improving in-house technical and marketing skills (Freel, 1999, p. 77). Freel goes on to suggest that there is a need for training courses to be developed which address the specific problems of SMEs (see Gibb, 1997): 'The tendency towards delivering large firm marketing courses to small firms with the attendant prescriptive solutions and unrealistic resource requirements must give way to a more flexible approach.'

One of the most systematic examinations of innovation in SMEs (Cobbenhagen, 2000) utilises resource-based theory which stresses the way in which internal factors including knowledge, skills, patents and brands are combined in unique ways by means of managerial capabilities (Grant, 1998). This combination of resource and capabilities leads to the creation of core competencies which help establish the firm's competitive advantage (Prahalad and Hamel, 1990). The study was based on 63 Dutch SMEs in a range of sectors including chemicals, electronics, insurance, banks and consultancies. As far as possible, firms were selected in 'matched pairs' of 'front-runners' and 'pack members' based on similarities of size, sector and ownership. Front-runners were distinguished from pack members on the basis of their *innovation success* which can be summarised as the economic exploitation of innovation by the introduction of new products and process as well as the enhancement of services (Cobbenhagen, 2000, p. 71). 'Innovation success' is distinguished from 'innovation', which simply indicates that a firm has renewed products and services without necessarily obtaining economic returns. To test his hypothesis that a combination of competences (technological, market and organisational) would best predict innovatory success, Cobbenhagen performed multiple regression analysis with all variables entered stepwise. Table 9.1 summarises the results, combining three competences which identified six separate factors with an R^2 of 0.72 (0.001).

A further factor which emerged from the study of front-runners was the importance of an 'internal locus of control'. This is similar to the psychological element which differentiates between individuals with an internal or external orientation (Rotter, 1966). 'Internals' believe that they control their own choices and actions while 'externals' believe that they are subject to events over which they have little control. Cobbenhagen (2000, p. 268) argues that SMEs with a strong internal locus of control were more proactive and managers believed that they had some influence over their environment. In contrast, external firms (pack members) were much more likely simply to react to events as they occurred. Finally, the study demonstrates that even successful innovators concentrate on evolutionary rather than revolutionary change.

Very few writers on innovation in smaller firms have stressed the importance of links to corporate strategy. Key exceptions are Dodgson and Rothwell, who set out five major features of corporate innovation strategy in smaller firms by examining data from three earlier studies (Dodgson and Rothwell, 1989; Dodgson, 1990; Rothwell and Dodgson, 1991). Although Dodgson and Rothwell's model (1991) has utility in evaluating strategic innovation management in SMEs, it does not capture the full range of organisational activities. 'External orientation' is a key dimension of innovation strategy and includes links with government schemes, public sector institutes (including HEIs), subcontracted and collaborative R&D,

TABLE 9.1 Factors influencing innovatory success

Factors	Organisational activities
1. Multidisciplinary projects	Bringing together people from different disciplines and functions during the innovation process
2. Relative R&D spend	Percentage R&D spend as a percentage of industry average (higher spend equates with success)
3. Market driven	Establishing effective links with market and utilising a wide range of information sources
4. Cooperate with customer	Establishing effective links with appropriate customers but not being totally driven by their requirements
5. Absorptive capacity	The ability to identify, acquire and utilise relevant market and technological knowledge
6. Policy timing	Focus on product/process innovation, recruitment, training and emphasis on quality

and marketing/manufacturing relations. Jones and Smith (1997) utilise the work of Dodgson and Rothwell (1991) as a framework for a detailed study of a firm, Otter Controls, in which managers and engineers were attempting to introduce a range of new technology-based products. Despite widespread recognition that networks are crucial for innovation, Freeman (1991) contends that they have received very little attention from researchers; 'informal networks are extremely important, but very hard to classify and measure.' Recent work carried out by researchers associated with Aston Business School in Birmingham, the UK, has begun to redress this imbalance by examining the role, nature and importance of formal and informal links in the development of successful technological innovations (Conway, 1995, 1997; Steward and Conway, 1996; Jones *et al.*, 2001).

Entrepreneurial Networks and Change Agents

In recent years it has increasingly been acknowledged in the literature that networks are central to effective innovation management. While it is recognised that innovation networks have existed for many years: 'information technology has led to the widespread diffusion of modes of networking which were previously far less common' (Freeman, 1991, p. 510). Similarly, Rothwell's (1992) 'fifth generation model' of innovation management emphasises the importance of IT as a facilitator of inter-organisational linkages (see Rothwell, 2002). Hence the need to develop a revised research agenda: 'With growing complexity, a focus on the role of innovation networks will be more appropriate than the behaviour of specific firms in isolation' (Tidd, 1997, p. 16). Because owner-managers usually have a dominant role, the small-firm literature concentrates on so-called 'entrepreneurial networks'. For example, Johannisson and Peterson (1984, p. 1) note the apparent paradox that, on one hand, entrepreneurship 'personifies individualism and independence' while on the other hand individuals are 'very dependent on ties of trust and cooperation'. Competent entrepreneurs draw on personal networks to extend strategic competences and help resolve acute operating problems by supplementing internal resources (Birley *et al.*, 1990; Conway, 1997; Conway and Shaw, 1999; Jones and Conway, 2000; Johannisson, 2000).

Leonard-Barton (1984, p. 113) suggests that 'entrepreneurs who, for geographic, cultural or social reasons, lack access to *free* information through personal networks, operate with less capital than do their well-connected peers.' Equally, it is recognised that effective personal networks 'must become as complex and as heterogeneous as the daily activities of the venture' (Johannisson and Peterson, 1984, p. 4). Inherent in the maintenance of such networks is the need for entrepreneurs to continually create *weak ties* to prevent a few strong ties from closing their network to opportunities and alternatives (Leonard-Barton, 1984; Aldrich and Zimmer, 1986). A comparative study of entrepreneurship established the importance of managerial education in encouraging the creation of networks (see Brereton and Jones, 2001). A lack of experience in higher education means that entrepreneurs have neither the personal contacts (which are a source of information) nor any real understanding of the expertise available through links with universities (Jones *et al.*, 1997). Much of this work is based on Granovetter's (1973) concept of weak ties that are an important potential source of knowledge and information (see Fletcher, 1998; Shaw, 1998). Strong ties constrain access to innovatory ideas and knowledge sources, whereas weak ties open up networks which provide access to new areas of expertise. At the same time, entrepreneurial activity is embedded in complex networks of social relations which are based on family, state, educational and professional background, religion, gender and ethnicity (Granovetter, 1985). The weakness of this literature is that it is based on the assumption that owner-managers will be the key actors in developing innovation networks. As Carrier (1996) notes, there is a 'somewhat surprising' absence of research into intrapreneurship in smaller firms, particularly given that such organisations are often ideal incubators.

It is suggested here that the key change agent role can be undertaken by actors other than the entrepreneur. To illustrate this point, two key studies of change agents in action are briefly discussed. To examine their hypothesis that strategic leadership is particularly important during periods of rapid change, Denis *et al.* (1996) studied two hospitals in Quebec, Canada. They analysed the dynamics of change under ambiguity by collecting documentary records, 16 retrospective interviews and 'ethnographic' data collected by one author who worked as a consultant in a community health department attached to one of the hospitals. The authors draw on the work of Hinings and Greenwood (1988) in arguing that an organisation's structural characteristics are supported by 'interpretative schemes' which in turn are based on collective ideas, beliefs and values. The 'leadership role constellation' and 'influence tactics' are conceptualised as the two key dimensions of the change process and link interpretative schemes and organisational structure. Leadership is seen as a team rather than an individual phenomenon (Pettigrew, 1992) and constellation effectiveness is influenced by three factors: *specialisation*, which refers to the extent to which roles have narrow areas of expertise; *differentiation*, the division of roles to ensure that there is not too much 'overlap'; and *complementarity*, the interlocking of roles (Denis *et al.*, 1996, p. 693). Organisation influence tactics (Pfeffer, 1981) describe the way in which individuals and groups attempt to influence the course of events by selective use of criteria such as agenda-setting, coalition building and symbolic management (Denis *et al.*, 1996, p. 693). Tactics have three different outcomes: first, symbolic changes based on modifications to existing interpretative schemes, second, substantive change based on organisational restructuring and, third, political change based on formal–informal power relations and the evolution of leadership roles. The case analysed by Denis *et al.* (1996, p. 689) 'illustrates the essentially collective and fragile nature of leadership in ambiguous organisations.'

Day (1994) carried out a questionnaire-based survey of 136 internal corporate ventures to examine the role of the 'principal champion'. She distinguishes between bottom-up champions who are close to the technical or market interface and top-down champions who are particularly important in times of major changes because they initiate substantive and symbolic actions. A third category, the dual-role champion, combines the role of product champion (bottom-up) and organisational sponsor (top-down) through their ability to mobilise knowledge, information and power. The study adopted innovation (timing, life-cycle, technological newness) as the dependent variable. Independent variables included the principal champion (product champion or organisational sponsor), hierarchical level and organisation location (proximity to core). A number of control variables such as size, age, diversity, R&D spend, market size, location and supporting assets, were also included. The results indicate that organisational size did not impact on innovativeness but provided 'weak support for the argument that firms ossify as they age' (Day, 1994, p. 164). R&D spend was positively related to innovation, and diversity had a negative relationship with the introduction of new products because, Day surmises, there is less incentive to innovate or to enter new markets. While the overall level of explanation, with an R^2 of 0.25 significant at the 0.001 level, means 'much is left unexplained, these results are very promising' (Day, 1994, p. 164). Dual role champions were found to be more common (36 per cent) than either bottom-up (30 per cent) or top-down (20 per cent) champions.

Intrapreneurs and Innovation

In most small, mature companies 'managers believe the industry is stable with slow demand growth and incremental changes in technology' (Baden-Fuller and Stopford, 1994, p. 4). However, the authors go on to argue that in mature sectors managerial choice rather than industry structure is the most important determinant of profits and growth. This proposition is based on the work of Schumpeter (1934) who pointed out that progress is only achieved by making people inside a business perform more effectively. Baden-Fuller and Stopford suggest that mature businesses can be rejuvenated via the 'strategic staircase' which creates new capabilities. At the lower level, IT is used to improve processes so that the organisation can deliver higher-quality products with fewer rejects. This gradually leads to lower costs and, perhaps, greater variety in the products offered by the company. Eventually, as employees develop IT skills, the company will begin to produce innovative products. Baden-Fuller and Stopford (p. 113) outline five features of entrepreneurial organisations: teams, aspirations, experiments, capabilities and dilemmas.

Kanter (1983) studied the role played by 'change masters' in helping 'progressive' companies innovate earlier than their rivals (see Merriden, 1998; Kanter, 2000). Segmentalism leads to a 'local rationality' in decision-making and this fragmentation discourages problem-solving, creates structural barriers, and stifles entrepreneurship and the spirit of innovation. An integrative approach emphasises the importance of aggregation which creates conceptual unity by loosening boundaries to encourage problem-solving and organisational change. Three sets of new skills are required to manage change effectively in integrative, entrepreneurial organisations (Kanter, 1983, p. 35): first, power skills for persuading others to invest information, support and the resources demanded for entrepreneurial initiatives; second, the ability to manage in an innovatory manner requires greater use of teams and higher levels of employee participation; and third, there is a need to integrate individual, micro-changes with the macro-changes resulting from strategic reorientation. Kanter (1983, p. 291) then sets out five major building blocks associated with organisational change:

> *Departing from tradition*: innovating companies change tradition as a result of deliberate intrapreneurial actions. Management control must be 'loose' enough to promote local experimentation. Small-scale innovations are important in demonstrating organisations can take productive action.

Galvanising events: segmentalist organisations are less well-equipped to respond to external events. Integrative organisations have better flows of information and this helps mobilise a broader-based response to environmental turbulence.

Strategic decisions: integrative organisations are able to balance the 'creative tension' between lower-level innovation and the strategic decisions taken by senior managers.

Individual prime movers: prime movers (ideas champions) help create an unequivocal commitment to organisational change. This entails regular communication to employees at all levels of the organisation about the importance of innovation and new ideas.

Action vehicles: the structure surrounding change must be institutionalised so that it becomes part of a legitimate and ongoing practice infused with value and supported by other aspects of the system. (Kanter, 1983, p. 299)

Entrepreneurial commitment to innovation is based on 'the willingness to move beyond received wisdom to combine ideas from unconnected sources, to embrace change as an opportunity to test limits' (Kanter, p. 27). Entrepreneurs operate on the edge of their competence instead of focusing on what they already know. Integrative thinking that embraces change is more likely in companies whose culture and structure is integrative. Segmentalism is anti-change because 'it compartmentalises action, events and problems' (Kanter, p. 28). Companies with such cultures are more likely to have compartmentalist structures with little communication between departments. In this study, Kanter's framework is utilised to analyse the role of change agents (intrapreneurs) in the implementation and institutionalisation of new technologies, new working practices and new routines. I concentrate on the specific activities of the prime mover (change agent) and therefore extend Kanter's category by the addition of two dimensions:

- Intrapreneurship is not based on the activities of a single individual but is essentially a collective effort which demands high levels of collaboration to achieve successful transformation. Managerial actions to initiate change can have three different outcomes: symbolic, substantive and political change (Denis *et al.*, 1996).
- Initiators of intrapreneurial actions can adopt one of three roles: top-down champion, bottom-up champion or dual-role champion. This illustrates the importance of recognising that even though change must be a team effort there will generally be one individual who acts as the champion in taking on responsibility for building and motivating 'collective transformational leadership' (Day, 1994).

In the following sections, this framework is utilised to analyse the processes associated with the introduction of new products and processes in two mature manufacturing organisations. Both organisations could be described as 'low-tech' although their internal competences were very different and the key change agents varied in terms of their power and status.

Research Methods

Although single cases do raise issues of generalisability, longitudinal studies of the innovation process are rare (Parker, 1982; Thomas, 1994; Van de Ven *et al.*, 1999). In stating the advantages of case study research, Yin (1994) claims that observing a 'chronological sequence' permits investigators to 'determine causal events over time'. My view is that establishing causality in highly complex social organisations is extremely difficult, whatever methodology is adopted. Rather, I concur with Barley (1986, p. 81) who argues that mapping 'emergent patterns of action' demands a detailed qualitative approach: 'Retrospective accounts and archival data are insufficient for these purposes since individuals rarely remember, and organisations rarely record, how behaviours and interpretations stabilise over the course of the structuring process.' In discussing the shift from micro- to macro-levels, Hamel *et al.* (1993) argue that the objectives are more important than the number of confirmatory cases. This refers to the distinction between statistical generalisation (Yin, 1994), in which inference is made about a specific population, and analytical generalisation, in which empirical data are compared with a theoretical 'template'.

The first study concerns MFD, a privately-owned manufacturing company founded over forty years ago to supply casting and machined components to the Ministry of Defence (MoD). Until recently, most products were batch-manufactured but there is now increasing emphasis on higher-volume work utilising flow-line assembly. MFD manufactured to contract and had little marketing expertise: 'If you took the customers away you would have difficulty identifying production of a specific product' (MFD manager). One expensive mistake was turning down a contract to manufacture Dyson's dual cyclone vacuum cleaner: 'The opportunity didn't fit the current profile of the business but Dyson also expected MFD to do the marketing' (Gareth Williams). Currently the firm relies heavily on two customers, BT and Lane Electronics. The company has been studied for more than three years and data have been acquired from a variety of sources including observation, company documents and fifteen interviews carried out over a two-month period at the end of 1999.

RSL is a family-owned business which has been in existence for 40 years, has 70 employees and manufactures office supply equipment. There were two main source of information. First, as academic supervisor of a TCS programme, I visited the company for half a day every fortnight for the two years the scheme was in operation. The majority of this time was spent in providing help and guidance to the TCS associate and in team meetings involving the academic supervisor, associate and the managing director (industrial supervisor). In meetings, which lasted between one and two hours, progress in the previous two-week period was discussed and targets set for the next meeting. The second source of data was the associate himself who acted as a participant-observer during his two years in RSL. Information was passed informally to the academic supervisor during regular meetings and formally in the submission of a MSc dissertation (Craven, 1999; Jones and Craven, 2001). The MD had two main objectives for establishing the TCS: first, to strengthen the company's market position by introducing a range of new products, and second, to create a 'more innovatory culture' within the company by institutionalising the search for new ideas and the mechanisms for turning those ideas into new products.

While both companies were engaged in change programmes, the key change agents were very different in status and attachment to the organisations. In MFD, change was initiated by the owner and managing director Mike Frost who was concerned about declining activity within the company as a result of fewer defence contracts. In this case the change agent was a middle manager who, in contrast to most other white- and blue-collar workers, joined the company under a year before the change programme began. Similarly, change was initiated in RSL by the MD, who recognised the need to become more proactive in the introduction of new products. On a day-to-day basis, the initiator of change was a TCS associate responsible for both the development of new products and the institutionalisation of new 'routines' within the company.

Managing Innovation in MFD

MFD is a family-owned, paternalist firm and the initiative for change had to come from the top. One factor stimulating change was the decline in defence spending in the UK because until 1992 MoD contracts had accounted for 60 per cent of MFD's business. The firm was heavily reliant on Mike Frost's personal contacts in the MoD to generate new contracts. Reductions in defence spending and the move away from cost-plus contracts to a market-based approach meant that by 1998 MFD had lost all its MoD work. Defence contracts were based on traditional, low-volume engineering skills and it was extremely difficult to find suitable replacement work. It gradually became apparent that if MFD were to survive it would be necessary to develop other activities. BT provided an opportunity because MFD were involved in the refurbishment of payphone coin-boxes. Senior managers negotiated a contract with BT to assemble telephone handsets, but this work was very different to the firm's previous engineering-based activities. Further changes initiated by owner Mike Frost included the recruitment of two outsiders with experience in different industries (Table 9.2). Gareth Williams had spent more than 20 years working for a large domestic appliance manufacturer which was organised according to Fordist principles. His ideas on material flows and

TABLE 9.2   Summarising the changes

	MFD	RSL
Galvanising events	Loss of MoD business	Declining market share
	Decline in batch engineering	Increasing customer power
	Improve labour utilisation	Need for new products
	Prompting from customer	
Strategic decisions	Substantial investment	Participate in TCS
	Recruit 'outsiders'	Invest in IT system
	Switch to electronics	Develop new products
	Emphasis on marketing	Incremental innovation
Departing from tradition	Regular management meetings	Delegate to MC
	End working in 'arrears'	Management meetings
	MD 'on shopfloor'	Information transparency
	Batch to mass production	Strategy 'away day'
Prime movers	MF (owner/MD)	WW (owner/MD)
	GW (middle manager)	MC (TC associate)
Action vehicles	Retaining Lane business	TCS
	Purchase of MRPII	NPD committee
	Welsh Development Agency	Idea generation form
	Eliminate WIP	Company newsletter

the elimination of WIP were revolutionary to most long-serving employees and were particularly important in developing the new 'telecommunication' business. Improvements in labour productivity and better stock control secured the BT contract and gradually Lane Electronics also began use MFD for the supply of telephone-handsets and printed circuit boards.

According to Denis *et al.* (1996) effective change needs to be managed through high levels of collaboration. Furthermore, the effect of strategic leadership can be categorised according to three outcomes: symbolic, substantive and political change. There was evidence of all three factors in MFD. Symbolic change occurred as a result of Mike Frost's willingness to spend more time in the plant talking to supervisors and managers. This new approach was regarded as a reflection of broader changes across the organisation which encouraged greater openness and trust between managers and shopfloor workers. Substantive change occurred as a result of two major investments, the first of which was an IT system costing £250 000, approved in 1998. Gareth Williams was initially given responsibility for the control of labour costs via the issue of standard times. He quickly realised that a wide range of factors influenced the inefficient use of labour, including an ancient and inflexible MRP (manufacturing resource planning) system which made it extremely difficult to track flows of material through the factory. This was a crucial factor because as a result of the unavailability of components, operator waiting time, paid at average earnings, was high. The work of white-collar staff was also inefficient as supervisors, foremen and store-keepers spent a considerable amount of time searching for missing materials. After carrying out a detailed analysis, Williams decided that the only way to improve efficiency was to purchase a new mainframe computer with software, including MRPII, capable of dealing effectively with the complexity of operations within MFD. Williams presented his recommendations to Ken Chalmers (works director) with an estimate of the total cost of the project including the employment of two or three new technical staff. Following discussions with Mike Frost, Ken Chalmers approved the project and Gareth Williams's department was given responsibility for the purchase, installation and commissioning of the new system. More effective labour utilisation was crucially important during the transition from batch to mass-production.

Second, in December 1999 Williams persuaded Mike Frost to invest £350 000 in a process line for printed circuit boards, and to reorganise the assembly shop to give a logical workflow and elimination of excessive work-in-progress (WIP). This was partly to satisfy the demands of Lane Electronics who wanted MFD to adopt a more professional approach which would impress their own customers, who sometimes visited subcontractors. Another change which had symbolic and substantive elements was ending the practice of working in 'arrears'. By ensuring that work was carried out two, three, four or even more weeks behind schedule, managers and supervisors knew that shopfloor activity could be maintained at least until arrears were cleared. This way of thinking had been encouraged by the 'cosy' relationship between suppliers and the MoD who seemed not to expect deliveries on time. New customers such as Lane Electronics and BT were unwilling to tolerate this practice.

The introduction of 'outsiders' to key middle-management positions influenced organisational change in a number of ways. First, obviously there had to be modifications to the managerial hierarchy to accommodate newcomers. Second, new mechanisms were created for the dissemination of information such as regular management meetings, committees and team-working arrangements. Third, and perhaps most importantly, Gareth Williams brought new ways of thinking and emphasised the importance of accessing knowledge and expertise from external sources. For example, when purchasing the MRPII system, rather than utilising a company with which MFD had previously done business, Williams initiated an evaluation procedure in which ten IT companies were required to submit detailed proposals (including technical specifications and costs). Williams also encouraged Ken Chalmers to take advantage of a programme developed by the Welsh Development Agency to improve manufacturing techniques in smaller companies. The WDA project, which emphasised the importance of Kanban and shopfloor teams, in combination with the MRPII system helped MFD shift towards the principles of lean manufacturing. However, Lane Electronics was the most significant action vehicle for ensuring that change within MFD was accepted and institutionalised. Engineers and managers from Lane Electronics encouraged a much more professional approach within MFD and, at the same time, prime movers such as Gareth Williams were able to use links with Lane Electronics as a 'lever' to minimise resistance to change.

Managing Innovation in RSL

RSL's main site in Birmingham manufactures a variety of sheet manila files, folders and wallets, and also houses a print department which now accounts for 20 per cent of turnover. Sheet metal products such as cabinets and trolleys are manufactured at the Bristol site. Office wholesalers (Spicers, John Heath, Kingfield), contract stationers (Guilbert, Niceday) and direct mail companies (Viking Direct) account for 50 per cent of RSL's sales, while direct sales account for the remaining 30 per cent. In the mid-1990s, RSL was acquired by a family trust fund. The White brothers were appointed to senior managerial positions: William, MD; Matthew, marketing director and Edward, operations manager. Change does not take place in organisations without someone recognising the potential for improvement. The new owners were galvanised by a lack of innovation in the company and declining market for the majority of their products (Table 9.2). Participation in the Teaching Company Scheme was a very significant strategic decision taken by the new management team. It was also decided that developing a positive approach to innovation meant that early projects had to succeed. Redesigning an existing product to reduce manufacturing and assembly costs was less likely to fail than creating entirely new, untested products.

The appointment of Martin Craven as TC Associate was in itself a significant departure from tradition for RSL. If the TCS was to succeed then he had to have access to resources and be fully supported by senior managers. Although Craven was inexperienced, he was enthusiastic, committed and hard-working. Also, given the low-tech nature of RSL's products, it was relatively easy for him to become familiar with the manufacturing processes. He also demonstrated his competence by quickly creating a bill of materials for each product which significantly improved stock control. This breakdown was also the basis for deciding the best areas for potential improvement. As a consequence of his successes, Craven was given greater autonomy to initiate broader organisational change. He encouraged sales representatives and service staff to listen more carefully to customers as a way of identifying new opportunities. Craven also designed a simple idea capture form that was distributed to all employees, and proposed that a new product development committee (NPDC) be formed to evaluate suggestions.

William White (MD) was clearly the prime mover who recognised that RSL had to become more innovatory and took the first step by participating in the TCS. White's support for the development of new products was a crucial factor in moving RSL from a basic operating pose to a strategic innovation pose (Clark and Staunton, 1993). In the first instance, his decision to participate in the Teaching Company Scheme and employ Martin Craven as TCS Associate provided the organisation with a resource which was entirely dedicated to the innovation of new products. Equally significant was White's regular attendance and active participation in New Product Development Committee (NPDC) meetings which demonstrated his continuing commitment to innovation and helped institutionalise this activity as a key innovation routine. However, on a day-to-day basis Craven's role was central to the creation of new products and processes. In particular, he was the catalyst for the introduction of ten new 'routines' during the course of the TCS (Jones and Craven, 2001). For example, employees at all levels realised that the idea capture form provided a mechanism by which their suggestions could be brought to the attention of senior managers. Many employees also engaged in regular discussions about how processes could be improved, and compared ideas for new products. It was necessary to ensure this was not a transitory effect after which everyone lapsed back into their previous ways of working. Employees were kept informed about the progress of their ideas, and a regular newsletter provided information on how the new products were contributing to improvements in the 'bottom line'. The new product development committee (NPDC) was certainly central to the changes observed in RSL.

Discussion: Change Agents and Innovation

Both MFD and RSL are mature manufacturing companies which have been successful in developing cultures conducive to innovation. A more competitive market stimulated the owner of MFD to make a substantial investment (more than £1m) over the last three years to help the transition from a batch manufacturer of engineering products to a mass producer of electronic components. This transition has been successful, with the company acquiring major contracts from BT and Lane Electronics. RSL's owners introduced a range of modifications to existing products which had an immediate impact on turnover. Staff employees at all levels became much more aware of the opportunities presented in their everyday work activities to improve existing products and processes, as well as suggest completely new ideas. Relationships with customers (major office supplies catalogue companies) were also transformed, as buyers began to perceive RSL as an organisation that was dynamic and innovative. This was particularly important as these companies were rationalising suppliers and were only interested in those which could deliver on price as well as maintain a stream of new products. The question addressed here is, how were managers in two conservative companies able to instigate successful change programmes?

Part of the explanation is that both companies are family-owned and are therefore free from external interference in business decisions. Proprietorship also meant that the initiators, in both cases the MD, had considerable power to ensure that everyone in the organisation accepted the need for change. That is not to say that all employees agreed with the proposals, but it was difficult to legitimise an alternative vision of how MFD and RSL should adapt to the increasingly competitive environment. In both organisations, the main change agents were recent recruits: Gareth Williams had more than twenty-years experience with a major white-goods company working in a variety of engineering and managerial roles. His experience of mass manufacturing contrasted with the majority of MFD managers, whose experience was primarily low-volume batch production. At the time of his appointment, Craven had very little business experience other than a placement year during his engineering/business degree. In the early stages his activities were legitimated through the MD's support. Gradually, as he successfully completed a number of projects, Craven established a major role for himself as the initiator of change within RSL.

Although both Martin Craven and Gareth Williams acted as change agents, they were very different in status as well as in terms of their access to resources, power, legitimacy and authority. The initial focus of Williams's role was improving the utilisation of direct labour but this provided him with the opportunity to extend his role by taking on responsibility for the introduction of a major new IT system. The computer system was primarily intended to resolve problems associated with stock control and labour inefficiency, but was also designed to link all major functions within MFD. This meant it was necessary for the new system to be 'sold' to departmental heads, obtaining their cooperation in making transparent the nature of their current activities so that their requirements could be incorporated into the specification. One of the most intriguing aspects of MFD was the management style of Ken Chalmers (works director) who, to the frustration of some departmental heads, never held management meetings. Rather, Chalmers's approach was to discuss such changes on an informal basis, obtaining the views of each individual manager. This provided Williams with the opportunity to take the initiative in organising management meetings to discuss the implementation of the new system in which he was able to outline his view of the company's future direction. For Martin Craven, the primary focus was incremental improvements to a range of existing products. However, he gradually recognised that changing products also meant changing other activities within RSL. So, Craven (with support from industrial and academic supervisors) initiated a number of new 'routines', including the NPDC and the idea generation form, which stimulated substantial changes to activities at all organisational levels. In Day's (1994) terms, Craven acted as a 'bottom-up' champion and Williams typified the 'dual-role' champion by acting as corporate sponsor for two major capital investment projects and at the same time initiating numerous minor changes on the shopfloor.

The conventional literature generally focuses on individual attributes (person-ality and behavioural) of change agents and I do not dispute that both possessed the entrepreneurial characteristics of risk-taking, hard work and resilience (Wickham,

2001, p. 39). In her study of intrapreneurship in small firms, Carrier (1996) found that 'the structural and relational aspect' was by far the most important factor in building an intrapreneurial environment. Therefore, I argue that in order for change agents to be successful it is necessary for the appropriate structural conditions to be in place. First, within both companies there was broad acceptance throughout the management team of the need for change. Second, and perhaps most important, although very different in experience and authority, both change agents had the full, unambiguous support of their respective MDs (and in MFD, the works director). This meant that anyone resisting change was challenging the owners' ultimate authority rather than simply threatening the change agents. In larger organisations where power is more fragmented, with competing coalitions based in different departments or different geographic locations, such a unitary vision would be much more difficult to achieve (Carr, 1999). Third, because Craven and Williams enjoyed senior management support they were also able to access both symbolic and substantive resources. William White's presence at every NPDC committee clearly signalled to others within the organisation that this was an important project which he fully supported, while investment in the TCS as well as the allocation of resources to evaluate and develop new ideas provided tangible evidence of managerial commitment. In MFD, the willingness of owner Mike Frost to invest very large sums of money in a new computer system as well as manufacturing equipment for printed circuit boards had enormous symbolic significance. The other factor which seems to be central to the creation of innovatory cultures in both organisations was recognition of the centrality of networks. Both Gareth Williams and Martin Craven spent a considerable amount of time building internal networks because (as pointed out by Denis et al., 1996) intrapreneurship is essentially a collective effort based on collaboration rather than relying on the efforts of one individual (see Morris et al., 1993). Furthermore, both recognised the need to access external knowledge by building more effective knowledge-based networks with suppliers, customers and public sector organisations (the Welsh Development Agency in the case of MFD and two universities in the case of RSL).

The literature is littered with examples of management 'fads' such as quality circles, TQM, BPR, HRM and organisational culture, which have failed to deliver the expected benefits in terms of improved organisational performance (Grey and Mitev, 1995; Sturdy, 1997). Part of the explanation for their failure is that management teams are unwilling to make the long-term commitment necessary for change programmes to succeed. Instigating new approaches is relatively easy, but managers must accept that patience and persistence are key elements in managing change processes. Within both companies there was a broad acceptance that innovation was a process rather than a one-off event. In line with Atherton and Hannon's (2000) model, change began with an examination of the external environment and an evaluation of internal capabilities. This was followed by attempts to match opportunities to capabilities in the development of new products and processes. However, it is necessary to 'institutionalise' new ways of working if fundamental change is to be achieved. The respective 'action vehicles' played a very significant role in ensuring successful implementation in RSL and MFD (see Table 9.2). Initially, the main action vehicle in MFD was Lane Electronics because everyone knew that long-term survival probably depended on convincing their representatives that MFD could become a major supplier of electronic components. Ending the practice of working in arrears and eliminating shopfloor WIP were achieved because these changes were demanded by representatives of Lake Electronics. The purchase of the new computer system also proved an effective mechanism for institutionalising change because Williams organised regular management meetings to provide a forum in which a wide range of interested actors were fully involved in the decision-making process. Within RSL, activities associated with TCS such as the NPDC, the idea generation form and the newsletter provided the mechanisms by which managers and employees at all levels began to focus on creating and implementing new ideas. In particular, monthly meetings of the NPDC ensured that projects considered to have serious potential were allocated to a committee member for further investigation, and their report had to be ready for the subsequent meeting. As a result, the management team was able to allocate appropriate resources to those ideas considered to have the most potential for improving organisational performance.

Conclusion

In this chapter I have analysed the change process in two mature manufacturing SMEs, MFD and RSL. They are the subject of longitudinal studies of the change process, which began early in 1997. Data were obtained from a variety of sources but mainly from regular site visits which included formal interviews, informal discussions and general observation. Developing a comprehensive understanding of change processes demands a longitudinal methodology.

Change in MFD has been much more fundamental than in RSL. The overall strategy has been to gradually move away from a business based on batch-produced engineering products to high-volume assembly work associated with the telecommunications industry. Nevertheless, the company has made steady, if not spectacular, progress over the last five years in which turnover has grown from £12m to £14.5m and pre-tax profits have increased from £510 000 to £720 000. Equally important, the company has overcome its reliance on the MoD and is gradually building up a portfolio of customers in high-technology areas. Lane Electronics has been particularly important in helping MFD make this transition by providing explicit guidelines about what they require of their telecommunications suppliers. This has certainly helped to 'change the culture', with employees and managers now having greater awareness of the need to be market-focused. The MD is strongly committed to the firm's long-term survival as a family business and has become much more active in day-to-day managerial activities. The employment of a senior manager with responsibility for marketing was one important outcome of his engagement.

Initially, innovatory activity within RSL focused on improving two existing products which were losing out to competitors because of high manufacturing costs and unattractive design features. Relatively simple design changes to both products improved market attractiveness and helped to reduce manufacturing costs. These products were selected because we judged that incremental, though significant, changes to existing products had a higher chance of success than more radical innovations. Within two years of the project beginning, redesigned products had contributed an additional £312 000 to sales and in the third year of operation this increased to almost £600 000. Company turnover at the start of the

TCS project was £2.5 million and consequently, a modest investment in the TCS of £35 000 has had a very significant impact on company finances. William White's (MD) clear criteria for the introduction of new products has helped to ensure that there was a strong link between innovation and improved competitive advantage. White stressed that his target was to introduce a minimum of three new products per year which each contributed at least £50 000 to turnover. While this may not appear to be very ambitious, the objective was to build a basis for RSL's long-term success by constantly introducing new products and improving processes. More subjective measures of improvement in RSL are also available. The idea capture form (ICF) was a catalyst for changing the way in which RSL employees performed their day-to-day activities. Employees at all levels realised that the ICF provided a mechanism by which their ideas could be brought to the attention of senior managers. Many employees also engaged in regular discussions about how processes could be improved and compared ideas for new products. There is strong evidence of an innovatory culture within RSL as employees and managers now recognise that it is possible to combine their day-to-day responsibilities with a commitment to the development and evaluation of new products. Equally important were changes in the perception of RSL by major customers such as office equipment wholesalers and contract stationers. The company is now widely regarded as being innovative and forward-thinking, which was not the case prior to the TCS programme.

Change in both organisations is evaluated by means of Kanter's (1983) framework which has five analytical categories: galvanising events, strategic decisions, departing from tradition, prime movers and action vehicles. While both companies were engaged in change programmes, the key change agents were very different in status and attachment to the organisations. In MFD change was initiated by the owner and managing director, Mike Frost, who was concerned about declining activity within the company as a result of fewer defence contracts. In this case, the change agent was a middle manager who had joined the company less than one year before the change programme began. Similarly, change was initiated in RSL by the MD, who recognised the need to become more proactive in the introduction of new products. On a day-to-day basis the initiator of change was the Teaching Company associate who was responsible for both the development of new products and the institutionalisation of new routines within the company. While I accept that individual change agents are important, it is argued that the appropriate structural conditions must be in place if change is to be successfully managed. This draws attention to the need for appropriate prime movers to be identified and empowered while appropriate action vehicles are introduced, to ensure that change mechanisms are institutionalised within the organisations.

References

Aldrich, H. and Zimmer, C. (1986) 'Entrepreneurship through social networks', in D. Sexton and R. Smilor (eds) *Art and Science of Entrepreneurship*. Ballinger, Cambridge, MA.

Atherton, A. and Hannon, P.D. (2000) 'Innovation processes and the small business: A conceptual analysis', *International Journal of Business Performance Management*, 2:4, 276–292.

Baden-Fuller, C. and Stopford, J.M. (1994) *Rejuvenating the Mature Business: The Competitive Challenge*. Harvard Business School Press, Boston, MA.

Barley, S. (1986) 'Technology as an occasion for structuring: evidence from observation of CT scanners and the social order of radiology departments', *Administrative Science Quarterly*, **31**, 79.

Barnett, E. and Storey, J. (2000) 'Managers' accounts of innovation processes in SMEs', *Journal of Small Business and Enterprise Development*, **7**:4, 315–324.

Beckhard, R. (1969) *Organizational Development: Strategies and Methods*. Addison-Wesley, Reading.

Beer, M. (1980) *Organization Change and Development. A Systems View*. Scott, Foresman and Company, London.

Bennis, W.G. (1964) 'The change agents', in R.T. Golembiewski and A. Blumberg (eds) *Sensitivity Training and the Laboratory Approach*. Itasca, Peacock.

Bennis, W.G., Benne, K.D. and Chin, R. (1969) *The Planning of Change*, 2nd edition. Holt, Rinehart & Winston, New York.

Bird, M. (1992) *Effective Leadership: A Practical Guide to Leading Your Team to Success*. BBC Books, London.

Birley, S., Cromie, S. and Myers, A. (1990) 'Entrepreneurial networks: their emergence in Ireland and overseas', *International Small Business Journal*, **9**:4, 56–74.

Brereton, D. and Jones, O. (2001) 'Social networks and business startups: a first-hand account of entrepreneurship', MMU Working Paper RP01/21.

Carr, C. (1999) 'Globalisation, strategic alliances, acquisitions and technology transfer: lessons from ICL/Fujitsu and Rover and BMW', *R&D Management*, **29**:4, 405–421.

Carrier, C. (1996) 'Intrapreneurship in small businesses: an exploratory study', *Entrepreneurship: Theory and Practice*, **21**:1, 5–21.

Cobbenhagen, J. (2000) *Successful Innovation: Towards a New Theory for the Management of SMEs*. Edward Elgar, Cheltenham.

Conway, S. (1995) 'Informal boundary-spanning communication in the innovation process', *Technology Analysis and Strategic Management*, **7**:3, 327–342.

Conway, S. (1997) 'Informal networks of relationships in successful small firm innovation', In D. Jones-Evans and M. Klofsten (eds) *Technology, Innovation and Enterprise: The European Experience*. Macmillan, London, pp. 236–273.

Conway, S. and Shaw, E. (1999) 'Networking and the small firm', in S. Carter and D. Jones-Evans (eds) *Enterprise and Small Business: Principles, Policy and Practice*. Addison-Wesley Longman, Harlow.

Clark, P. and Staunton, N. (1993) *Innovation in Technology and Organization*. Routledge, London.

Craven, M. (1999) 'Innovation: a matter of routine', Unpublished MSc dissertation, Aston Business School, UK.

Cummings, T. and Worley, C. (1997) *Organizational Development and Change*, 6th edition. ITP, Cincinnati, OH.

Dale, A. (1974) 'Coercive persuasion and the role of the change agent', *Interpersonal Development*, **5**:2, 102–111.

Day, D.I. (1994) 'Raising radicals: different processes for championing innovative corporate ventures', *Organization Science*, **5**:2, 148–172.

Denis, L., Langley, A. and Cazale, L. (1996) 'Leadership and strategic change under ambiguity', *Organisation Studies*, **17**:4, 673–699.

Dodgson, M. (1990) *Celltech: The First Ten Years of a Biotechnology Company*. Special Report, Science Policy Research Unit, University of Sussex, UK.

Dodgson, M. and Rothwell, R. (1989) 'Technology strategies in small and medium-sized firms' in M. Dodgson (ed.) *Technology Strategy and the Firm: Management and Public Policy*. Longman, Harlow.

Dodgson, M. and Rothwell, R. (1991) 'Technology strategies in small firms', *Journal of General Management*, **17**:1, 45–55.

Dodgson, M. and Rothwell, R. (1993) 'Technology-based SMEs: their role in industrial and economic change', *International Journal of Technology Management, Special Edition – Small Firms and Innovation*, 8–22.

Duncan, W.J. (1978) *Organizational Behaviour*. Houghton Mifflin, Boston.

Eden, C. and Huxham, C. (1996) 'Action research for the study of organizations', in S.R. Clegg, C. Hardy and W. Nord (eds) *Handbook of Organization Studies*. Sage, London.

Edwards, T. (2000) 'Innovation and organizational change: developments towards an interactive perspective', *Technology Analysis and Strategic Management*, **12**:4, 445–464.

European Commission (1999) *Innovation Management: Building Competitive Skills in SMEs*. EC, Luxembourg.

Fletcher, D. (1998) 'Swimming around in their own ponds: the weakness of strong ties in developing innovative practices', *International Journal of Innovation Management*, **2**:2, 137–160.

Freel, M. (1999) 'Barriers to product innovation in small manufacturing firms', *International Small Business Journal*, **18**:2, 60–80.

Freel, M. (2000) 'External linkages and product innovation in small manufacturing firms', *Entrepreneurship and Regional Development*, **12**, 245–266.

Freeman, C. (1991) 'Networks of innovators: a synthesis of research issues', *Research Policy*, **20**:5, 499–514.

Gibb, A. (1997) 'Small firms' training and competitiveness: building upon the small firm as a learning organization', *International Small Business Journal*, **15**:3, 13–29.

Granovetter, M. (1973) 'The strength of weak ties', *American Journal of Sociology*, **78**:6, 1360–1380.

Granovetter, M. (1985) 'Economic action and social structure: the problem of embeddedness', *American Journal of Sociology*, **91**:3, 481–510.

Grant, R.M. (1998) *Contemporary Strategy Analysis: Concepts, Techniques and Applications*, 3rd edition. Blackwell, Oxford.

Greiner, L. and Schein, V. (1988) *Power and Organization Development: Mobilizing Power to Implement Change*. Addison-Wesley, Reading.

Grey, C. and Mitev, N. (1995) 'Re-engineering organizations: a critical appraisal', *Personnel Review*, **24**:1.

Hamel, J., Dufour, S. and Fortin, D. (1993) *Case Study Methods: Qualitative Research Methods Series 32*. Sage, London.

Hartley, J., Benington, J. and Binns, P. (1997) 'Researching the roles of internal change agents in the management of organizational change', *British Journal of Management*, **8**, 61–73.

Havelock, R.G. and Havelock, M.C. (1973) *Training for Change Agents*. Institute for Social Research, University of Michigan, USA.

Hinings, R. and Greenwood, R. (1988) *The Dynamics of Strategic Change*. Blackwell, Oxford.

Hoffman, K., Parejo, M., Bessant, J. and Perren, L. (1997) 'Small firms, R&D, technology and innovation in the UK: a literature review', *Technovation*, **18**:1, 39–55.

Hussey, D. (1998) *How to be Better at Managing Change*. Kogan Page, London.

Johannisson, B. (2000) 'Networking and entrepreneurial growth', in D.L. Sexton and H. Landstrom, *The Blackwell Handbook of Entrepreneurship*. Blackwell, Oxford.

Johannisson, B. and Peterson, R. (1984) The Personal Networks of Entrepreneurs. Third Canadian Conference, International Council for Small Business, Toronto, 23–25 May citing W. Ashby (1956) *Introduction to Cybernetics*, Wiley, New York.

Jones, O. and Conway, S. (2000) 'Social-embeddedness and geographical reach in entrepreneurial networks: the case of James Dyson', *International Entrepreneurship: Researching New Frontiers*, McGill, Montreal (September).

Jones, O. and Craven, M. (2001) 'Beyond the routine: innovation management and the Teaching Company Scheme', *Technovation*, **21**:5, 267–285.

Jones, O. and Smith, D. (1997) 'Strategic technology management in a mid-corporate firm: the case of Otter Controls', *Journal of Management Studies*, **34**:4, 511–536.

Jones, O., Cardoso, C.C. and Beckinsale, M. (1997) 'Mature SMEs and technological innovation: entrepreneurial networks in the UK and Portugal', *International Journal of Innovation Management*, **1**:3, 201–227.

Jones, O., Conway, S. and Steward, F. (eds) (2001) *Social Interaction and Organisational Change: Aston Perspectives on Innovation Networks*. Imperial College Press, London.

Jones, O., Edwards, T. and Beckinsale, M. (2000) 'Technology management in a mature firm: structuration theory and the innovation process', *Technology Analysis and Strategic Management*, **12**:2, 161–178.

Kanter, R.M. (1983) *The Change Masters: Corporate Entrepreneurs at Work*. Unwin Hyman, London.

Kanter, R.M. (2000) 'When a thousand flowers bloom: structural, collective and social conditions for innovation in organization', in R. Swedberg, *Entrepreneurship: The Social Science View*. OUP, Oxford.

Leigh, A. and Walters, M. (1998) *Effective Change: Twenty Ways to Make it Happen*. IPD, London.

Leonard-Barton, D. (1984) 'Interpersonal communication patterns among Swedish and Boston-area entrepreneurs', *Research Policy*, **13**:2, 101–114.

Lewin, K. (1947) 'Frontiers in group dynamics', *Human Relations*, **1**, 5–41.

Lippitt, R., Watson, J. and Westley, B. (1958) *The Dynamics of Planned Change*. Harcourt, Brace & World, New York.

Merriden, T. (1998) 'Kanter saw it coming', *Management Today*, February, 87–88.

Morris, M.H., Avila, R.A. and Allen, J. (1993) 'Individualism and the modern corporation: implications for innovation and entrepreneurship', *Journal of Management*, **19**:3, 596–612.

Murray, G. (1997) 'A policy response to regional disparities in the supply of risk capital to new-technology based firms in the EU: the European Seed Capital Fund scheme', *Regional Studies*, **32**:5, 405–419.

Parker, R.C. (1982) *The Management of Innovation*. Wiley, Chichester.

Pettigrew, A. (1992) 'On studying managerial elites', *Strategic Management Journal*, **13** (Special Issue), 168–182.

Pfeffer, G. (1981) *Power in Organizations*. Pitman, Marshfield, MA.

Prahalad, C.K. and Hamel, G. (1990) 'The core competence of the corporation', *Harvard Business Review*, **68**:3, 79–81.

Robertson, M., Scarbrough, H. and Swan, J. (2000) 'Knowledge, networking and innovation: a longitudinal analysis of the design, diffusion and implementation of CAPM technology', British Academy of Management Conference, Edinburgh.

Rogers, E.M. and Shoemaker, F.F. (1971) *Communication of Innovations: A Cross-cultural Approach*, 2nd edition. Free Press, New York.

Rothwell, R. (1984) 'Technology-based small firms and regional innovation potential: the role of public procurement', *Journal of Public Policy*, **4**:4, 307–332.

Rothwell, R. (1989) 'Small firms, innovation and industrial change', *Small Business Economics*, **1**:1, 51–64.

Rothwell, R. (1992) 'Successful innovation: critical factors for the 1990s', *R&D Management*, **22**:3, 221–240.

Rothwell, R. (2002) 'Towards the fifth-generation innovation process', in J. Henry and D. Mayle, *Managing Innovation and Change*, 2nd edition. Sage, London.

Rothwell, R. and Dodgson, M. (1991) 'External linkages and innovation in SMEs', *R&D Management*, **21**:2, 125–137.

Rotter, J. (1966) 'Generalised expectancies for internal versus external control of reinforcement', *Psychological Monographs*, **80**:609, 1–28.

Schumpeter, J.A. (1934) *The Theory of Economic Development*. Harvard University Press, Cambridge, MA.

Shaw, E. (1998) 'Social networks: their impact on the innovative behaviour of small service firms', *International Journal of Innovation Management*, **2**:2, 201–222.

Stein, R.G. and Pinchot, G. (1998) 'Are you innovative?' *Association Management*, **50**:2, 74–77.

Steward, F. and Conway, S. (1996) 'Informal networks in the origination of successful innovations', in R. Coombs, A. Richards, P. Saviotti and V. Walsh (eds) *The Dynamics of Cooperation in Industrial Innovation*. Edward Elgar, Cheltenham.

Sturdy, A. (1997) 'The consultancy process: an insecure business', *Journal of Management Studies*, **34**:3.

Thomas, R.J. (1994) *What Machines Can't Do: Politics and Technology in the Industrial Enterprise*. University of California Press, Berkeley, CA.

Tichy, N.M. (1975) 'How different types of change agents diagnose organizations', *Human Relations*, **23**:5, 771–779.

Tidd, J. (1997) 'Complexity, networks and learning: integrative themes for research on the management of innovation', *International Journal of Innovation Management*, **1**:1, 1–19.

Tidd, J. (2001) 'Innovation management in context: environment, organization and performance', *International Journal of Management Reviews*, **3**:3, 169–183.

Tidd, J., Bessant, J. and Pavitt, K. (2001) *Managing Innovation: Integrating Technological, Market and Organisational Change*, 2nd edition. Wiley, Chichester.

Van de Ven, A., Polley, D., Garud, R. and Venkataraman, S. (1999) *The Innovation Journey*. OUP, Oxford.

Vossen, R.W. (1998) 'Relative strengths and weaknesses of small firms in innovation', *International Small Business Journal*, **16**:3, 88–94.

Wickham, P.A. (2001) *Strategic Entrepreneurship: A Decision-Making Approach to New Venture Creation and Management*, 2nd edition. Pearson Education, Harlow.

Yin, R.K. (1994) *Case Study Research: Design and Methods*, 2nd edition. Sage, Thousand Oaks, CA.

Yu, T.F.-Y. (2001) 'Towards a capabilities perspective of the small firm', *International Journal of Management Reviews*, **3**:3, 185–197.

Chapter 10

NETWORKING CAPABILITY: THE COMPETITIVE ADVANTAGE OF SMALL FIRMS

David Taylor and Krsto Pandza

Introduction

Those writing on small firms have started to acknowledge the contribution of personal contact networks and, in particular, the networking of the owner-manager to the success of the small business. It is argued that these networks provide the owner-manager with access to a range of complementary experiences and expertise that, if managed effectively, help to reduce risk and speed up decision-making, and act as a safe environment where ideas can be tested out with trusted others (McQuaid, 1996).

These networks are not restricted by organisational boundaries. Rather, they emerge out of the many interactions that each owner-manager has with other people. The limited nature of any network is down to the quality and productivity of the network resource and the capability of the owner-manager to use, manage and develop the network. It is this proactive and directed networking capability and the uniqueness of the relationships developed that helps to differentiate a small firm from its competitors, thus creating a potential for competitive advantage. While networking is viewed as an important requirement in enterprises of all sizes, these learning opportunities are argued to be of particular importance to small firms in order to offset the fragility of size (Szarka, 1990) acting as the key determinant of organisational success.

Success is regarded here as a highly idiosyncratic concept when used in the small-firm context (Thorpe, 1988). The view that success is associated with the achievement of an exceptional return on investment and growth in the small firm has been challenged since the 1971 Bolton Report, which argued that success is primarily related to the desire of the owner-manager to achieve personal involvement, responsibility and an independent lifestyle (Jennings and Beaver, 1997). Therefore, the development of competitive advantage is seldom a readily visible process in the small business, as it often arises accidentally out of particular circumstances and is linked to the aspirations, perceptions and capabilities of each owner-manager, who enacts strategic management in a highly personalised manner (Jennings and Beaver, 1997). It is the sustained satisfaction of these characteristics that the owner-manager would view as a legitimate measure of success.

This exploration of the role of networks of relationships on competitive advantage in small firms is looking to make recommendations to develop more synchronous support mechanisms to assist the network management and development processes, and ultimately the learning, of owner-managers. In line with the work of Conway and Steward (1998) a 'network graphic' is used to portray the subtle relationships at the level of the individual.

As discussed previously, an important factor in satisfying these aspirations is the quality of the small-firm owner-manager's network of relationships and how the owner-manager learns from and manages those relationships. This synchronous support mechanism functions as an enabling resource that the owner-manager can draw upon. Effective entrepreneurs are likely to undertake actions that increase their network density and diversity in support of their business vision (Centre for Enterprise, 2001). This capability is a necessary ingredient for effective management and by placing more emphasis on the development of their network of relationships owner-managers are helping to create the conditions for *learning*, the root cause of sustaining competitive advantage in the longer term (Gibb, 1997). An effective network forms part of the valuable, rare, inimitable and non-substitutional strategic resource that underpins the resource-based view of the firm (see Chapter 3; Teece *et al.*, 1997; Verona, 1999). It is this network resource that needs to be enriched and the networking capability of the owner-manager that needs to be developed in order to create more competitive small firms.

This notion of capability development is closely tied to the process of learning, and it is here that our investigation into small firm networks begins. We then explore the nature of the network with regard to a particular critical incident in the life of a small joinery business in the south-east of England. Finally, we look at each of the relationships within this network to gain insight into the network management process.

Learning and Networks

Organisational learning in small firms has become the subject of much research over the last thirty years, in particular the link between performance and training (Bolton, 1971; Curran, 1986; Gibb, 1997; Cosh *et al.*, 1998; Storey, 1994). Research by Storey (1994) and Gibb (1997) concludes that there is little evidence of training having an impact on organisational performance in any direct or tangible way. A study undertaken by Cosh *et al.* (1998) for the Department for Education and Employment (DfEE, now DPES), although not conclusive, found that training had only a limited significance in the survival and growth of the firm. To improve the competitiveness of small firms, a better understanding of the nature of learning is needed, an understanding that emphasises a connectedness of knowledge creation to context, where knowledge can be speedily and effectively transferred to the business.

One of the best-recognised and valued contributions to management learning is the 'hypothesised skills/qualities model' developed by Burgoyne and Stuart (1976). Here the authors relate to the individual's ability to interact with and make sense of his environment. The selective and interpretative nature of data input, knowledge acquisition and understanding, and behavioural choice highlighted in the model is not objective and value-free, as previous mental models will reflect the type of information collected, how it is interpreted and how it is used. This means, what has worked well, or well enough, in the past is considered valid in a similar situational scenario. That said, successful managers demonstrate meta-qualities that involve double-loop learning (Argyris and Schön, 1978), where learning is based on a questioning approach that seeks out the causes rather than dealing simply with the symptoms of an incident or problem in the business, in other words 'doing the right things' (effectiveness) as opposed to simple 'doing things right' (efficiency) (see Figure 10.1).

This learning process has a social dimension. Owner-managers are constantly, through engagement with and influence of others, making sense of the flows of activities in which they find themselves, in order to make decisions and satisfy their aspirations. It is this ongoing process that sets the arena within which small-firm owner-managers learn. To examine these wider contextual issues, there is a need to focus on relationships outside the firm and not limit our understanding of the learning processes involved.

From the authors' point of view, learning is located squarely in the processes of co-participation (Thorpe, 1990; Lave and Wenger, 1991; Thorpe *et al.*, 1998), highlighting the growing concern that current learning theories (see Burgoyne and Stuart, 1976; Revans, 1982; Kolb, 1984; Pedler, 1997) often fail to account adequately for the wider context in which learning takes place, where the social dynamic is limited to 'getting things done through people'. Exploring this dimension gives a 'richer picture' of small firm owner-managers' learning. For example, Pavlica *et al.* (1998) argue for a social and conversational model of experiential learning that complements Kolb's theory of experiential learning (1984). Holman *et al.* (1996) believe that Kolb's account of learning is fundamentally

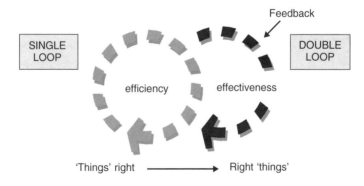

FIGURE 10.1 Single-loop and double-loop learning

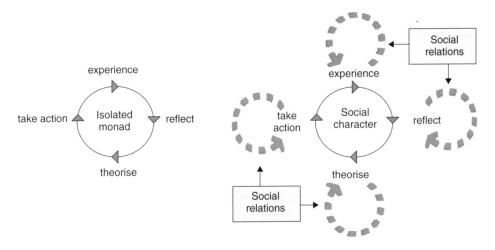

FIGURE 10.2 Two views of learning

cognitive, ignoring the influence of social relations. Here Kolb's view of the learner is as an 'intellectual Robinson Crusoe . . . isolated from their fellow beings' (Pavlica *et al.*, 1998, p. 301). The social process always mediates 'what is known' and 'how it is known' (Macharzina *et al.*, 2001). These writers suggest that learning can be considered as a process of argumentation in which reflecting, theorising, experiencing and action are viewed as different aspects of the same process, rather than stages in a process, and, more significantly, that when an individual reflects and theorises to themselves their thoughts have a 'social character' (Pavlica *et al.*, 1998, p. 302) (Figure 10.2).

Of particular interest here is the work of Wilson and Lupton (1959), who investigated the leakage of information about the Base Rate from the Bank of England in 1957. Wilson and Lupton demonstrated that knowledge transfer often had an informal social dynamic; a dynamic that allows the subject to emerge, never alone, never a pristine individual, but rather always entangled with and generously gifted by a collective (Gomart and Hennion, 1999).

All this points to the current interest in networks. The assumption about independent and isolated firms competing in an impersonal marketplace is increasingly inadequate in a world in which owner-managers are embedded in networks of social, professional and exchange relationships with other actors (Granovetter, 1985; Gulati, 1998). The term network is not used here to represent a definable spatial entity made up of a finite, identifiable set of individuals such as a breakfast club, business unit or cluster. Here the network is viewed as indeterminate, unique to each individual and incident, and can in principle ramify almost indefinitely. These networks emerge out of what Rogers and Agarwala-Rogers (1976) call the patterned communication flows of a given individual, clique or total system.

Research acknowledges the importance of network-centred learning (Birley, 1985; Granovetter, 1992; Nohria and Eccles, 1992; McQuaid, 1996; Dragoi, 1997; O'Donnell and Cummins, 1999; Collinson and Shaw, 2001). An integral part of this learning process is the complex network of relationships of the small-firm owner-manager (Taylor, 2000) (that is, all individuals that the owner-manager has contact with which in some way contribute to owner-manager decision-making).

By definition, therefore, these are not restricted to economic or permanent relations (Granovetter, 1992). Nohria (1992) states that while typically the term network is used to describe observation, it is just as likely to be used normatively to advocate what organisations, or indeed owner-managers, must do within today's competitive business environment. It is from these networks of relationships that learning and influence emerges as part of an ongoing negotiated process (Lave and Wenger, 1991).

Exploring the Network

The role of networks has been well researched by those studying ethnic businesses in Britain (Janhuha and Dickson, 1999; Ram et al., 1999) and in the Far East (Yeung, 1998; Liu, 1999; Redding, 1998, 1999) and was in evidence as early as the Hawthorne Experiments (Roethlisberger and Dickson, 1939). However, many studies of small businesses, while looking separately at networks and learning, had not considered, in any comprehensive manner, these aspects together. Furthermore, much of the quantitative and qualitative analysis has only taken into account work-related networks, which, no matter how informal or socially-based, limits our understanding of how decisions might be arrived at (see Dragoi, 1997; Wilkins, 1997; Törnroos and Nieminen, 1999). Complementary research using 'soft' approaches gives a richer understanding of learning within this deeply heterogeneous sector (see Holliday, 1995; McQuaid, 1996; Cummins et al., 1999; O'Donnell and Cummins, 1999; Shaw, 1999; Collinson and Shaw, 2001).

Taylor and Thorpe (2000) adopted a problem-centred approach in order to assess how owner-managers learn to solve problems and arrive at their decisions. Deakins and Freel (1998) support this view by arguing that the process of learning is characterised by significant and critical learning events. It is these learning events or critical incidents that Taylor and Thorpe use as catalysts for investigating learning in the small firm. Earlier research by Chell et al. (1991, pp. 74–75) used critical incidents, within semi-structured interviews, as a focus for respondents to elaborate on their behaviour in the context of these incidents, to later deduce the personality of the respondents. While the complex set of traits that underlie an entrepreneurial personality are seen to play a role in small-firm owner-manager decision-making (Chell et al., 1991), it is the collective and social dimensions of decision-making that were explored by Taylor and Thorpe (2000) in order to gain a 'richer picture' of small-firm owner-managers' learning.

The key issues and themes highlighted in Taylor and Thorpe's work have been restated here using examples from an owner-managed joinery business. Their research made the connections between owner-manager networks and the 'solving' of significant problems. This 'biographical approach' centred on critical incidents gave an indication of the role of the personal network of the owner-manager (known here as Robert Teece). This case is one of a number of owner-managed manufacturing firms located in the south-east of England that the researchers have, with the support of the Engineering Employers Federation and the Chamber of Commerce, been granted access to. This case study involved six in-depth interviews with Robert Teece and a single interview with each of six actors from within his network with regard to a particular critical incident.

Case Study: Everest Joinery

Background

Everest Joinery was founded in 1980 and is one of the largest joinery-based building companies in the south-east, employing over 40 people. Contracts vary from garden gates to £150 000 pub-restaurants. Large contracts come predominantly through their key customer Build Best Inc. As barriers to entry are low in joinery, there are numerous micro-firms operating out of garden sheds or lock-ups that undercut more established businesses. However, it is the larger firms that have been able to compete for tenders from the building industry, an industry that has recently sought to outsource its joinery requirements in order to maintain competitiveness. This has resulted in larger joinery firms forming increasingly dependent relations with the building industry, which has led to the loss of independence for some joinery businesses. In part, these changes have been driven by those in the leisure industry who prefer dealing with building firms that have a guaranteed capability to make quality craft joinery products. This is the arena within which Robert Teece, the owner manager of Everest Joinery, was operating.

Emerging Networks

Robert Teece was interviewed six times between September and December 2000. During early exchanges, he implied that the skills needed to manage the business were intrinsic to the entrepreneur. He argued that entrepreneurs are continually managing crises, and that it is the innate ability that gives him the skills to overcome such crises. The following extracts from the first interview transcript depict the entrepreneur as an 'isolated being'.

> This is my job, to make decisions; others depend on me to make the right decisions.

> Someone has to identify it's the right thing to do. Once you have decided it's the right thing to do, you can't talk to anybody, because that's not the right thing to do, you've sorted it out.

> I was quick to see his potential and gave him opportunities to develop ... my hunches usually prove right, otherwise I wouldn't be successful.

Later exchanges revealed the importance or value of the actors within Robert's network of personal relationships at particular 'life or death' decision points for the firm. Robert referred to a number of actors, his relationship with them and his perception of their worth to the business. The role of the wider network was much in evidence in the particular 'life or death' decision point highlighted below.

The Critical Incident

In April 1997, Robert had turned down an offer from a large building firm to buy his company, retaining him as managing director, even though the capital that such a development would bring was much needed for the expansion of the business. Robert wanted to retain autonomy and independence, and believed that the company offered considerably more potential for profitable growth. He decided not to sell and explained his decision as follows:

> I think partly because it certainly wasn't the time to sell, and I think generally it's going back to the entrepreneur. Most entrepreneurs are inveterate gamblers and you always think that next year will be even better than this year and the other thing is if someone is interested in buying you it must be a good business. There's got to be another reason for you to need to sell generally.

Robert contrasted his decision not to sell Everest Joinery with Jackie Stewart's decision to sell Stewart Formula One. He argued that Jackie Stewart's reason for selling to Ford was the existing resource limitations at his disposal and his high aspirations for Formula One success – something he could not achieve without building a close relationship with a significant automobile company. He believed that Jackie would not have sold for any other reason. Robert, on the other hand, was able to decline the purchase offer and source the appropriate level of finance from his major customer and not lose independence. He decided to raise the needed capital through the sale of non-voting B shares to Build Best Inc.

Initially, Robert suggested that he alone had come to this decision. However, he went on to recognise the important role that others had played in his decision-making process. He recognised the role of his former wife, though he regarded her support as simply helping him through his thought processes – 'bouncing his ideas off her', rather than contributing ideas or solutions. He later revealed that he had a short discussion with a fellow commuter on the London–Manchester shuttle, who had pointed out this way of raising capital without losing control. Moreover, Robert had checked out this idea with Andrew Poole (accountant) and David Duncan (solicitor), before making proposals to Barry Wright at Build Best Inc, his major customer. Sophie, Gerard and David are contained within the clique of significant actors (Figure 10.3). An indication of the dialogue emphasising the social aspects of decision-making are listed below:

> It's essential in the one-off joinery business that you have someone you can talk to, and share problems.

> I probably talked it through with my wife, I can't really remember – it's a while back. But generally, it's a bit like talking to yourself.

> I met this guy on the shuttle and he gave me the idea. He'd had a similar problem.

> I tend to check these things out with Andrew and David.

> I had ongoing discussions with Barry Wright.

Robert slowly revealed the roles of the actors that contributed to this particular decision. Taylor and Thorpe's (2000) findings imply a social dynamic in owner-manager learning, supporting the contention that entrepreneurs are not intellectual Robinson Crusoes (Pavlica *et al.*, 1998; Thorpe *et al.*, 1998) (Figure 10.4).

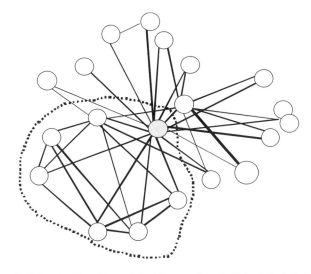

FIGURE 10.3   The clique of significant actions (within dotted circle)

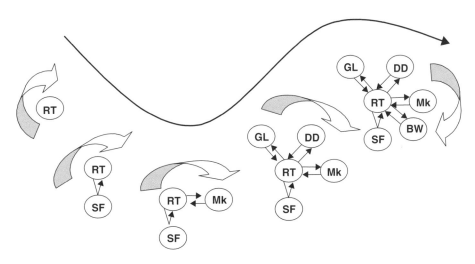

FIGURE 10.4   'Peeling the onion': owner-manager reflections on his decision-making process

The series of follow-up interviews with a range of actors from within the network gave support to the argument that owner-manager personal networks influence decision-making processes. Interviews were conducted through a series of face-to-face and/or telephone interviews with actors across Robert's network. These interviewees included some of those actors that Robert had highlighted as having a direct influence on the decision to sell non-voting B shares to his key customer and a range of other actors from across the network that reside both inside and outside the clique of significant actors. The findings from these interviews has been briefly summarised here.

Accountant

Andrew Poole pointed out that the search for a solution to this problem had started almost four years ago (early 1997). Robert was looking for a way of raising capital without losing control of the business and Build Best Inc needed to develop a closer relationship with a joinery firm that had considerable capability in order maintain its current customers. If Everest Joinery was unable to offer a closer relationship, Build Best Inc would have had to start looking elsewhere. Gerard said that the sale of the non-voting B shares was his proposal. 'That was my idea originally. Robert's a very good businessman but of course what we're here for is to provide solutions to problems. And as a matter of fact by going down the B share route we were able to differentiate the A from the B shares.'

Architect

Fred Davies had known Robert for many years and had been approached quite early on about the potential for landscaping the site and adjacent land to build a brand new multipurpose warehouse. He did not believe he had any input into the proposal but knew that his assessment of the site was a key part in the decision to expand in the current location rather than move the business: 'I've known Robert a long time and he trusted me to do the job.'

Father

Fred Teece, like David Duncan, had acted as a sounding board and devil's advocate to the proposed change. Fred had been worried that his son would lose control if the proposed change took place, and it seemed to him that much of the agreement was unwritten and based on an 'understanding'. He did not believe his son valued his contribution: 'He doesn't listen to me.'

Landlord and timber supplier

Winston Gravel knew that Everest Joinery was in need of funds to purchase adjacent land and expand the site. Robert had talked with Winston about developing the site and had mooted the possibility of outright purchase. A closer relationship between Everest Joinery and Build Best Inc benefited Winston as, potentially, an expanded site could double the amount of timber ordered to £750 000. 'Our input has not been from a business point of view; it has been more of a landlord point of view. He wanted to expand the site and have outright purchase, which I didn't want to do. I could have been difficult, but it meant a lot more business in the future to have for us, so it's paramount that I work with him.'

Owner of adjacent land

Gerard Watts did not believe he had played any role in Robert's decision to sell non-voting B shares to Build Best Inc. Gerard had purchased the land around Robert's site ten years ago to build 37 flats. A fall in the housing market had meant the building never started, and as early as 1990 Robert had showed an interest in the site. Two years ago he started to rent a warehouse on Gerard's land, before purchasing the land. 'I bought the site which surrounded where they were existing. There's an existing warehouse on the site that Robert rented for two years with a view to buy if the business needed it. I sold them half the land so he can extend the business. I had the land, he wanted it; it's as simple as that really.'

Solicitor

David Duncan was personally against the move to sell non-voting B shares to Build Best Inc as he believed Robert would ultimately lose control and influence. He saw his role as one of first challenging and then of operationalising the sale. He forced Robert to think through the consequences of his actions by continually questioning each of the courses of action that Robert was proposing to take. He believed Robert values him as both a personal friend and a legal expert, though he went on to state that: 'No one remembers you make a difference as a solicitor.'

On the whole these actors did not see themselves as contributing to the decision made by Robert with regard to this critical incident. Yet they all played some role in the decision, either contributing directly or indirectly to the solution, or compelling Robert to think through and hone his argument. Contributions are like tiny pieces of a unique jigsaw puzzle, which slowly emerge through social interaction and are made sense of by the owner-manager.

The Network Graphic

Taylor and Thorpe (2000) use the network graphic to portray the subtle relationships between the actors that emerged during the time of the study in relation to a particular incident. However, the representation of the network in these graphics does not easily identify the intra- and inter-organisational relationships involved, nor does it inform how the network could be enriched in order to improve owner-manager learning.

To assist in this process, a more structured network graphic advocated by Conway and Steward (1998) has been used. This actor positioning template (Figure 10.5) facilitates the locating of actor networks in the context of the innovation process, thus better visualising social interaction. The ellipse in the centre of the template represents the intra-organisational dyads and the six outer segments represent the inter-organisational dyads. In line with Conway and Steward (1998) the network adopted by Taylor and Thorpe (2000) is centred on a key individual and includes other actors who have had a definable input into the learning process. What is apparent is that the actor positioning template does not easily represent the clique of significant actors that form the safe environment where Robert Teece tests out his ideas. Many of these actors operate on the fringes of the firm and do not reside within the template as it stands. These include family members, friends and professional advisors such as solicitors or accountants (see Figure 10.6).

The ellipse has been modified to include a professional periphery. It is argued that this group, while usually residing outside the firm, is closely linked with the small firm's internal resources. A second modification is the addition of the

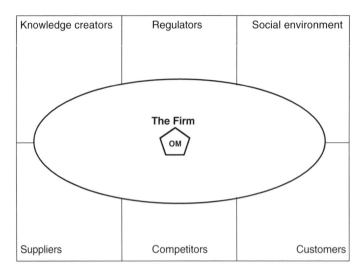

FIGURE 10.5   Conway and Steward's 'Actor Positioning Template'. *International Journal of Innovation Management*, Imperial College Press, **2**:2, Special Issue June 1998, p. 238

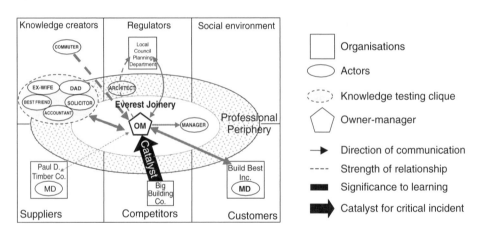

FIGURE 10.6   Adapted from Conway and Steward's 'Actor Positioning Template'. *International Journal of Innovation Management*, Imperial College Press, **2**:2, Special Issue, June 1998, p. 238

knowledge testing clique that has been positioned within the knowledge creators segment of the actor positioning template, replicating the clique of significant actors highlighted by Taylor and Thorpe (2000).

Managing and Enriching the Network

The argument is that by enriching this network resource and developing networking capability, owner-manager learning can be more effective. The Centre for Enterprise in Leicester supports this view, arguing that the building and maintaining of networks is central to the success of the small firm (Centre for Enterprise, 2001). Central to the enrichment process is the development of an owner-manager's networking capability to improve the productivity of the network resource. This entails the development of existing relationships and the introduction of new actors to complement and/or replace these relationships in line with current and future organisational requirements.

The critical incident from the Everest Joinery case study goes some way to suggest that owner-manager decision-making is in part dependent on and influenced by the network of relationships that each owner-manager has. There is evidence in this case that Robert Teece of Everest Joinery has used his network resource and network capability to better manage his business and inform his business-related decision-making. To gain a deeper insight into the network management and enrichment process, we will re-examine Robert Teece's social network by looking at each of the relationships within his network resource in more depth.

Joe Askew – Bank Manager (1979–1995)

Robert and Joe have a very close relationship that continues today in spite of Joe retiring in 1995. His father had introduced Robert to Joe, who had been his bank manager and friend for a number of years. Robert believed his excellent overdraft facility at the bank was in part due to his and his father's long-standing relationships and their development of mutual trust.

Maurice Bright and Suzy Bright – Backup Co

This personalised way of conducting business was evident in an example Robert gave of one of his subcontractors, Backup Co. This relationship came about because Suzy Bright, the wife of the owner-manager of Backup Co, kept dropping in, over a 12-month period, to ask if they needed any work subcontracting. She 'hassled' Robert until he agreed to subcontract some work to them. He said that he would never have done business with them but he admired the tenacity with which Suzy chased the business. Robert went on to explain that it had proven to be a mutually beneficial relationship because his main business was cyclical, they take only a minimal margin, and the subcontracting fills Backup Co's slack time.

Murray Bonner – Manager

Robert had worked with Murray before, in a previous company and in the early years of Everest Joinery. Murray had left Everest Joinery because his job had become increasingly office-based and he preferred to 'get his hands dirty'. He left the business on good terms and the two carried on a successful business and social relationship, regularly subcontracting to each other. Murray rejoined the business in 1988 to manage the workshop, leaving Robert free to develop the business more strategically. Murray can be trusted and is a good project manager.

Fred Davies – Architect

Robert has known Fred for a number of years. Fred was a well-respected local architect who had close dealings with the building industry. Robert had always maintained a close working relationship with Fred and always kept him in mind for any developments on the site. Their relationship was more professional than social.

David Duncan – Solicitor

Robert has known David since his early 20s. He cannot remember when they met. They get on well and trust each other implicitly.

Sophie Francis (Formerly Teece) – Ex-wife

His ex-wife Sophie was and continues to be a close friend and 'personnel' advisor. She works as a personnel officer for a well-known confectionery company. He sees her skills as invaluable and complementary to his own.

Jack Lambert – Best Friend

He had known Jack since childhood. Jack has moved around a great deal and has lived abroad for many years. They are regularly in touch. Robert says that Jack puts everything into perspective.

Stuart Learner – Account Manager at Bank (1999 – to date)

'BusyBank PLC' redefined Everest Joinery as a middle-sized business and moved his account to a regional centre. Robert does not believe that this relationship can be managed in a personalised way.

Gerard Lucas – Personal Friend and Tax Inspector

Gerard is a long-standing friend from school. They renewed their friendship after accidentally meeting in a local pub, and have kept in touch ever since. It is not unusual for them to meet up once a month to mix a little business and pleasure. Robert sees this as free and objective advice.

Andrew Poole – Poole, Meadows & Son Accountants

Recommended by his tax inspector friend, Gerard Lucas. He knew a little about the company as he had always lived locally. He didn't want someone too old. Andrew Poole was also the brother-in-law of his best friend, Jack Lambert.

David Poole – Insurance Brokers

Andrew Poole, his accountant, recommended David. He had known David from school where David was in the year above, and through his best friend's sister, who had married David.

James Pritchard – Bank Manager (1995–1999)

The relationship with James was professional but less personal. The business was considered to have a good track record with a strong financial footing. Maintaining such a close relationship was viewed as a lower priority. However, he still keeps in touch with James on a social basis for informal professional advice.

Barry Wright – Build Best Inc

Robert has close personal relationships with both of the directors of Build Best Inc. He meets Barry Wright (senior director) twice a month to discuss the business (these meetings are viewed by both parties as business/social occasions). The relationship has developed over the last twenty years.

As mentioned earlier, the network has the potential to be developed into a valuable, rare, inimitable and non-substitutional strategic resource. Effective networks contain a variety of dimensions and are managed in line with organisational need, dimensions that range from intensity, durability and reciprocity to diversity, transiency and redundancy. This intensity is evident in the writings of Dwyer (2000), who states that relationships with family members and friends based on trust and respect are of particular importance in times of need. Such need was evident in the Everest Joinery case study. These reciprocal and enduring relationships provide a sense of identity and a secure base. The degree to which actors are prepared to honour obligations within these relationships is a measure of the intensity of these parts of the network (Shaw and Conway, 2000), an intensity that informs the attitudes, values and behaviour of the actor anchored in the centre of his or her social network.

Diversity, transiency and redundancy play equally important roles, offering greater opportunities for acquiring information and advice. Granovetter (Shaw and Conway, 2000) argues that a narrow and tight network, one that is socially cohesive and containing actors with a narrow range and skills, knowledge and experiences, would offer fewer opportunities than a loose-knit, more outward-looking network. It is, however, the owner-manager who needs to be able to spot and exploit these opportunities. O'Donnell and Cummins (1999) found that often the most productive form of networking was 'opportunistic, intuitive and unplanned'. Such exploitation was evident in Robert Teece's managing of the critical incident in the Everest Joinery case study described earlier. A lack of vision from the owner-manager can limit the potential of the network resource. Competitive advantage emerges out of a combination of network resource and networking capability, where the network resource is influenced by the networking capability and vice versa (see Figure 10.7).

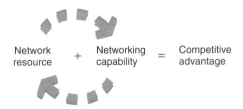

Network resource + Networking capability = Competitive advantage

FIGURE 10.7 The competitive advantage equation

Looking at the case study in this chapter, it was evident that the network resource helped to act as a force of influence on Robert's decision-making process, and a clique of significant actors existed where ideas were 'tested out'. While revealing a clique of significant actors, intensity and direction were not initially evident. Further exploration around a critical incident helped to highlight these variations, which Taylor and Thorpe (2000) argue hold the essence of the value of the relationship or combination of relationships to the decision-making process of the small-firm owner-manager.

Dwyer (2000) argues that there were three motives for an individual to be affiliated to others: social comparison, anxiety reduction and information seeking. We can use these descriptors to help identify the role affiliation played within the critical incident in the Everest Joinery case. In brief, Robert had turned down an offer from a large building firm to buy his company, retaining him as managing director, even though he needed the capital that such a development would bring for the expansion of the business. He decided to raise the capital himself through the sale of non-voting B shares to Build Best Inc., his main customer. He indicated that a number of individuals within his wider network had played some role in this decision. First, there was a fellow commuter, a businessman who had been through the same situation as Robert and had offered him reassurance from a position of knowledge. Dwyer (2000) argues that people like to discuss issues with someone who has been in a similar situation (social comparison). His ex-wife offered sympathy and emotional support which helped reduced anxiety. His accountant and solicitor offered reassurance based on their expertise and the level of trust and respect that had developed between them and Robert, so reducing anxiety and providing information.

It is evident that personal recommendations have played a significant part in developing Robert's personal network of relationships. Each actor seems to be a ready-made piece within a unique and complex network where mutual respect and trust play a central role. Reciprocity, intensity and durability are balanced with a diversity of complementary skills and experiences across the network that Robert Teece can draw upon and contribute to. Network enrichment and management is an ongoing process that is a necessary ingredient for the development for owner-manager learning and effective decision-making.

Conclusion

Success in the small firm is primarily related to the desire of the owner-manager to achieve personal involvement, responsibility and an independent lifestyle. An important factor in satisfying these aspirations is the quality of the small-firm owner-manager's network of relationships and how the owner-manager learns from and manages those relationships.

To this end, it is important for each owner-manager to establish a clearer understanding of his network of relationships. Some useful questions for an owner-manager would be:

- How diverse is my network?
- Do gatekeepers or brokers control access to key actors?
- Is the density of my network limiting opportunity?

- How durable are these relationships?
- How intense are the exchanges?
- How frequent are the exchanges?
- Am I optimising my network of personal relations?
- Where are the deficiencies in my network?
- How might I go about enhancing my network?
- How could I optimise my current network?

A network approach helps to better explain the complex learning environment of those managing small businesses. Effective decision-making is dependent on both the quality of the actors within an owner-manager's network and the ability of the owner-manager to manage and develop that network. It is this proactive and directed networking by the owner-manager and the uniqueness of the relationships developed that can help differentiate a small firm from its competitors, thus creating a competitive advantage. While the exploitation of competitive advantage in small firms is difficult to observe, initiatives that enrich owner-manager networks and get personal are beneficial for engaging with small businesses and promoting owner-manager learning.

References

Argyris, C. and Schön, D. (1978) *Organizational Learning: A Theory of Action Perspective*. Addison-Wesley, London.

Birley, S. (1985) 'The role of networks in the entrepreneurial process', *Journal of Business Venturing*, **1**, 107–117.

Bolton, J.E. (1971) *Report of the Committee of Inquiries on Small Firms*. HMSO, London.

Burgoyne, J. and Stuart, R. (1976) 'The nature, use and acquisition of managerial skills and other attributes', *Personnel Review*, **5**:4, 19–29.

Centre for Enterprise (2001) Building and Maintaining Networks. Session 7 on the Discovering Entrepreneurship Programme, Centre for Enterprise. Leicester.

Chell, E., Haworth, J. and Brearley, S. (1991) *The Entrepreneurial Personality*. Routledge, London.

Collinson, E. and Shaw, E. (2001) 'Entrepreneurial marketing – a historical perspective on development and practice', *Management Decision*, **39**:9, 761–766.

Conway, S. and Steward, F. (1998) 'Mapping innovation networks', *International Journal of Innovation Management*, **2**:2, Special Issue (June 1998), 223–254.

Cosh, A., Duncan, J. and Hughes, A. (1998) *Investing in Training and Small Firm Growth and Survival: An Empirical Analysis for the UK 1987–95*. Department for Education and Employment, Research Report No. 36.

Cummins, D., O'Donnell, A., Carson, D. and Gilmore, A. (1999) *A Qualitative Study of Networking in SMEs*. AMA Research Symposium on Marketing and Entrepreneurship.

Curran, J. (1986) *Bolton Fifteen Years On*. London, Small Firm Research: A Review and Analysis of Small Business Research in Britain (1971–1986), Small Business Research Trust, September.

Deakins, D. and Freel, M. (1998) 'Entrepreneurial learning and the growth process in SMEs', *The Learning Organization*, **5**:3, 144–155.

Dragoi, S. (1997) *Entrepreneurial Networks as Learning Environments in Small and Medium-sized Enterprises*. Transfer Report from MPhil to PhD, University of Derby, England.

Dwyer, D. (2000) *Interpersonal Relationships*. Routledge, London.

Gibb, A.A. (1997) 'Small firms' training and competitiveness. Building upon the small business as a learning organisation', *International Small Business Journal*, **15**:5, 13–29.

Gomart, E. and Hennion, A. (1999) 'A sociology of attachment: music, amateurs, drug users', in J. Law and J. Hassard (eds) *Actor Network Theory and After*. Blackwell, Oxford, pp. 220–247.

Granovetter, M. (1985). 'Economic action and social structure: a theory of embeddedness', *American Journal of Sociology*, **91**, 481–510.

Granovetter, M. (1992) 'Problems of explanation in economic sociology', in N. Nohria and R.G. Eccles (eds) *Networks and Organizations: Structure, Form & Action*. Harvard Business School Press, Boston, MA, pp. 25–56.

Gulati, R. (1998) 'Alliances and networks', *Strategic Management Journal*, **19**:4, 293–317.

Holliday, R. (1995) *Investigating Small Firms: Nice Work?* Routledge, London.

Janhuha, S. and Dickson, K. (1999) *Transitional Challenges within South Asian Family Businesses*. Paper presented to the Small Firm and Enterprise Development Conference, the University of Leeds, 22–23 March.

Jennings, P. and Beaver, G. (1997) 'The performance and competitive advantage of small firms: a management perspective', *International Small Business Journal*, **15**:2, 63–75.

Kolb, D.A. (1984) *Experiential Learning*. Prentice Hall, Englewood Cliffs, NJ.

Lave, J. and Wenger, E. (1991) *Situated Learning: Legitimate Peripheral Participation*. Cambridge University Press, Cambridge.

Liu, H. (1999) 'Globalisation, institutionalisation and social foundation of Chinese business networks', in H.W. Yeung and K. Olds (eds) *Globalisation of Chinese Business Firms*, Macmillan, Basingstoke, pp. 105–125.

Macharzina, K., Oesterle, M. and Brodel, D. (2001) 'Learning in multinationals', in M. Dierkes, A. Berthoin Antal, J. Child and I. Nonaka (eds) *Handbook of Organizational Learning and Knowledge*, Oxford University Press, Oxford, pp. 631–656.

McQuaid, R.W. (1996) 'Social networks, entrepreneurship and regional development', in M.W. Danson (ed.) *Small Firm Formation and Regional Economic Development*. Routledge, London, pp. 118–131.

Nohria, N. (1992) 'Face-to-face: making network organizations work', in N. Nohria and R.G. Eccles (eds) *Networks and Organizations: Structure, Form and Action*. Harvard Business School Press, Boston, pp. 288–308.

Nohria, N. and Eccles, R. (1992) *Networks and Organizations: Structure, Form and Action*. Harvard Business School Press, Boston, pp. 288–308.

O'Donnell, A. and Cummins, D. (1999) 'The use of qualitative methods to research networking in SMEs', *Qualitative Market Research: An International Journal*, **2**:2, 82–91.

Pavlica, K., Holman, D. and Thorpe, R. (1998) 'The manager as a practical author of learning', *Career Development International*, **3**:7, 300–307.

Pedler, M. (1997) *The Learning Company: A Strategy for Sustainable Development*, 2nd edition. McGraw-Hill, London.

Ram, M., Sanghera, K., Khan, D.R. and Abbas, T. (1999) 'Ethnic matching in enterprise support', *Journal of Small Business & Enterprise Development*, **6**:1, 26–36.

Redding, G. (1998) 'The changing business scene in Pacific Asia', in F. McDonald and R. Thorpe (eds) *Organisational Strategy and Technological Adaptation to Global Change*. Macmillan, London.

Redding, G. (1999) 'What is Chinese about Chinese family business? And how much is family and how much is business?', in H.W. Yeung and K. Olds (eds) *Globalisation of Chinese Business Firms*. Macmillan, Basingstoke, pp. 31–54.

Revans, R. (1982) *The Origins and Growth of Action Learning*. Chartwell-Bratt, Bromley and Lund, London.

Roethlisberger, F.J. and Dickson, W.J. (1939) *Management and the Worker*. Harvard University Press, Cambridge, MA, pp. 501–509.

Rogers, E.M. and Agarwala-Rogers, R. (1976) *Communication in Organizations*. Free Press, New York.

Shaw, E. (1999) 'A guide to the qualitative research process: evidence from a small firm study, *Qualitative Market Research: An International Journal*, **2**:2, 59–70.

Shaw, E. and Conway, S. (2000) 'Networking and the small firm', in S. Carter and D. Jones-Evans (eds) *Enterprise and Small Business*. Financial Times/Prentice Hall, London. pp. 367–383.

Storey, D.J. (1994) *Understanding the Small Business Sector*. Routledge, London.

Szarka, J. (1990) 'Networks and small firms', *International Small Business Journal*, **8**:2, 10–23.

Taylor, D.W. (2000) Learning as a process of interaction: An iterative exploration of small firm owner-manager networks. Research in Management and Business Working Paper Series, Manchester Metropolitan University, WP 00/01 (August).

Taylor, D.W. and Thorpe, R. (2000) *Learning as a process of co-participation: An iterative exploration of small-firm owner-manager networks*. Working paper presented to the British Academy of Management Conference, the University of Edinburgh (September).

Teece, D.J., Pisano, G.P. and Shuen, A. (1997) 'Dynamic capabilities and strategic management', *Strategic Management Journal*, **18**:7, 509–533.

Thorpe, R. (1988) An exploration of small business 'success': the role of the manager. Thesis, Lancaster University, School of Management.

Thorpe, R. (1990) 'An alternative theory of management education', *Journal of European Industrial Training*, **14**:2, 3–15.

Thorpe, R., Pavlica, K. and Holman, D. (1998) 'The manager as a practical author and mediator of learning – a conversational view of learning and managing people in organisations', *Applied Industrial Psychology*, **XXXII**:3–4, 89–96.

Törnroos, J.A. and Nieminen, J. (eds) (1999) *Business Entry in Eastern Europe*. Kikimora Publications, Helsinki.

Verona, G. (1999) 'A resource-based view of product development', *Academy of Management Review*, **24**:1, 132–142.

Wilkins, G. (1997) How does networking contribute towards the success of small firms in the advertising industry? Paper presented to the Small Business and Enterprise Conference, Sheffield (March).

Wilson, C.S. and Lupton, T. (1959) The social background and connections of 'top decision-makers', the bank rate tribunal: a symposium. The Manchester School of Economic and Social Studies, Vol. XXVII, Department of Economics, University of Manchester (January).

Yeung, H.W. (1998) *Transnational Corporations and Business Networks*. Routledge, London.

Section 3

FUNCTIONAL MANAGEMENT

Chapter 11

THE ADOPTION OF E-BUSINESS TECHNOLOGY BY SMEs

Paul Windrum and Pascale de Berranger

Introduction

This chapter seeks to identify key factors influencing the adoption of e-business technology by SMEs. An important issue that is highlighted is the need to reorientate communication behaviour of the businesses along the supply chain and within the organisation itself. As part of the research, this chapter draws upon a range of literatures on the diffusion of new information and communication technologies (ICTs), many of which have hitherto been treated as separate. It is an exercise that seeks explicitly to draw lessons from research conducted on the adoption of previous ICT technologies. The reasons for this are twofold. First, e-business technologies are the latest in a line of new ICT technologies. When exploited successfully, these ICTs have increased firm competitiveness either by raising the efficiency of internal communication and organisation and/or supply chain relationships, or by facilitating the development of new/improved products and services. Second, it is hypothesised that many of the factors affecting the successful adoption of new technologies are generic in nature. With regard to SMEs specifically, consideration of earlier research may assist us in identifying a set of enablers and barriers to e-business adoption. Hence, by acknowledging the context and prior history of research in the area, we are able to map out the dimensions of future theoretical and empirical research in an e-business adoption by SMEs.

In addition to drawing together factors identified by previous research, we highlight the implications of network externalities for the timing of technology investments and the returns that accrue to early and late adopters. We also draw attention to a number of problems associated with the analytical concept of 'the SME'. The research proceeds by clearly defining the technological and organisational characteristics of the e-business model and by briefly considering the trends in adoption in the UK *vis-à-vis* adoption in the other G7 countries. Together these set up a detailed consideration of the internal and external factors influencing adoption. A qualitative approach, in the form of a detailed case study, is then used to explore the potential usefulness of the identified categories of factors. The results of our findings are then drawn together in the concluding section of this chapter.

Stages to E-Business

E-business is the integration of the Internet and related ICTs into the business organisation, and has two facets. One is the integration of the supply chain in such a way that production and delivery become a seamless process. The other is the creation of new business models based on open systems of communication between customers, suppliers and partners. Where the integration of the supply chain provides increased efficiency and significant cost advantages through waste minimisation, the development of new products and services is facilitated by new ways of conducting business based on internetworking between organisations and individuals.

It is possible to trace a number of stages through which firms pass as they progress towards e-business. Each stage is associated with a higher degree of internetworking and sophistication in communication modes, the progression from traditional commerce to e-commerce business models requiring an increasingly radical restructuring of the internal structures of the organisation. The first stage is the adoption of e-mail. E-mail is a cost-effective and fast method of communicating and sending files that can improve the efficiency of internal communications within an organisation and also external communications with customers and suppliers. The adoption of e-mail for internal communications is closely correlated with the setting up of a local area network (LAN) to link computers within a building. Compared with a wide area network (WAN) that links computers between sites, setting up a LAN is relatively simple and so the costs of implementation are much lower. Both types of network facilitate electronic communication in the form of e-mail, file sharing and data back-up within an organisation. The second stage on the path to e-business is the establishment of a web presence. In the past, the first company website was often a 'flat ad website'. This is the simplest form of website, consisting of a one- or two-page document providing background information on the company, its contact address and telephone number. In the past, a flat ad website did not always have an e-mail link, although this is now a standard feature. A more sophisticated web presence is provided by a 'brochure website'. This provides details of product/service specifications, price and availability, and may make use of graphical illustrations of products much in the manner of a mail order catalogue. A brochure website also opens up the possibility of online ordering and payment. Online selling provides a relatively low-cost means of reaching a large number of customers. Additionally, the geographical reach of a website is far greater than that of a traditional retail outlet. If a digital commodity is being sold, then multiple copies can be distributed across the Internet at zero marginal cost. If the commodity cannot be digitised then a means of physical delivery, e.g. overnight carriers, needs to be organised. As Rosenberg observed some twenty years ago, important epochs in economic history are marked by the emergence of clusters of new, interrelated technologies rather than single technologies (Rosenberg, 1982, p. 59). The introduction of online selling invariably requires large-scale changes in information systems supporting outbound logistics – including stock and inventory control, warehouse management and delivery planning and control – and marketing and sales. This often requires the introduction of new complementary ICTs, new competences and business practices, and a degree of organisational restructuring.

Applying Porter's value chain model to the current discussion, we see that higher degrees of organisational restructuring are associated with each of the stages up to e-business. E-mail is relatively easy to adopt because its introduction affects those internal information systems linked to support activities in the value chain. By contrast, online selling requires a higher degree of organisational restructuring because its introduction affects outbound logistics and marketing, both of which are primary activities in an organisation's value chain. A still higher degree of organisational restructuring is required for businesses making the transition to e-business itself. As noted, e-business involves both the restructuring of supply chains and the reconfiguration of the business–customer interface with the aim of constructing a seamless web between customers and suppliers along the supply chain. This restructuring affects all of the primary activities of the organisation's value chain: inbound logistics, operations/manufacturing, outbound logistics, marketing and sales, and after-sales support. The Internet provides a common, interoperable platform for this new business model. A set of additional elements arise in the e-business model. Interactive websites, incorporating technologies such as dynamic databases and videoconferencing, facilitate multilateral communications between client and provider regarding product design. Extranets enable a business to share part of its information or operations with suppliers, vendors, partners, customers or other businesses. These can be used to check raw material requirements, investigate stock availability, or check the progress of an order. For many businesses, this represents an important step in the adoption of new working practices with partners. Internally, new ways of working are also being explored by offering employees remote access. Marketing and sales are further transformed by the development of after-sales support underpinned by database records of customers and telephone call centres. Finally, e-business requires the introduction of new financial management practices and support systems due to its high degree of complexity and the need for continuous information collection and monitoring in order to optimise a business' cash flow, in real-time.

The different types of communications required for e-business have been highlighted in the literature (e.g. Venkantraman, 1994; Gonzalez, 1998). The Internet is an inherently two-way medium that requires the development of new styles of conversation between an organisation and its clients/suppliers. It is still possible for organisations to use the Internet to conduct unidirectional interactions, e.g. completing and dispatching forms, sending and receiving messages via e-mail or voicemail. However, what is novel about the Internet is the ability to converse with someone while both parties work on an application, see the conversant, and transfer documents as the conversation continues. Gonzalez (1998) distinguishes four types of communication, each requiring a higher degree of organisational sophistication: the publication mode, the asymmetrical mode, the symmetrical mode and the synchronous virtual environment mode. The publication mode is the traditional unidirectional model of previous ICTs in which the sender formulates a static document that the receiver reads. The asymmetrical mode is a bidirectional, time-delayed didactic communication with one participant formulating a written question or statement and the other responding after a time lag. The symmetrical mode differs from the asymmetrical mode in that it has multidirectional communication with numerous feedbacks that takes place in real time and which extends the degree of interactivity. Finally, the synchronous virtual environment mode uses real-time, dynamic, multidimensional communication to support key business processes.

There remains enormous scope for extending the use of e-commerce in UK SMEs. We have suggested that the commercial benefits of e-business lie in six areas. First, significant opportunities exist for SMEs to expand their geographical reach. Second, important cost benefits lie in improved efficiency in procurement, production and logistics processes. Third, there is enormous scope for gaining competitive advantage through improved customer communications and management. Customer care websites are now becoming increasingly common. Fourth, the Internet reduces barriers to entry for new market entrants and provides an opportunity for small firms to reorientate their supply chain relationships to forge new strategic partnerships. Where proprietary electronic data interchange (EDI)[1] systems were promoted by large organisations as a means of tying in smaller suppliers to their needs, and of securing market power, open Internet-based platforms provide small firms with a far greater degree of strategic manoeuvre and negotiating power. Fifth, the technology facilitates the development of new types of products and new business models for generating revenues in different ways. Sixth, there is the opportunity to transform SMEs into information-driven businesses. The technology offers, for the first time, an affordable means of capturing and processing the information generated through electronic transactions. Through techniques such as data mining, this information can be translated into knowledge about what the company sells and can be linked to how the company operates, resulting in an integrated approach to knowledge management.

Recent Trends in the Adoption of E-Business Technologies by UK SMEs

The UK government's 1998 White Paper 'Our Competitive Future – Building the Knowledge Driven Economy' (HMSO, 1998) set targets for the numbers of micro enterprises, and SMEs becoming wired up to the digital marketplace. The targets were specified in terms of the adoption of key e-business technologies. Taking into account the current range of available technologies, this was interpreted as the adoption and use of external e-mail, websites and EDI. Numerically, the target set was for adoption of these underpinning technologies by one million micro enterprises and SMEs by 2002. When the White Paper was published, an estimated 350 000 micro enterprises and SMEs possessed these technologies. In 2001, some 1.9 million micro enterprises and SMEs had either adopted e-mail or an

EDI system, or set up a website (Spectrum/DTI, 2001). Still, UK SMEs are only beginning to experiment with new e-business solutions.

While 70 per cent of small firms in the UK have some form of Internet access (Spectrum/DTI, 2001), this remains limited to the exchange of e-mails or a static company website. Very few UK SMEs (or large firms for that matter) use the Internet as a fully interactive e-commerce platform. Usage remains confined to the provision of product information and to generic intra- and interfirm communication. According to sector studies conducted by the Office for National Statistics (ONS, 2001), nearly £57bn of goods and services were sold over the Internet in 2000.[2] Putting this into perspective, this represents 2 per cent of total sales in these sectors. The UK experience is in line with trends in other countries. Indeed, it has been suggested that, in terms of online trading, the UK ranks equal highest with Canada among the G7 countries (Spectrum/DTI, 2001). The ONS data suggest there is a positive association between company size and the proportion of UK firms engaged in online trading, defined as both ordering and paying online with either customers or suppliers. As in other countries, business-to-business (B2B) transactions constitute the majority of online trade in the UK. More than four-fifths of total online transactions were between firms, with an estimated value of £47bn. Again, the volume of transactions carried out electronically represents a small percentage of the total transaction volume in the UK. Interfirm electronic information flows remain centred on 'traditional' proprietary networking technologies such as EDI via direct lines and value added network (VAN) applications. At present there is a wide range of proprietary e-commerce solutions, including e-commerce interfaces and support applications built upon various enterprise resource planning (ERP) platforms and proprietary database systems.

There is a continued steady increase in nearly all measures of ICT uptake and usage in the UK, and the once enormous gap with the USA is closing. A noticeable gap remains, however, with US businesses still more likely to use ICTs across a wide range of business processes. Furthermore, the earlier adoption by US enterprises may well mean that they are using ICTs more intensively than their Canadian, Japanese and European counterparts (ownership measures are a crude indicator of usage since they do not indicate intensity of use). Comparing the UK experience with that across the G7, UK SMEs are ahead of their counterparts in Japan, France and Italy but lag behind US, Canadian and German enterprises. Indeed, whereas UK enterprises used to be reported as having a lead over their counterparts in European nations such as Germany, this is no longer true. A feature of the data noted by the recent Spectrum/DTI report is the distribution of performances according to the size of enterprises. The spread of performance between the smallest and the largest companies in the UK is greater than for the other reported G7 countries. This is illustrated in Figure 11.1 below which indicates the percentage of micro, small, medium and large respondents in the USA, Canada, UK, Japan, Germany and France that report the establishment of a company website, external e-mail, EDI installations and online selling systems.

At the national level, UK enterprises are among those most likely to have both local area networks (LANs) and wide area networks (WANs). Indeed, the pattern of internal e-mail adoption was found to be closely correlated with that of LANs. Of all respondents contacted, UK respondents had the highest reported use of videoconferencing (22 per cent of all UK respondents). This may reflect both the relative evenness of the geographical spread of population in the UK, and the high proportion of multisite and multinational businesses operating in the UK. However, the reported incidence of UK enterprises with Internet access, websites, external e-mail, EDI and online selling do not compare favourably with competitors in Canada, the USA and Germany. Twenty-seven per cent of UK businesses allow their customers to order online compared with 40 per cent of businesses in Germany, 28 per cent in USA and Canada, 20 per cent in Italy and Japan, and 17 per cent in France. Breaking down the figures by company size (Figure 11.1), the incidence of online provision in small and medium-sized businesses is the same as for large firms in the UK, at 28 per cent. Just 54 per cent of small and 65 per cent of medium-sized enterprises in the UK report they have a marketing website. This compares with 54 per cent and 71 per cent in Canada, and 64 per cent and 66 per cent in the USA. Interestingly, UK SMEs measure favourably compared to their German counterparts, who have a reported provision of 50 per cent and 63 per cent respectively. The overall picture is worse due to the lower provision reported among micro and large business organisations in the UK compared to their German counterparts.

The empirical studies conducted by ONS and Spectrum/DTI provide a valuable resource for those interested in the current diffusion of e-business ICTs in the UK. However, these reports do not explore in detail the key factors affecting adoption. Additionally, indicators such as EDI penetration are not suited to a discussion

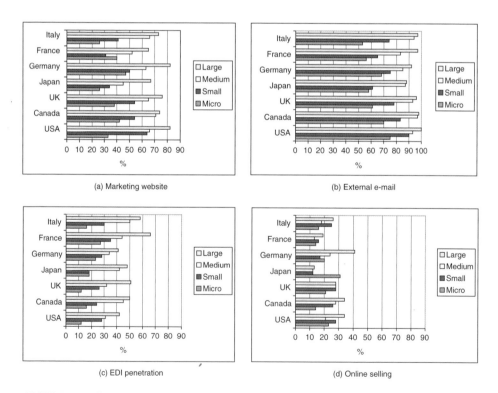

FIGURE 11.1 G7 comparison of micro, small, medium and large businesses using e-business ICTs (weighted by business size) (%). Source: Spectrum/DTI, 2000

of e-business diffusion. As highlighted above, e-business is associated with the adoption of systems based on open, Internet-based standards. These systems seek to displace older EDI technologies. Second, as stated earlier, ownership is a crude indicator of use because it neither indicates the purpose to which a technology is applied nor its intensity of use. For example, having a web presence does not indicate that an SME has an interactive website that supports e-business. Third, we have discussed how the establishment of effective e-business systems requires the integration of marketing, purchasing and human resources (HR). E-business requires more than the adoption of one or more key technologies; it requires the development of an interoperable ICT platform that integrates all three of these key business functions. An important research question is therefore, to what extent have UK SMEs integrated their organisational computer systems? We will turn our attention to this and other research questions in the remainder of this chapter.

In order to expand the discussion of the factors affecting the adoption of e-business ICTs, we shall consider two bodies of relevant literature. The first is the research on adoption that has been developed in the information systems (IS) literature. The second is the body of research that has been developed in the literature on technological innovation. These are examined in the following two sections.

Organisational Factors Affecting Adoption by SMEs

In this section we consider factors affecting the adoption of ICTs that have been highlighted in the information systems (IS) literature. This body of research focuses on internal factors within the business organisation, marrying technical implementation issues with business strategy issues. In principle, one would like to treat information systems as a separate factor of production and then measure the contribution of this factor input to overall profitability. However, this is problematic for two reasons. First, the artefactual aspects of information systems are varied in character; they comprise elements ranging from http and TCP/IP protocols to databases to processor chips to cables. Second, information systems have an organisational as well as an artefactual dimension, i.e. a particular information system technology has an associated set of organisational structures and procedures. What is more, different information systems typically have different sets of associated structures and procedures. The upshot is that information systems, unlike labour, do not have a common unit of measurement. Consequently, researchers have sought alternative ways in which to proceed. As yet, no commonly agreed method exists in this literature. In different ways, researchers have sought to investigate factors affecting the 'successful implementation' of new ICT systems. The most common indicators used are measures of user satisfaction (typically managers' subjective evaluations), expenditure on ICTs, evaluations of the degree to which systems accomplish the original set of specified objectives, and subjective estimates (again typically those of managers) of the payoffs of system implementation to the organisation.

Turning to the factors affecting successful implementation that have been highlighted, we follow the Yap *et al.* (1992) schema. This clusters factors reported as affecting the successful adoption of ICTs by SMEs into five major classes:

organisational characteristics, organisational action, system characteristics, internal expertise and external expertise.

Organisational Characteristics

As in other literatures, the IS literature notes that company size influences the probability of ICT adoption with smaller companies less likely to adopt new technologies than their larger counterparts. Smaller organisations typically have less complex organisational structures than larger organisations and, hence, have lower internal requirements for extensive communication technologies. With smaller volumes of information to be communicated and stored, the need for ICTs to manage information is less compelling.

ICT experience and the presence of in-house processing capabilities are well-documented factors affecting ICT adoption. In addition to technical knowledge and competences (Raymond, 1985; Yap *et al.*, 1992; Chapman *et al.*, 2000), the literature highlights the importance of application capabilities. The latter category involves a strategic understanding of the market opportunities afforded by new ICTs, their organisational implications, and the ability to successfully implement them in order to leverage competitive advantage (Venkatraman, 1994; Mullins *et al.*, 2001; Tetteh and Burns, 2001). Research on UK SMEs consistently indicates problems in both categories. Spectrum/DTI (2001) highlights the inability of UK SMEs to take advantage of the opportunities afforded by e-business ICTs. Tetteh and Burns suggest that 'few SMEs realise that they need a strategic appreciation of the dynamic of the web and that they will have to develop the capabilities for managing the information infrastructure for an e-business' (2001, p. 171). Furthermore, Chapman *et al.* (2000) and Spectrum/DTI (2001) suggest that UK SMEs tend to lack the in-house technical skills necessary to successfully implement e-business strategies. This is despite the wide range of support offered to SMEs (Hamill and Gregory, 1997; Fariselli *et al.*, 1999). In addition to national initiatives, the European Union has been funding a range of initiatives aimed at boosting ICT take-up by SMEs. Yet, despite this effort, technology take-up has remained much slower in SMEs than in large enterprises (Lebre La Rovere, 1998).

Spectrum/DTI (2000) estimates that some 63 per cent of UK businesses provide formal ICT training for their employees. This compares very favourably with respect to their findings in the other G7 countries (73 per cent in France, 71 per cent in Germany, 61 per cent in Canada, 50 per cent in the USA, 47 per cent in Italy, 41 per cent in Japan). However, clear differences exist according to firm size, with an estimated 58 per cent of medium-sized firms and just 50 per cent of small firms providing formal training, compared with 74 per cent of large firms. This accords with empirical studies by Lange *et al.* (2000) and Mullins *et al.* (2001) who also find a distribution of training according to size. In their study of Scottish SMEs, Lange *et al.* (2000) highlighted a number of factors affecting the upgrading of in-house human capital. First, training was perceived by those managers contacted to be a costly investment. Search costs are high, with managers reporting a bewildering number and variety of training initiatives provided by both public and private sector agencies. This makes it difficult for SMEs to ascertain which train ing is most suitable for their needs. However, the study additionally reported that managers view investment in the upgrading of in-house skills as risky. This raises some concerns about managers' limited expectations of the returns on investment in human capital. Additionally, worries were expressed regarding the dangers of subsequently losing trained staff to other organisations. The basis for this fear of a free-rider problem is open to question. Research conducted by Mullins *et al.* (2001) on European SMEs suggested there may be a recognition problem. Only half the managers they surveyed made a link between the quality of staff skills and the effective exploitation of e-business ICTs. A research issue that needs to be addressed is the degree to which a lack of awareness of the available opportunities, rather than a scarcity of in-house skills and competences, inhibits the automation of key business functions within SMEs.

Three further resource constraints in SMEs are frequently cited in the literature: financial resources, management resources and time. The scale of many small businesses is such that they are more exposed to cash-flow problems, have less resources to devote to the sophisticated management of financial instruments and, since they do not enjoy the economies of scale and market power enjoyed by large organisations, SMEs do not enjoy the preferential interest rates offered by banks to large organisations (Fariselli *et al.*, 1999; Foong, 1999; Premkumar and Roberts, 1999). Ein-Dor and Segev (1978) additionally note that there are considerable economies of scale in computing operations themselves. Hence banks may reasonably expect returns on investment in SMEs to be smaller than for large enterprises. The stronger financial constraints facing smaller organisations is a key factor, it is suggested, in explaining why smaller companies tend to be more sensitive to cost, and why they have longer replacement cycles. Additionally, binding financial constraints give rise to the possibility of suboptimal investment decisions when SMEs choose to adopt lower-cost, second-best (or worse) options that do not satisfy users' needs.

In addition to financial constraints, it has frequently been asserted that SMEs face severe time constraints compared to larger companies. There are multiple reasons for this. First, the organisational structures of small firms tend to be flatter than in large firms, with management performing multiple organisational tasks. In addition to potential losses of efficiency due to a lack of task and skill specialisation, managers in SMEs have little time to spare for upgrading their own knowledge and competence base (Lange *et al.*, 2000). Second, Ein-Dor and Segev (1978) and Malone (1985) discuss the shorter management timeframes found in SMEs. Tighter timeframes are one consequence of the oft-cited ability of SMEs to respond quickly to changing market conditions. When combined with pressures arising from multitasking within flat management structures, managers in SMEs are constrained to the day-to-day running of their businesses with little or no time to devote to forward planning. This helps explain the lack of willingness to upgrade either their staff's or their own skills base. Third, experience is a time-related variable. Empirical research conducted by Yap *et al.* (1992) supports Raymond's (1985) suggestion that the successful implementation of new ICTs is positively associated with the duration of an SME's ICT experience. Raymond reasoned that problems relating to ICT implementation require time to be resolved and, hence, measured success will be time-dependent. Fourth, time is an inherent influence affecting the path dependency of ICT investments. Previous experience gained through past investment in older ICTs, such as EDI, assists companies in identifying and understanding the organisational and strategic issues raised by investments in e-business ICTs.

Our own view is that the category 'SME' is problematic since it places under one roof companies that differ enormously in nearly all conceivable dimensions, not only in terms of numbers of employees and turnover but also in their business activities (manufacturing and services), degree of international exposure, customer bases, sector characteristics and technological sophistication. *Ex ante*, one would expect that, in bridging these very different internal and external forces, a variety of organisational structures could evolve, some of which would more closely resemble categorisations traditionally associated with large businesses than those associated with micro or very small businesses.

Organisational Action and System Characteristics

Studies in large organisations have established the importance of top management support in facilitating successful ICT adoption (Cerveny and Sanders, 1986; Earl, 1996; Daft, 1998). In SMEs, the focus has fallen on the support of CEOs because most small businesses are managed by an owner who also acts as the CEO. Additionally, as previously noted, SMEs tend to have a flat organisational structure. Within such structures, the CEO typically performs multiple roles in the daily running of the business, takes the majority of decisions, and has full control over the organisation's resources (Raymond and Magnenat-Thalmann, 1982; Steinhoff and Burgess, 1986). CEO support is therefore essential for establishing appropriate ICT goals, identifying critical business information needs, and allocating the requisite financial resources. DeLone (1988) and Yap *et al.* (1992) have highlighted the importance of CEO support in the implementation phase. Support in decision-taking in ongoing implementation is important, not only by indicating serious commitment but also for ensuring effective delegation and staff direction, and for the conduct of progress reviews when necessary. As with previous ICTs, dependence on CEO's support to drive the adoption of Internet technologies and the subsequent development of e-business solutions has been highlighted in empirical research conducted by Igbaria *et al.* (1998) and Premkumar and Roberts (1999).

Research conducted by Palvia and Palvia (1999) has suggested that the age and experience of the owner/CEO is the single most important factor governing successful ICT adoption. However, it is important to note that the median size of businesses included in the study was just four employees. It is not surprising to find that the owner is the primary IT user in micro businesses and, consequently, that the personal characteristics of the owner correlate closely with recorded satisfaction levels. In addition to variables such as the age and experience of the owner, the findings of the study suggested that gender is a statistically significant variable. By comparison, empirical research conducted by Igbaria *et al.* (1998) on a sample of firms with between 20 and 100 employees found that gender differences in the use of spreadsheets, data management packages, programming languages and software packages were not significant when controls were added for education, age and the experience of employees. Thus, while male respondents used more computer packages than female respondents, this reflected differences in their organisational functions, experience and training. In contrast to the research conducted by Palvia and Palvia, that conducted by Igbaria *et al.* included staff in many different positions/functions, rather than just profiles of CEOs. An interesting counterpoint to this is provided by Spectrum/DTI (2000). It asked managers across the G7 the extent to which they were enthusiastic about ICTs. The study found that the degree of expressed enthusiasm among its respondents was statistically related to neither ICT uptake nor usage.

Small businesses with a large number of administrative applications have the potential to provide better support for management control, operational control and administration. Raymond (1985) has argued that, as managerial task specialisation is less pronounced in small businesses, a manager must resolve a wide range of decisional and functional problems. Thus, it is expected that a small business manager will have a higher level of satisfaction with an ICT system that addresses a greater number of his problems. Raymond found some evidence to support the hypothesis that success is positively related to the number of administrative applications. However, the study conducted by Yap *et al.* (1992) found no evidence to support this hypothesis. Only when distinguishing between different types of administrative applications did they find a positive correlation for one particular class of application: financial and accounting applications.

Internal and External Expertise

Montazemi's (1998) empirical study of 40 SMEs found a positive correlation between ICT success and the presence of a systems analyst. As Montazemi himself noted, the mere presence of a knowledgeable systems analyst does not guarantee successful ICT adoption. The match between a firm's information system and its business strategy requires a detailed action plan that exploits and integrates the analyst's expertise (also see Galliers, 1991; Earl, 1996; Daft, 1998).

A knowledgeable systems analyst may perform a number of important roles within the firm. To begin with, he may act as a 'technology gatekeeper' for the firm. An effective systems analyst facilitates the implementation process by moderating extreme views or positions taken by external consultants, vendors or colleagues within the SME. A technology gatekeeper additionally plays an important role in shaping realistic expectations within the SME regarding the likely benefits of new ICTs. Second, the system analyst plays an important role as 'translator' between users within the organisation and the technology, providing in-house technical support, user assistance and perhaps even basic training or instruction. This role positively contributes to the rate of technology assimilation within the organisation. Third, the analyst often has an important role in the codification and transmission of knowledge within the organisation. User manuals, work procedures and system documentation are typically written and maintained by systems analysts. Finally, the systems analyst can play an important strategic role in system development since he possesses the technical background to improve and develop the implemented technology.

The diffusion of innovations is a process of social as well as technical adaptation. For Rogers, innovativeness is the 'degree to which an individual . . . is relatively earlier in adopting new ideas than other members of a social system' (Rogers, 1983, p. 245). In common with the introduction of any radically new product, e-business ICTs are currently characterised by a high degree of uncertainty and fluidity.

Doubts with respect to market size, combined with high rates of change in the underpinning technologies and rapid rates in experimentation of alternative business models, give rise to a high degree of uncertainty. In the presence of such technological uncertainty, the literature highlights the importance of networks within the information gathering process.

Social networks may be personal or commercial. Research conducted by Johnson and Keuhn (1987) indicates that SMEs rely on their commercial networks much more than on government sources for their information search. These networks may comprise suppliers, research centres and other private/public agencies involved in the transfer of information, industrial associations, competitors and consultants providing specialised services or know-how (Julien, 1995; Gibb, 1997). The importance of trust as a factor underpinning social networks has been highlighted by a number of authors (e.g. Hill and McGowan, 1996; Charlton et al., 1997; Meldrum and de Berranger, 1999). Trusted external sources may to some extent offset the internal information gathering and processing constraints of SMEs arising from limited time, financial and other resources. Lee (1994) suggests that the extent to which SMEs exploit their social networks is influenced by their internal culture, which can either hinder or encourage the sharing of new knowledge and information. This contrasts with research conducted by Howard (1997). Howard reports that the SMEs in her sample had relatively few external contacts and that they had difficulties in obtaining impartial expert advice (the experiences of SMEs in Howard's sample vary according to industrial sector and company size).

Data collected by Yap et al. (1992) suggests that, for those SMEs with external consultancy, successful ICT adoption is positively related to the quality of external advice provided by consultants to SMEs. Gable (1991) adds that the manner in which SMEs manage the relationship is a crucial factor determining the benefits of this interaction. He argues that SMEs need to actively focus consultants' advice and that three issues are crucial for a successful relationship: firm–consultant compatibility, the identification and addressing of specific organisational goals, and the ability to accommodate evolving project objectives. The research conducted by Yap et al. finds a positive relationship between successful adoption and the level of vendor support. This suggests that vendors also play an important role in the computerisation of SMEs, with small businesses relying on vendors to propose alternative ICT options and to provide after-sales service and training.

Industry-Level and Macro-level Factors Affecting E-Business Adoption and Exploitation

Much of the discussion relating to firm size and organisational structure is predicated on (what in industrial economics, at least, is seen as) a rather old-fashioned comparative approach – the organisational structure–performance approach – in which a set of idealised structures for SMEs and large organisations are stipulated. Relatively flat owner-led SME organisational structures are said to have advantages in terms of their ability to adapt to market changes when compared to the more complicated and hierarchical bureaucratic structures of large organisations. On the other hand, large organisations are said to enjoy significant advantages in terms of access to financial and human capital resources (Rothwell and Dodgson, 1991;

Vossen, 1998). Unfortunately, these ideal types have been found seriously wanting in their ability to explain the competitive innovative performance of a company, or speed of technological adoption. The comparative approach has fallen out of favour in, for example, industrial economics, as other, potentially more relevant, factors have been highlighted. These include the characteristics of the industrial sector in which the firm operates, its geographical resources, culture and other macro (national) factors, and factors relating to the nature of the technology itself (Hennart, 1982; Rogers, 1983; Casson, 1987; Porter, 1990; Hofstede, 1991; Lundvall, 1992; Freeman and Soete, 1997).

Sector and Supply Chain Factors

Examining the data provided by the 2000 Spectrum/DTI report, knowledge-intensive industries rank the highest in their use of key external networking technologies, i.e. company websites, use of external e-mail, EDI and online selling systems (see Figure 11.2). Technology-intensive manufacturing sectors (chemicals, vehicle components, defence and aerospace) and service sectors (advertising and insurance services) are significantly more likely to make frequent use of external networking applications than are clothing, road haulage and retail sectors. We observe that the life-cycle of an industry can have an effect on ICT usage, with usage likely to be higher in new sectors than in mature sectors. Firms in mature industries face particular challenges posed by the introduction of new technologies and practices that displace pre-existing technologies and practices.

Decisions to adopt e-business technologies are also influenced by supply chains. An important link may exist between industrial sector and supply chains. An interesting finding of the Spectrum/DTI (2000) report is a pronounced preference for EDI and external e-mail in different industry sectors. Road haulage, clothing, vehicle components and insurance companies were found to strongly favour EDI systems whereas the majority of advertising, chemicals and defence companies use e-mail for external communications.[3] Here the work of Bolisani on EDI is of particular interest (Bolisani *et al.*, 1999). EDI permits the communication of structured messages between customers and suppliers using agreed formats, and

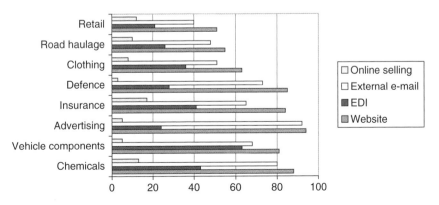

FIGURE 11.2   Percentage of UK companies frequently using e-business ICTs (by sector). Source: Spectrum/DTI, 2000

allows data to be fed directly into an electronic business process. The technical complexity of EDI is such that the costs of installation and maintenance are only justifiable when the technology is employed to underpin long-term, high-value relationships. The diffusion of EDI technologies has largely been associated with the development of tight supply chains that are focused around a leading company with significant market power. This leading company can ensure that its business partners conform to its requirements. Moreover, it is not unknown for the leading company to assist smaller SME partners, both financially and/or through technical support, in implementing the requisite systems. In manufacturing and retailing, the implementation of EDI has commonly resulted in the development of 'hub-spoke' EDI networks around the leading company (Zwass, 1996). These hub-spoke networks are limited in flexibility; it is very difficult to alter the connected partners, message formats and transaction procedures. Thus, although EDI was claimed to offer great potential for smaller businesses, the role of SMEs in hub-spoke EDI networks is often marginal. In many cases they are simply embedded in a closed system of relationships, the conditions of entry and action being determined by their larger partners. Indeed, there are instances of SMEs needing to run two different EDI systems on different equipment in order to participate in more than one network.

Picking up on Rosenberg's observation regarding the emergence of clusters of interrelated technologies making up a technology system, Windrum (2001) notes that technological substitutions can occur within system components. The substitution of EDI by open TCP/IP technology is a case in point. The diffusion of EDI has been closely tied with the diffusion of just-in-time production (JIT), electronic point of sale (EPOS), automated billing systems, and electronic inventory technologies. JIT production has been a particularly important factor in manufacturing sectors, its chief benefit being a significant reduction of inventory costs. Successful implementation of JIT requires the output of each stage of the production process to be fed into the next stage without undergoing an intermediate storage stage of indefinite length. In addition, the organisation needs to manage the delivery of external inputs from other organisations along the supply chain to ensure that inventory stocks are minimised. Automated billing systems and EDI have further increased the strength of the couplings between organisations within supply chains. The nature of the supply chains found in a particular sector can thus be a key factor affecting technological diffusion. In vehicle components sectors, for example, EDI diffusion has been facilitated by the close supplier relationships demanded by the few, large automobile manufacturers of their first- and second-tier suppliers in order to manage their JIT manufacturing processes. Similarly in the clothing sector, a small number of powerful actors – this time large retailers – have championed EDI technology and pushed it down the supply chain in order to gain greater control over their supply chains as a prerequisite for the need to control quality and the timing of delivery of their inputs. By contrast, the scale of operations of most small retailers is such that they do not justify investment in EDI-based JIT processes.

Turning to sectors such as advertising, where there are low adoption rates of EDI but high adoption rates of external e-mail, there is not a demand for high volumes of data interchange with one specific consumer or supplier. In addition, suppliers do not tend to make long-term commitments to advertisers, but usually offer new campaigns to competitive tender. This makes expenditure on EDI a risky investment. In contrast to EDI, the setting up of e-mail is technically simple and does not require large initial financial investments. Indeed, it is often a standard package delivered by an Internet service provider (ISP). Sillince *et al.* (1998) found that the most important issue affecting the decision of UK SMEs contacted in their study was whether customers, suppliers and other organisations with which they regularly communicate also have e-mail. Thus, in the absence of monopolistic buyers or monopsonistic suppliers dominating supply chains, adoption decisions are affected by network externalities. Here the perceived value of a network technology – in this case e-mail – increases according to the number of other users who are currently using the same technology. This has been formalised in Metcalfe's Law, which states that the value of a network is proportional to its number of users (Windrum and Swann, 1999).

Locational Factors

It has been proposed that the development and diffusion of Internet-based e-business will be associated with a reshaping of interfirm and firm–consumer relationships. Such changes are likely to have important implications for the geography of production (of both manufactured goods and services) and consumption. While ICTs may reduce the necessity of geographical proximity, they do not eliminate the existence of agglomeration economies (Pratt, 2000). Wever and Stam (1999) distinguish between classical resources munificence theory and the learning economy approach. In the former it is proposed that some regions have a more favourable resource base than others, e.g. a better-educated workforce, more and better knowledge centres, more venture capital companies, more high-quality services. The probability of innovation within a region is therefore related to the range and quality of the resources located within it. The learning economy approach views innovation as a process of interaction between customers, suppliers and knowledge centres. Geographical proximity, together with an institutional framework that encourages interaction, will stimulate the formation of regional clusters of innovative activities (Lundvall, 1992; Nelson, 1993; Storper, 1995; Morgan, 1997).

A distinction is made between two types of agglomeration economies within classical munificence theory (Moulaert and Djellal, 1995; Malmberg *et al.*, 2000). 'Urban economies' arise from urban concentration and include access to a diversified workforce, physical infrastructures and a range of diversified activities (particularly services). These factors are external to the firm and the industrial sector to which it belongs. By contrast, 'localisation economies' are internal to the industry and are related to the degree of industrial specialisation within a locality. Specialised inputs, for example, may be natural endowments (e.g. weather, soil conditions) or created endowments (e.g. a skilled workforce). A locality may also contain networks of dedicated suppliers (Keeble and Wilkinson, 1999). These factors form the key elements of a firm's supply chain. Further, close proximity to similar firms (similarly attracted by location-specific advantages) promotes the diffusion of new knowledge and information among competing companies. The local nature of information and the geographical bounds of knowledge spill-overs have been highlighted by Antonelli (1988) and von Hippel (1994). Indeed, quantitative and qualititative research (e.g. Jaffé *et al.*, 1993; Feldman and Audretsch, 1996; Saxenian, 1994) support the proposition that the spatial proximity of industrial activities promotes informational externalities.

Turning to those factors that directly affect ICT adoption, access to a pool of diversified labour, the transmission of new practices for managing relations with clients and suppliers, as well as technical information, and access to suppliers of new technologies and consultants that assist firms in making efficient technology choices are all factors that may outweigh the transaction cost benefits of digital goods highlighted by the weightless economy school. This is supported by empirical research conducted by Funck and Kolawski (1990), Fisher and Johansson (1994), Blaas and Nijkamp (1994), and Karlsson (1995). Not only does this research find a positive association between ICT adoption and population density, the association is found to increase in strength as the technical complexity of ICTs increases. The main factors highlighted in these studies are the proximity to suppliers and other organisations providing information and knowledge about new ICTs, and a qualified workforce for their implementation.

The transition from single to multiple organisational units opens up a range of spatial configurations, as firms are free to relocate activities to regions offering superior resources. However, these benefits are gained at the expense of increased coordination costs. Regardless of absolute size, a company with multiple sites tends to have more complex internal communications requirements than one based in a single location. Further, companies with international sites require advanced ICT applications in order to manage their communications across long distances and different time zones (Chandler, 1977). This UK's history of foreign direct investment (FDI) has produced large multisite and multinational organisations compared with other European nations (Dunning, 1993; Jones, 1994). These organisations have a correspondingly greater complexity of internal communications and this is an important explanatory factor behind the differential national uptake of technologies such as internal e-mail, local area networks (LANs), wide area networks (WANs) and intranets[4] in the UK. The benefits of introducing more efficient Internet-based ICTs is the reduction of the communication costs associated with more spatially dispersed organisations.

Case Study

Having discussed a broad range of potential enablers and barriers to ICT diffusion, we now consider an empirical case study that illustrates how various factors can play themselves out at the local level. As suggested at the outset of this chapter, we find many of the factors that affected the diffusion of previous ICTs playing a significant role once more. In addition, the case study highlights the strategies and actions that have been taken in order to deal with the challenges posed by e-business. The SME we consider here is a printing company located in the north of England, employing some 75 staff. It provides a good example of a company that has struggled to catch up with the rapid pace of organisational and technological change that has occurred within its industry. The industry has seen a shift away from the production of highly standardised products made in large print runs to tailored products made in smaller quantities. New ICTs have played a key role in facilitating this change, not only by making small batches of printed materials economic for the first time but also by facilitating closer client–provider interaction and improved image quality (notably the introduction of affordable digital colour technology). As in other industries, new ICTs have reduced barriers to entry and radically cut production costs. In highly competitive market conditions, companies have seen prices fall and profit margins squeezed, forcing them to find new ways of adding value to their products. The case study company has sought to follow these trends, shifting its focus away from traditional products to a variety of new goods and services that involve closer contact with clients, shorter print runs and a greater use of new digital technologies.

The adoption of Internet technology has enabled the company to develop an integrated information system in which sales staff have up-to-date data on clients and their sales portfolios via an intranet, while existing clients can monitor the progress of their orders at each stage of the production process via an extranet. In addition to improving the speed of communications with clients, e-mail has facilitated the introduction of colour proofs. The ability to easily and quickly generate colour graphics (prohibitively expensive with previous technologies) has turned design specification into a WYSIWYG ('what you see is what you get') process. Combined with an ability to send images in JPEG file format over the Internet, this has enabled clients to play a far more active role in product/design specification while simultaneously reducing lead time. The company also offers potential clients the opportunity to inspect its current portfolio of products and services through its public website. This is done in a rather novel way. For each product/service category listed on the website, a case study is provided. Here an initial problem faced by a client is identified, after which there follows a description of how this problem was dealt with and a successful solution formulated with the assistance of the printing company. This indicates the extent to which the image presented by the company has shifted away from that of a producer of bulk items to that of a knowledge-intensive service provider offering solutions to clients' problems.

We have argued in this chapter that the successful adoption of Internet technologies in part depends on how these are used in conjunction with the other technologies and management practices that form a 'technology cluster'. Despite predictions that the new digital media and communication channels offered by the Internet would contribute to the demise of printed materials, ICTs have actually invigorated both our case study company and the printing industry in general. Interestingly, the case study provides an example of how, as part of a substitution process, Internet technology has extended the logic of an older technology to new areas. The nature of printing design – its non-standardised content and rate of product change – had precluded a widespread diffusion of EDI in the printing industry. Yet the potential advantages of JIT production remain. The case study company, for example, has sought to leverage these advantages through its 'Virtual Cupboard' service. Offered to its most valued clients, this service enables clients to reduce their stocks of printed materials to zero by guaranteeing the printing and delivery of any desired quantity of a specific item within 24 hours. This is achieved through the company holding electronic templates of the client's entire portfolio of printed materials.

Management has come a long way in turning what had been a traditional printing company into a modern business operation. Yet there remains much that needs to be done if it is to catch up with its leading competitors. This is clearly evident, for example, in its transition towards an e-business model. Despite the company's moves to reconfigure communications with clients through its website and extranet, it has not yet made the move to online sales. Further, the successful implementation of JIT depends on an organisation's ability to manage the delivery of externally sourced inputs in order to ensure that its inventory stocks are in turn minimised. We were informed by the managing director that basic supplies to the printing industry are controlled by a few, very large international companies and so, due to its lack of market power, the company is unable to insist on the JIT delivery of its supplies. Indeed, the company is forced to bulk-buy their inputs. We were informed that all SMEs in the printing sector face this problem. The upshot is that the company is being squeezed by larger firms on each side of the supply chain, which raises its exposure to risk. The company also has a narrow customer base, and is over-reliant on a few major customers. This is despite efforts to build up close business relationships with more blue-chip customers. Management is still searching for a strategy that will expand the company's client base. Online sales may offer it an important opportunity to reach new customers and broker new long-term relationships.

The strides made towards an e-business model form part of a wider organisational transformation of the company. As noted previously, e-business is predicated upon the integration of a set of interrelated ICTs within a new business structure. The company began with an information system that was partial and comprised a set of incompatible legacy systems. Thus, while computer automation was well established in design and administration, designers worked with Apple Macintosh hardware/software that was incompatible with the bespoke system used by administrative staff. Unfortunately, the company's first forays into Internet technology lacked a clear strategic objective, and its first website – a flat ad website that hosted an e-mail account – was not integrated with the other information systems. This e-mail account was hardly ever used for business communications. In part, this was due to the fact that only one computer was set up with an e-mail account, in part it reflected the fact that most of its customers did not use e-mail at this time! As the managing director noted in our discussions with him, the company then jumped on the industry bandwagon. It recognised a need to catch up with rivals who were starting to set up websites. With little or no thought given to what the Internet could actually do for the company or its competitive advantage, it followed suit.

The company simply lacked the knowledge needed to develop a coherent strategy. Not only did its existing personnel lack the requisite operational competence to set up and run a computer network, they also lacked an appreciation of what the Internet could offer the company. These constraints were quickly recognised by the company's management. Management were also keenly aware that there was no 'quick fix'. Financial constraints limited flexibility and its ability to invest in the upgrading of technology and skills, whether via the hiring of new staff or the retraining of existing staff. The company's social network provided little assistance, since other SMEs within the industry faced the same problems. Further, the time constraints faced by management meant that it could not quickly upgrade its skills/knowledge base. Rather, the upgrading of the information system and knowledge base would need to proceed incrementally, over time.

Following the discussion developed in this chapter, three research questions are of particular interest. First, what strategies did the company formulate in order to overcome these initial barriers? Second, what organisational role did the management team play? And third, what external sources were called upon? We have observed the emphasis placed on the CEO in motivating the diffusion of new ICTs in SMEs. This stems from two initial assumptions. First, the business is managed by an owner who also acts as the CEO and, second, SMEs have a flat organisational structure in which the CEO performs multiple administrative and organisational roles and has full control over the organisation's resources. Under these conditions, CEO support is essential for establishing appropriate ICT goals, identifying the business' information needs, and allocating the requisite financial resources. The picture within the case study company is not quite so simple, however. To begin with, the business is a limited company headed by two managing directors of equal status. The company's organisational structure is hierarchical. Under the two MDs there is an operations manager, a sales manager, a financial accounts manager, a production manager and (more recently) an IT manager. This organisational structure closely fits Williamson's classic description of the large, centralised and functionally departmentalised company (Williamson, 1975). This supports our contention that it is problematic to categorise SMEs because it places under one roof companies that differ greatly in their size and business activity. A question mark is also raised about the 'heroic' role of the CEO. It was not a single individual but rather a management team that spearheaded change within this company. This management team initially comprised one of the MDs, the marketing manager and the production manager. Again, discussions of management teams driving technological and organisational change are common within the large-firm literature, but not the SME literature, further highlighting the problems associated with the SME category.

A significant turning point was the attendance of an 'IT planning workshop' by the MD and the marketing manager. Run by the Manchester Metropolitan University (MMU) with the aid of EU funding, the workshop was targeted at small businesses. It provided the MD with an opportunity to examine issues surrounding the company's legacy information systems and ways in which the Internet can lever competitive advantage. The marketing manager was able to consider the business opportunities provided by e-business and gain a clearer understanding of the basic mechanics of the Internet. Following this external consultation, the IT management team identified two key initiatives. The first was the need to align the company's IT strategy with its overall business strategy. In order to realise this, the company would need to develop a single IT platform that integrated its various activities. The second initiative involved the upgrading of its knowledge base. A key aspect of this initiative involved the creation of a new post; that of an IT manager. The responsibilities of the new post would include the daily running of the new system, strategy formulation, keeping the company abreast of new technology, and staff training in IT. These twin initiatives formed the core of a policy document, produced by the management team, outlining the benefits of e-business, an assessment of the avenues open to the company, and the management team's recommended option. The document was presented to the rest of the company's management in an internal seminar.

Through the setting up of an open standards platform, it was possible to integrate some of the existing ICT investments. A contract was set up with an IT solutions provider to install an open TCP/IP network with the necessary new hardware and software. At the same time, e-mail access was widely distributed across all computers within the company. In addition to improving internal communication, e-mail could now be used to send proofs to clients and gain approval for contracts. More of the company's clients were also starting to set up their own e-mail accounts, so the benefits of developing e-mail communications increased significantly. The aims of the IT strategy were clearly defined by the IT management team: the new system needed to be flexible and ensure the effective flow of information and data between commercial, sales and production departments. The new system is central to the company's business strategy, which aims to increase profits through improving internal efficiency and raising the quality of customer service. The management team began to roll out its plans by first hiring an external solutions provider to install an administrative intranet. This provides all staff with up-to-date sales and production information. With the IT manager on board, and seeking to learn from their mistakes, the IT management team proceeded to radically overhaul the company website. Again with the aid of an external source, this time a web design company, the management team developed a second-generation website which ties the intranet with an extranet and a completely revamped front end in order to improve communication between the company and its clients. The password-protected extranet provides existing clients with direct access to the company. Meanwhile, the public website provides potential clients with the opportunity to inspect its current range of products and services.

Conclusions

Two key findings arise from the research discussed in this chapter, each of which is of particular note for those working in the innovation and IT fields. First, the benefits of information and communication technologies such as e-mail and websites depend on the size of their network externalities, i.e. the installed base of other firms and consumers who also adopt these technologies. In this respect they differ to previous generations of computer technologies whose benefits lay in reducing firms' internal transaction costs. This raises important strategic issues relating to the timing of new ICT investments. If a firm invests too early, i.e. when existing and potential customers and firms have not adopted the technology or will not adopt it within the payback period, then network externalities will be low and the competitive advantage of technology adoption will approach zero. If the firm adopts too late, then it faces the danger of falling so far behind its competitors that it cannot recover. We have noted that the appropriate timing of ICT investments are likely to differ according to the industrial sector and the particular supply chain structures within which a firm is located. The network externality issue appears to fundamentally recast existing discussions of first- and second-mover advantages of technology adoption.

The second issue raised in this chapter concerns the existence of commonality, in particular the recurrence of internal and external factors affecting the adoption of technologies within SMEs. All too often researchers have noted surprise at finding out that factors which were known to affect the adoption of previous technologies (ICT and otherwise) also had an influence on the adoption of a new technology. By short-circuiting yet another reinvention of the wheel, it should be possible to give greater direction and speed up future empirical research on the adoption of e-business technologies by SMEs. To this end, this chapter has drawn together research on adoption conducted in a range of (previously separate) disciplinary fields in order to identify a set of potentially important variables. The possible explanatory value of these variables in future quantitative research has been highlighted with the aid of exploratory qualitative research in the form of a detailed case study.

Turning, first of all, to the internal factors affecting e-business adoption, our research once again illustrates the important constraints imposed on SMEs by limited time, knowledge and financial resources. As highlighted in previous research, knowledge constraints take two forms. One concerns the ability to implement and run an e-business information system. The other concerns the ability to appreciate its strategic worth and the capacity to apply the new technology in new ways in order to lever competitive advantage over rival firms. Crudely speaking, improving the former is related to the quality of the workforce while the latter is related to the quality of management. The case study company sought to overcome its constrained resource base through the incremental improvement of its knowledge base, the piecemeal improvement of its information system, and a restructuring of the organisation. This involved an upgrading of existing managerial and staff skills together with a hiring of new staff, including the creation of a new IT managerial position.

With respect to previous literature on organisational action, we identified a number of problems associated with the 'SME' category when applied to the case study. First, the organisational structure of the company was not the classical 'flat' structure described in the small-firm literature. It is far closer to the U-form structure with centralised and functionally departmentalised management identified in large firms by Williamson (1975). Second, and probably related to the first finding, change is not being driven by a CEO but by a small management team, formed through a coalition of interests, that worked closely together to form an IT strategy that underpins the company's business strategy, and is now seeking to implement this IT strategy. This raises a serious question mark against the 'heroic CEO' description encountered in the small-firm and SME literature. Future research should consider, for example, more sophisticated analyses developed by managerial theories of the firm. Strategy is often the consensus that is reached through negotiations between managers holding (sometimes very) different views and interests. Subsequent implementation involves a further round of negotiations between management and the other members of the organisation, possibly leading to strategy revision. We raise these issues as being of potential interest for future research.

As the case study highlights, the process of strategy formulation and implementation may be far from smooth in practice. An initial lack of knowledge among the management team prevented the formation of a clear and coherent IT strategy. The management team was not aware of the potential to integrate all of its IT functions within an open Internet-based platform. Nor did it understand the implications of network externalities. As a result, the first company website was separate and incompatible with the other IT systems while its implementation of e-mail failed because it moved earlier than its customers and the other firms within its supply chain. Problems were compounded by the fact that an e-mail account was only set up on one of the company's machines and staff were not provided with training on how to use the new software.

Existing theoretical and empirical research on technology adoption draws attention to the importance of external expertise, notably the roles played by suppliers and external consultants as key sources of new knowledge and information, in such circumstances. This is supported by the case study. This particular company drew upon the services provided by two private sector service companies and a public sector institute, to improve its IT system and its knowledge base. In terms of the latter, important contributions from external sources were made in improving managerial competence (essential for effective strategy formulation) and for identifying methods for improving workforce competence (essential for effective strategy implementation).

Our research has identified the potential importance of sector-specific and location-specific factors in technology diffusion. The issues faced by an old firm in a mature industry are likely to be quite different to those faced by a start-up company in a new (high-tech) sector. Our case study company is faced with issues concerned with the implications of substituting old technologies and associated knowledge and organisation practices with new, more efficient ones. Innovations such as digital printing and e-business models are not sourced within the industry but are usually either introduced by suppliers or adapted using examples drawn from outside the industry. Such innovations are particularly difficult to deal with because they destroy existing competences. SMEs such as the case study company are therefore unable to draw upon social networks within the industry to gain information and knowledge because their contacts face the same set of problems. Finally, while it is difficult to establish the significance of locational factors without recourse to a comparative study, we observed that all the private and public consultants used by the case study company are based in the local region and it has been able to recruit new, more highly skilled staff (including its IT manager) locally.

To summarise, our research has highlighted a number of key factors that are likely to influence the adoption of e-business technologies in SMEs. Drawn together from a variety of research traditions, these enable one to map out the dimensions of future theoretical and empirical research. In addition, we have highlighted the importance of network externalities in determining the timing of technology investments, and discussed the first- and second-mover advantages of technology adoption. These we shall explore in our future research in the area.

References

Antonelli, C. (1988) 'Localized technological change, new information technology and the knowledge-based economy: the European evidence', *Journal of Evolutionary Economics*, **8**:(2), 177–198.

Blaas, E. and Nijkamp, P. (1994) 'New technology and regional development in the European snowbelt: towards a new emerging network?', in B. Johansson, C. Karlsson and L. Westin (eds) *Patterns of a Network Economy*. Springer-Verlag, New York.

Bolisani, E., Scarso, E., Miles, I. and Boden, M. (1999) 'Electronic commerce implementation: a knowledge-based analysis', *International Journal of Electronic Commerce*, **3**:3, 53–69.

Casson, M. (1987) *The Firm and the Market*. Blackwell, Oxford.

Cerveny, R.P. and Sanders, G.L. (1986) 'Implementation and structural variables', *Information Management*, **11**, 91–198.

Chandler, A.D. (1977) *The Visible Hand*. MIT Press: Cambridge, MA.

Chapman, P., James-Moore, M., Szczygiel, M. and Thompson D. (2000) 'Building internet capabilities in SMEs', *Logistics Information Management*, **13**:6, 353–360.

Charlton, C., Gittings, C., Leng, P., Little, J. and Neilson, I. (1997) 'Diffusion of the Internet: a local perspective on an international issue', Facilitating Technology Transfer through Partnership, Learning from Practice and Research, IFIP TC8 WG8.6 International Working Conference on Adoption and Implementation of Information Technology, 25–27 June, Ambleside, Cumbria, UK.

Daft, R.L. (1998) *Organization Theory and Design*, 6th edition. West Publishing Co, New York.

DeLone, W.H. (1988) 'Determinants of success for computer usage in small business', *Management Information Systems Quarterly*, **12**:1, 51–61.

Dunning, J.H. (1993) *The Globalization of Business*. Routledge, London.

Earl, M.J. (1996) *Management Strategies for Information Technology*. Prentice Hall, New York.

Ein-Dor, P. and Segev, E. (1978) 'Organizational context and the success of MIS', *Management Science*, June, 1064–1077.

Fariselli, P., Oughton, C., Picory, C. and Sugden, R. (1999) 'Electronic commerce and the future for SMEs in the global marketplace: networking and public policies', *Small Business Economics*, **12**, 261–275.

Feldman, M.P. and Audretsch, D.B. (1996) 'Innovation in cities: science-based diversity, specialization, and localized competition', *European Economic Review*, **43**, 409–429.

Fisher, M.M. and Johansson, B. (1994) 'Networks for process innovation by firms: conjectures from observations in three countries', in B. Johansson, C. Karlsson and L. Westin (eds) *Patterns of a Network Economy*. Springer-Verlag, New York.

Foong, S.Y. (1999) 'Effect of end user personal and systems attributes on computer based information systems success in Malaysian SMEs', *Journal of Small Business Management*, **37**:3, 81–87.

Freeman, C. and Soete, L. (1997) *The Economics of Industrial Innovation*, 3rd edition, Pinter, London.

Funck, R.H. and Kolawski, J.S. (1990) 'Innovation, new information technologies and the structure of urban regions', in R. Cappellin and P. Nijkamp (eds) *The Spatial Context of Technological Development*. Avebury, London.

Gable, G.G. (1991) 'Consultant engagement for computer system selection: a proactive client role in small business', *Information Management*, **20**, 83–93.

Galliers, R.D. (1991) 'Strategic information systems planning: myths, reality and guidelines for successful implementation', *European Journal of Information Systems*, **1**:1, 55–64.

Gibb, A.A. (1997) 'Small firms' training and competitiveness. Building upon the small business as a learning organisation', *International Small Business Journal*, **15**, 13–29

Gonzalez, J.S. (1998) *The 21st Century Intranet*. Prentice Hall, London.

Hamill, J. and Gregory, K. (1997) Internet marketing in the internationalisation of UK SMEs, *Journal of Marketing Management*, **13**, 9–28.

Hennart, J.F. (1982) *A Theory of Multinational Enterprise*. University of Michigan Press, Ann Arbor, MI.

Hill, J. and McGowan, P. (1996) 'Developing a networking competency for effective enterprise development', *Journal of Small Business and Enterprise Development*, **3**:3, 148–157.

Hippel E. von, (1994) 'Sticky information and the locus of problem solving: implications for innovation', *Management Science*, **40**:4, 429–439.

HMSO (1998) *Our Competitive Future – Building the Knowledge Driven Economy*. UK Government White Paper, December. Also available at www.dti.gov.uk.

Hofstede, G. (1991) *Cultures and Organizations*. McGraw-Hill, New York.

Howard, K. (1997) 'IT means business? A survey of attitudes in smaller businesses to information technology', *Institute of Management Research Report*, July, 1–39.

Igbaria, M., Zinatelli, N. and Cavaye, A. (1998) 'Analysis of information technology success in small firms in New Zealand', *International Journal of Information Management*, **18**, 103–119.

Jaffé, A.B., Trajtenberg, M. and Henderson, R. (1993) 'Geographical localization of knowledge spillovers as evidenced by patent citations', *Quarterly Journal of Economics*, **108**:3, 577–598.

Johnson, J.L. and Keuhn, R. (1987) 'The small business owner/manager's search for external information', *Journal of Small Business Management*, July, 53–60.

Jones, G. (1994) 'British multinationals and British business since 1850', in M.W. Kirby and M.B. Rose (eds) *Business Enterprise in Modern Britain from the Eighteenth to the Twentieth Centuries*. Routledge, London.

Julien, P.-A. (1995) 'New technologies and technological information in small business', *Journal of Small Business Venturing*, **10**:6, 459–476.

Karlsson, C. (1995) 'Innovation adoption, innovation networks and agglomeration economics', in C.S. Bertuglia, M.M. Fisher and G. Preto (eds) *Technological Change, Economic Development and Space*. Springer-Verlag, New York.

Keeble, D. and Wilkinson, F. (1999) 'Collective learning and knowledge development in the evolution of regional clusters of high technology SMEs in Europe', *Regional Studies*, **33**:4, 295–303.

Lange, T., Ottens, M. and Taylor, A. (2000) 'SMEs and barriers to skills development: a Scottish perspective', *Journal of Industrial Training*, **24**:1, pp. 5–11.

Lebre La Rovere, R. (1998) 'Small and medium-sized enterprises and IT diffusion policies in Europe', *Small Business Economics*, **11**, 1–9.

Lee, A.S. (1994) 'Electronic mail as a medium for rich communication – an empirical investigation using hermeneutic interpretation', *Management Information Systems Quarterly*, **18**:2,143–157.

Lundvall, B.-Å. (1992) *National Systems of Innovation: Towards a Theory of Innovation and Interactive Learning*. Pinter, London.

Malmberg, A., Malmberg, B. and Lundquist, P. (2000) 'Agglomeration and firm performance: economies of scale, localisation, and urbanisation amongst Swedish export firms', *Environment and Planning A*, **32**, 305–321.

Malone, S. (1985) 'Computerizing small business information systems', *Journal of Small Business Management*, April, 10–16.

Meldrum, M. and de Berranger, P. (1999) 'Can HE match the IS learning needs of SMEs?', *Journal of European Industrial Training*, **23**:8, 380–402.

Montazemi, A.R. (1988) 'Factors affecting information satisfaction in the context of small businesses', *Management Information Systems Quarterly*, **12**:2, 239–256.

Morgan, K. (1997) 'The learning region, institutions, innovations and regional renewal', *Regional Studies*, **31**, 491–503.

Moulaert, F. and Djellal, F. (1995) 'Information technology consultancy firms: economies of agglomeration from a wide-area perspective', *Urban Studies*, **32**:1, 105–122.

Mullins, R., Duan, Y. and Hamblin, D. (2001) 'A pan-European survey leading to the developement of WITS', *Internet Research: Electronic Networking Applications and Policy*, **11**:4, 333–340.

Nelson, R.R. (ed.) (1993) *National Innovation Systems: A Comparative Analysis*. Oxford University Press, Oxford.

ONS (2001) *E-commerce Inquiry*. Office for National Statistics, London.

Palvia, P. and Palvia, S. (1999) 'An examination of the IT satisfaction of small business users', *Information and Management*, **35**, 127–137.

Porter, M.E. (1990) *The Competitive Advantage of Nations*. Macmillan, London.

Pratt, A.C. (2000) 'New media, the new economy and new spaces', *Geoforum*, **31**, 425–436.

Premkumar, G. and Roberts, M. (1999) 'Adoption of new information technologies in rural small businesses', *Omega, International Journal of Management Science*, **27**, 467–484.

Raymond, L. (1985) 'Organisational characteristics and MIS success in the context of small businesses', *Management Information Systems Quarterly*, **9**:1, 37–52.

Raymond, L. and Magnenat-Thalmann, N. (1982) 'Information systems in small business: are they used in managerial decisions?' *American Journal of Small Business*, **6**:4, 20–23.

Rogers, E.M. (1983) *Diffusion of Innovations*. Free Press, New York.

Rosenberg, N. (1982) *Inside the Black Box: Technology and Economics*. Cambridge University Press, Cambridge.

Rothwell, R. and Dodgson, M. (1991) 'External linkages and innovation in small and medium-sized enterprises', *R&D Management*, **21**:2, 125–137.

Saxenian, A. (1994) *Regional Advantage*. Harvard University Press, Cambridge, MA.

Sillince, J., Macdonald, S., Lefang, B. and Frost, B. (1998) 'E-mail adoption, diffusion, use and impact within small firms: a survey of UK companies', *International Journal of Information Management*, **18**, 231–242.

Spectrum/DTI (2000) *Moving into the Information Age: International Benchmarking Study*. Available at www.ukonlineforbusiness.gov.uk/.

Spectrum/DTI (2001) *Business in the Information Age: International Benchmarking Study.* Available at www.ukonlineforbusiness.gov.uk/.

Steinhoff, D. and Burgess, J.F. (1986) *Small Business Management Fundamentals*, 4th edition. McGraw-Hill, New York.

Storper, M. (1995) 'The resurgence of regional economics, ten years later: the region as a nexus of untraded interdependencies', *European and Urban Regional Studies*, **2**, 191–221.

Tetteh, E. and Burns, J. (2001) 'Global strategies for SME business: applying the SMALL framework', *Logistics Management Information*, **14**:1/2, 171–180.

Venkatraman, N. (1994) 'IT-enabled business transformation: from automation to business scope redefinition', *Sloan Management Review*, **35**:2, 73–87.

Vossen, R.W. (1998) 'Relative strengths and weaknesses of small firms in innovation', *International Small Business Journal*, **16**:3, 88–94.

Wever, E. and Stam, E. (1999) 'Clusters of high-technology SMEs: the Dutch case', *Regional Studies*, **33**:4, 391–400.

Williamson, O.E. (1975) *Markets and Hierarchies.* Free Press, New York, and Macmillan, London.

Windrum, P. (2001) 'Late entrant strategies in technological ecologies: Microsoft's use of standards in the browser wars', *International Studies of Management and Organization, special issue on Innovation Management in the New Economy*, **31**:1, 87–105.

Windrum, P. and Swann, G.M.P. (1999) 'Networks, noise and web navigation: sustaining Metcalfe's Law through technological innovation', *Merit Research Memoranda* 1999/009, See www-edocs.unimaas.nl/abs/mer99009.htm .

Yap, C.S., Soh, C.P.P. and Raman, K.S. (1992) 'Information systems success factors in small businesses', *Omega, International Journal of Management Science*, **20**:5, 597–609.

Zwass, V. (1996) 'Electronic commerce: structures and issues', *International Journal of Electronic Commerce*, **1**:2, pp. 2–23.

Notes

1. EDI permits the communication of structured messages between customers and suppliers using agreed formats, and allows data to be fed directly into an electronic business process.
2. The ONS survey had 9000 businesses respondents with 10 or more employees.
3. The study found that EDI was used by 63 per cent of all respondents in the UK vehicle components sector, by 43 per cent in chemicals, 41 per cent in insurance, 36 per cent in clothing, 28 per cent in defence, 26 per cent in road haulage, 24 per cent in advertising and 21 per cent in retail. External e-mail was used by 94 per cent of UK respondents in the advertising sector, by 88 per cent in chemicals, 85 per cent in defence, 84 per cent in insurance, 81 per cent in vehicle components, 63 per cent in clothing, 55 per cent in road haulage and 51 per cent in retail.
4. An intranet is a service running on a company LAN or WAN which uses Internet (TCP/IP) standards and web file formats to distribute and display information to an organisation's employees. Intranets require considerable financial and human resources to implement and support.

Chapter 12

SUPPLY CHAIN MANAGEMENT: IMPROVING COMPETITIVE ADVANTAGE IN SMEs

Allan Macpherson and Alison Wilson

Introduction

Over the last two decades, strategic restructuring programmes within large organisations and the intensification of competition have resulted in a focus on supply chain management as a potential source of competitive advantage. Since the basic structure of any supply chain is the transactional and relational framework between or within organisations, supply chain management is concerned with the drive for greater efficiency and effectiveness through creating more integrated business systems to manage the customer–supplier relationship. Consequently, supply chain management involves establishing closer relationships with suppliers to add value through the supply chain (Fox, 1998). This, in turn, creates an opportunity for businesses with unique products and services to work with larger organisations for mutual competitive advantage. However, establishing and maintaining the type of collaborative supply chain relationship that will sustain competitive advantage requires time, effort and specific organisational capabilities. It would be rational, therefore, for this task to be undertaken only after a critical analysis of the advantages of such a strategy, which may not always be desirable (Forker and Stannack, 2000; Lamming *et al.*, 2000; Cousins, 2002). There will be a limited number of SMEs that will benefit from supply chain management initiatives. Moreover, this changing business context must have an impact on the competences required to support effective customer–supplier interactions (Croom, 2001), and only those suppliers with appropriate capabilities will be in a position to gain competitive advantage.

Suppliers, many of them SMEs, are increasingly being expected to provide levels of information and service that not only increase the pressures on their profit margins, but also call for more proactive and innovative customer support, including product development. As pressure is put on the supply chain, it seems logical that it will be those who are best able to respond to the changing context that will benefit most. Thus, if SMEs are to develop the types of competences that are to be useful, they will need to be able to analyse their own capabilities and seek support from appropriate agencies. Unfortunately, however, many SMEs find it difficult to identify their skills gaps, and to identify and benchmark their capabilities (Monkhouse, 1995). This is due to the lack of mechanisms and infrastructure for identifying skills gaps, the multifaceted and highly pressurised role of the owner-manager that limits the time they can spend on analysing skills gaps or training and development needs, and a lack of understanding on the part of SMEs of the higher skills and competence levels required to respond in today's changing business context (Lange *et al.*, 2000).

If the types of activities the corporate supply chain originators are expecting their supply chain 'partners' to undertake are changing, there is a consequent need for SMEs to develop new organisational capabilities if they are to improve and sustain their competitive advantage within a supply chain context. However, collaborative relationships are the antithesis of inter-organisational relations that have been, traditionally, market-based interactions. Thus, supply chain management is introducing an element of transformation to the customer–supplier relationship that may not be understood, or even desired, by SMEs, and this degree of change will require cultural issues to be addressed. In particular, the ability to lead and implement that change will be crucial to the success of supply chain management, and the ability to address and remove cultural barriers will be an essential component of any supply chain management programme. Therefore, this chapter focuses on the directions of change within supply chain management, the competences required to support that change, and the barriers or opportunities that they create for competitive advantage among SMEs.

Supply Chain Management – Theories, Directions and Competences

Supply Chain Management – A Theoretical Perspective

The nascent supply chain management literature includes confusing terminology and intersecting hypotheses and meanings that hamper the development of clear conceptual and theoretical positions (Croom *et al.*, 2000). Nevertheless, it is apparent that the premise of supply chain management is to seek cost reductions and competitive advantage through the development of integrated supply networks, creating a more competitive whole. Consequently, the focus of supply chain management theory must be on the development and control of inter-organisational interactions. Indeed, much of the supply chain management literature foregrounds the integrative activities of supply chain management and argues that it is through these unique relationships and activities that strategic competitive advantage is realised (for example, McDermott and Chan, 1996; Sinclair *et al.*, 1996; Arnold, 2000; Hoyt and Huq, 2000; Croom, 2001; Macpherson, 2001). Thus, supply chain management theory must consider the outsourcing decision, and the strategic merits of closer relationships with suppliers. This provides a framework for exploring the implications of supply chain management for SMEs.

The decision to outsource business processes and create supply chains outside the organisation is clearly one that requires an assessment of where the boundary of the organisation should reside. Coase's (1937) seminal text proposes that the boundary of the firm is defined by the relative transaction costs of organisation through either the market or vertical integration. Williamson (1979, 1981) develops this transaction cost view and argues that the management of recurrent transactions also includes the key dimensions of asset specificity and uncertainty. Since reliability and quality can be better controlled through the hierarchical and centralised decision-making of the firm, when elements of asset specificity and uncertainty are high, there is pressure to integrate the transaction within the boundaries of the organisation (Williamson, 1981; Hart, 1993; Sinclair *et al.*, 1996; Bolton and Scharfstein, 1998). In terms of asset specificity, this will include the strategic importance of the physical component, for which the supplier may hold copyright, and the technical, professional, communication, management and collaboration skills of the supplier. Many of these assets are intangibles that are difficult to measure, and, indeed, may only become apparent, or increase in value, over time (Boddy *et al.*, 2000).

With regard to uncertainty in the customer–supplier relationship, although this can be reduced with the introduction of formal contracts, it is impossible to cover all eventualities. The resulting 'incomplete contracts' create the opportunity for parties to exploit ambiguities, and to respond to changing priorities, for their own advantage (Bolton and Scharfstein, 1998). However, this opportunism can be reduced through informal contracts, where interactions are evaluated against socialised norms, built up through experience and reciprocity (Wren *et al.*, 1998; Weaver and Dickson, 1998). Breaches of norms of behaviour will degrade the relationship and introduce transactional inefficiencies. Failure to collaborate will also create information distortions that directly, or indirectly, increase transaction costs (Corbett *et al.*, 1999). It is in both parties' interests, therefore, to sustain the relationship and reduce transaction costs. Consequently, the transaction costs theory indicates a need for closer relationships with suppliers in order to reduce transaction costs and to benefit from the suppliers' unique capabilities. Moreover, to be effective, these relationships will require high levels of trust, communication and collaboration; they will take time to develop and they will increase in complexity throughout the life of the relationship. This complexity offers the opportunity of strategic competitive advantage.

From a resource-based perspective of strategy, sustained competitive advantage is gained where the resources are rare, imperfectly imitable and non-substitutable (Barney, 1991; Boxall, 1996). The importance of retaining core competences (Prahalad and Hamel, 1990), and the concomitant shift towards modularity and specialisation of knowledge in organisations and society, creates a need to access knowledge developments and information through organisations' networks (Brusoni and Prencipe, 2001). In supply chain relationships, then, this can be achieved by customers and suppliers developing high levels of trust and product knowledge, integrated communication structures and flexible inter-organisational relations (Hoyt and Huq, 2000). The complexity, quality and flexibility of these relationships may provide the *potential* to be a resource of sustained competitive advantage, provided the organisations have the capabilities to support and sustain them (Croom, 2001). Therefore, in terms of both transaction costs and resource-based strategy theories, there is a strong argument for moves to develop more integrated and more collaborative relationships with suppliers. Indeed, a recent study of successful SME innovation highlighted the importance of SMEs creatively configuring their customer relationships as a source of enhancing their own capability (Barnett and Storey, 2000). Achieving these relationships will require different capabilities and relationships than traditional, market-based, customer–supplier relations. Consequently, their success will be dependent on identifying and developing skills, structures and competences crucial to supply chain partnering, both in large organisations and in SMEs.

Directions and Competences of Supply Chain Management

There is evidence that supply chain management is increasingly considered as a potential source of competitive advantage, and that more companies are investing effort in this direction (Bendiner, 1998). Business activities include increased outsourcing, rationalisation of suppliers, longer-term and total contract solutions, developing supply chain networks, the development of e-purchasing, supply chain information and communication technology systems, and collaborative product development (see, for example, Rhodes and Carter, 1998; Graham and Hardaker, 2000; Matthews *et al.*, 2000; Croom, 2001; Macpherson, 2001; Ellram and Billington, 2001). However, it is not necessarily the case that all customer–supplier relationships will benefit from closer collaboration. Due to the costs and effort required to sustain a relationship of trust and cooperation, investment will only be appropriate in those relationships that are strategically important (Forker and Stannack, 2000; Christopher and Jüttner, 2000). Where SMEs cannot add value to the supply chain through their product or relational capabilities, it seems likely that they will be increasingly under direct competitive pressure from global sourcing through the use of e-purchasing or e-market systems (Rhodes and Carter, 1998). This will inevitably result in the reduction of local and/or UK SME suppliers. Thus, there is a need to identify, and then measure, the SME organisational capabilities and competences necessary to support supply chain management.

Although studies have been conducted into the effect of single competences on SMEs for supply chain partnering, for example, customer orientation (Appiah-Adu and Singh, 1998; Veitch and Smith, 2000; Hvolby *et al.*, 2001), holistic studies into the competences necessary to support collaborative supply chain management structures are limited (Croom *et al.*, 2000). Nevertheless, using a similar theoretical framework to the one outlined above, Croom (2001) conducted a comprehensive case study of collaborative product development. The outcomes of his research indicate that within a dyadic customer–supplier framework, there is a strong argument for strategic capabilities, within *both* of the organisations, that are based on product, structure and interaction competences. The reality of business relationships, however, is that it is generally the customer who has the power, and is the one 'selecting' their supply partner (Cox *et al.*, 2000). Therefore, if SMEs are to make themselves attractive as partners within a supply chain management framework, they must demonstrate the competences that *customers* consider

TABLE 12.1 Supplier competence requirements

Competence	Organisational implications
Business process competences	
Benchmarking	Competitive business processes delivering cost, quality and performance
Continuous improvement	Development orientation required across all business processes and staff
Flexibility	Adaptive products, processes, organisation and staff
Innovative approach	Change orientation to processes and products
Interactive competences	
Customer focus	Service orientation. Proactive in understanding and responding to customer requirements
Communication	Formal and ad hoc interactions. Quality information systems and information sharing. Collaborative approach, possibly multilevel and multifunctional
Production competences	
Performance	Delivery accuracy and cost are used as direct comparisons with competitors. Production optimisation should achieve this
Quality	The product must meet the appropriate national or internal quality standards. A quality culture should be evident in the supplier

(Source: Adapted from Macpherson, 2001)

important. A study of the attributes required by large manufacturing organisations (Macpherson, 2001) concluded that, similar to Croom's findings, suppliers were looking for more than just performance and quality of products. Indeed, these criteria were prerequisites for consideration; while companies were actively working within their supply chains – either formally or informally – to rationalise their suppliers, supplier selection and assessment were likely to include the range of competences included in Table 12.1. It will be the ability of the SME to provide *both* production and relation management capabilities that will be key to their retention as preferred suppliers.

In summary, then, specific competences will be a potential source of competitive advantage for SMEs working within a framework of supply chain management, and the study of supply chain competences is a strategically important area of research for them. If the intention is to create and sustain a relationship for mutual competitive advantage, relationship management will need to be a key strategic priority, in order that the context allows collaboration to evolve (Boddy *et al.*, 2000). Moreover, supply chain management is a developing business priority, and if SMEs are to take advantage of future opportunities, it will be important for SMEs to identify and address these competences. It is to the assessment of these competences within SMEs that we now turn.

Measuring and Assessing Supply Chain Competences within SMEs

In order to assess the SMEs' supply chain competences, it is necessary to understand the types of activities that SMEs are conducting in their day-to-day operations. The competences highlighted in Table 12.1 do not fit into traditional management functions, and require a range of activities *across* functions. Nevertheless, traditional functional competence maps do detail a wide range of business activities necessary to run a successful business. Therefore, using these 'best practice' functional activities as a base, and earlier empirical research on the competences expected by large organisations from their suppliers (Macpherson, 2001), a questionnaire was constructed consisting of 126 questions regarding the types of activity the SMEs 'should' be undertaking within their business, and within their supply chain. These questions were then grouped in relation to the competences listed in Table 12.1. However, competence is not just conducting an activity. Assessing competence requires the opportunity to observe and assess knowledge application, and a level against which competence can be benchmarked (Loan-Clarke *et al.*, 2000). Nevertheless, the frequency of conduct and level of importance attached to specific activities demonstrates a knowledge of the relative importance of that activity for the subject organisations, and also a relative degree of competence. Although this would not measure an absolute degree of capability, measuring the business activity in this way allows a measure to be computed for each competence and also provides an indication of supply chain orientation. Details were also gathered on the size, age and turnover of the organisations. All organisations were manufacturing SMEs, operating within the supply chains of larger organisations in the north-west of England. In total, 39 organisations participated; the mean age of these organisations was 32, and the mean size was 49 employees. Details on turnover were only made available by 25 firms. It is recognised that other structural characteristics may be relevant, particularly financial measures of success, but detailed accounts were not available for the research.

The mean computed scores for each of the competences are included in Table 12.2, and the degree of correlation between the competences and the age,

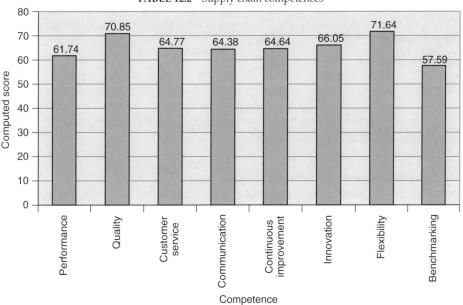

TABLE 12.2   Supply chain competences

TABLE 12.3 Structural correlation coefficients

	Performance	Customer service	Continuous improvement	Innovation	Communication	Quality	Flexibility	Benchmarking	
Age	0.050	0.048	0.035	−0.032	−0.111	0.055	−0.069	−0.049	Pearson correlation
n = 39	0.764	0.770	0.834	0.844	0.503	0.739	0.678	0.769	Significance
Size	0.013	−0.102	0.153	−0.154	0.080	0.042	−0.026	0.009	Pearson correlation
n = 39	0.939	0.538	0.352	0.349	0.628	0.801	0.875	0.959	Significance
Turnover	0.240	−0.033	0.122	−0.002	0.284	0.101	0.023	0.255	Pearson correlation
n = 25	0.249	0.877	0.562	0.993	0.169	0.632	0.914	0.218	Significance

*Correlation is significant at the 0.01 level (two-tailed)

TABLE 12.4 Competence correlation coefficients

	Customer service	Continuous improvement	Innovation	Communication	Quality	Flexibility	Benchmarking	
Performance	0.800*	0.737*	0.710*	0.762*	0.695*	0.804*	0.875*	Pearson correlation
	0.000	0.000	0.000	0.000	0.000	0.000	0.000	Significance
Customer service		0.792*	0.814*	0.780*	0.659*	0.873*	0.791*	Pearson correlation
		0.000	0.000	0.000	0.000	0.000	0.000	Significance
Continuous improvement			0.776*	0.832*	0.604*	0.884*	0.678*	Pearson correlation
			0.000	0.000	0.000	0.000	0.000	Significance
Innovation				0.841*	0.565*	0.786*	0.736*	Pearson correlation
				0.000	0.000	0.000	0.000	Significance
Communication					0.677*	0.783*	0.806*	Pearson correlation
					0.000	0.0000	0.000	Significance
Quality						0.632*	0.856*	Pearson correlation
						0.000	0.000	Significance
Flexibility							0.774*	Pearson correlation
							0.000	Significance

n = 39
*Correlation is significant at the 0.01 level (two-tailed)

size and turnover of the organisation is included in Tables 12.3 and 12.4. The standard deviations for the computed competence scores vary in the range 14.2 to 19.2. From Table 12.2, it can be seen that within the sample companies, there is a positive approach to the activities that support a supply chain capability. Perhaps this should not be surprising. Given that it is notoriously difficult to engage SMEs in research, those that do participate are likely to have considered the potential benefits of engaging with their external environment, and to consider interactions as a potential resource. Indeed, the SME innovation literature highlights the fact that it is important for firms to react to, collaborate with, and draw on their environmental resources through the network of opportunities available to them (Barnett and Storey, 2000). Moreover, Barnett and Storey note that less than 20 per cent of SMEs last more than six years; this research sample has a mean age of 32 years – with only one organisation under six years old – and significantly exceeded this statistic. Consequently, they are the exception rather than the norm, and it would be unwise to infer from this research that the general approach to supply chain issues will be as strong in other SMEs. Surviving for considerably longer than over 80 per cent of SMEs can also be considered a credible measure of success, which may also be reflected in the external orientation of the organisation. Nevertheless, even within these proactive and successful SMEs, there was still significant room for improvement in their supply chain orientation.

Of all of the scores computed, the benchmarking competence appears to be the most problematical. Again, however, this is not surprising since the SMEs complain that there are no relevant tools for them to conduct benchmarking, particularly in areas of intangible values such as flexibility and innovation (Monkhouse, 1995). The benchmarking that was conducted was primarily through recognised quality standards and key performance indicators from their customers. However, the use of the data was often patchy, and further evidence of weak evaluation was observed in the performance competence, where evaluation activity was intermittent and reduced the score in this competence. Issues of quality were clearly strongly addressed, often through either inspection or the attainment and maintenance of quality standards to meet legal or customer requirements. Flexibility was highly prized, particularly since this competence was required to meet the changing and short-term requirements of customers. Moreover, bearing in mind the move towards leaner production methods and reduced stock holdings in larger organisations, pressure is put on SMEs to respond quickly to fluctuations in demand, and activities to improve flexibility were important to the SMEs.

With regard to the degree of correlation, all of the competences are significantly correlated with each other. That is, if an organisation is strong on one competence, it is strong on them all. In addition, there were no significant correlations between the variations in age, size or turnover and variation in competence. Where similarities did exist between firms – operating within a declining sector of the economy and almost all having survived significantly longer than most small firms – it was not possible to compare this research sample with a comparable sample from another economic sector or younger companies. This would be an interesting direction for future research. Nevertheless, the fact that these companies were ready to engage with the external environment, evident in their willingness to participate in research and their relatively high supply chain competence scores, is worthy of further discussion. While the research results do not indicate that they are collaborating within a supply chain framework, they do highlight that these organisations have survived, and they have an external orientation. While there may be no causal link between these elements, it is worth considering that the external orientation may be part of the 'culture' of the organisation, and the relevance of this for SME development is also worthy of further discussion.

Competence, Change and Risk for SMEs in Supply Chain Management

As highlighted earlier, supply chain management seems set to be a significant and changing contextual factor with which SMEs will be faced. This will require SMEs to consider their integration with larger organisations in terms of information exchange, business activities and relationships. Although the results from this research indicate that the SMEs were reasonably oriented towards supply chain activities and competences, there were still significant areas for improvement among this sample, measured against the identified competences. Moreover, whatever theoretical perspective one takes on the implications of the environment for success of the organisation – resource dependence, population ecology or institutional theory – the importance of being able to interact with that environment for competitive advantage remains crucial to organisational success. Therefore, being able to identify and strengthen supply chain competences will be an important factor for SME competitive advantage and will be dependent on two major issues: the willingness and opportunity to develop of appropriate skills; and the belief or perception by the SME management that closer integration is important for their success. Both of these issues need further exploration.

Developing Competence

The strength of the supply chain competence correlation in Table 12.4 highlights the cross-functional nature of work within an SME and certainly the importance of developing competences that do not fall within the traditional structures of NVQ-based systems. This further strengthens the argument that competence-based NVQ programmes which focus on functional and skills competence are not relevant to the needs of SMEs, due their generic nature, which does not account for the diversity within the SME sector (Banfield et al., 1996; Connor and Haydock, 1997). Moreover, SME owners do not appear to value the certification process (Matlay and Hyland, 1997). Unfortunately, this stylised approach to training support is the predominant method of training delivery and support from government agencies, and reflects a supply- rather than demand-led approach (Vinten, 2000). Indeed, many studies of SME development have highlighted the dichotomies existing between the structural constraints and preferred methods of training within SMEs, and the current structures for SME support.

The structural constraints include time, cost, and the perception that benefits from training accrue to the individual rather than to the SME. This last point is particularly damaging, since even those SMEs which are development-oriented fear that their investment may ultimately benefit their direct competitors (see, for example, Westhead and Storey, 1996; Wong et al., 1997; Smith et al., 1999; Kerr and McDougall, 1999; Johnson, 1999). Furthermore, employees often perceive training programmes as a punishment for poor performance rather than an incentive or opportunity (Lange et al., 2000). The lack of evidence to link development directly to performance acts as a further disincentive, particularly since benefits from training take time to accrue, which does not sit well in the culture of many SMEs who have short-term priorities and require immediate solutions to current problems (Westhead and Storey, 1997). One further constraint is that the development of competence and managerial skills is closely linked to the firm's culture, which is, in turn, a product of the owner-manager's attitude, personality and values during the early years of the SME's development (Smith *et al.*, 1999). This clearly supports the implications of the research above, which indicates that supply chain orientation is organisationally consistent across all competences. Since the approach and attitude of the management are felt directly through the informal communication structures typical of SMEs, the supply chain orientation must be, at least partly, a product of the SME owner-manager and/or the management team influence.

Despite these structural and attitudinal barriers, many SMEs do participate in training and development. Participation occurs both formally and informally, with the former being used to tackle current and specific problems, or needs, directly within the SME (Homan *et al.*, 2000) and growing in importance as the size of the organisation increases (Penn *et al.*, 1998). However, the time to find relevant training from the plethora of training programmes available acts as a barrier to participation in formal training activities (Marshall *et al.*, 1995). Since, as highlighted earlier, formal competence and skills programmes are not seen as fit for purpose by the SME, training is sourced in a variety of other ways. Despite developments in distance learning technology and the expansion of open learning, the clear preference appears to be for consultants who will work on a one-to-one basis to ensure the organisation's specific needs are met (Lange *et al.*, 2000). Perhaps even more significant, in terms of supply chain management, is the fact that the nature of entrepreneurial learning is essentially different from traditional learning programmes, in that it is non-linear and discontinuous, with a significant emphasis on the ability to learn informally through networks and partnerships (Choeuke and Armstrong, 1998; Barnett and Storey, 2000). Indeed, the skills relating to networking, learning from experience, and sourcing of resources and expertise from outside the firm are considered key functions of the owner-managers of SMEs (Gibb, 1997; Deakins and Freel, 1998), and can be linked directly to the competences necessary to participate in a supply chain management environment (see Table 12.1). However, it is clear that these skills are not available through traditional formal training programmes.

The implications of these structural, attitudinal and developmental limitations of SMEs are important for those who wish to work and survive in a supply chain management environment. If, as Hill and Stewart (2000) argue, an SME's approach to development is directly related to its organisational context, then operating within a supply chain management structure should provide SMEs with significant opportunities to learn from their customers. Moreover, learning from other organisations within the supply chain appears to fit well with the development model preferred by SMEs; it is immediate, focused on real business issues, and addresses the specific business needs of the SME, albeit possibly from the perspective of the customer organisation. However, the attitude and approach of their customers will be a significant contextual factor, and the success and competitiveness of SMEs may well rest on the ability and desire of larger organisations to disseminate their learning through the supply chain. The concern is whether there will truly be a culture of collaboration within a supply chain management framework that will enable the SME to learn. This will require a major change to current relationship frameworks between customers and suppliers.

Changing the Context of Customer–Supplier Relationships

One of the crucial aspects of supply chain management, highlighted in the theoretical framework, is closer integration through collaborative and more trusting relationships between supply chain partners. In addition, in both the innovation literature and existing empirical research, it is clear that collaboration is critical to innovation and competitiveness (Barnett and Storey, 2000). Therefore, for SMEs, customers who are keen to implement a supply chain management framework *should* provide a strong, supportive and mutually beneficial source of collaboration, and therefore competitive advantage. However, a move to supply chain management will challenge existing transactional behaviours that are deeply ingrained. If we accept that behaviours are manifestations of deeper cultural influences (Schein, 1984), supply chain management will also require a change of culture in both customer and supplier organisations. The problem, as in all change initiatives, will be in identifying who will lead the change, what structures will be needed to support the change, and the difficulties to be overcome if change is to be mutually beneficial (Buchanan and Boddy, 1992).

Unless customer organisations are *leading* and *supporting* the change in inter-organisational relations, they will only be changing the context within which the customer–supplier interaction occurs. In this scenario, the customer will be expecting the SME suppliers to adopt and develop more relational competences by themselves. Moreover, although there may be a need for change, the changing context will be forced on the SME from the top of the supply chain. This factor means that change may not be welcome and may create varying degrees of dissonance (Burnes and James, 1995) both within and between organisations. Moreover, since culture is continually evolving, perceptions of changes that affect inter-organisational relations will be predicated on the existing cultural framework, developed through shared experiences (Schein, 1984; Hendry and Hope, 1994). Considering that traditional inter-organisational relations are based on inequalities of power, and that supply chains are easier to manage if the supplier is dependent (Cox *et al.*, 2000), then it is likely that any 'top led' change will be perceived by the SME as only supporting the agenda of the customer. These factors suggest that not only will existing structures and cultures within the organisation act as barriers to socialising new competences necessary for supply chain management (Scarbrough, 1998) but existing relations, structures and cultures between organisations may be significant factors to overcome. Thus, real change, if it is possible at all, will happen slowly and a significant cultural shift within the supply chain will require a significant and concerted effort from the customer, which presupposes that the customer is both willing and able to make this effort. This is far from certain, particularly since (based on a rational analysis of the uncertainty and asset specificity of suppliers) there will be a limited number of situations where this approach will be considered appropriate (Forker and Stannack, 2000; Cousins, 2002). This suggests the possibility that the positive supply chain orientation demonstrated by SME organisations can be, or is, adopted independently of the customer. In addition, given the nascent nature of supply chain management, this further strengthens the argument that a proactive approach to the supply chain may be in response to, rather than in collaboration with, their customers' activities. It suggests that the attitude or culture of the SMEs is crucial to developing the appropriate competences to support a supply chain focus, which clearly links strongly to both the correlation of competences across organisations (Table 12.4), and the acknowledgement that the development orientation of SMEs is strongly linked to the attitude of the owner-manager. Thus, both the development of SMEs' competences and the criticality of behavioural orientation of the SME indicate that the approach of SMEs to supply chains will depend on the institutionalisation of appropriate models of supply chain management. However, cultural and developmental barriers may not be the only factors limiting participation in supply chain management.

Risks and Supply Chain Management

There will also be real physical and financial implications for the SME in supply chain management. Closer integration with customers requires a commitment to a relationship, and a suitable context within which collaboration can flourish. To foster and manage that relationship requires time and effort, as well as attention to a number of structural processes, including technology, power, people, culture and finance (Boddy *et al.*, 2000). Whether the SME has the resources or inclination to do this will be dependent on its specific resource capabilities, in both business and relational terms, or at least its willingness and support to develop these resources, as highlighted above. However, even if SMEs do have resources, they will be finite. This, together with the time pressures that these organisations traditionally face, will mean that integration will be limited to, at best, a few key customers, which implies a strategic risk for the SME. This can be demonstrated using ICT as an example.

Introducing electronic or ICT systems to increase customer–supplier integration and responsiveness is currently expensive and requires a level of commitment from both the supplier and customer to longer-term relationships. While this may change with the development of more universal e-purchasing systems, the availability of expertise within the SMEs to understand and implement such systems is far from assured (Ritchie and Brindley, 2000), and the full extent and impact of integration through e-commerce is still uncertain (Rhodes and Carter, 1998). Moreover, unless systems architecture allows the integration of data from a variety of customers seamlessly into the production process, integration will only be possible for a limited number of customers. Closer integration with a reduced customer base will mean that the SMEs will be unable to spread financial risk. Moreover, information systems downstream that identify changing customer needs also create upstream pressures to increase flexibility. With the move to leaner and 'just in time' (JIT) supply chains, supply stock-holding is pushed down the supply chain and the suppliers are under pressure to respond quickly to changes in demand, with lead time and delivery precision used as important measures of success (Hvolby and Thortenson, 2000). If the information systems are truly integrated, the lead times should give the supplier SME time to respond to changing demand. However, the reality is that the SME is managing a number of customers with competing demands. In order to respond flexibly, the SME either has to hold higher stock levels, or incorporate increased capacity into the organisation (for example, through multiskilling or production capability). Both of these scenarios carry a real financial penalty and risk in terms of capital investment.

In terms of the opportunities for competitive advantage, then, the implications of change suggested by supply chain management and research suggests that *the attitude and approach of the SME to closer integration will be important for any change process*, but also that a move to closer integration is not without structural and financial problems. Consequently, if we consider the extra time, effort, development, change and risks associated with an SME's move towards closer collaboration in the supply chain, it is clear that the opportunities available for competitive advantage through supply chain management may be a fine balance between investment (developmental and financial), flexibility, service, integration and strategic risk. This will be a difficult balance to strike for many SMEs. Moreover, there is a significant degree of doubt over whether SMEs will be equipped to respond to the unprecedented levels of change and subsequent opportunities occurring through changes in supply chain activities by large companies (Nelder and Skandalakis, 1999).

Conclusion

There is an abundance of evidence to suggest that large organisations are focusing strategically on their supply chains as a source of competitive advantage, and the strength of the argument for closer relations based on transaction costs and resource-based strategy theories is compelling. However, there is also a strong theoretical argument that an integrated supply chain management approach will be the exception rather than the rule (Forker and Stannack, 2000). Nevertheless, increased strategic activity by large organisations within their supply chains will provide opportunities for SMEs, provided they have – or can develop – appropriate business, production and relational competences. Thus, the changes occurring within supply chains and supply chain management are creating *potential* opportunities for competitive advantage among SMEs. If supply chain management is really more than simply integration through physical and technological business systems, those SMEs that can develop the appropriate competences will have a competitive advantage.

It is also clear that, if customers are to be successful in leveraging change and in securing competitive advantage through supply chain management, an understanding and sensitivity to the issues of culture change will be crucial. From an SME perspective, the move to more collaborative inter-organisational relations will cause difficulties unless the appropriate competences already exist, or are developed within a culture that embraces change. If SMEs are not to miss out on opportunities that are emerging through supply chain management, they will need to measure their levels of organisational and relational competence against the dimensions identified by customers as critical to supplier performance. Thus, further research will be needed to benchmark and evaluate the competence levels of SMEs, to identify critical areas of underachievement, and to use this information to inform the support networks for SME development provision. Alternatively, and given the failure of current support systems to engage with SMEs, it may be that those SMEs that can foster relationships through supply chains will also be able to use their supply chain networks as a source of competitive advantages by creating learning opportunities within them (Barnett and Storey, 2000). The development of appropriate competences may be more about the attitudes of SME management, and the organisation's cultural orientation towards its external environment, than the formal support provided by government initiatives.

The full extent and implications of supply chain management for SMEs are unclear, and there is a need for further research in this area. Indeed, the ability or desirability of the SME adopting a supply chain management approach towards its own suppliers is still to be addressed. It may be that supply chain management is more rhetoric than reality, or it may only affect a small number of select companies with unique skills and products. If the latter is the case, it will be SMEs which can foster unique capabilities that will survive, particularly in the face of global- and e-sourcing. However, if customers do not embrace a more holistic approach to performance when selecting their suppliers, the future for the UK SME may continue to be bleak, particularly with ICT systems set to make the sourcing of suppliers more efficient and dynamic (Ritchie and Brindley, 2000). In addition, supply chain management may be an opportunity, but for how many SMEs, and at what risk? It may be putting more strain on SMEs by creating the extra costs of flexibility, but providing few of the benefits of collaboration. Competitiveness in the supply chain may be a balance between flexibility, service, integration and financial risk; this will be a fine line to tread for many resource-scarce SMEs.

References

Appiah-Adu, K. and Singh, S. (1998) 'Customer orientation and performance: a study of SMEs', *Management Decision*, **36**, 385–394.

Arnold, U. (2000) 'New dimensions of outsourcing: a combination of transaction cost economics and the core competencies concept', *European Journal of Purchasing and Supply Management*, **2**, 23–29.

Banfield, P., Jennings, P. and Beaver, G. (1996) 'Competence-based training for small firms–an expensive failure?' *Long Range Planning*, **29**, 94–102.

Barnett, E. and Storey, J. (2000) 'Managers' accounts of innovation processes in small and medium-sized enterprises', *Journal of Small Business and Enterprise Development*, **7**, 315–324.

Barney, J. (1991) 'Firm resources and sustained competitive advantage', *Journal of Management*, **17**, 99–120.

Bendiner, J. (1998) 'Supply chain software', *APICS–The Performance Advantage*, January, 34–38.

Boddy, D., MacBeth, D. and Wagner, B. (2000) 'Implementing collaboration between organisations: an empirical study of supply chain partnering', *Journal of Management Studies*, **37**, 1003–1016.

Bolton, P. and Sharfstein, D. (1998) 'Corporate finance, the theory of the firm, and organizations', *Journal of Economic Perspectives*, **12**, 95–114.

Boxall, P. (1996) 'The strategic HRM debate and the resource-based view of the firm', *Human Resource Management Journal*, **6**, 59–75.

Brusoni, S. and Prencipe, A. (2001) 'Managing knowledge in loosely coupled networks: exploring the links between product and knowledge dynamics', *Journal of Management Studies*, **38**, 1019–1035.

Buchanan, D.A. and Boddy, D. (1992) *The Expertise of the Change Agent: Public Performance and Backstage Activity*. Prentice Hall, Hemel Hempstead.

Burnes, B. and James, H. (1995) 'Culture, cognitive dissonance and the management of change', *International Journal of Operations and Production Management*, **15**, 14–33.

Choeuke, K. and Armstrong, B. (1998) 'The learning organization in small and medium-sized enterprises: a destination or a journey', *International Journal of Entrepreneurial Behaviour and Research*, **4**, 129–141.

Christopher, M. and Jüttner, U. (2000) 'Developing strategic partnerships in the supply chain: a practitioner perspective', *Purchasing and Supply Management*, **6**, 117–127.

Coase, R. (1937) 'The nature of the firm', in O.E. Williamson and S.G. Winter (eds) *The Nature of the Firm: Origins, Evolution and Development*. Oxford University Press, Oxford, pp. 18–33.

Connor, J. and Haydock, W. (1997) 'Management development in the small firm: do competence-based approaches work?' *Enterprise and Growth in the Small Business Sector*, collection of papers by Bolton Business School, Bolton, UK.

Corbett, C., Blackburn, J. and Van Wassenhove, L. (1999) 'Case study partnerships to improve supply chains', *Sloan Management Review*, Summer, 71–82.

Cousins, P. (2002) 'A conceptual model for managing long-term inter-organizational relationships', *European Journal of Purchase and Supply Management*, **8**, 71–82.

Cox, A., Sanderson, J. and Watson, G. (2000) 'Wielding influence', *Supply Management*, **6**, April, 30–33.

Croom, S. (2001) 'The dyadic capabilities concept: examining the process of key supplier involvement in collaborative product development', *European Journal of Purchasing and Supply Management*, **7**, 29–37.

Croom, S., Romano, P. and Giannakis, M. (2000) 'Supply chain management: an analytical framework for critical literature review', *European Journal of Purchase and Supply Management*, **6**, 67–83.

Deakins, D. and Freel, M. (1998) 'Entrepreneurial learning and the growth process in SMEs', *The Learning Organization*, **5**, 144–155.

Ellram, L. and Billington, C. (2001) 'Purchasing leverage considerations in the outsourcing decision', *European Journal of Purchasing and Supply Management*, **7**, 15–27.

Forker, L. and Stannack, P. (2000) 'Cooperation versus competition: do buyers and suppliers really see eye-to-eye?' *European Journal of Purchasing and Supply Management*, **6**, 31–40.

Fox, M. (1998) 'Supply chain challenge–to create virtual companies of integrated and synchronous supply chains', *APICS–The Performance Advantage*, January, 44–48.

Gibb, A. (1997) 'Small firms' training and competitiveness–building upon the small business as a learning organization', *International Small Business Journal*, **15**, 13–30.

Graham, G. and Hardaker, G. (2000) 'Supply chain management across the Internet', *International Journal of Physical Distribution and Logistics Management*, **30**, 286–295.

Hart, O.D. (1993) 'Incomplete contracts and the theory of the firm', in O.E. Williamson and S.G. Winter (eds) *The Nature of the Firm: Origins, Evolution and Development*. Oxford University Press, Oxford, pp. 138–158.

Hendry, J. and Hope, V. (1994) 'Cultural change and competitive performance', *European Management Journal*, **12**, 401–406.

Hill, R. and Stewart, J. (2000) 'Human resource development and small organizations', *Journal of European Industrial Training*, **24**, 105–117.

Homan, G., Hicks-Clarke, D., and Wilson, A. (2000) 'The management development needs of owner managers/managers in SMEs', *European Social Fund Project Report*, Manchester Metropolitan University, UK.

Hoyt, J. and Huq, F. (2000) 'From arms' length to collaborative relationships in the supply chain: an evolutionary process', *International Journal of Physical Distribution and Logistics Management*, **30**, 750–764.

Hvolby, H.-H. and Thortenson, A. (2000) 'Performance measurement in small and medium-sized enterprises' *Proceedings from the 3rd SMESME International Conference*, Coventry University, 17–19 April, 324–332.

Hvolby, H.-H., Jacques, H., Trienekens, J. and Carrie, A. (2001) 'Supply chain planning in small and medium-sized enterprises'. *Proceedings of the 4th SMESME International Conference*, Aalborg University, Denmark, 14–16 May.

Johnson, S. (1999) 'Skills issues in small and medium-sized enterprises', *Skills Task Force Research Paper 13*, December.

Kerr, A. and McDougall, M. (1999) 'The small business of developing people', *International Small Business Journal*, **17**, 65–74.

Lamming, R., Johnsen, T., Zheng, J. and Harland, C. (2000) 'An initial classification of supply networks' *International Journal of Operations Management*, **20**, 675–691.

Lange, T., Ottens, M. and Taylor, A. (2000) 'SMEs and barriers to skills development: a Scottish perspective', *Journal of European Industrial Training*, **24**, 5–11.

Loan-Clarke, J., Boocock, G., Smith, A. and Whittaker, J. (2000) 'Competence-based management development in small and medium-sized enterprises: a multistakeholder analysis', *International Journal of Training and Development*, **4**, 176–195.

Macpherson, A. (2001) 'Corporate directions in supply chain management: implications for SME competences and inter-organizational relations', *Research in Management & Business*, Manchester Metropolitan University, Working Paper Series, 01/15.

Marshall, J., Alderman, N., Wong, C., and Thwaites, A. (1995) 'The impact of management training and development on SMEs', *International Small Business Journal*, **13**, 23–34.

Matlay, H. and Hyland, T. (1997) 'NVQs in the small business sector: a critical overview', *Education and Training*, **39**, 325–332.

Matthews, J., Pellew, L., Phua, F. and Rowlinson, S. (2000) 'Quality relationships: partnering in the construction supply chain', *International Journal of Quality and Reliability Management*, **17**, 493–510.

McDermott, M. and Chan, K. (1996) 'Flexible intelligent relationship management: the business success paradigm in a stakeholder society', *The Learning Organization*, **3**, 5–17.

Monkhouse, E. (1995) 'The role of competitive benchmarking in small to medium-sized enterprises', *Benchmarking for Quality Management Technology*, **2**, 41–50.

Nelder, G. and Skandalakis, A. (1999) 'Benchmarking as the gateway to knowledge transfer in SMEs', *Industry and Higher Education*, October, 342–348.

Penn, W., Forster, R., Heydon, G. and Richardson, S. (1998) 'Learning in smaller organizations', *The Learning Organization*, **5**, 128–137.

Prahalad, C. and Hamel, G. (1990) 'The core competence of the corporation', *Harvard Business Review*, May–June, 79–91.

Rhodes, E. and Carter, R. (1998) 'Electronic commerce technology and changing product distribution', *International Journal of Technology Management*, **15**, 31–49.

Ritchie, B. and Brindley, C. (2000) 'Disintermediation, disintegration and risk in the SME global supply chain', *Management Decision*, **38**, 575–583.

Scarbrough, H. (1998) 'The HR implications of supply chain relationships', *Human Resource Management Journal*, **10**, 5–17.

Schein, E. (1984) 'Coming to a new awareness of organizational culture', *Sloan Management Review*, Winter, 3–15.

Sinclair, D., Hunter, L. and Beaumont, P. (1996) 'Models of customer–supplier relations', *Journal of General Management*, **22**, 56–74.

Smith, A., Whittaker, J., Clark, J.L. and Boocock, G. (1999) 'Competence-based management development provision to SMEs and the providers' perspective', *Journal of Management Development*, **18**, 557–572.

Veitch, K. and Smith, E.H. (2000) 'The evaluation of customer service performance and the small business–a case study within the packaging supply chain', *Proceedings from the 3rd SMESME International Conference*, Coventry University, 17–19 April, 216–221.

Vinten, G. (2000) 'Training in small and medium-sized enterprises', *Industrial and Commercial Training*, **32**, 9–14.

Weaver, M. and Dickson, P. (1998) 'Outcome quality of small- to medium-sized enterprise-based alliances: the role of perceived partner behaviours', *Journal of Business Venturing*, **13**, 505–522.

Westhead, P. and Storey, D. (1996) 'Management training and small firm performance: why is the link so weak?' *International Small Business Journal*, **14**, 13–24.

Westhead, P. and Storey, D. (1997) 'Training provision and the development of small and medium-sized enterprises', *DfEE, Research Report No. 26*.

Williamson, O.E. (1979) 'Transaction cost economics: the governance of contractual relations', *Journal of Law and Economics*, **22**, 233–262.

Williamson, O.E. (1981) 'The economics of organization: the transaction cost approach', *American Journal of Sociology*, **87**, 548–577.

Wong, C., Neil, J., Marshal, N., Alderman, N. and Thwaites, A. (1997) 'Management training in small and medium-sized enterprises: methodological and conceptual issues', *International Journal of Human Resource Management*, **8**, 44–65.

Wren, B., Simpson, J.T. and Paul, C. (1998) 'Market channel relations among small businesses', *International Small Business Journal*, **16**, 64–78.

Chapter 13

SUSTAINING VIABILITY IN SMEs: PERSPECTIVES ON INNOVATION IN FINANCIAL MANAGEMENT

Bob Sweeting, Tony Berry and Jitsuo Goto

Introduction

A healthy SME population is central to current policy in the UK (see Chapter 1) and other developed economies in North America, Europe and Japan. At the same time, failure rates among SMEs are high, one of the main reasons for which can be inadequacy in financial management (Keasey and Watson, 1993). Different managerial techniques, practices and competencies are required at different stages in the growth cycle of businesses (Miller and Friesen, 1984) and at any stage there has to be a 'fit' to the particular organisation (McDonough, 1986). However, overzealous application of financial disciplines has attracted adverse criticism. For example, overactive use of accounting and accountants was given as a major reason for economic decline in the USA in the 1970s, in that innovation and flair were stifled in businesses of all kinds (Hayes and Abernathy, 1981). In the 1980s, management accounting (and accountants?) were accused of having lost their 'relevance' to the managers and organisations they were there to serve (Johnson and Kaplan, 1987). These criticisms came at a time when Western businesses were facing severe global competition, particularly from Japan, and were failing in competitiveness. Some Japanese businesses were winning because it was perceived they had better service, quality and manufacturing methods coupled with a more open and transparent management culture. The way in which larger Japanese firms worked more closely with their suppliers, particularly smaller businesses, also came under close scrutiny (Turnbull *et al.*, 1992; Kato, 1993; Carr and Ng, 1995).

These circumstances put tremendous pressure on Western businesses to change, including changing their methods of financial management.

This chapter proceeds via reflections upon external influences on SMEs and changing perspectives on SMEs (with special reference to accounting and financial innovation) to report on some findings of a survey on the current accounting and financial management practices of a sample of SMEs in the north-west of England.

Some External Influences on SMEs

SMEs were subject to a number of external influences, including technology, accounting innovations and the rise of the new finance.

The Impact of Advanced Manufacturing Technology

Large Western manufacturing businesses invested in Advanced Manufacturing Technologies (AMT) that embraced not only new ways of 'cutting metal', for example computer-aided manufacturing, but also new logistical integration with Just-in-Time (JIT) manufacturing and new ideas in workforce integration with Total Quality Management (TQM). But even in these large firms, financial management and accounting practices, especially cost management, were criticised for not supporting this new world of manufacturing (Kaplan, 1984). This increasing sophistication led these businesses to expect more capability from their suppliers, including, of course, SMEs.

The Impact of Accounting Innovations

The principal thrust of accounting innovations was to turn accounting from a pre-occupation with internal costs towards accounting that would link businesses to their markets. Such innovations included activity-based costing, strategic management accounting, target costing and throughput costing. While the advancement of activity-based costing (ABC) was predicated to some extent on the need to handle changing internal cost problems (with a shrinking proportion of direct labour costs in products and overheads outweighed by heavy investment in new manufacturing technologies), ABC was capable of much wider application to the core activities of any kind and size of organisation (Cooper and Kaplan, 1988) and could facilitate better decision making and performance measurement improvements and redesign of business processes (Davies and Sweeting, 1995).

However, the use of these innovations was problematic. A study (Bright et al., 1992) to examine how well these innovations were integrated with one another and how well they were understood by managers noted some divergence of attitudes and practices. While in survey responses managers indicated a certain level of adoption and indeed necessary understanding, such acceptance was not reflected in workshops held with the managers. However, the study reported that managers were learning from their experimentation with the new accounting techniques and practices, and were being eclectic in putting together new financial systems. But the problems of change remained, as Smith (2000) reported, 'adoption rates in the US, UK and Australia of no more than 14 per cent, even for mature innovations such as ABC, are common.'

The Rise of the New Finance

Experimentation with new accounting techniques by large company managers (a process that in itself could be wasteful) allowed progress and learning to be achieved (Bright *et al.*, 1997). These large businesses had a wide resource base of professional managers, access to high-quality external consulting and the necessary financial resources. Eventually these collective innovations were focused into the New Finance movement (Fisher *et al.*, 1997) which called for the radical reshaping of the finance function away from an emphasis on transactional and conformance work towards decision support and performance-related work. The new accounting approaches were supportive of such new tasks. At the same time, large businesses were shifting from departmental or functional ways of operating towards working with business processes across functions. Financial managers and accountants required to support this new operating paradigm needed to develop new interpersonal skill sets in order to work more closely with managerial colleagues.

Changing Business Processes and Outsourcing

Attention to business processes through the introduction of new production and managerial techniques and practices (the 're-engineering' process) eliminated unnecessary processes and led to further outsourcing of non-core activities. While extensive outsourcing had a long history in Japan (Doi and Cowling, 1999) this was not the case in the UK. While many transactions can and do take place between large businesses in Japan, these large businesses also actively engaged with the small business sector (Doi and Cowling, 1999). Managers in large Japanese business also have a close engagement with the operations and management of their respective SME suppliers, giving these SMEs access to considerable financial and non-financial resources. There is an acceptance on the part of Japanese SME owner-managers that this engagement will take place, and in general they are willing to cooperate.

In the UK, SME owner-managers are frequently characterised as independent and keen to resist anything from outside that they either perceive as interference or becoming too dependent upon one customer. While the use of Japanese approaches to supply chain management in a UK context is unlikely, there has been some evidence of major UK companies leading radical change in supply arrangements including gain-sharing with SMEs (Berry *et al.*, 2000). The authors provide evidence of supply chains operating in partnership with larger customers leading to product, process and administrative innovation.

Larger businesses entering into extensive outsourcing through preferred supplier routes in a framework of supply chain management may represent an attempt to reduce their own costs by exploiting their power over SMEs. In this stress mode (Lamming, 1996) larger business customers in supply chains place considerable financial and management pressures on SMEs and also give them little management support.

Of increasing interest for both observers of SMEs and their managers is the transactional setting of a particular SME. These can range through: (a) autonomous actor; (b) serial dependence, recognising links in a supply chain; (c) reciprocal dependence, recognising interaction for change and product/service provision; and (d) mutual dependence, recognising jointness of endeavours between transactionally related businesses. In all of these forms, basic management control techniques such as budgetary planning and control, quasi-open book accounting, open project accounting and gain-sharing may be relevant (Berry *et al.*, 2000). The changing nature of supply chain management makes demands on SMEs to develop greater competence in financial management.

External Advice and the Changing Emphasis of Accounting Firms

Support for the development of financial management in SMEs in the UK comes from a variety of sources including business links, research centres, government departments, consultants of different kinds and accounting firms. Concurrent with the changes outlined above, accounting firms are now expanding their work as business advisors as opposed to merely servicing the statutory reporting, audit and tax needs of clients.

Changing Perspectives in SMEs

New Ideas and Sophistication

To be described as an innovation, a new idea needs to be widely diffused and understood by users (Van den Ven, 1986). Merely increasing the sophistication of financial management techniques does not necessarily improve matters, as observed by Rui and Ibrahim (1998) in their study of SMEs:

- Innovations are more likely to succeed if they are 'championed' by top management (Twiss, 1986).
- Successful innovation is more likely to result from markets via user 'pull' than technology 'push' (Twiss, 1986).
- Users themselves can be major producers of innovation through their own experimentation with different existing and new ideas (Von Hippel, 1977).

It was observed (Jewkes *et al.*, 1958) that while SMEs may have been a rich source of ideas for new products and services, their subsequent successful innovation generally took place in larger businesses that had a greater range and depth of resources. In the case of supply chains, new requirements and initiatives are emanating *from* large businesses *to* SMEs and therefore the situation observed by Jewkes is reversed. Moreover, it should be noted that in any relationship with an SME the larger business is normally in the dominant position regarding influence and decision-making. This can be particularly significant in supply chain relationships between large and small firms. Changes that may be regarded as trivial in larger businesses could be daunting to managers and employees in an SME (Berry *et al.*, 2000).

Ownership, Management, Dependencies and SME Growth

SME growth trajectories are influenced by the attitudes and competencies of managers and the interests of owners, whether institutional or family (Jarvis *et al.*, 2000). Simplistic growth phases are not really practical in the context of SMEs because there is so much variability as between, for example, ownership and industry (Mitra and Pingali, 1999). The legal form may also have a significant bearing on the scope and nature of business growth. These forms may be (a) sole trader; (b) partnership; (c) private limited liability; or (d) public limited liability. However, managers in any business can decide not to change further, having reached a size and form that suits them, and to reverse the process of development in legal form, by for example, reverting from public limited company to a private limited company status.

New Financial and Non-financial Management Techniques and Practices: Administrative Innovation

One of the ideas that has attracted the attention of managers in larger businesses in recent years has been developing and integrating multiple performance measures. This movement has been driven by work on the balanced scorecard by Kaplan and Norton (1992). Developments along similar lines can be traced back much earlier (for example, General Electric in 1952; Anthony *et al.*, 1989). The movement was driven largely by the need to assess managers (employees) and organisations in both operational and strategic terms. In SMEs, these pressures to assess performance, often because of the closeness of ownership and management, were not so acute. Given the expansion of external interdependencies and the concentration on the nature of their institutional environment (Keeble *et al.*, 1999), SMEs are no longer able to remain isolated from external assessments of performance. Also, while owner-managers may have a preoccupation with cash as the key performance measure, outsiders probably need a much more extensive set of metrics, hence the current interest in assessing the balanced scorecard for use in SMEs.

Performance measurement requires underpinning with relevant information flows and processing capabilities. It cannot be assumed that developments made in larger business settings can be easily used in SMEs. One of the main 'costs' is the time of owners and key managers, and many studies have shown this to be in very short supply. Coupled with this is the need for positive and sustained interest in the changes by these key people when they may be expected to have competing demands on their time.

Little research has been published on accounting and financial management in SMEs, and there is little understanding as to whether accounting and financial innovation was associated with improving performance. Hence, in order to increase understanding, a survey of SMEs was conducted in the north-west of England.

Observations of Financial Management Practice in SMEs

A study was conducted of 140 SMEs operating in a large industrial cluster in the north-west of England. The study was based on an administered questionnaire together with other industrial data. Only the financial study is reported here. Of the sample (see Table 13.1), 42 companies were manufacturers with a mean age of 18.41 years; 98 were service firms with a mean age of 13.4 years. The mean turnover

TABLE 13.1 The sample companies

	Sample	Manufacturers	Services
Number growing	62	19	43
Stable	35	10	25
Declining	30	11	19
No data	13	2	11
	140	42	98

for the whole sample was approximately £3.3m, with a mean employment of 15 persons, although manufacturers were larger than service firms.

In this section we present five areas of observation: growth and strategic focus, private companies, the adoption of new accounting ideas, the role of external advisors, cost management, and performance measurement, together with two case studies to illustrate the behaviour of firms.

Growth and Strategic Focus

Nearly all the SMEs used only one growth strategy. Companies reported growth approaches via involvement in acquisition (24/140), new markets (121/140), improving competitiveness (88/140) and new product development (90/140). These proportions were almost identical between the two subsamples, manufacturing and services. While acquisition was the least commonly used in this sample, it was the most effective means of growing in turnover terms. Clearly, financial growth performance is bought at the time of acquisition whereas the other approaches are more systemic and take time to improve turnover, profits and cash flow.

The manufacturers were growing at an average of 12 per cent per annum (11/42 were shrinking, 10/42 were stable and 19/42 were growing). The service firms were growing with a mean of 17 per cent per annum (19/98 were shrinking, 25/98 were stable and 43/98 were growing). Overall, service firms were growing substantially faster than the manufacturers.

Private Companies and New Accounting Ideas

Most (over two-thirds) of the SMEs in our study were private limited companies. These private companies, compared to the others, had the most extensive deployment of financial management techniques. Private companies exhibited most use of the four growth strategies and the most extensive use of cost management techniques. There was relatively less use of these techniques among smaller businesses. This was primarily because smaller businesses had less capability and resource whereas larger businesses had experience of using a range of these techniques.

External Advisors

Firms sought external advice in a number of areas of management, as shown in Table 13.2.

TABLE 13.2   Firms seeking advice

Area in which advice was sought	Proportion seeking	Growing	Declining	Stable (no data)
Statutory	98/140	46	19	25 (8)
Financial management	44/140	27	10	6 (1)
General business advice	46/140	21	8	14 (3)
Emergency advice	52/140	21	8	17 (6)

Apart from advice on statutory matters, firms in decline were least likely to seek external advice. Those growing were most likely to seek advice on financial and general business matters. Private companies were peak users (compared to others) of external advisors of all kinds. We suggest that (a) these businesses were most 'open to not knowing', realised their needs and limitations and were prepared to access different sources of help; (b) smaller businesses did not know or understand where to go or how to get help, and hence made limited use of external advisors; (c) larger businesses were better resourced, more knowledgeable, aware and focused, and in less need of external advice (Littler and Sweeting, 1990). Hence private companies were perceived as more innovative than those in the other categories.

Cost Management

One of the most disturbing (but not necessarily surprising) findings was the poor and relatively sparse understanding of organisational costs. This led to the relatively low use of business relevant techniques and practices. 'Cash and tax are king' was the dominant message, a finding in line with other research (Jarvis *et al.*, 2000). There was very patchy use of cost information for obvious purposes; e.g. the limited use of cost information in budgeting was very surprising (see Table 13.3).

In this table we observe a wide variation in the systematic use of cost management information in SMEs. There was scope for innovation but the use of most of these techniques was not related to growth. It is interesting to note from Table 13.3 that the use of cost for investment justification was highly associated with the growing businesses where the techniques were used (but also note the low relative usage). In terms of particular financial techniques (Table 13.4), break-even (39 per

TABLE 13.3   Use of cost information

Use of cost information	Proportion using	Growing	Declining	Stable (no data)
In budgetary control	70/140	41	12	13 (4)
Investment justification	54/140	34	8	6 (6)
New product decisions	56/140	29	11	10 (4)
Procurement decisions	90/140	43	19	21 (7)
Cost reduction	80/140	41	18	15 (6)

TABLE 13.4   Finance techniques

Practice or technique	Proportion using	Growing	Declining	Stable (no data)
Break-even	55/140	26	13	13 (3)
Activity-based costing	37/140	22	5	8 (2)
Target costing	28/140	15	6	5 (2)
Cost of quality	23/140	14	3	5 (1)

cent) was most widely used and 26/55 who did use it were growing, while 13/55 were declining and 13/55 were stable. The use of activity-based costing and cost of quality were also weakly in evidence, but note that two-thirds of the users were also growing. The use of target costing was also related to growth. Here we see that the use of market-related accounting techniques was related to growth of the business, but we cannot infer causality. The relative popularity (compared to the data of Smith, 2000) of some of these techniques may reflect promotion in recent years by advisors and other business commentators.

Performance Management

Relatively few SMEs had a mixed financial/non-financial portfolio of performance measures. The most frequently used financial and mixed measures are shown in Table 13.5.

In general, a very low proportion of companies used any other measures of performance. But, again, growing firms were more likely to use financial or non-financial measures of performance, providing some evidence that financial and accounting innovation was associated with growth and probably also with increasing complexity. Whether growth preceded the accounting innovation or was preceded by it is a question that we will seek to answer in future studies.

TABLE 13.5   Frequently used financial measures

Most frequently used financial measures	Proportion using	Growing	Declining	Stable (no data)
Profit/sales	106/140	53	21	26 (6)
Budget variance	68/140	36	11	14 (7)
RoCE	35/140	6	18	8 (3)
Mixed measures				
Debtor days	84/140	48	12	18 (8)
Creditor days	81/140	44	13	18 (6)
Inventory turn	36/140	22	5	5 (4)
Customer profitability	36/140	23	4	6 (3)
Product profitability	38/140	24	7	5 (2)

The case studies in this chapter were chosen to represent two approaches to accounting practice common to the SMEs in our study. The first shows how simple techniques were being replaced by more bureaucratic procedures. The second shows how simple real-time accounting was adequate for many businesses.

Cerise Ltd

Cerise Ltd operated in the north-west of England as a subcontract engineer. The primary competence of the founder and owner was in engineering and sales. It provided parts and subassemblies to other manufacturers. In 1990 the owner purchased a second company and after five managing directors had been hired and sacked, a relation of the owner was appointed as MD. The ensuing period demonstrated that the company lacked rigorous financial management across all areas, including a lack of both formal operational budgeting and capital expenditure, which was undertaken without using financial models. The MD used last year's performance as a 'yardstick' to assess current performance and came to place greater emphasis on financial control, including significant attention to cash flow. In the late 1990s the firm's debt increased and debt payments were sourced from a more effective collection of invoices from a major customer. Late in 2000, it was decided to reduce costs via consolidation of the two companies. Finance was sought from their bank. However, the bank, after requiring a report from the company's external auditors refused to increase its exposure to the company. This has led to three things:

1. The MD to actively manage both businesses, and the owner to concentrate on sales.
2. A move away from day-to-day involvement and an attempt to drive the businesses strategically.
3. An attempt to reduce debts, improve bank relationships and improve the balance sheet.

Comment: management initially operated in 'real time' with minimal accounting, against a trading model rather than a business model. The resulting problems led to a more formal approach which might take the manager's eye off the 'real time' business process.

Rouge

Karel Jones, with experience as an engineer and in sales, founded Rouge as a sole trader in 1984 to supply engineering parts. He took on the role of parts supplier to a number of customers, building business links with a number of local manufacturers. He developed the business around a fast service idea, using his engineering expertise as a basis for decisions. He held no stock, always providing parts to order, minimising working capital by negotiating favourable payment terms to suppliers and from customers. The business grow to £500 000 turnover in 2000. Throughout the company's life Karel Jones has practised financial management by following a simple business model. No computer systems were in use. Invoices were raised manually and sales and purchase day books maintained. There were minimal overheads, so gross margin (GM) and sales volume were used as key performance measures. A running day total of the gross margin was kept. This was transformed into weekly, monthly and year-to-date totals and compared to the estimated break-even point of the business. A calculation of monthly gross margin was used as the basis for profit, which enabled the proprietor to adjust the salary he took from the business. Order lead times were very short, so sales were used as a basis of cash-flow. All stocks were minimal, and supplier payments and debtor collection were closely monitored. Periodic payments of VAT and business tax were factored into cash-flow management. Financial advice and input has been obtained regularly from his external chartered accountant through the process of preparing annual accounts for quarterly VAT payments and taxation purposes.

Comment: This is an example of a real-time simple system of business for a trader, essentially operating a JIT approach. The immediacy of the business activities are well matched by the immediacy of the business information and the rudimentary accounting procedures, supported by a professional accountant's services and advice. There is no need for, and perhaps no value in, further financial complexity.

Discussion

Paths of Change

From the discussion above, the data from our survey and the two case studies it may be observed that many SMEs operated with unsophisticated, indeed simple, accounting and financial management procedures. Any innovation that had taken place was mostly in private limited companies. Furthermore, despite information from the accounting profession and the advice industry, firms have been slow to develop more sophisticated administrative systems. There had been some innovation in accounting procedures, but it appeared that in this population of SMEs there was much scope for improvement. There have been a number of suggestions as to why SMEs apparently resist such innovation: a lack of understanding, irrelevance, uncertainty and shortening business time cycles, complexity and cost. It is, however, too simple to assume that remedying these apparent causes would lead to greater innovation.

The grounded theory research of Jarvis *et al.* (2000) described managers as using a number of simple real-time performance measures (order books, sales shipped, cost of materials, cash at bank) and only using accounting in relation to year-end statements and tax purposes, which they see as lagging information. So the invitation from advisors and accountants to use more complex leading (budgets etc.) and lagging (reports) or different cost measures (e.g. ABC) are invitations to move out of 'real time' or immediate measures into abstract and disengaged time. These are also invitations to mirror the accounting systems in use in larger companies. There was some indication in the findings of our survey companies that when firms had innovated in the past (as evidence of more complex practice), such innovation was to a significant extent associated with growth.

While the actual pathways of change were not visible to us in our survey findings, we conjecture that innovation was much more likely to have been a combination of a 'shock' event (cf. Van den Ven, 1986) coupled with seeking advice to help deal with the ramifications. It was as though firms had crises and only then faced the need to make a decision. We do not know how firms recognised (or failed to recognise) these 'shocks' as decision points, or how they dealt with them. It may have been that the conditions for the firms were different. The case study firms had made some innovations but still managed with simple accounting systems.

Explaining Accounting Innovation

Models of change in accounting (Laughlin, 1991) were defined in a skeletal manner as operating at three levels: the interpretive schemes, which are the meaning frames within which actors make senses of their experience and from which they act; design archetypes, which are the operating procedures such as accounting; and subsystems, which are the systems for doing work. Laughlin (1991) argued that change directed at the design archetypes and the subsystems which does not involve change in the interpretative schemes but which challenges existing schemes is likely to be rebutted, and the design archetypes and systems will return to something like their previous state.

In the case of accounting innovation, then, it is not surprising that the values and beliefs (interpretive schemes) of the owner-managers of SME are central. Where owners are open to or have interpretive schemes that include a more complex business model, perhaps (as our data indicates) triggered by a kick or shock, then accounting innovation is more likely to occur and to persist. It could be observed from the two case studies and from the grounded theory observations of Jarvis *et al.* (2000) that the single owner-manager SME is an unlikely candidate for accounting innovations that require new interpretive schemes. Our survey data reflect this proposition, where we observed that firms with legal forms of private companies were most likely to have innovated. But it was noted from our survey data that these innovations were the relatively simple adoption and use of accounting practices.

Indeed, Laughlin (1991) was at pains to note that change did not happen on its own but required a stimulus (a 'kick'). From our data it seems unlikely that advice on its own was responsible for innovation, but it may have been that advice, following upon a significant business problem, may have given an owner-manager new understanding about changes needed in both accounting and systems. One of the case studies reported here, Cerise, is an example of potential innovation (learning) in response to a financial problem with advice from auditors, bank and accountants. This raises the question of the professional as agent of change, perhaps concentrating upon the technicalities and issues of the design archetypes without either wishing or being able to work at the level of the schemas. This might become a frustrating role, as acceptance of proposed change would appear to be at the whim of the owner-manager. In this survey we were not seeking direct evidence of the pathways of innovation. Malmi (1999) suggested four perspectives from which ABC accounting innovation might be viewed. These were efficient choice (the basis of professional advice as they see it); forced selection (by dominant customers in supply chains); fad; and fashion (which might explain the limited innovations noted by Smith (2000)). But it was clear from our survey data that it may become necessary to explain the limited scale of accounting innovation.

Implications for an Ideal Innovation Path

Perhaps both innovation and the lack of innovation are related to pressure within the SME for the development of competitive advantage. If, following Porter (1985), we acknowledge three main stances to competitive advantage – niche positioning, cost leadership and differentiation – then it is clear that the each of these require a thorough understanding of cost management. Clearly, the growing firms were innovators in this sense, perhaps suggestive of a relationship between growth, innovation and competitive advantage. These findings require further research.

From these considerations we propose an ideal path of innovation in accounting for SMEs in relation to accounting and reporting as follows.

Stage 1   The real-time simple scorecard in use.

Stage 2   Recognising their limitations (surprises, loss of control), companies are encouraged to create leading and lagging information systems and also add complexity to match the business complexity. Ideas related to the balanced scorecard are suggested.

Stage 3   Proposed or suggested innovation is resisted; and relatively simple measures continue to be used.

Stage 4   A new pathway might be emerging in which SMEs use the new ideas (ABC, cost management, investment decision-making) to produce a real-time complex scorecard, contextualised in a set of leading and lagging statements.

Here the innovation (that is, the evolution from simple to complex) is rooted in the acceptance of ideas that support the real-time, hands-on nature of SME management. What is problematic to understand is how this new pathway is taken. From our data, many firms have little or no growth strategy; they appear to meander in their markets and in the economy, subject to 'shocks' which appear to stimulate innovation, but are also likely to miss opportunities for innovation and growth. Yet others are clearly on purposeful journeys where opportunities and 'shocks' are understood in their business context and where change and innovation can take place. Reid and Smith (2000) demonstrated that their sample of micro firms could be classified as adaptive, running blind and stagnant, and that the development of management accounting systems was dependent on the timing of contingent events and external and internal contingencies.

Conclusion

1.   The results from our survey are part of a wider cross-national study. Our classification, SME, refers only to size and hides a wide variety of differences in business processes that are only partly addressed by the distinctions of manufacturing and service. Hence, generalisations and indeed attempts to construct explanations of firm behaviour based on simple classifications were avoided.

2.   We wanted to explore whether the strategic search for competitive advantage was affected by a firm's capability to innovate its administrative procedures for accounting and financial management. We observed that administrative innovation in accounting was both very patchy (as Smith (2000) had noted) and was particular to the owner-manager and circumstances, especially in private limited companies. However, there was a substantive relationship between accounting/financial innovation and growth. It is not clear whether the stimulus of growth provoked such innovation or whether the innovation

contributed to growth, but there is clear evidence of association. We also observed innovation via embedded approaches taken by professional service firms. It was observed here that the path from 'simple real-time' scorecards (contextualised by annual accounts and professional advice) to complex leading and lagging systems compensating in some technical ways for absent ideas was very unclear and appears not to be valued by SME managers. It was probably the case that innovations were based on some ideal economic and managerial rationality (the core idea of bureaucracy) borrowed from larger businesses. It may be that these complications missed the emerging managerial perspectives of 'real-time complex scorecards' contextualised by better ideas and missed the particularity of a given SME, observations similar to those of Perren and Grant (2000).

3. In relation to Laughlin's model of change we observed that the values and beliefs of owners about the business and its role dominates the technical work of accounting which is at the level of the design archetypes. Of itself, the design archetypes cannot change the values of the owners, but the values of the owners may lead to a rebuttal of any innovation at the level of the design archetypes. This may explain some of the perceived resistance of owner-managers to accounting innovation and openness to innovation when the legal form of the business changes and growth (and hence change) is central to their agendas.

4. However, explanations of administrative innovation in SMEs with respect to accounting and financial systems and practices have not addressed its relationship to the underlying business model. We suggest that the process of accounting innovation needs to be studied in relation to three dimensions: (a) the underlying business model in the minds of the managers; (b) the growth strategies of the firm; and (c) the routes/pathways of change.

5. Further research is needed to develop better explanations of the relationship between financial management and accounting innovations and the search for competitive advantage.

References

Anthony, R.N., Dearden, J. and Bedford, N.M. (1989) *Case Study: General Electric Company in Management Control Systems*, 6th edition. Irwin, Homewood, IL.

Berry, A.J., Ahmed, M., Cullen, J., Dunlop, A. and Seal, W.B. (2000) *The Consequences of Inter-firm Supply Chains for Management Accounting*. CIMA, London.

Bright, J., Davies, R., Downes, C. and Sweeting, R. (1992) 'The deployment of costing techniques and practices: a UK study', *Management Accounting Research*, **3**, 201–211.

Carr, C. and Ng, J. (1995) 'Total cost control: Nissan and its UK supplier partnerships', *Management Accounting Research*, **6**, 347–365.

Cooper, R. and Kaplan, R.S. (1988) 'Measure cost right: make the right decisions', *Harvard Business Review*, Sept–Oct, 96–103.

Davies, R.E. and Sweeting, R.C. (1995) 'Industrial innovation and parallel accounting developments', *Technovation*, **15**:5, 289–301.

Doi, N. and Cowling, M. (1999) 'Transaction structure in Japanese small business sector', *Small Business Economics*, **12**, 85–95.

Fisher, J., Morrow, J. and Sweeting, R.C. (1997) 'Views on the "new finance"', *Financial Focus, ICAEW*, **32**, 3.

Hayes, R.H. and Abernathy, W.J. (1981) 'Managing our way to economic decline', *McKinsey Quarterly*, Spring, 2–23.

Hippel von, E. (1977) 'Transferring process equipment innovations from user-innovators to equipment manufacturing firms', *R&D Management*, **8**:1, 3–22.

Jarvis, R., Curran, J., Kitching, J. and Lightfoot, G. (2000) 'The use of quantitative and qualitative criteria in the measurement of performance in small firms', *Journal of Small Business and Enterprise Development*, **7**:2, 123–134.

Jewkes, J., Sawers, D. and Stillerman, R. (1958) *The Sources of Innovation*. Macmillan, London.

Johnson, H.T. and Kaplan, R.S. (1987) *Relevance Lost: The Rise and Fall of Management Accounting*. Harvard University Press, Boston, MA.

Kaplan, R.S. (1984) 'Yesterday's accounting undermines production', *Harvard Business Review*, July–August, 95–101.

Kaplan, R.S. and Norton, D.P. (1992) 'The balanced scorecard – measures that drive performance', *Harvard Business Review*, Jan–Feb, 71–79.

Kato, Y. (1993) 'Target costing support systems: lessons from leading Japanese companies', *Management Accounting Research*, **4**, 33–47.

Keasey, K. and Watson, R. (1993) *Small Firm Management*. Blackwell, Oxford.

Keeble, D., Lawson, C., Moore, B. and Wilkinson, F. (1999) 'Collective learning processes, networking and "institutional thickness" in the Cambridge region', *Regional Studies*, **33**:4, 319–332.

Lamming, R. (1996) 'Squaring lean supply with supply chain management', *International Journal of Operations and Production Management*, **16**:2, 183–196.

Laughlin, R.C. (1991) 'Environmental disturbances and organisational transitions and transformations: some alternative models', *Organisation Studies*, **12**:2, 209–232.

Littler, D.A. and Sweeting, R.C. (1990) 'The management of new technology based business: the existential firm', *OMEGA*, **18**:3, 231–240.

Malmi, T. (1999) 'Activity-based costing diffusion across organisations: an exploratory empirical analysis of Finnish firms', *Accounting, Organisations and Society*, **24**, 649–762.

McDonough, E.F. (1986) 'Matching management control systems to product strategies', *R&D Management*, **16**:2, 141–149.

Miller, D. and Friesen, P.H. (1984) 'A longitudinal study of the corporate life cycle', *Management Science*, **30**:10, 1161–1183.

Mitra, R. and Pingali, V. (1999) 'Analysis of growth stages in small firms: A case study of automobile ancillaries in India', *Journal of Small Business Management*, July, 62–75.

Perren, L. and Grant, P. (2000) 'The evolution of management accounting routines in small businesses: a social construction perspective', *Management Accounting Research*, **11**:4, 391–412.

Porter, M. (1985) *Competitive Advantage*. Free Press, New York.

Reid, G.C. and Smith, J.A. (2000) 'The impact of contingencies on management accounting system development', *Management Accounting Research*, **11**:4, 427–450.

Rui, L.W. and Ibrahim, N.A. (1998) 'The relationship between planning and sophistication and performance in small business', *Journal of Small Business Management*, October, 24–32.

Smith, M. (2000) 'Innovation diffusion', *Management Accounting*, **78**:6, 40–41.

Turnbull, P., Oliver, N. and Wilkinson, B. (1992) 'Buyer–supplier relationships in the UK automotive industry: Strategic implications of the Japanese manufacturing model', *Strategic Management Journal*, **13**, 937–954.

Twiss, B. (1986) *'Managing Technological Innovations'*, 3rd edition. Pitman, London.

Van den Ven, A.H. (1986) 'Central problems in the management of innovation', *Management Sciences*, **32**:5, 590–607.

Chapter 14

RETAIL AND SERVICES MARKETING

Steve Baron[1]

Introduction

In Chapter 1, the retail sector was identified as an exception to the rising trend in the number of small firms in the 1970s. Indeed, there has been a steady decline in the number of small retailers since the 1970s. For example, numbers of non-affiliated, independent food and grocery retailers fell from 24 000 in 1996 to 22 000 in 1998 (Gordon and Walton, 2000). Similarly, there has been a decline in small service firms operating in business-to-consumer (B2C) markets, such as opticians, which fell from 2990 in 1995 to 2652 in 2001 as a result of 'tough competition from the multiples' (Retail Intelligence, 2001). Independent public houses also fell from 36 113 in 1996 to 28 352 in 2000 'indicating the tough trading environment in which independents have been competing' (Leisure Intelligence, 2001). What is common to both the retail and B2C service sectors is that the traditional small-business competitive advantage based on 'convenience' and long opening hours are being eroded by the strategies of the large (multiple outlet) organisations and by the advent of Internet-based home shopping. That is not to say that small businesses cannot create competitive advantage, but there must be more focus on organisational flexibility if independents are to survive in these sectors. To illustrate the challenges facing small retailers in the twenty-first century, the main trends in convenience retailing[2] are outlined in the following section.

UK Convenience Retailing since the 1970s

Dawson and Kirby (1979) identified the main advantages of independent retailers in the 1970s. They consisted of convenience in location and opening hours, home delivery, friendly and personal service and informal financial services (for example, Christmas clubs). Independent retailers did, however, tend to charge higher prices than the multiples, but this was believed not to be a problem as the view at the time was that there was a polarisation of the shopping landscape (Bates, 1976). Large, multiple retailers were at one end of the spectrum with small independents at the other. In the 1980s, polarisation theory was still used as an explanation for retailing trends (Brown, 1987) although it was increasingly recognised that 'convenience' was becoming an important consideration for customers in decisions where to shop (Kirby, 1987). By the late 1980s, Davies and Harris (1990) had identified 'three planks' that underpin successful independent retail businesses: product specialisation, service and location. Here, again 'convenience' plays a major role both through location and the 'open all hours' philosophy that was considered to be a key element in the service provided by small independents.

Although numbers of small retail businesses were falling during the 1970s and 1980s there was a relatively clear formula for competing with the larger organisations: convenience, friendliness and product specialisation. Convenience was regarded as the most important competitive advantage of small retailers and Kirby (1987) provided the following definition: 'a self-service store, usually between 1000 and 3000 square feet, located close to housing with some parking facilities, offering a wide range of goods including grocery and CTN (confectionery, tobacconist, newsagent) products, chemist sundries, alcohol and possibly other lines including video hire, fast foods or petrol, opening long hours including Sundays.' The 1990s heralded a change in perceptions of the shopping landscape held by both retailers and consumers. Retailers from both ends of the spectrum were gravitating towards the centre by offering 'convenience' to food and grocery shoppers. Consequently, the polarisation theory no longer offered an adequate explanation of the competitive environment. Many specialist and independent retailers, such as CTNs, bakers, grocers and off-licences, moved into convenience retailing, creating a new grocery market sector labelled 'traditional retailing/developing convenience' (Gordon and Walton, 2000, p. 19). At the same time, large multiple retailers and fuel companies recognised the convenience food sector as a major business opportunity, which led to new formats such as Tesco's Metro stores and Sainsbury's Local stores. There were also alliances between supermarket groups and fuel companies to operate petrol forecourt stores (Safeway and BP Amoco; Tesco and Esso) (*Financial Mail on Sunday*, 1999). In addition, the out-of-town superstores were affecting the trade of town and district centre independent retailers. A Verdict report in 1999 estimated that 'out-of-town superstores are likely to kill off more than 20 000 small retailers by 2001' (*Daily Mail*, 1999). An academic study of market town communities, carried out in the late 1990s, reached a similar conclusion: 'Through time it emerges that the community has not been able to sustain its trading opposition to a large format intruder' (Hallsworth and Worthington, 2000, p. 207).

By 2001, many of the large supermarket groups had outlets that were open 24 hours a day Monday to Saturday and a further six hours on Sunday. The total opening time of 150 hours a week was far above that offered by any independent retailers (109 hours per week being the maximum opening hours per week of independent retailers surveyed by Smith and Sparks, 2000). Thus, one of the main distinguishing features of convenience traditionally offered by independent retailers, longer opening hours, had been eliminated by large supermarkets. Furthermore, goods bought via Internet shopping could be purchased and delivered to consumers at times convenient to them with shop location no longer a factor. These changes cast doubt on whether convenience alone represented a source of sustainable competitive advantage for the small, independent food and grocery retailers at the start of the twenty-first century.

This brief summary of changes in food and grocery retailing since 1970 is mirrored in many respects by similar problems for other small retailers and B2C services. In particular, the challenges posed in the late 1990s by the multiples and consumer alternatives offered by the Internet are common to many small retail businesses. From a consumer perspective, small businesses no longer offer locations or opening hours that are any more 'convenient' than those offered by multiples or by the Internet. Arguably, these alternatives have become *more convenient* for consumers to purchase goods and services than the small, independent retail/service organisations. For example, clients seeking veterinary advice about their pets now have the option of obtaining advice from a website such as www.pets-pyjamas.com for 18 hours each day. The same website sells pet products and has a chat room.

Support for Retail/Service SMEs

Support for retail/service SMEs from trade associations tends to consist mainly of government lobbying to protect these businesses against rising costs. Again, using the convenience retailing sector as an example, the Association of Convenience Stores was formed in 1995:

> ... to proactively develop the whole of the professional convenience store sector, for the current and future benefit of retailers, wholesalers and suppliers, through acting as the voice of the sector with government and policy makers; campaigning on key issues to give members a voice in discussion on matters that affect them; providing benefits and services to help members develop their businesses; providing them with a forum for the exchange of ideas and relevant information (www.cstoreretailing.co.uk/about.html)

There have also been calls for government intervention to maintain a healthy independent retail sector (Pickering *et al.*, 1998; Peston and Ennew, 1998). Surveys of both retailers and consumers pointed to the *social need* for the continued existence of independent retailers (Peston and Ennew, 1998). However, as McNicholas and Turnbull (2001, p. 91) point out: 'The public is inherently sympathetic to the perceived plight of small stores and most in theory support the underdog in the retail marketplace. In practice, this sympathy is rarely translated into action.'

Thus, at the start of the twenty-first century, small retail and B2C service businesses have representatives lobbying government on their behalf and have (some) public sympathy, but their numbers are still declining and 'convenience' (their traditional competitive advantage) is being seriously challenged. Small retailers have been accused of adopting a short-term tactical outlook and have been advised to develop a more strategic approach to their businesses (McNicholas and Turnbull, 2001). The next section presents the results of a national survey of owners and/or managers of independent food and grocery shops/stores carried out in 2000. The study was designed to examine the views of owner-managers on six themes that influenced their future strategies: factors contributing to success, response to changes in the environment, relationships with consumers, reactions to technological developments, growth and succession constraints, and perceived skill levels.

Surveying Independent Food and Grocery Retailers

A postal questionnaire survey was completed by 142 owners and/or managers of independent food and grocery retailers. The details of the sampling procedure, the profile of respondents and the questions posed are to be found in Baron *et al.* (2001). The key findings demonstrate their views that:

- shops/stores are centres for social exchange;
- the majority of retailers had not adopted the latest technologies, although many that had done so were experiencing rapid growth;
- they had a tendency to operate in isolation from other traders in the same location;
- closer cooperation with suppliers was often not implemented;
- there was a general, if reluctant, admiration for store operations of multiple retailers.

More detailed evidence to illustrate each of the findings is now presented.

The shops/stores are centres for social exchange

There was an overwhelmingly strong level of agreement expressed by the respondents to the statements 'My customers like to talk to the staff' and 'My customers often talk to other customers on the premises.'

The responses confirm the social value given by independent retailers throughout the UK. Respondents consistently held the view that the provision of product advice was integral to the service offered and that their staff aimed to offer a friendly service to customers with increasing demanding expectations.

The majority of the retailers had not adopted the latest technologies

Only 15 per cent of respondents had an Internet website and 47 per cent operated an EPOS (Electronic Point of Sale) system. Furthermore, owners and/or managers who had *not* set up websites believed that it was difficult, required specialist advice and that the creation and maintenance of the site would be costly. This is in contrast to the experiences of those who *had* set up websites, although they often had difficulty in finding time for updating the site. Retailers that had created websites sometimes used them to provide information rather than simply as a mechanism for selling more products (for example, www.unicorn-grocery.co.uk). However, others had created websites to complement their existing store operations in a 'clicks and mortar' strategy (DTI, 2000). For example, Bells Stores in north-east England, a family-owned convenience store group, have embraced the development of retail technology and created an Internet site 'Bells Direct' in addition to their usual outlets.

The tendency to operate in isolation from other traders in the same location

In the UK, many small retailers are located on high streets or in shopping precincts shared by other small retailers. Although marketing by networking is acknowledged to be a 'naturally inherent aspect of SME owner-manager decision-making'

(Gilmore *et al.*, 2001, p. 7) many respondents did not admit to networking or even discussing trade with other independent retailers in the same vicinity. The opportunities for combined voices were being missed. However, there are examples of retailers in the same location working together: small businesses trading in Beech Road, Chorlton (Manchester) have created a joint, street website (www.beechroad.com). As well as promoting shops and public houses in the area, the site provides information on local history, panoramas and postcards, as well as news of forthcoming events such as the autumn food festival.

Closer cooperation with suppliers was often not implemented

The survey results did demonstrate a trend towards greater cooperation between suppliers and independent retailers. Furthermore, respondents were clearly interested in finding out more about supply chain-related issues such as category management and efficient consumer response. There was, however, less evidence that they discussed product packaging and display with suppliers and increased cooperation had not, in general, resulted in changes to the range of goods and services offered. Although there was evidence of a willingness to operate more closely with suppliers in theory, with some notable exceptions, this willingness did not extend to the implementation of new, agreed practices. It is doubtful whether many owners and/or managers saw their relationships with suppliers as a key source of competitive advantage or as a business philosophy (Hines, 2001).

There was a general, if reluctant, admiration of the store operations of the multiple retailers

There was a very high level of agreement among respondents with the statement: 'I believe that the large retailers' convenience store formats will be successful.' In addition, most respondents felt that it was important to learn from the operation of convenience stores owned by large retailers.

It was argued in Chapter 2 that many 'large firm' concepts are relevant to owner-managers who are trying to improve their firms' competitiveness. In retailing, one major issue is how methods and ideas associated with multiple retailers are made accessible to independent retailers. Byrom *et al.* (2000) provide a useful audit of the training needs, materials and systems for independent retailers, but learning delivery is still a major issue. One possibility is the provision of programmes to support workplace learning and establish a support network between small and large retailers, National Training Organisations and higher education. An example of such a programme is the 'Towards a Healthy High Street' project (Byrom *et al.*, 2001), which aims to foster learning in the high street, and encourage liaison between large and small retailers. The cost of this initiative, to the small retailers, is subsidised by the European Social Fund.

General Strategies for Small Retailers and B2C Service Companies

The above survey reflects the views of independent food and grocery retailers in 2000. Many of the themes are, in varying degrees, relevant to independent retailers in other sectors and also to B2C service organisations.

Centres for Social Exchange and Communities

Consider the following quotations from the autobiography of Richard Branson in which he discusses the opening of the *first* Virgin record shop:

> We continued to work on different ideas to make our customers as welcome as possible. We offered them headphones, sofas and beanbags to sit on, free copies of the *New Musical Express* and *Melody-Maker* to read, and free coffee to drink. We allowed them to stay as long as they liked and make themselves at home. Word of mouth began to spread, and soon people began to choose to buy records from us rather than from the big chains. It was as if they thought that the same album by Thin Lizzy or Bob Dylan somehow had greater value if bought at Virgin rather than Boots. (Branson, 1998, p. 76)

The second quotation relates to the opening of another shop, some months later.

> When we opened our Virgin Records shop in Bold Street, Liverpool in March 1972, I saw proudly that we took £10 000 in the first week. A week later, the figure was £7000 .... By the middle of the summer (takings) had dropped to £2000 .... There were rockers all jammed into one corner, mods in another, and hippies draped all over the floor near the till. All kinds of music were playing. But nobody was buying anything .... For the next month we had someone at the door who gently warned people as they went in that they were going into a shop not a nightclub .... It was a narrow line between maintaining the shop's atmosphere and keeping it profitable. The takings at last recovered. (Branson, 1998, p. 99)

The first quotation provides a clear example of the potential competitive advantage for independent retailers in *their provision of a centre for social exchange* as well as a place of trade. In this respect they have well-recognised advantages over multiple operators, which can be enhanced by a careful strategic approach. But, as the second quotation illustrates, there is a narrow line between maintaining a centre for social exchange and making a profit. Creating an environment that attracts consumers while at the same time not making it too comfortable to stay for long periods without making a purchase requires considerable social skills on the part of the staff and management.

Offering a centre for social exchange does not necessarily involve the provision of a physical environment. Waymark Holidays is a provider of cross-country skiing and walking holidays which are sold directly to customers (Baron and Harris, 1995). Staff spend a considerable amount of time talking to customers on the telephone to ensure they obtain the exact holiday they are seeking in terms of both the level of difficulty and in compatibility with other members of the group. As a consequence, over 75 per cent of bookings are from existing customers, many of whom have forged lasting friendships with group leaders and other customers from previous holidays. The Waymark website (www.waymarkholidays.co.uk) provides information about the company and its products as well as allowing customers to order their brochures.

Rather than providing training related to general retail and selling skills (which staff may already possess), these examples suggest that small retail and service businesses should improve the facilitation and improvisation skills of staff to help them create a friendly and social environment for their customers. Such a goal is in line with a wider governmental concern about the health of local communities. A recent DTI Foresight Report, quoted in Davies and Ward (2001, p. 137), states:

> Commercially viable small shops that supply the goods and services that local customers need can significantly enhance the quality of life through jobs and the provision of local produce, as well as a hub for the local community. If they are innovative and provide cafes, social credit, and web ordering facilities they can attract more people into the area and create interest in and demand for local products.

Flexibility in the Adoption of Latest Technologies

Reports on retail and service SMEs agree that their levels of success in the future may depend on their willingness and ability to adopt new technologies. Peston and Ennew (1998) argue strongly that independent retailers must improve their technology and management systems in order to satisfy customer desires. The DTI (2000), in a Foresight Report, pointed out significant benefits of e-commerce for SMEs advising that: 'Some local retailers and service providers will be able to extend their markets and offer enhanced low-cost services using new technologies' (p. 20). It is noticeable, however, that those small retail and services business which successfully incorporate new technology do so because it supports a clearly defined business 'purpose'. That is, owner-managers have a clear focus (not necessarily articulated as a strategy) that can be maintained and enhanced using new technologies. Furthermore, the technologies may extend beyond the use of the Internet or the introduction of EPOS systems. Two cases (a micro business and a small business) are now presented as examples in the adoption of new technologies.

The first case is *Blue Lagoon*, a fashion shop in the north-west of England, which was founded in 1987 by Anna Fern. The shop sells casual wear for men and women as well as more expensive designer wear for women, and has a coffee shop on the premises. Information technology systems (IT) were first introduced in 1993 to establish a basic customer record-keeping system. This was followed by a computerised stock-control system in 1997 which was updated in 2000 and incorporated:

- an Excel 'buying' calculator at point of ordering;
- automatic barcoded stock on the database;
- automatic stock replenishing on a daily basis;
- monitoring sales and profitability; and
- monthly analysis of stock movements by brand, item, colour and size.

The customer database is a key factor in business success, with 5900 customers on a typical mailing list. From this, Fern can establish when, what and how customers make purchases, segment her customer base according to how much they spend, and send personal invitations by e-mail to organised events at the shop. She has no interest in mail order sales as she believes that this takes away the personal and social element that she values highly. Consequently, the website (www.BlueLagoon.co.uk) was done to stimulate interest, brand the business, promote events and collect customer e-mail addresses rather than develop online sales. The website was created in-house but was professionally designed and maintained, which allows new information to be added on a monthly basis.

The second case concerns *Outside*, a climbing and outdoor leisure retailer founded in 1987 by Richard Turnbull who emphasises that climbing is what he and his staff enjoy. Turnbull has four *Outside* outlets, two in the Derbyshire Peak District, one in Snowdonia and one in Sheffield. Their customers vary in age and ability from dog walkers to Himalayan mountaineers. A typical store has a rock hardware counter at the back which displays serious climbing gear, but also doubles as a meeting place for climbers. This provides an environment in which staff and customers can engage in discussions and knowledge-sharing about climbing. The *Outside* website (www.outside.co.uk) was set up to extend the existing mail order facility and bring in new customers. Turnbull found that many online customers regularly visit a store but used the Internet to make additional purchases. Hence, the website, which has low overheads and high profit margins, is a valuable but peripheral service which provides back-up to the retail stores.

The two cases are typical of the more successful attempts by micro or small retail/service businesses to incorporate new technologies. Technology is harnessed *to support their existing purpose* (strategy) in as many ways as possible by building up their relationships with customers and helping to increase their potential market. As the Virgin and Bells Stores examples illustrate, the retail and B2C service sector is characterised by the speed by which successful micro/small businesses can become medium-sized or even multiple enterprises. For example, Pet Doctors Ltd, a seven-clinic veterinary group, was incorporated in 1998. One of the partners, Garret Turley, relinquished his clinical duties in 1999 to concentrate on expansion and the aim is expand to about 40 clinics. Turley is fully aware of the competitive environment:

> I qualified nine years ago and I know that the huge change I have seen in that nine years will pale into insignificance with the introduction of more communications and technology, with increased client awareness and expectation of quality service, with clients mentally attuned to what they will and will not accept, and of course with the changing force that is money. (Turley, 2000, p. 5)

Nevertheless, the partners are investing cautiously in their website (www.pet-doctors.co.uk/practices.php). It was set up to complement their regional clinics in the south-east of England and yet in the first year of operation only 32 per cent of 'hits' were from the UK. Pet Doctors see the real value of a website as a means by which existing clients can book appointments, get details on the post-operative conditions of their pets and to obtain (paid-for) advice. Further expansion of their web-based activities is dependent on a clear conception of how it will contribute to future business success.

Horizontal and Vertical Networks

Gilmore *et al.* (2001) conducted in-depth interviews with a total of 45 SME owner-managers (in several sectors) in the UK and Australia, and concluded that 'there is considerably more communication between the SME owner/manager and his/her competitors than is widely reported in the literature' (p. 8).

In practice, such horizontal alliances between SMEs were often facilitated through Trade Associations which created opportunities for social encounters between owners and managers. Opportunities for such horizontal alliances are even greater in the retail and B2C service sector because they are often physically located close to each other (on a high street or precinct) and are often in contact on a daily basis. The real competitors, confirmed by the survey results above, are the multiples. Yet the survey also suggested that initiatives such as that in Beech Road are the exception rather than the rule. There are clear potential benefits for small retailers to engage in horizontal alliances with traders in the same location (Pickering *et al.*, 1998).

Other *online* communities (Rowley, 2001) offer further opportunities for horizontal integration. For example, over 40 craft shops and workshops in the Yorkshire Dales are represented on the website www.dalesmade.co.uk where details of their products and locations are included in a 'guide' around the Dales. Websites supporting 'communities of interest' are often helpful in publicising small retail and service businesses. Ethical Junction administer a website (www.ethical-junction.org) that is dedicated to helping consumers make ethical choices regarding a wide range of potential purchases in construction, catering, finance, transport and travel as well as retailing. Several pages of the site are devoted to an ethical shopping centre with opportunities for SMEs offering fair-trade goods to create awareness among those interested in ethical purchases.

Vertical alliances with suppliers (see Chapter 12) also have great potential for improving competitiveness. Jackson Family Food Stores in East Yorkshire, for example, have worked with Cadbury Trebor Bassett on controlled experiments designed to establish the effects of different ways of merchandising confectionery, with the retailer devoting resources to learning and innovating. In the future, the role of retail/service stores acting as a 'hub' (Davies and Ward, 2001), supporting online and in-store purchasing, may redefine the supply chain. According to a Foresight Report:

> The use of community services such as the milk round, mobile libraries, etc., could reach those social groups potentially otherwise excluded with varying points of delivery, e.g. local shop, post office or community centre. Evening, weekend and other 'out of hours' delivery may become commonplace, accompanied by built-in 'smartness' such as alert functions which inform both supplier and purchaser (DTI, 2000, p. 19)

Learning from Multiples

The survey of independent food and grocery retailers confirmed that they could learn from large multiples. This is primarily because owner-managers are acutely aware of the investments that multiples have made in improving their operations and levels of service. In addition, retail SMEs know of the existence of systems employed by multiple retailers such as category management and efficient consumer response, but only have a vague knowledge of what they actually do. The mechanisms for passing good practice from large to small retailers are difficult even though there is often a publicly expressed willingness by large retailers to share knowledge (although not necessarily to SMEs in the same retail sector). Some initiatives to aid this process have been established by National Training

Organisations (NTOs). For example, in 2000, the Bakery NTO engaged the help of retired senior managers of large retail organisations to work with small bakers on adapting their methods of merchandising to respond more effectively to increases in consumer demands for ready-made sandwiches and other meals and snacks. This concept of experienced individuals from large stores acting as mentors for SMEs has been adopted in a European Social Funded (ESF) project facilitated by Manchester Metropolitan University (Byrom *et al.*, 2001). In this project:

> The establishment of an online mentoring brokerage system will also, it is hoped, aid independent retailers in the growth of their businesses, providing such a system avoids the pitfalls outlined by O'Dwyer and Ryan (2000), who note that the risk of a breach of confidentiality, and the danger of being drawn into using systems that work for a larger business but not necessarily a smaller one, may negate against the successful deployment of a mentoring scheme. (Byrom *et al.*, 2001, p. 64)

These examples confirm the potential for SMEs in their use of Higher Education Institutions, ESF and NTOs as part of their external networks (see Figure 2.2 in Chapter 2).

Marketing Implications

The marketing concept has been defined as 'the achievement of corporate goals through meeting and exceeding customer needs better than the competition' (Jobber, 2001, p. 3). In many areas of the service sector, including retailing, it has been argued that SME's main competitors are the multiples. So to be competitive in this sector, SMEs need to improve their levels of customer service to at least the same level as the multiples. With regard to operational efficiency, including individual transactions with customers, multiples are likely to be ahead of smaller firms by virtue of the investments they can and do make in these areas. Many of the general strategies and courses of action suggested earlier for small retailers and B2C service companies lie within the province of *relationship marketing*, rather than transactional marketing.

Relationship marketing (in the form of *market-based relationship marketing*) draws attention to the importance of *retaining* as well as attracting customers with emphasis on the development of long-term relationships with existing customers. *Network-based relationship marketing* focuses on enhancing relationships with the internal market (employees) and with external markets including suppliers, recruitment markets, referral markets and influence markets (Christopher *et al.*, 1991). It has been argued that 'personal relationships, interactions and social exchange are the most important core elements of relationship marketing' (Zineldin, 2000). As small businesses flourish on personal contacts and networking, it is important to recognise that this fits the relationship marketing framework rather than transactional marketing which concentrates on the attraction of new customers through offensive strategies using promotions or price reductions (Fornell and Wernerfelt, 1987).

To what extent can ideas emanating from relationship marketing help small businesses in the B2C markets? In Chapter 2, the importance to small firms of their business networks was emphasised and, in many ways, relationship

TABLE 14.1   Market-based relationship marketing: advantages and disadvantages

	Advantages	Disadvantages
Customer	• Can contribute to sense of well-being, stability and quality of life	• Can be irritating
	• Can be part of a social support system	• Can be intrusive
	• Can make it unnecessary to incur high switching costs	
Organisation	• Can result in customers spending more	• Can stifle innovation and employee creativity
	• Can result in lower marketing costs	• Can raise customer expectations
	• Can result in free, positive word-of-mouth advertising	
	• Can increase *employee* retention	

marketing simply reiterates this view. Relationship marketing means taking a customer- and network-focused approach to facilitate an increase in customer loyalty and retention. There are both advantages and disadvantages, for customer and company, in applying market-based relationship marketing ideas, and these are summarised in Table 14.1.

Arguably, since SMEs in the service sector are closer to their customers they should be able to capitalise on potential advantages and avoid disadvantages better than the multiples. By providing a personal service for 'regular' customers, small service organisations such as retailers, hairdressers, restaurants and pubs can establish a strong relationship and a sense of loyalty which is difficult to replicate in larger firms. Customers do switch services, but not always without some cost or anxiety. Not every customer wants a 'relationship' with every service provider, especially the unseen and unknown representatives of large organisations such as banks, travel companies or credit card firms. In such cases, attempts by large organisations to build relationships can be irritating and even intrusive, especially where they are perceived to be exploiting customer databases to promote unwanted services. Because of the more personal relationships between provider and customer in smaller service companies, such alienation of customers should be less likely. Therefore, by adopting market-based and network-based relationship marketing strategies (which many successful ones do, without necessarily recognising it) SMEs can reap a number of organisational advantages:

- greater customer spend (customers tend to spend more each year they trade with an organisation);
- lower marketing costs (attracting new customers is more costly than retaining existing customers);
- positive word of mouth (services, being intangible, rely on word of mouth to reassure potential customers);
- higher levels of employee retention (employees tend to feel happier in long-term relationships with customers).

Long-term relationships with customers do have some disadvantages, and those listed in Table 14.1 may be more likely in SMEs than in multiples. First, employees that have regular, and similar, service encounters with loyal customers may feel frustrated at the lack of variety in their work and the lack of opportunity to display different talents. Second, because loyal customers are given 'special' treatment by the service firm or its employees, this may raise their expectations to a level beyond which it is possible to satisfy. This creates the potential for negative word of mouth, which is particularly damaging for small businesses. Overall, the application of relationship marketing by SMEs in the B2C sector seems both sensible and achievable. Competitive advantage can be improved by providing centres of social exchange, and by a willingness to be flexible and to learn from customers and network partners. Flexibility is particularly important for SMEs if they are to avoid turning the advantages of relationship marketing into disadvantages.

Conclusion

Numbers of independent businesses in the retail and B2C service sectors have been steadily declining since the 1970s, despite increases in government initiatives to support small firms during the period (see Chapter 1). SMEs in these sectors are clearly in competition with each other, but the principal reason for their decline is competition from large multiple retailers. Not only are multiples changing the retail geography of many cities, towns and villages in the UK with increasing numbers of superstores, they are also moving into the 'convenience' sector with small store formats such as Tesco's Metro stores. The impact of new technologies, especially increased consumer access to the Internet, has also influenced consumer behaviour in these sectors. Most Internet-based businesses (dot-coms) have had limited success. The evidence so far points to retail/service businesses of all sizes preferring to adopt a 'clicks and mortar' strategy using websites to support their shop. However, in some areas of retailing such as book-selling, music and travel, dot-coms such as Amazon have changed the nature of competition with some SMEs under threat from disintermediation (Ellis-Chadwick, 2001).

Competitive advantage through convenience, which served the retail and B2C SMEs in the last three decades of the twentieth century, seems unlikely to be sustainable. The survey, reported in this chapter, adds weight to the argument that independent operators do have a major advantage over multiple operators in their ability and capability to provide *a locus for social and informational exchange* (McGrath and Otnes, 1995) using their affinity with customers as a key strength (Leisure Intelligence, 2001). Sometimes, this potential competitive advantage is taken for granted by both providers and customers. Also, while customers claim they want to see a healthy independent sector, largely because of these perceived benefits, their actual purchasing behaviour often does not match their intentions. Therefore, SMEs need to be proactive in developing strategies that support their role in providing centres for social exchange and community.

Figures 2.2 and 2.3 are particularly helpful in illustrating the need for organisational flexibility and change management. Successful retail and B2C service SMEs, such as those cited in this chapter, have demonstrated their ability to adopt new technologies in support of a clearly focused business 'purpose' (where there is an explicit aim to foster social interactions with customers). In many respects, these SMEs have adopted relationship marketing strategies, although they may not be articulated as such. There is focus on external networks to constantly improve vertical and horizontal alliances. In general, such firms are aware that they lack the operational expertise of large multiples but are capable of making incremental innovations based on ideas from these competitors, as well as from their customers. Unfortunately, less successful SMEs tend to passively absorb successive blows dealt by large multiples and changes in customer expectations with no obvious attempt to manage the change process or to consider more active ways of responding to the challenges. Despite lobbying behaviour on their part, these firms find it more and more difficult to remain profitable.

References

Baron, S. and Harris, K. (1995) *Services Marketing: Text and Cases*. Macmillan, Basingstoke.

Baron, S., Harris, K., Leaver, D. and Oldfield, B.M. (2001), 'Beyond convenience: the future for independent food and grocery retailers in the UK', *International Review of Retail, Distribution and Consumer Research*, **11**:4, 383–402.

Bates, P. (1976) *The Independent Grocery Retailer*. Manchester Business School, Manchester.

Branson, R. (1998) *Losing my Virginity*. Virgin Publishing, London.

Brown, S. (1987) 'An integrated approach to retail change: the multi-polarization model', *The Service Industries Journal*, **7**:2, 153–164.

Byrom, J.W., Harris, J. and Parker, C. (2000) 'Training the independent retailer: an audit of training needs, materials and systems', *Journal of European Industrial Training*, **24**:7, 366–373.

Byrom, J., Parker, C. and Harris, J. (2001) 'Towards a healthy High Street: identifying skills needs in small independent retailers', *Proceedings of the 2001 Annual Manchester Conference for Contemporary Issues in Retail Marketing*, Manchester Metropolitan University, 7 September, 50–67.

Christopher, M., Payne, A. and Ballantyne, D. (1991) *Relationship Marketing*. Butterworth Heinemann, Oxford,

Daily Mail (1999) 'Toys and shoeshops next in High Street wipeout', 10 March.

Davies, G. and Harris, K. (1990) *Small Business: The Independent Retailer*. Macmillan Education, Basingstoke.

Davies, B. and Ward, P. (2001) 'Wiring the hub: small stores and the Internet', *Proceedings of the 2001 Annual Manchester Conference for Contemporary Issues in Retail Marketing*, Manchester Metropolitan University, 7 September, 131–149.

Dawson, J.A. and Kirby, D.A. (1979) *Small Scale Retailing in the UK*. Saxon House, Farnborough.

DTI (2000), 'Clicks and mortar: the new store formats'. Foresight Report, Crown Copyright, February.

Ellis-Chadwick, F. (2001) 'From High Street multiple to High Street multiple.co.uk: an analysis of retailer uptake of the Internet in the UK', *Proceedings of the 2001 Annual Manchester Conference for Contemporary Issues in Retail Marketing*, Manchester Metropolitan University, 7 September, 2–16.

Financial Mail on Sunday (1999) 'Store giants think small', 25 July.

Fornell, C. and Wernerfelt, B. (1987) 'Defensive marketing strategy by customer complaint management: a theoretical analysis', *Journal of Marketing Research*, **24**:4, 337–346.

Gilmore, A., Carson, D. and Grant, K. (2001) 'SME marketing in practice', *Marketing Intelligence and Planning*, **19**:1, 6–11.

Gordon, D. and Walton, J. (2000), *Convenience Tracking Programme: Market Review 1999*. IGD Business Publication, Letchmore Heath.

Hallsworth, A.G. and Worthington, S. (2000) 'Local resistance to larger retailers: the example of market towns and the food superstore in the UK', *International Journal of Retail and Distribution Management*, **28**:4/5, 207–216.

Hines, T. (2001) 'Developing digital supply chains to satisfy customer demand – it's time to remove the weakest link – Goodbye!', *Proceedings of the 2001 Annual Manchester Conference for Contemporary Issues in Retail Marketing*, Manchester Metropolitan University, 7 September, 18–48.

Jobber, D. (2001) *Principles and Practice of Marketing*, 3rd edition. McGraw-Hill, Maidenhead.

Kirby, D. (1987) 'Convenience stores', in E. McFadyen (ed) *The Changing Face of British Retailing*. Newman, London, pp. 94–102.

Leisure Intelligence (2001) *Independent Pubs and Bars*. Mintel Publications, June.

McGrath, M.A. and Otnes, C. (1995) 'Unacquainted influencers: when strangers interact in the retail setting', *Journal of Business Research*, **32**, 261–272.

McNicholas, C. and Turnbull, A. (2001) 'Retail SMEs and e-tailing: expectations and aspirations', *Proceedings of the 2001 Annual Manchester Conference for Contemporary Issues in Retail Marketing*, Manchester Metropolitan University, 7 September, 69–94.

O'Dwyer, M. and Ryan, E. (2000) 'Management development issues for owner/managers of micro enterprises' *Journal of European Industrial Training*, **24**:6, 345–353.

Peston, L. and Ennew, C.T. (1998) *Neighbourhood Shopping in the Millennium.* University of Nottingham Business School Discussion Paper, XII, October.

Pickering, J.F., Greene, F.J. and Cockerill, T.A.J. (1998) *The Future of the Neighbourhood Store.* Durham University Business School Publications, September.

Retail Intelligence (2001) *Opticians.* Mintel Publications, June.

Rowley, J. (2001) 'Online communities: stabilising e-business', *Proceedings of the 2001 Annual Manchester Conference for Contemporary Issues in Retail Marketing*, Manchester Metropolitan University, 7 September, 114–129.

Smith, A. and Sparks, L. (2000) 'The role and function of the independent small shop: the situation in Scotland', *International Review of Retail, Distribution and Consumer Research*, **10**:2, 205–226.

Turley, G. (2000) 'Are you putting marketing theory into practice?', *The Veterinary Business Journal*, **37**, June, 5–13.

Zineldin, M. (2000) 'Beyond relationship marketing: technologicalship marketing', *Marketing Intelligence and Planning*, **18**:2, 9–23.

Notes

1. The author acknowledges the contributions of Kim Cassidy, David Leaver and Brenda Oldfield in the collection and interpretation of the survey data referred to in this chapter.
2. The Institute of Grocery Distribution (IGD) divides the UK grocery market into four main sectors: 'convenience retailing', 'traditional retailing/developing convenience', 'supermarkets and superstores' and 'alternative channels'. Independent retailers competing in the 'convenience retailing' sector consist of non-affiliated and symbol group members from the first IGD sector, and specialists such as CTNs, grocers, off-licences, greengrocers, butchers, fishmongers and bakers from the second IGD sector.

Chapter 15

CONCLUSION

Oswald Jones and Fiona Tilley

Introduction

As discussed in the Preface, this book was undertaken in response to the broad range of SME-related activities undertaken by MMUBS staff. A considerable amount of European structural funding (ESF and ERDF) has been obtained to help smaller firms improve the way in which they are managed. Projects include a number concerned with supply chain management (Chapter 12), 'Towards a Healthy High Street' (Chapter 14) and a recent ERDF-funded project to help improve the competitiveness of SMEs in the north-west of England. This engagement with the small-firm community provides MMUBS staff with clear insight into problems associated with managing such firms. Throughout the book, our aim has been to draw on this experience to help provide a better understanding of why competitive advantage is important to SMEs as well as improving understanding of mechanisms by which owner-managers can improve the performance of their firms. While acknowledging that SMEs are not 'little big firms' (Dandridge, 1979; Welsh and White, 1981) we do suggest that many large-firm concepts such as HRM, strategic management and supply chain management are directly relevant to owner-managers trying to improve the performance of their firms. MMUBS's long experience in dealing with the small-firm community has led to the recent creation of a Centre for Enterprise (CfE). Two major projects are currently being undertaken within the CfE:

- The New Entrepreneur Scholarship Scheme (NES), which is a Treasury initiative that seeks to address the issue of social exclusion by providing assistance to those from disadvantaged backgrounds wishing to start their own businesses (Jones and Boles, 2002).
- Substantial ERDF funding has recently been obtained to help improve competitiveness among SMEs in the north-west of England.

In addition, there are a number of doctoral researchers associated with the Centre and topics under investigation include learning networks in SMEs; internationalisation and small firms; creativity and innovation in start-up businesses; and drug development in biotechnology-based firms. In recent years, the Business School has established a wide range of contacts with SMEs including student placements, research projects (ESF/DfEE/S), consultancy and management training. The Centre for Enterprise will build on these contacts by providing a mechanism for regular interaction between Business School staff and the small-firm community. Existing research staff have wide-ranging experience and skills associated with SMEs including:

- government/regional policies related to entrepreneurship and SMEs;
- sustainable management in SMEs;
- risk management;
- performance management;
- quality management;
- innovation (new products and processes) management.

Therefore, this book is intended to provide an overview of work carried out in MMUBS which directly relates to improving competitiveness in SMEs. At the same time, we as editors recognise that this is an extremely dynamic area and we also try to use this experience to suggest areas for future research.

Towards a Strategic Approach

In Chapter 1, Tilley and Tonge review a number of issues related to the role of SMEs in the UK economy. Smaller firms certainly became increasingly visible during the Thatcher era with talk of the need to create an 'enterprise culture'. Greater focus on individualism was consistent with the New Right's argument that the corporatism associated with the 1960s and 1970s was responsible for economic decline in the UK. Entrepreneurship and associated business start-ups had potential advantages in terms of decreasing the high levels of unemployment which resulted from monetary economic policies pursued by the first Thatcher government (Hutton, 1995). As a consequence, the many government small-firm policy initiatives introduced during the 1980s were designed to encourage higher levels of employment (Scase, 2000). New Labour has, for the most part, adopted a very similar rhetoric to the preceding Tory administrations in terms of the need to create an enterprise culture in the UK. At the same time, the focus of attention has shifted from small firms as a mechanism to create new jobs to the need to improve the productivity of SMEs. In recent years, Gordon Brown has announced a number of initiatives designed to improve small-firm performance including R&D tax credits (to stimulate innovation) and stock options to encourage the movement of experienced managers from large to small firms (*Financial Times*, 2000). However, the central argument made by Tilley and Tonge is that researchers still do not fully understand why some firms grow successfully and others do not.

Much of the literature associated with small firms and entrepreneurship is focused on the psychological attributes of owner-managers (McClelland, 1961;

Kickul and Gundry, 2002). In this book we have, for the most part, concentrated on the organisation rather than the individual as the unit of analysis. While not wishing to disregard the importance of 'the entrepreneur' to the performance of SMEs we, as editors, have encouraged contributors to apply concepts which are more usually associated with larger organisations. This emphasis is strongly apparent in Section 1 of this book (on general management issues) in which the authors examine the following topics: competitive advantage, strategic management, corporate governance and sustainability. The term competitive advantage is mostly closely associated with the work of Michael Porter (1980, 1985, 1990). Considering competitive advantage in terms of SMEs, it is important to note that owner-managers may have a range of objectives rather than a narrow focus on 'profit maximisation' (see Jennings and Beaver, 1997). Our view is that competitive advantage related to SMEs should incorporate the consideration of objective factors such as ROI (return on investment), ROA (return on assets), market share, revenue and profits as well as subjective factors such as improved reputation with customers and suppliers, better service quality and stronger competitive position. A recent contribution by Man and Chan (2002) illustrates the complexity of competitive advantage even in a small-firm context. The authors develop a sophisticated model (see Chapter 2) which incorporates competitive scope (external), entrepreneurial competences (including recognition of market opportunities) and organisational capabilities (internal). Similar complexity is evident in the work of Cobbenhagen (2000) who distinguishes between market, technological and organisational competences.

There is certainly a range of macro factors, including access to finance and low levels of education and training, which can inhibit the search for competitive advantage in SMEs. Equally, there are numerous internal factors which also limit the productivity of smaller firms (and large firms) such as an unwillingness to seek external assistance, limited investment in capital equipment (particularly ICTs), training and R&D. Beginning the process of improving competitive advantage in SMEs means that owner-managers (or management teams) should initiate a broad strategic review of the firm's internal capabilities and its relative strengths and weaknesses in the marketplace. Marsden and Forbes (Chapter 3) point out that the small-firm research community tend to be suspicious of 'top down' approaches to management (Jennings and Beaver, 1997; Smallbone and Wyer, 1998). The basic argument is that because small firms are very different than large firms, managers have to respond in different ways. For example, SMEs are much less able to influence their environment than are large firms, who exert considerable political 'clout' at both regional and national levels. Nevertheless, Porter's generic strategies are an appropriate template for small firms and there may be advantages in pursuing a differentiation strategy (quality) rather than attempting a cost-based approach which will usually favour economies of scale associated with larger firms. We certainly agree that smaller firms are constrained in terms of their managerial resources in comparison to larger firms. But, as Marsden and Forbes argue, it is important not to assume that all small firms are homogeneous. Significantly, Hannon and Atherton (1998) suggest that, within SMEs, it is the planning process which is important rather than the degree of formality. This mirrors the approach of some mainstream strategy writers (Mintzberg, 1978, 1990) who are critical of the 'classical' approach (Ansoff, 1965) and suggest that the most effective approach is 'logical incrementalism'. One of the key strategic decisions for owner-managers is whether to expand the business and the 'stages of growth' has received a considerable amount of academic attention (Greiner, 1972; Churchill and Lewis, 1983). Smallbone and Wyer (1998) posit that growth depends on a range of factors including entrepreneurial resources, firm capabilities and strategy (market position for example). According to Marsden and Forbes, Gibb and Scott's (1985) model has the strongest links to large-firm strategy-making. The emergence of resource-based strategy is certainly an appropriate tool for smaller firms, particularly given its genesis in Penrose's analysis of firm growth. The methods associated with RBT (resource-based theory) are particularly relevant when consideration is given to improving broader competitive advantage rather than simply focusing on growth. Links between RBT and Porter's approach are discussed below.

Corporate governance deals with an issue that is of fundamental importance to the strategy of SMEs. One major decision facing owner-managers, as Warren points out, is whether or not to adopt limited liability. Pros include limits to shareholder risk, ease of attracting external funds and the opportunity for entrepreneurs to realise wealth otherwise tied up in the firm. More negatively, limited liability potentially creates a 'moral hazard' by transferring risk of failure from owners to creditors (see Freedman, 2000). Traditional forms of ownership such as sole trader, partnerships and unlimited liability may be more appropriate for the vast majority of start-up firms, particularly where there is no commitment to rapid growth. Once again, Porter's influence is recognised, as Warren recommends that the 'firm infrastructure' (board of directors for example) should be included in any value chain analyses. SMEs, certainly in the early stages, are unlikely to feature the separation of ownership and control identified by Berle and Means (1932). As Warren argues, the transition from owner control to corporate governance is likely to present any small firm with a 'formidable challenge'. Equally, there may be substantial benefits by introducing non-executive directors who can bring in expertise which is important in providing a stronger strategic focus. In summary, Warren is optimistic that a realistic approach to corporate governance in SMEs can directly improve competitive advantage because of increased emphasis on a professional approach to managerial decision-making. Although, it has to be recognised that at present there is very little research evidence to indicate that corporate governance issues are taken seriously in anything but the minority of SMEs.

Sustainability, the third broad strategic issue which we consider, is concerned with links between environmentally sensitive business practices and competitive advantage. Tilley *et al.* argue in Chapter 5 that the sustainability agenda has shifted from a focus on environmental protectionism and social equity to a recognition that economic prosperity must also be considered. Corporate environmentalism is strongly associated with Al Gore, at least in the early stages of the first Clinton administration, and Michael Porter (Porter and van der Linde, 1995). Perhaps surprisingly, Porter has been a strong advocate of the need for high regulatory standards in developed countries. In fact, Porter identifies direct links between sustainability and competitive advantage in terms of greater efficiency in the use of materials, better quality products, reduced exposure to risk, lower insurance premiums and better corporate reputation. This win-win approach discussed by Tilley *et al.* is represented by the concept of eco-efficiency which simply means doing more with less. As is the case with corporate governance, SMEs lag behind larger firms in recognising the benefits of sustainable business practices. The government acknowledges the need for a more positive approach to sustainability among SMEs. Tilley *et al.* evaluate the failure of initiatives and interventions designed to promote sustainability. The authors argue that there is a need for greater emphasis on training and education for those employed in SMEs if there is to be more widespread 'environmental literacy'. Better understanding of sustainability within SMEs would not only help improve competitive advantage by reducing costs and improving the quality of products and services; it would also have a positive impact on the environment in which we all live.

Other topics, including innovation and HRM, also have strategic links with the creation of competitive advantage in SMEs. Our argument is that the factors discussed in the preceding sections are genuinely strategic in the sense that the attitude of owner-managers (or management teams) to these issues will set the agenda for all other activities within the firm. In Section 2, 'Managing People', attention is turned to focus on people-related issues within SMEs, such as on HRM, performance-related pay, creativity, innovation and networking.

Managing People for Productivity

HRM emerged as a important academic discipline in the early 1980s as the USA responded to Japanese economic success (Tichy *et al.*, 1982; Fombrun *et al.*, 1984; Beer *et al.*, 1984). The two factors which distinguish HRM from personnel management are greater emphasis on the individual and a more strategic approach to people issues. While the practice of HRM began as a large-firm phenomenon, Taylor *et al.* (Chapter 6) point out that a number of US studies carried out in the 1990s claim to have identified HRM in SMEs (the US definition includes firms with up to 499 employees). However, the authors are critical of these studies, because most were based on self-report data from managers and their claims to be practising HRM were not independently verified. An IPD (Institute of Personnel Directors) study carried out in the UK found that although managers in SMEs claimed to be aware of 'best practice', few had actually implemented coherent HRM policies in their own firms. None of this will surprise students of the small-firm sector because the Bolton Report (1971) identified a fundamental paradox more than thirty years ago. Conditions of employment (pay, holiday entitlement and employment rights) in SMEs were generally worse than in large firms but employees were more satisfied. This was partly explained by the friendlier 'family atmosphere' which prevailed in many smaller firms. However, there has since been a substantial amount of research which paints a more negative picture of most employees' experience of SMEs (Curran and Stanworth, 1979; Moule, 1998; Rainie, 1989; Scase, 1995; Jones, 2003). Taylor *et al.* suggest that this may be explained by changes in employment legislation over the last thirty years that have increased the formality of employee–employer relations; although this tends not to apply to small firms in which informal approaches to personnel issues are still dominant. A lack of commitment to HRM does have direct implications for competitiveness, because it means that basic activities such as recruitment, selection, training, development and succession planning are done in an ad hoc manner. Hence, few SMEs are equipped to generate the levels of employee commitment and motivation which are central to high levels of organisational performance.

Employee motivation, a topic central to HRM and personnel management, is discussed in relationship to share ownership schemes. Government attempts to improve UK productivity have led to increasing interest in the use of share-based reward schemes. Pendleton (Chapter 7) points out that it is difficult to estimate exactly how many SMEs operate such schemes, but it certainly seems to be less than 5 per cent, compared to 24 per cent of large firms which use share option schemes (WERS98, 2000). Take-up is low because employee share ownership is seen as less relevant to smaller firms and because regulatory barriers discourage participation. Five schemes are identified by Pendleton, of which the share option plan is the most widely used. The advantages are that employees are exempt from income tax on share acquisitions although they may eventually be subject to capital gains tax. Share option schemes are attractive to politicians because of the perception that employees with a financial stake in their employer's business will be more highly motivated and hence contribute to improvements in productivity. It seems reasonable to hypothesise that such schemes should be more effective in smaller firms where there are more direct links between individual effort and firm performance. A counter argument is that the day-to-day involvement of owner-managers is a more direct form of motivation for employees. Pendleton identifies three main barriers to the adoption of share option schemes in SMEs: financial and ownership structures (corporate governance), approaches to people management (HRM), and the implications for management control. The latter issue is particularly important given that owner-managers usually have strong proprietorial interests which mean they are reluctant to cede any element of control to other actors. Share option schemes are most strongly associated with the rise of the dot-com phenomenon, in which they were often used as a pay substitute when a firm's financial value was rising rapidly. Such schemes remain extremely valuable in knowledge-based small firms (such as biotechnology and software) because they help 'lock in' those employees vital to future growth. Perhaps the most practical way in which share option schemes can contribute to competitive advantage in SMEs is by attracting experienced managers through the potential for major capital gains. The deferred nature of benefits from share option schemes means that newly recruited managers must remain committed to a firm for some years if they are to realise the full extent of their financial rewards. At the same time, they have a strong motivation to ensure that the firm is successful, which will increase the financial value of their share options.

Creativity is linked to resource-based theory (RBT) by Banks et al. (Chapter 8) because it provides opportunities to exploit an organisation's unique attributes in the search for competitive advantage. Although much of the creativity literature focuses on individual psychological attributes, the authors concentrate on examining the role of management in developing an environment which encourages creativity at a broader organisational level. Furthermore, Banks et al. argue that the shift towards a knowledge-based economy makes creativity an increasingly important factor in organisations of all sizes. Links between creativity and competitive advantage are investigated by studying SMEs in creative industries. Two

ESF projects provide detailed qualitative material on a number of small, creative firms which the authors use to identify three different managerial approaches to the management of creativity:

- organised looseness – in which managers attempted to ensure that individual employees had high levels of autonomy and freedom;
- organising and controlling – a top-down approach in which the creativity of employees was seen as something which could be closely managed;
- 'laying it on the line' – a traditional authoritarian management style in which employees were expected to fulfil client requirements within narrowly defined criteria.

As the authors conclude, somewhat surprisingly, even creative firms in which it might be anticipated employees would be given high levels of freedom managers emphasised short-term, task-based solutions. However, there was a negative correlation between creativity and firm size as younger, smaller firms were more likely to encourage creativity. Banks *et al.* go on to suggest that if creativity is to be harnessed as a source of competitive advantage in SMEs, managers need to recognise that it is not amenable to a top-down approach.

A key debate in the literature is whether large or small firms provide the best environment for innovation. Large firms have advantages in terms of formal management skills, specialised (technical) labour, R&D, economies of scale and the ability to protect innovation by patenting. Smaller firms have advantages because they are less bureaucratic, decision-making is more rapid, they are closer to the customer and can therefore respond more effectively to market signals (Vossen, 1998; Tether, 1999). In recent years, there has been much emphasis on innovation as a process rather than as a single 'one-off' event (Atherton and Hannon, 2000). RBT has also been influential in studies of innovation in SMEs (Cobbenhagen, 2000) and this literature stresses the importance of mobilising the firm's unique resources. Despite the importance of innovation management in SMEs there is, as Carrier (1996) notes, surprisingly little focus on the role of change agents, corporate entrepreneurs or intrapreneurs. Jones (Chapter 9) uses Kanter's (1983) work on organisational change as a framework for the analysis of two firms. RSL (with 70 employees) and MFD (with 240 employees) are both traditional manufacturing companies operating in declining sectors. Management teams in both companies adopted a strategic response to innovation management as a result of what Kanter describes as 'galvanising events'. The capabilities required to manage innovation effectively need to be acquired through experiential learning and experimentation (Stopford and Baden-Fuller, 1994). The terms used in Chapter 9 to describe this process are 'departing from tradition' (Kanter, 1983) or 'changing the routine' (Jones and Craven, 2001) which indicate that innovation should be introduced gradually beginning with small-scale, incremental change. As capabilities are expanded throughout the firm (management and employees), then more radical innovation will become feasible. In both companies, the owners were responsible for initiating change at a strategic level, but other actors were responsible for managing the day-to-day tasks and consequently operated as change agents. There are a number of important points which can be drawn from the cases:

- The status of the change agent is less important than full support of owner (management team).
- The mobilisation of symbolic and substantive resources is crucial to successful change programmes.
- Structural and relational elements are central to the creation of an organisational culture that supports innovation and intrapreneurship.
- Networking (both internal and external) is crucial in firms attempting to make the transition from maturity to entrepreneurship.

Networking is also the focus of Chapter 10 in which Taylor and Pandza utilise a detailed case study to investigate the process of entrepreneurial learning. The authors draw on current theories of learning which emphasise the importance of social relations. Networks, as defined by Taylor and Pandza, are indeterminate and may be unique to a single event which encourages a research approach centred around 'critical incidents' that stimulate a problem-centred approach to learning. The study concentrates on the activities of Robert Teece, owner-manager of Everest Joinery, and his utilisation of knowledge networks to improve decision-making. The critical incident concerned his decision not to sell out to a large building firm because he wanted to retain his independence and autonomy. A network of actors who provided Teece with a range of information and expertise was gradually revealed during the research. This network, including solicitor, accountant, architect and supplier, is mapped onto a template developed by Steward and Conway (1998) but extended to incorporate a 'professional periphery'. The importance of networks has long been established in the entrepreneurship literature (Leonard-Barton, 1984) but Taylor and Pandza add to our understanding by stressing the importance of both family and other long-standing relationships. In other words, strong ties are central to the creation of competitive advantage in owner-managed firms. The key factor is that entrepreneurs need to recognise the potential of their network and adopt a strategic approach to its exploitation. The importance of strong ties probably declines as firms grow in size and the direct influence of the owner-manager has less direct influence on day-to-day activities within the firm (Birley *et al.*, 1990).

Functional Approaches to Competitive Advantage

In Section 3 on functional management we include chapters dealing with e-commerce, supply chain management, financial management and retailing. While we do not suggest that these are the only factors which must be considered by SME managers, they are areas of particular importance to improved competitive advantage. The integration of Internet and related ICTs (e-business) is fundamental to SMEs in terms of improving both internal and external communications. Many small firms utilise e-mail and may even have introduced websites but there is still enormous scope for the use of e-commerce in SMEs. Windrum and de Berranger (Chapter 11) suggest that the benefits are related to six areas of activity: extended geographical reach, greater efficiency in procurement, better communication with customers, opportunities for new strategic partnerships, facilitation of the innovation of new products/services and, finally, a shift towards an information-based business. UK governments have been particularly keen to promote the potential of e-commerce as a mechanism for improving productivity among SMEs (DTI, 1998). A key factor inhibiting the adoption of newer technologies is the lack of technical skills in smaller firms, despite many recent national and EU initiatives. Other significant restrictions include limited financial resources and pressure on management time. These restrictions are important, but lack of expertise in dealing with external technical experts is also a barrier for many owner-managers (Chapter 11). There are obviously sectoral variations in the adoption of e-commerce, with high-tech industries more likely to have integrated supply chains than more mature sectors. However, the case study discussed in Chapter 11 does indicate that SMEs in relatively low-tech sectors (in this case, printing) can use e-commerce technologies as a basis for significant improvements in organisational performance. While it is difficult to draw general conclusions from a single case, Windrum and de Berranger argue that, in combination with an analysis of the literature, it is possible to suggest ways in which SMEs can overcome their inherent difficulties in the adoption of new technologies. The authors emphasise the need for a team-based approach to implementation rather than relying on the individual owner-manager. Second, it is suggested that obtaining external advice on the most appropriate technologies is essential if the management team lack technical expertise. Third, given the 'competence-destroying' (Tushman and Anderson, 1986) nature of e-commerce, it is essential that a strategic approach is adopted to both evaluation and implementation of this particular technology.

Supply chain management is concerned with the effective management of inter-organisational relationships. Closer linkages help to reduce transaction costs and increase trust and opportunities for knowledge-sharing, which has the potential to benefit all parties, although we acknowledge that SMEs, in particular, are coming under increasing pressure as a result of rises in global sourcing with the advent of e-purchasing. In their contribution, Macpherson and Wilson (Chapter 12) identify three sets of supply chain competences (business process, interaction and production) which provide a framework for the analysis of activities within SMEs. A survey of 39 manufacturing SMEs with an average size of 49 employees was carried out to evaluate their supply chain activities. Responses indicated high levels of competence associated with organisational flexibility and quality while 'benchmarking' and 'performance' were rated significantly lower. More significantly, as Macpherson and Wilson point out, companies were generally consistently strong or weak in the full range of competences. The positive findings about supply chain management among this set of firms must be considered in the light of their willingness to participate in the research. It is suggested by the authors that such openness may indicate that these companies may not be typical in terms of their management skills. Perhaps the most important finding from the study is the need for the development of more cross-functional competences. Most training and development offered to SMEs through government agencies concentrates on NVQ-style functional competences, which are relatively easy to deliver. Certainly there are risks to any SME engaged in close relationships with other companies, particularly if there are imbalances in power. At the same time, improving competitive advantage in SMEs means that it is essential that management teams are aware of the competences necessary for effective supply chain management and consider ways (benchmarking and training) that such activities can be improved in their own organisations.

Issues related to the financing of small firms have probably attracted more attention from academics and policy-makers than any other topic. In their discussion of financial innovations, Sweeting *et al.* (Chapter, 13) examine the adoption by SMEs of performance management techniques such as the balanced scorecard. The authors report on a study of 140 small firms operating in Trafford Industrial Park (Manchester, UK). Data from the study revealed that there was a low penetration of cost-management techniques such as cost of quality, net present value, activity-based costing and life-cycle costing. In contrast, a relatively large proportion (39 per cent of the sample) used break-even analysis, defined by the authors as an 'old cost management technique'. As Sweeting *et al.* point out: 'one of the most disturbing findings was the poor understanding of organisational costs.' The results are also disturbing because they indicate that owner-managers seem unwilling to access information from the accounting profession or other advice agencies. Strategy decisions (cost leadership or differentiation) demand that managers have a thorough understanding of their firm's cost base. The pessimistic conclusion from this study is that owners and managers of small firms have to pay much greater attention to newer, more dynamic accountancy techniques if there are to be substantial improvements in overall competitiveness.

Independent retailers are most notable for their decline since the 1970s. Increasing competition from multiple stores, often located on out-of-town sites, has made it extremely difficult for small retailers to survive on the basis of extended opening hours typical of the sector. Baron's report (Chapter 14) on a survey of 142 independent retailers provides information on how such businesses are responding to the new competitive landscape. Some of the issues discussed by Baron (such as creating opportunities for social exchange) are less applicable or practicable outside retailing. Other factors, including the flexible adoption of ICTs, horizontal and vertical networks and learning from large firms, could be adopted by SMEs across a range of sectors. In two of the cases discussed in this chapter, retailers used ICTs to build and maintain relationships with customers. Most importantly, new technologies were utilised as a means of supporting, rather than replacing, existing strategy. Evidence of small retailers collaborating to compete more effectively against their larger, better resourced rivals again emphasises the importance of networking. Third, observing the activities of large firms can provide SMEs with an effective method of learning. As Baron points out, some training organisations have recruited retired managers from large retail firms to act as mentors to SMEs. We suggest that all three of these approaches can aid smaller firms in a wide range of sectors to improve their competitive advantage.

Conclusion

A recent survey identified Porter's (1985) 'five forces' as the theoretical concept most widely used in practice by MBA students (Bahra, 2002). The importance of Porter's contribution to debates about the nature of competitive advantage is also acknowledged throughout this book. Certainly, exposure to basic analytical tools such as the value chain and the five forces could help many owner-managers to adopt a more rigorous approach to improving the competitiveness of their organisations. At the same time, it is recognised that debates in strategic management have moved on to incorporate resource-based theory (RBT) which originated with

Penrose's analysis (1959) of firm growth. Once again, most contributors have mentioned the significance of RBT for the effective management of smaller firms. While this approach is clearly relevant, it is less straightforward to move from theory to practice than in the case of Porter's work. Resource-based theory is premised on the idea that, rather than industry structure determining competitive advantage, the firm's accumulated assets (including knowledge, resources, skills, structure, culture and ownership) are the main source of sustained competitiveness (see Wenerfelt, 1984; Barney, 1995; Foss, 1997). The distinction between the 'outside-in' approach of traditional industrial economics (on which Porter's work is based) and the 'inside-out' approach of RBT seems, initially, to be irreconcilable. However, in recent years a number of attempts have been made to identify the complementary aspects of Porterian approaches and the resource-based perspective (Conner, 1991; Amit and Schoemaker, 1993; Hoskisson *et al.*, 1999). Spanos and Lioukas (2001, p. 912) draw on Wernerfelt's work (1984) to posit a 'fundamental compatibility' between the two approaches, which they believe constitute two sides of the same coin. The authors suggest that RBT provides the 'strengths–weaknesses' element of SWOT, while industry analysis provides the 'opportunities–threats' element. A further similarity is that both approaches acknowledge that the attainment of 'above normal' returns are possible for firms with favourable strategic positions. Following the development of a conceptual framework, Spanos and Lioukas (2001) test their hypothesis that sustained competitive advantage stems from a combination of industry effects and resource availability. The empirical data are based on a questionnaire survey of 147 CEOs representing Greek manufacturing firms with an average size of 160 employees. Results indicated the co-existence of three 'distinct but complementary' factors which influence performance: strategy configuration, industry effects and firm-specific factors (p. 920). In other words, those small firms that concentrate on matching their internal, knowledge-based resources to the external environment appear to be the most successful in sustaining competitive advantage. To summarise, improving competitiveness within SMEs means owners and managers must take a strategic approach to decision-making. Exposure to the basic tools of strategic management including the value chain, five forces and SWOT analysis would certainly help those involved with the management of most small firms to make more informed decisions about future directions.

Another theme that permeates the book is that of networks and networking. Of particular significance here is Gibbs's (1997) article, in which he argues that various external linkages constitute the firm's 'learning environment' which is central to improved performance. This emphasis on 'informal learning' is important in the case of SMEs where there are generally high levels of scepticism related to the value of formal training (Matlay, 2000). Certainly the case study discussed by Taylor and Pandza (Chapter 10) illustrates ways in which entrepreneurs can make effective use of their learning environment by accessing a wide range of information from both strong and weak ties. In fact, this very point was emphasised by Leonard-Barton (1984, p. 113) in her early study of networks established by owner-managers: 'entrepreneurship is both constrained and facilitated by linkages between the resources and opportunities that are created via the social network of the entrepreneur'. Entrepreneurs build successful businesses by maximising their opportunities, and social networks are a crucial resource for business owners

(Birley *et al.*, 1990; Lawton-Smith *et al.*, 1991; Rothwell and Dodgson, 1991). Networks incorporate a wide range of social relationships including family, friends and neighbours as well as customers, vendors and creditors. Birley *et al.* (1990, p. 59) note the evolutionary nature of these relationships: 'entrepreneurs, at an early stage of enterprise development, rely heavily on an informal network of friends, family members and social contacts from the local neighbourhood to gather relevant data.' Gradually, entrepreneurs extend their networks to include bankers, accountants, lawyers, suppliers, government agencies, customers and consultants. Research on the growth of small firms (McGhee *et al.*, 1995) confirms the importance of entrepreneurial teams which 'expand the organisation's network of contacts and provide the balance of expertise required to profit from certain types of cooperative activity' (Birley and Stockley, 2000, p. 289). Entrepreneurs with good cultural and social networks can attract more capital and are more likely to be successful than those with limited networks (Shaw, 1998). Some linkages are planned, some are accidental and others are established with organised groups, such as Chambers of Commerce, that help enhance entrepreneurial scope. However, Chell and Baines (2000) note that some authors (Blackburn *et al.*, 1991; Curran *et al.*, 1993) report that small business owners have little time for networking and place more emphasis on independence via a 'fortress enterprise mentality'. In explaining the contradictory evidence, Chell and Baines (2000, p. 205) found that networking positively related to business growth, being significantly higher in expanding or rejuvenating businesses than in those that were plateauing or declining. In other words, effective networking is strongly associated with those firms which adopt a strategic approach to building and exploiting their various business relationships.

An emerging area of research which complements the network perspective is related to 'social capital'. In their recent review of the literature, Adler and Kwon (2002, p. 23) point out that the concept of social capital is 'gaining currency' in a range of areas related to organisations: career success (Burt, 1992), job search (Granovetter, 1995), product innovation (Tsai and Ghoshal, 1998), intellectual capital (Hargadon and Sutton, 1997), corporate entrepreneurship (Chung and Gibbons, 1997), new business formation (Walker *et al.*, 1997), supply-chain relations (Uzzi, 1997), regional production networks (Romo and Schwartz, 1995) and interfirm learning (Kraatz, 1998). The core of social capital is that goodwill drawn from wide-ranging network relationships provides firms with valuable resources including information, influence and solidarity (Sandefur and Laumann, 1998). According to Woolcock (1998, p. 155) social capital can be defined as the 'norms and networks facilitating collective action for mutual benefit'. Cooke and Wills (1999) examine the creation of social capital among SMEs in Wales, Denmark and Ireland. Data were obtained by means of an extensive questionnaire in which respondents were asked about improvements in business performance as a result of involvement with a range of domestic and EU innovation programmes. The authors demonstrate how such programmes improve business performance by promoting interfirm collaboration. The research makes a positive contribution to our understanding of how SMEs in different countries create social capital by engagement with a range of innovation programmes. Social capital is distinctive from other forms of capital in that it cannot be owned by individuals or organisations. However, our argument is that owner-managers concerned with improving the competitive position of their firm must think about their personal and their organisational networks in a strategic manner. The importance social capital plays in improving competitive advantage in SMEs is only now beginning to be recognised. It reinforces the need for broad-ranging skills acquisition and knowledge sharing across the organisation. Skills and knowledge can be accessed via existing networks as well as by building links with universities and training providers. Social capital also has implications for the retention of those highly skilled staff who are central to the performance of many SMEs. This issue is raised in Chapters 4 and 7, which discuss the related topics of share ownership and corporate governance.

In conclusion, our view is that the links between strategic management, networking and social capital as well as education and training suggest there needs to be a more dynamic approach to improving competitiveness in SMEs. The problem for both academics and policy-makers is that few of those people owning and managing small firms recognise the value of external knowledge and advice. This is clearly evident from the low response rate to various initiatives designed to help SMEs discussed by Tilley and Tonge in Chapter 1. Sweeting *et al.* (Chapter 13) confirm that there is considerable reluctance among owner-managers to seek external advice from professional groups and other advice agencies. Unfortunately, this does not augur well for encouraging such firms to use more sophisticated accounting practices or to consider how owner-managers might improve performance by the effective mobilisation of social capital within their firms. However, based on the MMUBS experience of engaging with SMEs, we believe that it is possible for academics to encourage the small-firm community to seek new sources of knowledge and information. This experience suggests that engagement with the small-firm community should be seen as an experience which is mutually beneficial based on what Gibb (1997) describes as 'informal learning'. In other words, owner-managers are rightfully suspicious of academics claiming to know more about running their business than they themselves do. Within MMUBS, there is a long tradition of using action learning which emphasises the importance of experiential learning and critical reflection (Thorpe, 1990; Thorpe *et al.*, 1998). Action learning (Revans, 1980; Marsick and O'Neil, 1999) has been identified as an appropriate method for responding to the problem-centred needs of entrepreneurs (Gibb, 1983; Gold *et al.*, 2000). Perren *et al.* (1999, p. 353) suggest 'that owner-managers need context-specific and timely support rather than generic training programmes.' Action learning engenders a personal, situational and emergent process in which 'groups of equals' are encouraged to develop a questioning and critical approach to solving their problems (Beaty *et al.*, 1997; Downing, 2000). This process-oriented approach allows learning to emerge from participant interactions and action (Simon, 1991; Lave and Wenger, 1991; Holman *et al.*, 1996; Pavlica *et al.*, 1998; Leitch and Harrison, 1999). In conclusion, what we are suggesting is a more active engagement with those involved in the day-to-day problems of managing small firms. In this way, we believe that academics can make a positive contribution to the creation of competitive advantage in SMEs.

References

Adler, P. and Kwon, S. (2002) 'Social capital: prospects for a new concept', *Academy of Management Review*, **27**:1, 17–40.

Amit, R. and Schoemaker, P. (1993) 'Strategic assets and organizational rents', *Strategic Management Journal*, **14**:1, 33–46.

Ansoff, H.I. (1965) *Corporate Strategy*. McGraw-Hill, New York.

Atherton, A. and Hannon, P.D. (2000) 'Innovation processes and the small business: a conceptual analysis', *International Journal of Performance Management*, **2**:1, 276–292.

Bahra, P. (2002) 'MBA experience: new tools for the trade', *Financial Times*, 21 January.

Barney, J.B. (1995) 'Looking inside for competitive advantage', *Academy of Management Executive*, **9**:4.

Beaty, L., Lawson, J., Bourner, T. and O'Hara, S. (1997) 'Action learning comes of age – Part 3: Action learning for what?' *Education and Training*, **39**:5, 184–188.

Beer, M., Spector, B., Lawrence, P., Quinn Mills, D. and Walton, R. (1984) *Managing Human Assets*. The Free Press, New York.

Berle, A.A. and Means, G.C. (1932) *The Modern Corporation and Private Property*. Harvest, New York.

Birley, S. and Stockley, S. (2000) 'Entrepreneurial teams and venture growth', in D. Sexton and H. Landstrom (eds) *The Blackwell Handbook of Entrepreneurship*. Blackwell, Oxford.

Birley, S., Cromie, S. and Myers, A. (1990) 'Entrepreneurial networks: their emergence in Ireland and overseas', *International Small Business Journal*, **9**:4, 56–74.

Blackburn, R., Curran, J. and Jarvis, R. (1991) 'Small firms and local networks: some theoretical and conceptual explorations', in M. Robertson, E. Chell and C. Mason (eds) *Towards the Twenty-first Century: The Challenge for Small Business*. Nadamal Books, London, pp. 105–122.

Bolton Report (1971) *Report of the Committee of Enquiry on Small Firms*. Cmnd 4811, HMSO, London.

Burt, R. (1992) *Structural Holes: The Social Structure of Competition*. Harvard University Press, Cambridge, MA.

Carrier, C. (1996) 'Intrapreneurship in small businesses: an exploratory study', *Entrepreneurship: Theory and Practice*, **21**:1, 5–21.

Chell, E. and Baines, S. (2000) 'Networking, entrepreneurship and microbusiness behaviour', *Entrepreneurship and Regional Development*, **12**, 195–215.

Chung, L. and Gibbons, P. (1997) 'Corporate entrepreneurship: the roles of ideology and social capital', *Group and Organization Management*, **22**, 10–30.

Churchill, N.C. and Lewis, V.L. (1983) 'The five stages of small business growth', *Harvard Business Review*, **6**:l.

Cobbenhagen, J. (2000) *Successful Innovation: Towards a New Theory for the Management of SMEs*. Edward Elgar, Cheltenham.

Conner, K. (1991) 'An historical comparison of resource-based theory and five schools of thought within industrial economics: do we have a new theory of the firm? *Journal of Management*, **17**, 121–154.

Cooke, P. and Wills, D. (1999) 'Small firms, social capital and the enhancement of business performance through innovation programmes', *Small Business Economics*, **13**:3, 219–234.

Curran, J. and Stanworth, J. (1979) 'Work involvement and social relations in the small firm', *Sociological Review*, **27**:2, 317–342.

Curran, J., Jarvis, R., Blackburn, R. and Black, S. (1993) 'Networks and small firms: constructs, methodological strategies and some findings', *International Small Business Journal*, **11**:2, 13–25.

Dandridge, T.C. (1979) 'Children are not little "grown-ups": small business needs its own organisational theory', *Journal of Small Business Management*, **17**:2, 53–57.

Department of Trade and Industry (DTI) (1998) *Our Competitive Future: Building the Knowledge Driven Economy*. UK Government White Paper, the Stationery Office. London. Also available at www.dti.gov.uk.

Downing, S. (2000) 'Action learning for entrepreneurs: key issues in the design and delivery of programmes', *ISBA National Small Firms Policy and Research Conference*, Aberdeen Business School, November.

Financial Times (2000) 'Tax break encourages employee share ownership along US lines', Budget Report, 22 March.

Fombrun, C., Tichy, N. and Devanna, M. (1984) *Strategic Human Resource Management*. Wiley, New York.

Foss, N.J. (1997) *Resources, Firms and Strategies: A Reader in the Resource-Based Perspective*. OUP, Oxford.

Freedman, J. (2000) 'Limited liability: large company theory and small firms, *Modern Law Review*, **3**:63, 317–354.

Gibb, A. (1983) 'The small business challenge to management education', *Journal of European Industrial Training*, **7**:5.

Gibb, A. (1997) 'Small firms' training and competitiveness: building upon the small firm as a learning organisation', *International Small Business Journal*, **15**:3, 13–29.

Gibb, A. and Scott, M. (1985) 'Strategic awareness, personal commitment and the process of planning in the small business', *Journal of Management Studies*, **22**, 597–631.

Gold, J., Devins, D. and Johnson, A. (2000) 'What is the value of management development in a small business?' Small Business and Enterprise Development Conference, University of Manchester, April.

Granovetter, M. (1995) *Getting a Job: A Study of Contacts and Careers*, 2nd edition. University of Chicago Press, Chicago.

Greiner, L. (1972) 'Evolution and revolution as organisations grow', *Harvard Business Review*, July/August.

Hannon, P.D. and Atherton, A. (1998) 'Small firm success and the art of orienteering: the value of plans, planning and strategic awareness in the competitive small firm', *Journal of Small Business and Enterprise Development*, **15**:2.

Hargadon, A. and Sutton, R. (1997) 'Technology brokering and innovation in a product development firm', *Administrative Science Quarterly*, **42**, 716–749.

Holman, D., Pavlica, K. and Thorpe, R. (1996) 'Rethinking Kolb's theory of experiential learning: the contribution of social construction and activity theory', *Management Learning*, **26**:4, 485–504.

Hoskisson, R., Hitt, M., Wan, W. and Yu, D. (1999) 'Theory and research in strategic management: swings of a pendulum', *Journal of Management*, **25**:3, 417–456.

Hutton, W. (1995) *The State We're In*. Jonathan Cape, London.

Jennings, P. and Beaver, G. (1997) 'The performance and competitive advantage of small firms: a management perspective', *International Small Business Journal*, **15**:1, 66–75.

Jones, O. (2003) 'The persistence of autocratic management in small firms: TCS and organisational change', *International Journal of Entrepreneurial Behaviour and Research* (forthcoming).

Jones, O. and Boles, K. (2002) 'New entrepreneurs and social capital: building support networks through action learning', Institute for Small Business Affairs Conference, Brighton.

Jones, O. and Craven, M. (2001) 'Beyond the routine: innovation management and the Teaching Company Scheme', *Technovation*, **21**:5, 267–285.

Kanter, R.M. (1983) *The Change Masters: Corporate Entrepreneurs at Work*. Unwin Hyman, London.

Kanter, R.M. (2000) 'When a thousand flowers bloom: structural, collective and social conditions for innovation in organizations', in R. Swedberg, *Entrepreneurship: The Social Science View*. OUP, Oxford.

Kickul, J. and Gundry, L. (2002) 'Prospecting for competitive advantage: the proactive entrepreneurial personality and small firm innovation', *Journal of Small Business Management*, **40**:2, 85–98.

Kraatz, M.S. (1998) 'Learning by association? Interorganizational networks and adaptations to environmental change', *Academy of Management Journal*, **41**, 621–643.

Lave, J. and Wenger, E. (1991) *Situated Learning: Legitimate Peripheral Participation*. Cambridge, Cambridge University Press.

Lawton-Smith, H., Dickson, K. and Smith, S. (1991) 'There are two sides to every story: innovation and collaboration within networks of large and small firms', *Research Policy*, **20**, 457–468.

Leitch, C.M. and Harrison, R.T. (1999) 'A process model for entrepreneurship education and development', *International Journal of Entrepreneurial Behaviour and Research*, **5**:3, 83–109.

Leonard-Barton, D. (1984) 'Interpersonal communication patterns among Swedish and Boston-area entrepreneurs', *Research Policy*, **13**:2, 101–114.

Man, T. and Chan, T. (2002) 'The competitiveness of small and medium enterprises: a conceptualization with focus on entrepreneurial competencies', *Journal of Business Venturing*, **17**, 123–142.

Marsick, V.J. and O'Neil, J. (1999) 'The many faces of action learning', *Management Learning*, **30**:2, 159–176.

Matlay, H. (2000) 'Training and the small firm', in S. Carter and D. Jones-Evans (eds) *Enterprise and Small Business*. FT-Prentice Hall, Harlow.

McClelland, D.C. (1961) *The Achieving Society*. Van Nostrand, Princeton, NJ.

McGhee, J.E., Dowling, M.J. and Meggison, W.L. (1995) 'Cooperative strategy and new venture performance: the role of business strategy and managerial experience', *Strategic Management Journal*, **16**, 563–580.

Mintzberg, H. (1978) 'Patterns in strategy formation', *Management Science*, **14**, 934–948.

Mintzberg, H. (1990) 'The design school: reconsidering the basic premises of strategic management', *Strategic Management Journal*, **11**, 171–195.

Moule, C. (1998) 'The regulation of work in small firms: a view from the inside', *Work, Employment and Society*, **12**:4, 635–654.

Pavlica, K., Holman, D. and Thorpe, R. (1998) 'The manager as a practical author of learning', *Career Development International*, **3**:7, 300–307.

Penrose, E. (1959) *The Theory of the Growth of the Firm*, revised edition, 1995. OUP, Oxford.

Perren, L., Berry, A. and Partridge, M. (1999) 'The evolution of management information, control and decision-making processes in small growth-oriented service sector businesses: exploratory lessons from four cases of success', *Journal of Small Business and Enterprise Development*, **5**:4.

Porter, M. (1980) *Competitive Strategy: Techniques for Analysing Industries and Competitors*. Free Press, New York.

Porter, M. (1985) *Competitive Advantage: Creating and Sustaining Superior Performance*. Free Press, New York.

Porter, M. (1990) *The Competitive Advantage of Nations*. Free Press, New York.

Porter, M. and van der Linde, C. (1995) 'Green and competitive: ending the stalemate', *Harvard Business Review*, **73**:5 (September/October), 120–137.

Rainie, A. (1989) *Industrial Relations in Small Firms: Small Isn't Beautiful*. Routledge, London.

Revans, R. (1980) *Action Learning: New Techniques for Management*. Blond & Briggs, London.

Romo, F.P. and Schwartz, M. (1995) 'Structural embeddedness of business decisions: a sociological assessment of the migration behavior of plants in New York state between 1960 and 1985', *American Sociological Review*, **60**, 874–907.

Rothwell, R. and Dodgson, M. (1991) 'External linkages and innovation in SMEs', *R&D Management*, **21**:2, 125–137.

Sandefur, R. and Laumann, E.O. (1998) 'A paradigm for social capital', *Rationality and Society*, **10**, 481–501.

Scase, R. (1995) 'Employment relations in small firms', in P. Edwards (ed.) *Industrial Relations: Theory and Practice in Britain*. Blackwell, Oxford.

Scase, R. (2000) 'The enterprise culture: the socio-economic context of small firms', in S. Carter and D. Jones-Evans (eds) *Enterprise and Small Business*. FT-Prentice Hall, Harlow.

Shaw, E. (1998) 'Social networks: their impact on the innovative behaviour of small service firms', *International Journal of Innovation Management*, **2**:2, 201–222.

Simon, H.A. (1991) 'Bounded rationality and organisational learning', *Organization Science*, **2**:1, 125–134.

Smallbone, D. and Wyer, P. (1998) 'Growth and development in the small firm', in S. Carter and D. Jones-Evans (eds) *Enterprise and Small Business: Principles, Practices and Policies*. Financial Times/Prentice Hall, Harlow, Essex.

Spanos, Y. and Lioukas, S. (2001) 'An examination into the causal logic of rent generation: contrasting Porter's competitive strategy framework with the resource-based perspective', *Strategic Management Journal*, **22**:10, 907–934.

Steward, F. and Conway, S. (1998) 'Situating discourse in environmental innovation networks', *Organization*, **5**:4, 479–502.

Stopford, J.M. and Baden-Fuller, C. (1994) 'Creating corporate entrepreneurship', *Strategic Management Journal*, **15**:7, 521–536.

Tether, B. (1999) 'Small firms, innovation and employment creation in Britain and Europe: a question of expectations', *Technovation*, **20**:2, 109–113.

Thorpe, R. (1990) 'An alternative theory of management education', *Journal of European Industrial Training*, **14**:2, 3–15.

Thorpe, R., Pavlica, K. and Holman, D. (1998) 'The manager as a practical author and mediator of learning – a conversational view of learning and managing people in organisations', *Applied Industrial Psychology*, **XXXII**:3–4, 89–96.

Tichy, N., Fombrun, C. and Devanna, M. (1982) 'Strategic human resource management', *Sloan Management Review*, **23**:2, 47–61.

Tsai, W. and Ghoshal, S. (1998) 'Social capital and value creation: the role of inter-firm networks', *Academy of Management Journal*, **41**, 464–478.

Tushman, M.L. and Anderson, P.A. (1986) 'Technological discontinuities and organizational environments', *Administrative Science Quarterly*, **31**, 439–465.

Uzzi, B. (1997) 'Social structure and competition in interfirm networks: the paradox of embeddedness', *Administrative Science Quarterly*, **42**:1, 35–67.

Vossen, R.W. (1998) 'Relative strengths and weaknesses of small firms in innovation', *International Small Business Journal*, **16**:3, 88–94.

Walker, G., Kogut, B. and Shan, W. (1997) 'Social capital, structural holes and the formation of an industry network', *Organization Science*, **8**, 109–125.

Welsh, J.A. and White, J.F. (1981) 'A small business is not a big business', *Harvard Business Review*, **59**:4, 18–32.

Wernerfelt, B. (1984) 'A resource-based view of the firm', *Strategic Management Journal*, **5**:2, 171–180.

WERS98 (2000). 'Workplace Employee Relations Survey 1998' (special issue), *British Journal of Industrial Relations*, **38**:4.

Woolcock, M. (1998) 'Social capital and economic development: towards a theoretical analysis and policy framework', *Theory and Society*, **27**, 151–208.

INDEX